Southern California:
An Island on the Land

SOUTHERN CALIFORNIA
AN ISLAND ON THE LAND

by Carey McWilliams

PEREGRINE SMITH BOOKS
SALT LAKE CITY

© Published by Gibbs Smith, Publisher, 2010
P.O. Box 667 Layton, Utah 84041

Copyright © 1946, 1973 by Carey McWilliams

Book cover design and illustration by Don Weller,
Weller Institute for the Cure of Design
Manufactured in the United States of America
ISBN 13:978-0-87905-007-8
ISBN 0-87905-007-1
Library of Congress Catalog Card Number;
73-77787

Dedicated

to

ROBERT WALKER KENNY,

— Native Son —

INTRODUCTION

If years before I wrote *Southern California: An Island on the Land*, I had planned to write it, then it could be said that I picked exactly the right time to settle in the region, that my work experience was providential, and that I selected precisely the right group of friends. But of course I did not plan to write the book; it grew out of my experiences in a perfectly natural way. Let me explain.

First about the timing. In one sense the growth of Southern California has been continuous but it is also true that its growth has been characterized by quantum leaps, great surges of migration. In the period, say, from 1900 to 1920, the region had grown steadily and many significant developments had taken place. But most of this growth and development was essentially prologue to the extraordinarily rapid expansion that took place after 1920. Modern day Los Angeles might be said to date from 1920; as late as 1925 it was aptly characterized by Louis Adamic as an "enormous village." The mere mention of oil and motion pictures is enough to suggest what began to happen after World War I.

I arrived in Los Angeles in the first years of the 1920 decade. No migrant ever arrived in the region knowing less about it than I did. I had never visited the state before I came to live there. I remember that I left Denver for Los Angeles in a blizzard a day or two after St. Patrick's Day, 1922. The snow storm is an important detail because those who set out for Southern California under such circumstances are always the more impressed by the warm and affable climate they encounter on arrival. The bit about St. Patrick's Day is also of minor importance. I had celebrated the occasion much too enthusiastically, certainly, for a freshman who was already on probation at the University of Denver for some similar, and earlier, antics. So the authorities, deeply imbued as they were in those days with the Methodist ethos, were naturally, and justifiably, a bit nettled, and suggested that the time had come for me to leave. And where do you go when you leave Colorado? I did what many other residents of the Rocky Mountain states were doing in the 1920s (although for different reasons), I set out for Southern California. My mother had preceded me and my brother would soon join us in Los Angeles. My father, a promin-

ent cattle rancher, a member of the State Senate, and one of the
pioneer settlers of Northwestern Colorado, had been clipped in the
disastrous post-World-War I collapse of the cattle market. (For
his story and the early history of Northwestern Colorado see:
Where The Old West Stayed Young by John Rolfe Burroughs,
Wm. Morrow & Company, 1962; see also my interview with
Studs Terkel in *Hard Times*, Pantheon Books, 1970, pp. 240-244).
The end of World War I marked the end of what was still left,
by that time, of the open range cattle industry in the West. More
than one large cattle rancher suffered the fate that befell my
father. For him the experience was such a shock—the impact so
traumatic—that, in effect, it killed him. So detaching herself from
the rubble and ruin of what had been one of the minor cattle "em-
pires" in Colorado, my mother, with the same admirable courage
and enterprise that she had shown in helping to build that empire, set out for Southern California. She had a brother there, a
Canadian citizen by naturalization—he had taken part in the
Klondike stampede of 1897-1898 and had later settled in Prince
Rupert, British Columbia—who had come to Los Angeles to retire around 1918 or 1919. And it was there that I joined her, a
drop-out, in disgrace, acutely impoverished, an inter-state migrant
with dim prospects but high hopes.

The journey was made, of course, by train. And what an admirable trip it was in those days of leisurely Southern Pacific
travel, with stops at splendid Fred Harvey eating houses along
the way. Like other migrants to California I was impressed by
the hundreds of miles of desert and mountain terrain—largely
uninhabited wasteland—that had to be crossed en route to the
promised land. I had known New Mexico only as a place to which
my father used to go to buy thousands of steers which were
shipped to Northwestern Colorado to be fattened in mountain
parks and forest reserve areas and then shipped to the Denver
stockyards. Crossing the Colorado desert was an experience; I
dreaded to think of what Los Angeles might be like. Like most
migrants, too, I was homesick for Colorado before I had even arrived in the land of giant geraniums, poppies, oranges, and perpetual sunshine that was even then beginning to be widely advertised as a kind of far western paradise facing the Pacific.

Like most migrants, also, I was not prepared for the scenes I
encountered. My dear uncle—the kindest man I have ever
known—met me at the old Southern Pacific station, said not one
word about my unfortunate St. Patrick's Day antics, and drove me
out Sunset Boulevard to the white-stucco six-unit flat he owned

near the corner of Normandie and Sunset. It seemed like a long trip although it can be made in minutes today on the freeway. I was impressed by the cool gray mist and above all, by the extraordinary greenness of the lawns and hillsides. It was the kind of green that seemed as though it might rub off on your hands; a theatrical green, a green that was not quite real. My uncle's flat building seemed large and the lawns quite spacious—by Denver standards. And the absence of snow was quite shocking. That same night my uncle took me to a benefit performance that a group of motion picture stars had organized for some charity. It was held in a large circus-type tent that had been set up at the southeast corner of Sunset and Vine which was then, so to speak, unoccupied territory. I thought it quite exciting to be so close to all those movie stars and remember that Wallace Reid played a saxophone solo; (he would die of drug addiction the next year).

In the days that followed, I discovered, bit by bit, what was then called "downtown Los Angeles." Sid Grauman had opened the Million Dollar Theater at Third and South Broadway in 1918, as part of a grandiose scheme to make Broadway "the Great White Way of Los Angeles." And for a few brief years it was. The Rialto, built in 1917, was remodeled by Grauman in 1923. The Orpheum was built in 1926, Loew's State in 1923, Pantages in 1920. The old Alexandria Hotel was still quite elegant. "People were coming downtown," write Bill and Nancy Boyarsky (*Westways*, November, 1971), "from all over the city—the rich in big cars, the less affluent on public conveyances, making a noisy confusion of rattling streetcars, clattering autos and an occasional bewildered horse, left over from the previous era." It wasn't until the late twenties, in fact, that the movie stars and the well-to-do began to desert downtown Los Angeles. In 1922, Pershing Square was not quite so bedraggled as it is now but it was even then inhabited by the same floaters and drifters and professional sitters and loungers; some even had bench seats reserved by custom and long usage. A curving arcade ran between Broadway and Spring, between Fifth and Sixth, which was lined with cheap shops; over this arcade the present-day Spring and Broadway Arcade Buildings were erected. I was not impressed by the stores in "downtown" Los Angeles; those in Denver seemed, in fond retrospect, more elegant. In fact the whole downtown section struck me as being somewhat dreary. But what did impress me instantly were the crowds—the aimless, restless movement of armies of people with nothing much to do who were not going any place in particular. On my first visit I was short-changed in one of the numerous phoney curio shops that lined Hill Street and quickly got the feeling that, sociologically speaking, Los Angeles was a very strange community.

My uncle had told me that the best way to get a job was to watch the bulletin board in the employment office of the YMCA. This I did. And I got a succession of part-time jobs: addressing envelopes in a small directmail advertising agency; tending a machine in a lithograph plant; typing letters in the office of the president of a furniture store who, day after day, was engaged in horrendous quarrels with his brother. Then one day the bulletin board carried an announcement that there was an opening at the Los Angeles *Times* in the business office. After my recent experiences the prospect of a job, any kind of job, on a newspaper, seemed too good to be true. So I raced up to the *Times*, got the job, and stayed there, in several different capacities, until I graduated from law school in 1927. These years at the *Times* were a rewarding experience.

The *Times* was then located at First and Broadway, in a fortress-like structure that had been rebuilt in the image of the old building that had been destroyed by dynamite in 1910—an act which climaxed the bitter fight to organize "open shop" Los Angeles. My job was to serve as typist-stenographer-assistant and general flunkey for the awesome M. E. Hillis, who had for years been the head of the credit department. Awesome, because he was the terror of the business office and the scourge of all the thousands of deadbeats who tried—often successfully—to avoid payment of their advertising bills. His temper tantrums were legendary. Later I learned that I had been given the job so quickly—almost without an interview—because he had driven a succession of earlier secretaries from the office in fear and trembling. I should say that I had no qualifications for the job, none. I could type, yes, a bit. But I knew no shorthand (later I learned some). I had had no office or business experience of any kind. So not surprisingly I suffered acutely the first months I was there from the tyrannical whims and ferocious temper of the Great M. E. Hillis. He made my life a hell-on-earth, as he had, I discovered, for all those who had preceded me. I could do nothing right. Again and again he complained loudly and bitterly to C. O. Denning, who had hired me, that I must go, right then, immediately, on the double. But Denning, who had grown tired of interviewing applicants, would say yes and then not do anything about it while pleading with me to stay on if only for a few more weeks.

And then one day the attitude of the Holy Terror, as he was

known, changed suddenly, miraculously. Overnight I became the "fair-haired boy": I could do no wrong. His partiality and paternalism were almost obscene. From then on, I had the run of the office. And of course I discovered that he was, beneath that forbidding exterior, a kindly man, at least toward those he had come to like. We became great friends. We often lunched together at the old Fern Cafeteria at Third and Hill, one of the few really fine "early day" cafeterias in Los Angeles. His wife fancied herself as a patroness of the fine arts and I was incited to various poetry-readings and concerts in their home. I had only held the job a short time when I explained to Mr. Hillis that I wanted to resume my interrupted college education. So he most obligingly let me arrange my own work schedule so that I could enroll, first in the old City College on Vermont Avenue (later UCLA), and, the next year, at the University of Southern California, where I wrote editorials for *The Trojan*, tried to be funny in the pages of *Wampus*, the college humor magazine, and edited *The Wooden Horse*, a literary magazine. In view of all the sassy editorials I wrote on compulsory chapel and other sacred subjects, I was surprised but pleased years later to be asked to write a foreword to the first official history of USC (*Southern California Its History: A History of USC*, by Manuel Servin and Iris Higbie Wilson, Ward Ritchie Press, 1969). I had not planned to study law, but after three years I got tired of driving to and from the campus in my old Model-T Ford, and decided to enroll in the Law School which was then located in a building right across the street from the Los Angeles *Times*. For me it proved to be most fortunate that I got that job at the *Times* which no one wanted. It enabled me to hold down what was, in effect, a full-time job, while attending the university. But more to the point, my years at the *Times* constituted a marvelous introduction to the Los Angeles of the 1920s.

As the decade opened, the *Times* and the *Examiner* were locked in mortal combat. One or the other would emerge as the dominant morning paper. The competition, at all levels, was ferocious—for news, advertising, good newsstand corners, political clout. With Los Angeles—and other Southern California communities as well—beginning to "boom" in the wake of World War I, classified advertising soared, mostly real estate advertising but other categories too. The *Times* was on its way to winning, for the first time, the distinction of running more classified advertising than any newspaper in the country. The policy of the paper was to run almost any advertising copy that was submitted—even so its standards were a cut above the *Examiner's*—and to extend credit in a reckless way. So in effect a kind of guerilla warfare existed between the deadbeats and con men and fly-by-night promoters, trying to avoid payment for advertising which was their life blood, and the business office. In the process we became first rate investigators, skilled in ferreting out bank accounts, locating hidden assets, and tracking down debtors as they changed names, addresses and phone numbers. We built up excellent "intelligence" files and astonishing "memory banks," without the aid of computers. We could spot a deadbeat's advertising copy by the style, the lingo, even though a different name and address had been used. Our running feuds and encounters with these bad check artists and flimflam promoters simulated guerilla warfare in which no tricks were barred—on either side. Our "mission" was to collect as much as we could while the *Times* was winning the advertising sweepstakes.

As a result of this stimulating experience— I actually enjoyed the combat phase of it—I was given an extraordinary insight into the seamy side, the under side, of booming Los Angeles. What I saw and came to understand was not the whole story by any means but it was most revealing all the same. After all, is there a better way to understand a community than to be exposed to the chicanery, fraud, desperation and hardship, and the very real tragedies that one encounters in this kind of business "under world?" Near the *Times* was the old Music and Arts Building. I got to know the building and its tenants as perhaps no one else knew them. The place was alive with colorful fakers and con men. The various "studios" were occupied by a constantly changing collection of voice teachers, "masseurs," swamis, mind readers, graphologists, yogis, divine teachers, faith healers, spiritualists, old thesbians who wanted to teach neophytes, fake publishers, fake literary agents, and other exotic types. And this was merely one building, one collection. In our frantic efforts to minimize the *Times'* losses from running advertising it should never have accepted in the first place and certainly not unless accompanied by a certified check, we came to know a fine cross-section of men and women "on the make," mostly recent migrants to Los Angeles, enticed there by dreams of health, fame, and easy money. Some of our adversaries later became prominent figures in the business and financial life of the community—in motion pictures, oil, and real estate. Men who later became millionaire "realtors" and joined the California Club feuded with us as though we were revenue officers at war with moonshiners. The cliche has it that it is fun to work on newspapers because you meet so many interesting people. I certainly met my share in the five years (1922-1927) that I worked at the *Times.*

I graduated from law school in 1927, full of the crammed learning, brashness and specious wisdom of all law school graduates, and promptly got a place in an "old" Los Angeles firm. "Old" has ironic meaning when applied to any Los Angeles institution. Daniel Marion Hammack of Illinois, where he represented the Burlington Railroad, came to Southern California in 1887. He brought his family of four on $1 passes, each, which he had obtained from the railroad. His son, Daniel Stewart Hammack, graduated from Occidental College (at that time located at North Figueroa and Avenue 50), and then took a year at Princeton. Many Occidental men, of that period, went on to Princeton; Occidental prided itself on being "the Princeton of the West." At Princeton he met Alfred L. Black, Jr., who was also a member of the Class of 1906. Their fathers had also graduated from Princeton. The Blacks had originally practiced in Bellingham, Washington, but moved to Los Angeles around 1918 and formed the firm of Black, Hammack & Black, the senior Hammack having died in 1918. When I joined the firm the second generation was in charge, both fathers having died. A second generation law firm in Los Angeles in the 1920s was as rare as a six generation firm would be in New York or Chicago. The offices in the old American Bank Building, Second and Spring Streets, can only be described as Dickensian. The offices were sprawling. The library was huge but old-fashioned and largely unusable. Alfred L. Black, Jr. had a rocking chair in his office in which he loved to doze and he dozed most of the day. The office files were voluminous but wildly disorganized; there was a general air of friendly chaos about the place.

Both partners were delightful men. Dan Hammack, long active in the Occidental Alumni Association, had been a classmate of Robinson Jeffers. He had a lively interest in the history of Southern California and knew a great deal about it. Dr. Robert Cleland, the California historian, also a graduate of Occidental, was a great friend of his. The two Hammacks represented a large group of families, mostly of Presbyterian persuasion, who lived in such communities as Highland Park, Eagle Rock, San Marino, South Pasadena, and Pasadena. In Los Angeles terms these were "old money, first families." The money was of the genteel, 7-per-cent-interest-first mortgage variety. The two hundred or so wills in Dan's safe constituted, when I joined the firm, a fine collection of well-known early-day Los Angeles residents, including any number of rich spinsters and widows, not enormously or vulgarly rich but well beyond the pressure of need or stress. Many of them were graduates of Occidental or had sons and daughters, and grandchildren, who went there.

Some of the most famous names in "early" Los Angeles history were clients of the firm, for example, Joseph Mesmer, for many years prominent in Southern California historical circles. The firm also represented the Blondeau family. The Blondeaus once owned a roadside inn called Cahuenga House—at that time Hollywood was known as Cahuenga Valley. Travellers used to stop there for lunch enroute to and from San Fernando Valley. The inn was located on property at Sunset Boulevard and Gower, where the CBS studios were later built. Alfred L. Black, Jr., the other partner, could not have cared less about Southern California history, but he and his father represented some clients who helped shape the economy of the region. A fairly good history of the early phase of the oil industry in Southern California might be written around the figure of J. W. Jameson, who was one of the first to prove the rich Huntington Beach field. One of the wells he drilled there, named the Laura J after his wife, was for years the finest producing well in the field. In brief, the office files, ancient and modern, in that office contained a wealth of historical raw material. Although I was not aware of it at the time, my experience with the firm was very much part of my initiation into the history of the region. Fortunately for me, neither of the senior members liked courtroom work, one because he was naturally shy, the other because he was naturally lazy. So I was given a free hand and actually urged to try cases far beyond my experience and competence. One can learn a lot about a community in the courts, trying cases, examining jurors, and cross-examining witnesses.

If the firm represented, as it did, highly conservative interests, the clients that I managed to bring in were quite a different type. Miraculously neither partner ever expresesd concern or distaste over the clients I represented although I am sure they were less than enchanted by the character of my practice. I had some personal clients, of course, who were as conservative as theirs, but I also took civil liberties cases of all sorts and represented quite a number of trade unions. No doubt I was drawn to this kind of practice in part by the circumstance that I had graduated from law school on the eve of the depression. A lot of the firm's work, in fact, during these years was by way of trying to salvage something for clients who had been hard bit by the 1929 stock market crash. In any case, I was the first attorney for the Newspaper Guild in Los Angeles and represented the Guild in its first significant negotiation—with the Los Angeles *Herald-Express*—and during the bitter strike at the Hollywood *Citizen-News* (see: *A History of the Los Angeles Labor Movement*, 1911-1941, by Louis B. Perry and Richard S. Perry, 1963, pp. 476-480). I also represented a number of Hollywood trade unions, including a group of courageous rank-and-file members of the International Alliance of Theatrical and Stage Employees. These clients sought to challenge the high-handed, strong-arm tactics of the union which, at that time, was gangster controlled, and to have the courts set aside a collusive closed shop agreement with the industry. In pressing this litigation, I managed to turn up, with the assistance of my old friend, Elmer Gertz, the distinguished Chicago attorney, the criminal backgrounds and connections of George Browne and Willie Bioff of the IATSE. I also succeeded in inducing my law school classmate, William Mosely Jones, then Speaker of the Assembly, to have a state legislative committee investigate the racket-dominated IATSE. The committee held a public hearing in the auditorium of the State Building in Los Angeles which attracted wide interest and intensive news coverage. But the IATSE shrewdly retained a member of the firm with which Jones was associated, and that was the end of the investigation. The background is set forth in rich detail in the Philbrick Report on legislative corruption; copies of this report became collectors' items soon after it was published. But the fight continued. Westbrook Pegler got interested and his columns helped publicize the facts. By luck we turned up some curious stock certificates and the number of a brokerage account, data which was turned over to the U.S. Attorney's office. The upshot was the arrest and conviction of Joseph Schenck for income tax evasion and the subsequent arrest and conviction of Browne and Bioff on a charge of extorting something like $3,000,000 from the industry. Later Browne and Bioff testfied for the government in a case involving Frank Nitto, their real boss (see: "Hollywood Labor Dispute: A Study in Immorality" by Father George H. Dunne, "You Don't Choose Your Friends" by Herbert Knott Sorrell, part of the Oral History Project, UCLA, 1963, and hearings in the matter of the Estate of Joseph Nitto vs. Commissioner of Internal Revenue, Dockets 8840, 8841, and 8842, Sept. 24 to Oct. 4, 1958). As a footnote, Bioff was later killed when, after his release from prison, he stepped on the starter of his car in Phoenix and his energetic and colorful career came to a dramatic end in the explosion that followed.

The long struggle against the IATSE which my clients initiated and which cost them dearly—one was savagely beaten at a union convention in Cleveland—constitutes the indispensable background to an understanding of the Conference of Studio Unions lockout of 1946 which changed the social landscape of Hollywood and would have to be regarded as a major event in the social history of the community. This strike in turn provides the background to the case against the Hollywood Ten (see: 80th Congress, 2nd Session, House of Representatives, Committee Report No. 13, also *The Imperfect Union* by James Hutchinson and "Pickets in Paradise" a Ph.D. dissertation by Dan Biederman, New York University. Of special interest also is a fine study by Grace Franklin and Bernard McMahon, Institute of Industrial Relations, UCLA which, I am told, has somehow vanished from the files). I also served as one of the first Trial Examiners named by the National Labor Relations Board for the Southern California region and heard, among other proceedings, a famous case involving the American Potash and Chemical Company of Trona, California. These experiences, to put it mildly if perhaps immodestly, were highly educational. And so too were my investigations of migratory farm labor and the four years I served as Chief, Division of Immigration and Housing (1938-1942) in the state government.

Even before I graduated from law school, I had begun to write for magazines and newspapers. While at the *Times*, I wrote book reviews and articles for the weekend magazine. I reviewed books regularly for the San Diego *Union* and wrote for a variety of long since forgotten "little" magazines: *The Dum Book, San Francisco Review, The Double Dealer, Sports & Vanities, The Fortnightly, Game and Gossip*, the *San Franciscan, The Clipper, Hesperian, Contempo, Panorama, The Frontier*, and others. I became a regular contributor to the Los Angeles weekly *Saturday Night* edited by Samuel T. Clover,—some graduate student in search of a subject should investigate this man's fascinating career—as well as *The Overland Monthly* and *The Argonaut*. I also contributed to the *Haldeman-Julius Monthly* (mostly pieces about odd Southern California types). Later I began to write for *The American Mercury, The Bookman, Saturday Review*, PM, Baltimore *Sun*, *Common Ground, Southwest Review, Antioch Review, North*

American Review, the University of California *Chronicle, South Atlantic Quarterly, Harper's, Commentary, Holiday* (a piece about California cults later included in *The California Dream*, edited by Dennis Hale and Jonathan Eisen, Collier Books, 1968 p. 279). At the same time I was working most of the decade of the 1920s on a biography of Ambrose Bierce which was published in 1929. Much of this writing had to do, in one way or another, with California and, more particularly, the Southern California scene. It constituted, in a way, a further apprenticeship.

One phase of my apprenticeship had a special relevance to the writing of this book. Among my friends in Los Angeles, from an early date after my arrival, was Phil Townsend Hanna, dapper man-about-town, expert on Californiana, and editor of the monthly publication of the Automobile Club of Southern California, then as now a key institution in the region. At one time the monthly was called *Touring Topics*, then the name was changed to *Westways*. The magazine has always had a large circulation since it is a membership publication. In 1933, Phil asked me to contribute a monthly feature, consisting usually of two pages in type, about California folklore and related themes. The first appeared in the August, 1933, issue under the title "California Curiosa"; later the caption was changed to "Tides West" and it continued until August, 1939. Having to write this feature once a month made me do something I very much enjoyed doing but would not otherwise have done, namely read a large number of California newspapers and a lot of writing, fiction and non-fiction, about California, more particularly Southern California.

In the spring of 1939, my book *Factories in the Field* was published and I was caught immediately in the heated controversy over migratory farm labor that was triggered by publication of *The Grapes of Wrath*. An important official of the Auto Club was Standish Mitchell, who was related to Ruth Comfort Mitchell, the California novelist. The lady novelist, married to a large grower, took violent exception to my book, so she complained to Standish Mitchell who "spoke to" Phil Hanna. One day Phil took me to lunch and broke the bad news: the feature would have to be dropped. I did my best to assure him that I understood why he felt that he had to do what he did. In fact I felt far more sorry for him than I did about not being able to write the monthly feature or for the loss of income which this implied. He had his own problems at the time and it was really most unfair that he should have been caused distress because of this incident. In retro-

spect I am most grateful to him. Those years in which I re-
searched and wrote "Tides West" added to my store of information about the region and my interest in it.

During the 1920s I came to know an interesting group of Southern California intellectuals—the first intellectuals, in a very real
sense, to emerge in modern day Los Angeles. We constituted, after a fashion, a group or coterie. Among these individuals were
Jake Zeitlin, the bookdealer and publisher; Grace Marian Brown,
a commercial artist; Paul Jordan Smith, literary editor of the
Times; Dr. Jose Pijon, the art historian; Phil Townsend Hanna;
Will Connell, the photographer; Lloyd Wright, son of Frank
Lloyd Wright; Merle Armitage, the impressario; Hildegarde Flan-
ner, that very fine poet; (see my paper "The Cultural Climate of
California" to be found in *The Cultural Arts: California and The
Challenge of Growth*, UCLA, April 5-7, 1963), Herbert Klein, the
journalist, Ken Weber, who designed furniture, Louis Adamic, and
others, including at a later date Ward Ritchie, the printer, and
Lawrence Clark Powell, the librarian and critic. For a time we
published a little magazine called *Opinion* (from October, 1929, to
May 1930). We used to meet for dinner at Rene & Jean's French
restaurant on West Sixth Street where you could get a good meal
for seventy-five cents. Each of these individuals was, in his or
her own special field, a fine resource for anyone interested in
Southern California, its history, culture and folkways. Then, too,
I had the good fortune to know some of the best of the modern
architects who settled in Los Angeles, specifically, Richard Neutra,
R. W. Schindler, and Harwell Harris. Stanley Rose, the Hollywood bookdealer, was an old and dear friend. With Leslie Baird,
I used to visit the downtown studio of S. MacDonald-Wright, at
the Arts Students League, in an old loft building near Second and
Spring, the painter and brother of Willard Huntington Wright
(S. S. Van Dyne). I remember driving to Santa Ana, in September, 1927, to help assemble the props and stage sets for MacDon-
ald's one act play "The Infidelity of Madame Lun," at the first
annual Southern California Tournament of one act plays. It was
also my good fortune to have as close personal friends Duncan
Aikman, who was for some years West Coast correspondent for
the Baltimore *Sun*, and Robert Walker Kenny, jurist, state senator, and Attorney General of California, to whom this book is
dedicated. A native son, Bob Kenny was, and is, a one-man library
of information on California politics; no one knows the politics of
the state as well as he does. For a brief time, Bob and his friend
Roy Allen, published a little news weekly called *Midweek* (1933-

1934) which was largely written by Duncan Aikman. Since then Judge Kenny has prepared a draft autobiography as part of the Oral History Project at UCLA; the transcript is entitled: "My First Forty Years in Southern California Politics, 1922-1962." With Dunc Aikman I used to trail along as he covered meetings and conventions for the Baltimore *Sun* and interviewed visiting celebrities such as Bertrand Russell and Paul Elmer More. Also the two of us compared notes on Aimee Semple McPherson (see the chapter I did about her, "Sunlight in My Soul," which appears in *The Aspirin Age*, a book of articles about the period 1919-1941 which Isabel Leighton edited in 1949, and for which I supplied the title, borrowed, of course, from Scott Fitzgerald).

Several friends, in particular, helped stimulate my interest in Southern California. One was George Sterling, the poet. I knew Sterling quite well. I visited him at the Bohemian Club in San Francisco, and drove him around Los Angeles when he came to visit his sisters. He encouraged me to write about his mentor, Ambrose Bierce, and talked to me for hours about Bierce, Jack London, Mary Austin, and his life in Carmel and San Francisco. His letters to me, edited by John R. Dunbar, have been published in the California Historical Society *Quarterly* (September, 1967). In 1926, H. L. Mencken came west to visit Sterling and I had a chat with him at the Ambassador Hotel in Los Angeles where he had stopped enroute to San Francisco. We both knew that Sterling, with great difficulty, had been staying "on the wagon," preparatory to celebrating Mencken's visit. Mencken did see him at the Bohemian Club—"we had a brief and friendly palaver" he wrote—but Sterling had by then slipped off the wagon and was quite ill. The next day when Mencken returned he could not see Sterling; the door was locked. And the following day—November 17, 1926—Sterling was found dead, apparently a suicide. Of him Mencken said, with truth and insight, that "no artist ever kept his peculiar faith more resolutely . . . he was one of the last of the free artists." Of his passing Robinson Jeffers wrote that he would be

> "remembered utterly generous, constraining sorrow,
> Like winter sundown, splendid
> Memory to ennoble our nights."

(I wrote the note about Sterling which appears in the *Dictionary of American Biography*, Vol. 17, p. 585).

On September 11, 1926, Sterling wrote with enthusiasm about a story he had just read in the July issue of *The American Parade* by a young man named Louis Adamic whom he had just met. He had urged Adamic to get in touch with me, which he did a few days later. Louis had come to this country as a Slovenian immigrant in 1913, alone, fifteen years of age, speaking virtually no English. He had enlisted in 1916 and served most of his term in Panama, Louisiana, and Hawaii. Most of his postwar duty was performed at Fort MacArthur, San Pedro, California. When he was mustered out, in January, 1923, he decided to stay there and got a job as clerk in the municipal port pilot's office. I remember that we had dinner on that first meeting at a long since forgotten restaurant—Agazoni's—and a good session it proved to be. We became and remained close friends—he dedicated *Grandsons* to me—from that first meeting until his tragic death on September 4, 1951, at his home in Milford, New Jersey (see the article I did about him for *The Nation*, September 22, 1951). During the years that I knew him we were in constant communication, by correspondence and long talk sessions in Los Angeles, New York and Milford. We compared notes about Southern California frequently and often took junkets together. I once took him to visit Robinson and Una Jeffers at Tor House—in 1928—about which he wrote in *Robinson Jeffers: A Portrait* in the University of Washington Chapbook Series. From New York, we once drove down to Baltimore to have lunch with Mencken. We had many of the same interests, shared many enthusiasms, and held basically the same political views (although we had some arguments now and then). It would be difficult to count the hours we spent—many in the old pilot station office near the end of the breakwater at San Pedro—rapping about Southern California and laughing our heads off at this or that social absurdity. (See: *Louis Adamic: A Checklist*, by Henry A. Christian, Kent State University Press, 1971).

I also knew Mary Austin and saw her frequently. She had known an earlier Los Angeles quite well and used to talk to me about Charles Fletcher Lummis and George Wharton James and other writers of the period who then lived in Southern California. She also gave me a great deal of information about Owens Valley, where she had lived for some years; her husband had been a government land agent there. In San Francisco, Clarkson Crane, the novelist, and Oscar Lewis, the biographer-historian, were friends who provided many helpful hints about the California scene. I was fortunate, also, to have some good friends among Hollywood film writers, including Humphrey Cobb (in the years he lived in Southern California), and Frank Fenton, John Fante, and Ross Wills, all mentioned in this volume. With Fante and

Wills I have explored Southern California from the Mexican border to the Tehachapi Range, not once but many times. We were co-explorers of the region. I learned also from some of the Easterners to whom I was privileged to introduce aspects of Southern California, including Edmund Wilson (see p. 259).

So it should be clear, from this too lengthy introduction, that I did not just happen to write this book: I lived it. I was more than an observer; I was an active participant in the community during a period when I was growing up and Los Angeles was becoming a city. It should also be clear from this introduction that I had many collaborators, friends who shared with me their special insights and broadened my understanding about the region. Not long after the book was published I wrote *California: The Great Exception* which tried to do for the state what this book did for Southern California, that is, interpret it and provide the framework for a better understanding. After it was published I was asked to come east to edit a special civil liberties issue of *The Nation*, and stayed on as associate editor, editorial director, and editor (since 1955). The date of my departure from Southern California—which I had not realized was to be for such a long term—was symbolically of a part with the fortunate date of my arrival. Those years, from 1922 to 1951, mark a definite period in the history of the region. These were the years when it began to make a real impact on national and world opinion and when papers other than *Time*, began to write it Southern California.

—Carey McWilliams
1973

FOREWORD

SINCE this volume does not follow the well-worn path of most books about Southern California, a word or two of explanation, by way of charting its course, may be helpful. I have assumed that all Californians and others interested in the history of the state are by now painfully aware of the fact—they have been reminded of it often enough—that Juan Rodriguez Cabrillo discovered the Bay of San Diego on September 28, 1542; that they know the story of Sir Francis Drake and the *Golden Hind*; that they are familiar with the explorations and travels of Onate and Vizcaino, Portola and Kino; and that they are sophisticated enough to realize that nothing much happened in Southern California between Cabrillo's voyage of exploration and the arrival of Father Junipero Serra at San Diego in 1769, a library of Ibero-Americana to the contrary notwithstanding. I have therefore deliberately ignored Cabrillo and Drake, Onate and Vizcaino, Portola and Kino. Should this brusque procedure offend the tender sensibilities of chronic collectors of Californiana, I wearily point to the library of volumes about the Spanish explorations. In the same spirit, I have sought to tell the story of the Missions not in the conventional manner, that is, from the point of view of the Franciscans, but from the point of view of the real parties in interest, namely, the Indians of Southern California. Similarly, in dealing with that almost completely misunderstood period, "the days before the gringo came," I have tried to examine, with a degree of realism, the actual structure of social classes in Alta California. Much of the celebrated "romance" of early Southern California is pretty pallid stuff at best, but, for those chronically addicted to this sort of thing, I refer to the romances of Stewart Edward White, Gertrude Atherton, and Helen Hunt Jackson.

The chapter on the Indians of Southern California is largely based upon the monumental research of Dr. S. F. Cook of the University of California. Full details can be obtained from his fascinating volumes: *The Conflict Between the California Indian and White Civilization* (in four volumes, 1943); and *Population Trends Among the California Mission Indians* (1940). These volumes have superseded all

prior studies of Indians in California. I am indebted also to James
Rorty for permission to reprint several poems; to *The New Yorker* for
permission to reprint the poems of Theodore Spencer and Ogden
Nash; to B. A. Botkin for an item from his valuable collection of
American folklore; to Random House for permission to quote from
Nathanael West's novel, *The Day of the Locust*, and from Frank
Fenton's *A Place in the Sun*; to Louis Adamic and *Harper's* for per-
mission to quote from *Laughing in the Jungle*; to Agnes Smedley and
to Coward-McCann for permission to quote from *Daughters of Earth*;
to Reynal & Hitchcock for permission to quote from *The Smart Set
Anthology* and to the University of California Press for permission to
quote from *Study Out the Land* by T. K. Whipple.

I am also indebted to a number of individuals for their generous
assistance, notably Dr. Elmer Belt, R. W. Schindler, Richard Neutra,
John Anson Ford, Dr. Murray Abowitz, Dr. Talbot Hamlin, Harwell
Harris, Clifford Clinton, Dr. Esref Shevky, Lawrence Clark Powell,
Jake Zeitlin, and Ross B. Wills. For three years I did a page about
Southern California happenings for the magazine *Westways* and I
am indebted to Phil Townsend Hanna, editor of *Westways*, for permission to include some of this material. The chapters "Cathay in
the South" and "The Growth of a Legend" first appeared in *Common Ground* and are reprinted by permission of its editor, Margaret
Anderson to whom I am also indebted for much valuable assistance
in preparing the manuscript; the chapter "Californios and Mexicanos"
appeared in the review *ORT* and is reprinted by permission of its editor, and my good friend, Louis Boudin; while the chapter on the utopian politics of Southern California appeared in *Science and Society*
and is reprinted by permission of its editors. Had it not been for a
fellowship which I received from the Guggenheim Foundation I
should not have been able to complete the research upon which this
volume is based. I wish, therefore, to acknowledge my indebtedness
to the trustees of the foundation and to Mr. Henry Allan Moe.

CAREY McWILLIAMS

Los Angeles,
California.

CONTENTS

SOUTHERN CALIFORNIA
AN ISLAND ON THE LAND

"O bury me not in the North countree,
But plant me South of the Tehachapi."

CHAPTER I

SOUTH OF TEHACHAPI

REALISTIC observers of their northern province, the Spaniards always spoke of "The Californias"—Baja California and Alta California; Lower California and Upper California; New California and Old California. Later, still more Californias, more regional entities, were distinctly etched: the Mother Lode Country, known to the natives as *Superior California;* the Delta district; the Redwood Empire; the great Central Valley; and the Desert Country. While most of these regions and sub-regions are clearly delineated, none is more sharply defined, geographically and socially, than the area now known as Southern California.

The name itself is rather new. In the past the region has been variously titled, usually with eloquence or contempt, with devotion or repugnance. Not a neutral land, it has long aroused emotional reactions ranging from intense admiration to profound disgust. In years gone by, it was called California del Sur, the California of the South. Under early American rule, the counties which make up Southern California were invariably known as the Cow Counties. Still later the region was labeled "sub-tropical California." But, by 1920, the practice of capitalizing the "s" in Southern California was well established.

While no one has ever questioned that Southern California is a distinct regional entity, its boundaries have occasionally been misplaced. In a special issue of the *Saturday Review of Literature* for

3

October 30, 1943, the northern boundary of the region was placed as far north as the Monterey County line. While egregious errors of this sort have frequently been made, there has never been any real uncertainty about the region's boundaries. Southern California is the land "South of Tehachapi"—south, that is, of the transverse Tehachapi range which knifes across to the ocean just north of Santa Barbara. Once this range has been crossed, as Max Miller has said, "even the ocean, as well as the land structure, as well as the people, change noticeably." In the political parlance of the state, Northern California candidates have always "come down to the Tehachapi" with a certain majority. In the vast and sprawling state of California, most state-wide religious, political, social, fraternal, and commercial organizations are divided into northern and southern sections at the Tehachapi line. When sales territories are parceled out, when political campaigns are organized, when offices are being allocated, the same line always prevails. The Tehachapi range has long symbolized the division of California into two major regions: North and South. While other states have an east-west or a north-south division, in no state in the Union is the schism as sharp as in California. So sharp is the demarcation in California that, when state-wide meetings are held, they are usually convened in Fresno, long the "neutral territory" for conventions, conferences, and gatherings of all sort.

1. The Region

From San Francisco south, the coast-line extends in a north-south direction until Point Conception is reached at latitude 34.30 degrees; then the line swerves abruptly east and the shoreline begins to face almost due south. Once Point Conception has been rounded in an ocean liner, once the Tehachapi range has been crossed by train or car, even the most obtuse observer, the rankest neophyte, can *feel* that he has entered a new and distinct province of the state. If Southern California is entered from the east, through El Cajon Pass or San Gorgonio Pass, the impression is even more vividly sensed. On the Pacific side, the coast range turns east. The mountains no longer shut off the interior from the sea. The air is softer, the ocean is bluer, and the skies have a lazy and radiant warmth. South of Point Conception, a new Pacific Ocean emerges: an ocean in which you can actually bathe and swim, an ocean that sparkles with sunlight, an ocean of many and brilliant colors. Here is California del Sur, the Cow Counties, sub-tropical California, the land South of Tehachapi.

Physically the region is as distinct, as unlike any other part of the state, as though it were another country. But this separateness is not accurately reflected in county boundaries. Southern California, properly speaking, is one of the smallest geographic regions in America. It includes part of Santa Barbara County (the portion south of Tehachapi), all of Ventura, Los Angeles, and Orange Counties, and those portions of San Bernardino, Riverside, and San Diego Counties "west of the mountains." It does not include Imperial County, for Imperial Valley belongs, geographically and otherwise, to the Colorado River basin. Southern California is a coastal strip of land—"the fortunate coast" as Hamlin Garland once called it—275 miles in length and with a depth that ranges from a few miles to nearly a hundred miles "from the mountains to the sea." The land area itself embraces approximately 11,729 square miles.

As a region, Southern California is rescued from the desert by the San Bernardino and San Jacinto Mountains on the east and is walled off from the great Central Valley by the transverse Tehachapi range which, running in an east-west direction, unites the Sierra Nevada and the coast ranges. Not only do these towering mountain ranges serve to keep out the heat and dust of the desert, but they are high enough to snatch moisture from the ocean winds and to form clouds. The land itself faces west, toward the Pacific, from which the winds blow with great regularity. It is this combination of mountain ranges, ocean breezes, and semi-desert terrain that makes the "climate," and the climate in turn makes the land.

Offshore are the Channel Islands, definitely a part of the region although traditionally detached from its social life. At one time several of the islands were thickly populated with Indians, but the Spaniards removed the Indians to the mainland, leaving the islands as deserted as they are today (with the exception of resort-ridden Santa Catalina). To the north, near Point Conception, are the islands of the Santa Barbara group: perennially fog-bound San Miguel, the Anacapas, Santa Rosa, Santa Cruz, and San Nicolas well offshore. About a hundred miles south of Santa Barbara are the Catalina Islands: Santa Catalina and San Clemente; while still further south, near San Diego, are the islands of the Los Coronados group.

In all of Southern California, there are no fully mature soils.

Stretching from "the Sierras to the Sea," the lowlands are covered with huge coalescing alluvial fans formed of materials washed down from the mountains. The coastal plains are broken, here and there, by branches of the Sierra Madre range and by three of the driest rivers in America: the Los Angeles, the San Gabriel, and the Santa Ana. It was surely of these rivers that Mark Twain spoke when he said that he had fallen into a California river and "come out all dusty." Today the three rivers carry only a limited amount of surface and drainage waters, although each has an excellent underground flow. Here, in Southern California, as J. Russell Smith has observed, "rain makes possible the homes of man where otherwise there would be only jack rabbits, pastures, a little extensive farming, and a few small irrigated oases."

Basically the region is a paradox: a desert that faces an ocean. Since it is desert or semi-desert country, maximum sunshine prevails most of the year. The sunshine makes up for what the soils lack—a discovery that both Anglo and Hispano settlers were slow to make. Before man completely changed the ecology of the region, the natural landscape was not particularly prepossessing. The native vegetation consisted of chaparral on the moist mountain slopes and bunch grass on the lowlands. The real richness of the land is not to be found in the soils but in the combination of sky and air and ocean breezes. The wisecrack that Los Angeles is half wind and half water describes a real condition. As a region, Southern California lacks nearly everything: good soils; natural harbors (San Diego has the one natural harbor); forest and mineral resources; rivers, streams, and lakes; adaptable flora and fauna; and a sustaining hinterland. Yet the region has progressed amazingly by a succession of swift, revolutionary changes, from one level of development to another, offsetting natural limitations with an inventive technology. Its one great natural asset, in fact, is its climate.

The climate of Southern California is palpable: a commodity that can be labeled, priced, and marketed. It is not something that you talk about, complain about, or guess about. On the contrary, it is the most consistent, the least paradoxical factor in the environment. Unlike climates the world over, it is predictable to the point of monotony. In its air-conditioned equability, it might well be called "artificial." The climate is the region. It has attracted unlimited resources of manpower and wealth, made possible intensive agricultural development, and located specialized industries, such as motion pictures. It has given the region its rare beauty. For the charm of Southern California is largely to be found in the air and the light. Light and air are really one element: indivisible, mutually interacting, thoroughly interpenetrated. Without the ocean breezes, the sunlight would be intolerable; without the sunlight and imported water, virtually nothing would grow in the region.

When the sunlight is not screened and filtered by the moisture-laden air, the land is revealed in all its semi-arid poverty. The bald, sculptured mountains stand forth in a harsh and glaring light. But let the light turn soft with ocean mist, and miraculous changes occur. The bare mountain ranges, appallingly harsh in contour, suddenly become wrapped in an entrancing ever-changing loveliness of light and shadow; the most commonplace objects assume a matchless perfection of form; and the land itself becomes a thing of beauty. The color of the land is in the light and the light is somehow artificial and controlled. Things are not killed by the sunlight, as in a desert; they merely dry up. A desert light brings out the sharpness of points, angles, and forms. But this is not a desert light nor is it tropical for it has neutral tones. It is Southern California light and it has no counterpart in the world.

The geographers say that the quality of Southern California's climate is pure Mediterranean—the only specimen of Mediterranean climate in the United States. But such words as "Mediterranean" and "sub-tropical" are most misleading when applied to Southern California. Unlike the Mediterranean coast, Southern California has no sultry summer air, no mosquito-ridden malarial marshes, no mistral winds. A freak of nature—a cool and semi-moist desert—Southern California is climatically insulated, shut off from the rest of the continent. As Helen Hunt Jackson once said, and it is the best description of the region yet coined, "It is a sort of island on the land." It is an island, however, of sharp contrasts. To William Rose Benet, the land suggests "a flowing life circle cut into contrasting angles . . . hills change over a week from garish green to golden brown; days are hot in the sun and cool in the shade; dense fog and spotless sky; giant trees or bare slopes; burnt sand or riotous flowers."

Traveling west from Chicago, the transition from one landscape to another although often abrupt is altogether logical. The rich, black Mississippi bottom lands shade off imperceptibly into the Kansas wheat lands; the Kansas plains lead naturally up to the foothills of the Rocky Mountains; once over the mountains, stretches of desert alternate with high piñon-covered plateaus; and, across the Colorado River, the desert climbs slowly to the last mountain range. Up to this point, the contrasting landscapes have seemed pleasing and appropriate; the eye has not been offended nor the emotions shocked. But, once the final descent has been made from the desert, through Cajon Pass, to the floor of the coastal plain at San Bernardino, one has entered a new world, an island tenuously attached to the rest of the continent. "My first impression," wrote L. P. Jacks, "was such as one might receive on arriving in a City of Refuge, or alternatively on entering the atmosphere of a religious retreat. Here, it seems, is the place where harassed Americans come to recover the joy and serenity which their manner of life denies them elsewhere, the place, in short, to study America in flight from herself." Logically Southern California should be several miles offshore, so that one might be prepared for the transition from the desert and the intermountain West. But, if the long train trip is thought of, as it should be, as an ocean crossing, then the island-like character of the region is properly revealed.

Southern California is the land of the "sun-down sea," where the sun suddenly plummets into the ocean, disappearing "like a lost and bloody cause." It is a land where "the Sun's rim dips—at one stride comes the Dark." Of landward rolling mists, but not of clouds; of luminous nights, but not of stars; of evanescent light, but not of sunsets; of rounded rolling hills and mountains without trees. Here the sun glares out of a high blue sky—a sun that can beat all sense from your brains, that can be "destructive of all you have known and believed": a relentless, pounding, merciless sun. But when the mists roll in at evening, the skies brighten with "blue daylight" and the air is like "a damp cloth on the forehead of the hills." Cool and fragrant and alive, the nights engulf the glaring pavements, the white stucco homes, the red-tiled roofs, the harsh and barren hills. From Mt. Wilson, late at night, one can look down on a vast pulsating blaze of lights, quivering like diamonds in the dark. Here, as Frank Fenton notes, the land does not hug the sky; it is the sky that is solid and real and the land that seems to float. At times you feel as though you were far away "on the underside of the earth."

2. THE SEASONS

Most people believe that there are only two seasons in Southern California: "the wet" and "the dry." But this crude description fails to take account of the imperceptible changes that occur within the two major seasons. Actually, Southern California has two springs, two summers, and a season of rain. The first spring—the premature spring—follows closely upon the early rains in the late fall. In November the days shorten; the nights become cooler; the atmosphere clears (except when brush fires are burning in the hills); the air is stilled; and the land is silent. By November people have begun to listen for rain. The land is dry and parched and the leaves of the trees are thick with dust. The dry season has now begun to fray nerves, to irritate nostrils, and to bear down on the people. When the wind blows, it is full of particles of dust and dry leaves, of sand and heat.

And then come the first rains, drifting in long graceful veils, washing the land, clearing the atmosphere: the gentlest baptism imaginable. The people have known to a moral certainty that these rains would come; they have been expecting them; and, yet, they are forever delighted and surprised when they appear. The earth is reborn, the year starts anew, with the rains. James Rorty has perfectly captured the elation aroused by the first rains:

> Faultless in wisdom, at my window-pane
> Compassionate sweet laughter of the rain.
> The cowled hills, rising, met and kissed
> The grey-eyed daughters of the mist;
> Above the flawed and driven tide
> The white gulls flapped wet wings and cried;
> High on the slope the cattle lowed and ran,
> On every hill the meadow-larks began
> Their confident loud chime of Spring's rebirth;
> Iris and tooth-wort stirred the fragrant earth . .
>
> I, too, who let the blown rain whip my face,
> Received my portion of the season's grace.

After these first rains—which fall gently, never in torrents—the sun is softer: it no longer burns, the air is cool and fragrant, and the hills begin to change. In a miraculously short period—a matter of days—the country is green and fresh. It is not the "green-dense and dim-delicious" green of the poets of the English countryside. Rather the land is clothed in a freakish greenery, a green so bright that, at times, it is almost sickening. "It is a bright emerald hue," as one observer has noted, "and has a sheen upon it which is like that upon the rind of green fruit, but much stronger. This appearance is very rank, and looks as though it would come off on your hands."

The first spring has now arrived: "the little spring" that only lasts a few weeks. A premonition of spring, it tricks the senses of the people and deludes the plants and flowers which start to bud and blossom out of season. Often called "the false spring," it deceives the gullible semi-tropical plants which sometimes bloom weeks, and even months, in advance of their regular schedule. Jasmine, bougain-villea, privet, hibiscus, oleanders, and trumpet vines, usually dormant at this time of the year, suddenly start to bloom. Under the illusion that spring has arrived, bare-root roses blossom and the buds of peach and apricot trees begin to swell. But this is not spring, only a conceit of nature, a lovely winter mirage.

And then in January, February, and March come the real rains: heavy, torrential, soggy. These rains do not slant in from the sea, but, like emptied buckets of water, fall straight and level on the earth. The arroyos race with rain waters; the dry river beds overflow; the floods have arrived. The earth now smells wet and the chaparral begins to brighten. The last rains come in April—"grasshopper rains" they were once called—showers and squalls, fitful and intermittent. Before the last rains have fallen, the real spring has arrived. There is a sudden blaze of color on the land. The green has changed from its early vividness to the heavier dense green of the rains, and, as the season advances, the green begins to bleach and fade. This second spring is really an aborted summer.

The second spring ends with the first desert winds, which usually come in May and last for several days. The ocean breezes suddenly cease, as the hot dry desert winds come whirling down the canyons, through the passes, and rush out across the valleys. Harsh and burn-ing winds, they rip off palm leaves, snap branches, topple over eucalyptus trees, and occasionally carry off a flimsy roof. The desert winds bring dust and heat. The mountains stand out in the sharpest possible outline, so clear that you can see the rocks and boulders, so close that you can almost touch them. These are the winds once called "northers," but which the Spanish called "santannas." Dona Magdalena Murrillo, born on the Las Bolsas Rancho in 1848, said that the winds were called "Santa Anas" because they came down the Santa Ana Canyon. They were always very hot, she said, and stirred up a *polvareda grande*. When the Santa Anas came, no one dared light a fire, even in a stove. Don Jesus Aguilar, of San Juan Capistrano, said the wind was called *El Viento del Norte*; but Willa Cather, referring to hot desert winds in New Mexico, called them "santannas." The desert winds often precede the last rain of the season.

After the desert winds, comes June: cool and gray, with day-long mists and overcast. The summer flowers are at their loveliest; the lawns are damp and fragrant; and the leaves of the camphor tree, brightest and gayest of all the trees in Southern California, shimmer and dance in the air. But by late May it is already fall—in the hills; away from the fountains and the sprinklers. The hills are tawny and the black shade of the live oaks is dense and heavy. The full blaze of summer color has gone by July and the summer that follows is the long summer of the dry season, when the hills are brown as umber. August is "only the long-lingering afternoon of a long-lingering summer day." In late August the sea breeze dies and once again the desert winds sweep across the land. This is the hottest spell of the year: baking-hot, desert-hot, oppressive. Brush fires break out in the foothills just as they often do when the Santa Anas come in May. Heat from the brush fires, smoking and blazing in the foothills, makes the inland districts writhe and burn.

"Where had been a lush thicket of ferns," writes Stewart Edward White, "now the earth lay naked and baked, displaying unexpected simplicities of contour that had before been mysteriously veiled. So hard and trodden looked this earth that it seemed incredible that any green thing had ever, or could ever again, pierce its steel-like shell. The land was stripped bare. In the trees the wind rustled dryly. In the sky the sun shone glaringly." The fog banks, however, prevent the summers from being oppressive throughout the season. Forming beyond the islands, they can be seen moving in toward the coast "in long attenuated streamers and banners, as night comes on, filling up the valleys of the coast with great tumultuous seas." With the morning sunlight, the mists obligingly roll out to sea. Throughout the summer, one can see this fog bank, about a thousand feet thick, lying offshore on the water. It has the strange feature, wrote Van Dyke, "of moving in against a breeze—the land-breeze—and moving out against another—the sea-breeze."

Toward the end of the long summer, when the unirrigated sections of the land are a gray, sun-baked tan, one can see, as James M. Cain has observed, that "the naked earth shows through everything that grows on it." It is then that one notices the sparseness of leafage in relation to the land. The earth is naked and exposed in Southern California. It is like the skin of a sun-tanned body with the few indigenous trees standing out sharply, like the hairs on the body, and not, as in other areas, like a thick mat of hair on the head. There is no carpet on the earth. Everywhere exposed, the earth is brown and gray and only seldom green. Today the appearance of the region is deceitful and illusory, for essentially it is a barren, a semi-arid land.

3. City-State

One of the smallest geographic regions in America, Southern California is today one of the most intensively developed. Perhaps the most thoroughly urbanized region in America, it is made up of a network of cities and towns stretching from Santa Barbara to San Diego, from Santa Monica to San Bernardino. All of these cities and towns are, in a sense, suburbs of Los Angeles. No region in America, write the geographers White and Foscue, is dominated by one city to the extent that Los Angeles, with its 450 square miles of territory, dominates Southern California. The Los Angeles Times is the newspaper of the entire region, almost as widely read in the outlying communities as in Los Angeles proper. The whole region is closely tied together by a network of roads and highways, electrical transmission lines and aqueducts, islands within an island dominated by Los Angeles.

For all practical purposes, it is a non-rural region; there are few strictly rural districts. In effect, Southern California constitutes a single metropolitan district which should be characterized as rurban: neither city nor country but everywhere a mixture of both. Just as

Southern California is the least rural of all the regions in America, so, paradoxically, Los Angeles is the least citified of all the cities of America. "Nowhere in the United States," writes J. Russell Smith, "is it more difficult to draw a line between city life, suburban life, and country life, because the farms are so small, the roads so good, and the automobile so universal that large numbers of people are making their living or a part of it by growing fruit, vegetables, and poultry on farms so small, and therefore so close together, that the farm area seems like an Eastern residential suburb."

Like the entire region, Los Angeles, its heart and center, has developed in spite of its location rather than because of it. Southern California is man-made, a gigantic improvisation. Virtually everything in the region has been imported: plants, flowers, shrubs, trees, people, water, electrical energy, and, to some extent, even the soils. While potentially a rich and fertile region, the land required a highly developed technology to unlock its resources and to tap its amazing fertility. Given water and proper scientific cultivation, the land will raise more things, faster, and in greater quantities than any other section of America. It is difficult for persons not familiar with the region to believe that Los Angeles County is the richest agricultural county in America—a distinction that it has long enjoyed. It is a versatile and hospitable land. Most of the herbs, trees, shrubs, plants, and flowers to be found in the region today are immigrants. Trees that most visitors believe are indigenous, such as the eucalyptus, the acacia, and the pepper tree, are, nonetheless, importations (the first two from Australia, the latter from South America). Forage plants and grasses, as well as such vertebrates as the rat, the house-mouse, the English sparrow, and the pheasant, are likewise importations. Even the weeds of the region are not native.

Without lumber and minerals, with only one natural harbor, lacking water and fuels, and surrounded by mountains, desert, and ocean, there was seemingly never a region so unlikely to become a vast metropolitan area as Southern California. It is an artificial region, a product of forced growth and rapid change. Plants and flowers, crops and cities grow rankly in this region, in "a growth roused from its fiery sleep, striving in a day to make up for ages of helpless bondage." No region in America has experienced anything like the same rapidity of growth and social change that has characterized Southern California. The following table tells its own story:

Population of:

Year	Southern California	Los Angeles
1860...............	24,751	4,385
1870...............	32,032	5,728
1880...............	64,371	11,183
1890...............	201,352	50,395
1900...............	304,211	102,479
1910...............	751,310	319,198
1920...............	1,347,050	576,673
1930...............	2,932,795	1,238,048
1940...............	3,572,363	1,504,277

Today, over 4,000,000 reside in the region, of whom approximately 3,000,000 reside in the Los Angeles metropolitan district. The concentration is even more striking than these figures indicate, for included in the Southern California total for 1940, as I have given it, are 59,740 residents of Imperial County.

Walled off from the rest of the country by mountain ranges and desert wastes, Southern California is an island on the land, geographically attached, rather than functionally related, to the rest of America. The Spanish explorers who mistakenly thought of California, first, as an island, and, later, as a peninsula, were right in theory if wrong in fact. Explaining California's industrial problems, a spokesman for the War Production Board, in an interview of July 17, 1945, aptly said, "Those mountains and dry lands constitute the great wall of California. They are a barrier that separates the west coast industrially from the other states. California is an economic island, an entity that must look overseas for new markets." As Charles Fletcher Lummis once said, California is "the right hand of the continent." Long separated from the East and the other sections that make up the West, California developed in relative isolation a more-or-less self-centered culture, a culture that has matured more rapidly than the culture of the other western states. While all of California is, in this sense, an island, the insularity of Southern California presents a special case. To Southern Californians, the rest of California is ultramontane, remote, and unrelated. If California is a peninsula attached to the continent, Southern California is an island at the foot of the peninsula.

4. IRREDENTISM IN CALIFORNIA

"Mountains interposed make enemies of nations,
Who had else like kindred drops
Been mingled into one."   —William Cowper

The well-known rivalry between San Francisco and Los Angeles, between Northern and Southern California, has often been regarded as merely another up-state-down-state feud. But the issue involves far more than economic rivalry or competition for prestige. Actually the two sections of the state have long been separated by many barriers: historical and physiographic, social and cultural. Time has not bridged this rift nor is it likely to be bridged in the future.

Even under Mission rule, the Franciscans repeatedly suggested that the state should be divided, for administrative purposes, at the Tehachapi line. The Missions in Southern California were the oldest, the most prosperous, and the most densely settled. The College of San Fernando once offered to cede to the College of Orizaba the nine Missions south of Santa Ynez (in Santa Barbara County). The ten northern Missions were frequently referred to, in the Mission records, as "worthless skeletons." Under the period of Mexican rule, two political parties developed on the basis of the same divisionist sentiment: the *arribenos* or *nortenos* (the upper or northern people), and the *abajenos* or *surenos* (the lower or southern people). The Alvarados, Vallejos, and Castros of the north were invariably pitted against the Picos, Carrillos, and Bandinis of the south. A proposal for a division of the state was advanced at the first session of the Mexican legislature in 1822.

The same rift continued throughout the period of American rule. "Throughout the fifties," writes Dr. Caughey, "there was a strong undercurrent of feeling in favor of a division of the state." Fearing dominance by the newcomers of the north, the Southern California delegates raised the issue of state division at the constitutional convention in 1849. Important economic as well as political issues were involved. In 1852 the six Cow Counties of the south, with a population of 6,000, paid $42,000 in property taxes and $4,000 in poll taxes, while the northern counties, with a population of 120,000, paid only $21,000 and $3,500 in the same categories. The influential *Daily Alta*, published in the north, conceded that division was logical and desirable, since "no bound of connection or sympathy existed between their interests and those of the commercial cities and other sources of wealth in our infant state." In 1851, a convention to divide the state met in Los Angeles, at which a division, "friendly and peaceful but still complete," was advocated. In 1859 the people of Southern California, by a two-thirds vote, approved a measure for division which was forwarded to Congress. The proposal would unquestionably have been approved, but for the intervention of the Civil War.

From 1849 to 1860, the southern counties remained largely Spanish-speaking, a factor that aggravated the tensions between the two sections. Concentrated in the south, the Mexican-Spanish element looked with some favor upon the Confederate cause and tended to side with the Democratic Party, upon the assumption that secession of the southern states might enable Southern California also to secede. For years after 1849, the northern part of the state was dominated by miners and mining interests, but there was virtually no mining in the south. After the American conquest, the southern counties were isolated for twenty-five years from the north, a branch line of the Southern Pacific not being completed to the south until 1876.

Culturally, Northern California is western; Southern California is eastern (by longitude it is actually east of the northern or frontier part of the state). San Francisco, as Paul Schrecker has pointed out, had already developed features of its own when the invasion by mass production and uniform federal patterns began. It was therefore better prepared to resist the trend toward uniformity. The great California fortunes were made in the north and remained in the north. The northern part of the state was settled by single men; the south by families. The first great wave of migration to Southern California took place thirty years after the Gold Rush. Although the newer region, Southern California was settled by older people who came from Eastern and Middle Western regions thirty years more mature than the regions from which forty-niners had set forth for the gold fields. By 1880 the settlers of Northern California had come to think of themselves as native sons and believed they had a special mandate to rule the state. Adopting the habit of referring to San Francisco as "The City," they gave scant consideration to the views or interests of Southern California.

"There is a striking difference of physique," wrote Charles Fletcher Lummis in 1903, "between the street crowds of San Francisco and Los Angeles—a difference disheartening to those too innocent to know its why. The reason is simply that in San Francisco you see streets thronged with people who were born in California. In Los Angeles, on the other hand, I sometimes walk blocks without meeting, in all the crowd, one person who had ever seen California fifteen years ago—and I used to know every face in the town. That the real reason of the startling difference is only this, the children conclusively prove. The southern youngsters are just as stalwart-legged, just as thick-chested, just as surprisingly big for the eloquent calendar of their ruddy faces." Even earlier, in 1888, J. P. Widney had contended that "two distinct peoples are growing up in the state, and the time is rapidly drawing near when the separation which the working of natural laws is making in the people must become a separation of civil laws as well."

"A certain independence born of geographical location," writes Dr. Henry Harris in his history of the medical profession in California, "always characterized Southern California, as though the region were more an extension of the southwest than of the north." The sentiment itself is reflected in an article which appeared in a Southern California medical journal in 1866: "Distance, rugged intervening mountains and entirely diverse commercial and industrial interests, which are making of California two separate and distinct sections, have also in a great measure prevented a close union of the medical profession. Southern California has developed its own intellectual life and its own educational system. We believe that the time has come for the establishment of its own medical journals and societies."

Throughout the years, the sentiment for division always emanated from the south and was always resisted in the north. As population increased in the south, the sentiment intensified. The north had more rainfall than the south and much better water resources. As a consequence, a proposal was advanced in 1880 to divide the state upon the basis of the respective water-needs of the two sections: riparian rights in the north, the doctrine of appropriation in the south. When the doctrine of riparian rights was upheld as the common law of the state in 1884, after a long and bitter struggle involving actual violence and bloodshed, the south thought that it had been dealt a crushing blow. The issue was so fundamental that division would have resulted had not the doctrine of riparian rights been somewhat modified by legislation. In 1904 the south launched still another campaign to sever itself from the north. This time the mistake was made of including Tulare and Kern Counties (both north of the Tehachapi line) in the proposed new state, and, as a consequence, the proposal was stillborn. In 1909, Edwin T. Earl, publisher of the Los Angeles *Express*, once again raised "the bloody torch of division," and summoned a secession convention which met in Los Angeles. Mr. Earl wanted to divide the state at the Tehachapi line, but, in the meantime, the City of Los Angeles had reached out to Inyo County for water, a circumstance that made his proposal obviously unworkable.

Since the southern counties did not pass the northern counties in population until after 1920, it was only natural that the legislature should consistently favor the northern part of the state. For thirty-two years after California was admitted to the union, there was not a single state-supported institution in the south. Pressure for institutional appropriations finally resulted in a condescending gesture from the north: the legislature bestowed upon the "cow counties" an insane asylum and a reformatory! For many years virtually all the federal appropriations, under the river and harbor provisions, were spent in Northern California. Most of the early hospitals, schools, and colleges, which received public support, were located in the north, resulting in an institutional and cultural "lag" in the south which has persisted to the present day.

Throughout the years, the cultural rift has been pronounced. The Los Angeles *Herald* pointed out, in 1892, that "long ago the various religious bodies separated from their parent organizations in Northern California," and called attention to the fact that the secret fraternal societies had long followed the practice of dividing jurisdiction and authority at the Tehachapi as a means of preserving unity. As late as 1942, the Baptist convention considered a petition signed by 3,000 Baptists living in Southern California asking that they be permitted to affiliate with the Southern Baptist convention then in session at San Antonio. The story was reported in the press under the headline: "California Sudeten Problem Has Baptists Fighting Civil War Again." The Southern California "Sudeten" Baptists, furthermore, were granted a schism and permitted to join the southern wing of the church. In their booster activities, the southern counties always acted independently of the northern. Settlers were invited to come to *Southern* California, as though it were a separate state. Increasingly, the phrase Southern California has been used in corporate names, in promotional activities, and in the names of both public and private institutions. The northern part of Santa Barbara County once sought to sever itself from the portion south of Tehachapi and to form a new county of "Olive."

The cultural cleavage was strikingly indicated in 1922. In that year a referendum was proposed to apply prohibition in the state. The measure carried by a vote of 445,000 to 411,000. How did it happen that a wine-producing state such as California could have adopted this measure? Californians living north of the Tehachapi voted decisively against the measure, but the vote in the south was heavily affirmative. "The country is the same," wrote André Siegfried who was visiting California at the time, "with the same Andalusian atmosphere, but the people are very different." One could cite numerous examples showing how, in state elections, the cultural difference between the two regions has accounted for otherwise inexplicable results. "We of Southern California," writes Max Miller, "are foreigners to Northern California. We are two separate countries."

The cultural difference is pronounced in the field of architecture, with most of the Spanish and pseudo-Spanish influences being confined to the south. San Francisco is a consciously historical city, mindful of its traditions, enamored of its past; a city of parks and monuments and statues. One can look in vain for a statue in Los Angeles. Arthur Millier has even noted some "division between the art tendencies of north and south." The art of San Francisco, he believes, is more sophisticated, modern, and cosmopolitan, while in the southern part of the state the tradition of the outdoor American landscape painter is dominant. "Many of the artists came from the Middle West during the last twenty years, imbued with its native American spirit." The mural painters are of the north; the landscape artists of the south. "It seems almost an absurdity to divide the northern section of California from that of the south," wrote Everett C. Maxwell in an essay on California art in 1915, "yet it is necessary to approach the subject from almost opposite viewpoints." The northern artists live in San Francisco and Carmel; those of the south, in Los Angeles, Santa Barbara, and Laguna Beach. Working apart from each other, they hold separate exhibits. Even the landscape painting of the two sections is different. "In the south," writes Mr. Maxwell, "the wave-washed shores of the Pacific, with their sandy formations, grotesque cliffs, and fantastic headlands are as unlike the colder waters and the etched shoreline of Monterey and Santa Cruz as anything could well be." The same division is noted in the handling of news. The Los Angeles newspapers ignore happenings north of Tehachapi, and the San Francisco newspapers carry little news from the south. To follow political events in the state, it is necessary to read a San Francisco, a Los Angeles, and a Central Valley newspaper.

To some extent the sentiment for division has abated as the center of population has shifted to the south. Between 1880 and 1928, the center of population moved 165 miles south. In 1880, the southern counties had 7½% of the state's population; in 1890, 16%; in 1904, 20%; but by 1928, the southern counties had 53.3% of the population with Los Angeles and Orange Counties alone having 40% of the state's total. Once this point had been reached, the south did begin to secure some measure of equity at the hands of the state legislature. But reapportionment has never kept pace with population changes. It was not until 1933, in fact, that Southern California secured the representation to which it was entitled in Washington and in Sacramento and, even then, the northern counties, by a swift political maneuver, circumvented the south by restricting representation in the state senate to one senator for each county.

So sharply defined are north and south in California that I am convinced that some form of severance is inescapable. It is not likely, of course, that division will take the form of establishing a new state in the south. The cultural differences between the two regions have leveled off to such an extent that actual separation is not likely (although the idea echoed, again, in the 1945 session of the legislature). Division will come about through the granting, to the southern cities and counties, of an ever-increasing autonomy. Under its present charter, the City of Los Angeles is virtually free of state control. The County of Los Angeles, with 16,198 employees, 45 incorporated and 60 unincorporated communities, and a current budget of $90,287,165, is already a state within a state. By budget standards, number of employees, and size of population, it warrants comparison with some thirty-six state governments. What is actually happening is that a league of cities is coming into existence in Southern California under the hegemony of Los Angeles. One does not need to share all the illusions of the boosters to believe, as I believe, that the most fantastic city in the world will one day exist in this region: a city embracing the entire region from the mountains to the sea.

"Here the Indians gathered round them,
Here the crucifix adored,
While the vibrant bells' sweet music
On the sleeping air was poured."
—Eliza A. Otis

CHAPTER II

THE INDIAN IN THE CLOSET

A LAND of magical improvisation, Southern California has created its own past, with a special cast, and a script written by its favorite troubadours, John Steven McGroarty, George Wharton James, and Charles Fletcher Lummis. Unquestionably the production, with its improvised traditions and manufactured legends, has been a huge success. There have been few visitors to Southern California who have not made a tour of the Missions, purchased a postcard with a picture of Ramona's birthplace, and attended a performance of the Mission Play. With a boldness more comic than brazen, the synthetic past has been kept alive by innumerable pageants, fiestas, and outdoor enactments of one kind or another; by the restoration of the Missions; and by the establishment of such curious spectacles as Olvera Street in the Old Plaza section of Los Angeles.

The symbols of this synthetic past are three in number: the Franciscan padre praying at sundown in the Mission garden, lovely Ramona and brave Alessandro fleeing through the foothills of Mt. San Jacinto, and the Old Spanish Don sunning himself in the courtyard of his rancho. Around these sacred symbols, the legends have grown. According to the authorized version, the officially approved script, the Indians were devoted to the Franciscans, and, with the collapse of the Mission system, lost their true friends and devoted defenders. As Michael Williams puts it, "The poor, foolish, yet gentle and lovable sheep lost their shepherds, and upon them rushed the wolves of vice, of robbery, of cruel injustice." The other side of the legend has to do with the idyllic period "before the gringos" came, when the Spanish residents of Alta California, all members of one big happy guitar-twanging family, danced the fandango and lived out days of beautiful indolence in lands of the sun that expand the soul. Before explaining how this legend came into existence, it might be well to take a look at the facts.

If asked to define the areas of Indian influence in the United States, the average American would probably reply, "Oklahoma, New Mexico, Arizona, and the Great Plains." After a moment's reflection, he might add Wisconsin and the Northwest, and, if prodded sufficiently, he might even mention Florida and California. But it is extremely unlikely that he would think of Southern California, so thoroughly has the region buried its Indian dead. But the Indian skeleton is still there, in the closet, and of late such investigators as Dr. S. F. Cook of the University of California have been performing an interesting, if belated, post-mortem.

Indians have exerted a profound influence on the development of Southern California. Despite the fact that Indian influences have been frequently confused with Spanish influences (wherever possible the Spanish has been emphasized to the detriment of the Indian), the Indian influence is still perceptible throughout the region, primarily in the long since forgotten origin of such curious place-names as Anacapa, Azusa, Cahuenga, Camulos, Castac, Cosmit, Cucamonga, Cuyama, Cuyamaca, Guajome, Guatay, Hueneme, Jalama, Jamacha, Jamul, Jurupa, Lompoc, Malibu, Mugu, Muscipiabe, Nipomo, Ojai, Otay, Pocoima, Pala, Pismo, Saboba, Saticoy, Sespe, Tapu, and Yacaipa. "The Indian of Southern California," writes Owen H. O'Neill, "has left a greater imprint on the land than is generally known. He located all of the Spanish Missions of California. The padres built where the Indians were established in greatest numbers. Most of the cities of the coastal region are built squarely upon Indian village sites. The reason is a simple one: the Indians chose the most favored spot with a sure knowledge born of long experience in the region. He sought fresh water, a scarce commodity in early days; a smooth shoreline; and abundant vegetation." The Indian village of Yang-na became Los Angeles; Sibag-na is now San Gabriel; while Santa Ana is located on the site of the Indian village of Hutucg-na.

While not a living influence, the dead hand of the Indian is everywhere upon the land. Indian forced-labor is the key to the explanation of the rapid agricultural development, as it also explains the backward and restricted character of this development. Indians furnished the labor power for the far-flung Mission enterprises. They cleared the ground, planted the first vineyards, constructed the irrigation ditches and canals, and built the Missions. The Indian influence explains the singular dichotomy in the cultural traditions of the region between what is termed "Spanish," and is therefore valuable and praiseworthy, and what is termed "Mexican" and is therefore undesirable. For while Indian and Spanish are, in a sense, oppositional terms in this cultural tradition, the Indian and Mexican influences tend to merge. Lastly, the brutal treatment of Indians in Southern California in large part explains the persistence of an ugly racial arrogance in the mores of the region of which, alas, more than a vestige remains.

Somehow this Indian background got lost in the transition from Spanish to English. There was much lore and information about the Indians in the Spanish archives which did not reappear in English until long after most of the Indians had been exterminated. Even after the Spanish chronicles began to appear in English, the record remained incomplete and misleading. For there was much confusion and contradiction in the Spanish version, with Mission apologists being ranged against Mexican anti-clericals. Going back over these records in later years, the American historians popularized whichever version best suited their particular purposes. When the great commercial value of the Mission tradition was discovered around 1888— an event of major importance in the cultural history of Southern California—the healthy realism of such California historians as Bancroft, Forbes, and Hittell was largely forgotten and the Franciscan version of the Indian was accepted at face value. In a region of rapid social change, such as Southern California, traditions have a tendency to become lost, distorted, or confused, with part of the confusion being purposeful and part fortuitous. It is not surprising, therefore, that a bizarre pattern of cultural miscegenation should have developed in the region in which the Indian influence was almost wholly obscured.

"The poor California Indian," writes Dr. John Walton Caughey, "has almost never had a good word said for him." Neither the Spanish explorers and colonizers nor the Franciscan fathers were particularly impressed with the Indian in California. In fact they inclined to write the Indian down to the lowest level of humanity, as Stephen Powers once observed, "that the more conspicuous might appear that self-sacrificing benevolence which reached down to pluck him to salvation." If the Franciscans were condescending, the early Anglo settlers were contemptuous. When the great overland trek started, these settlers brought the term "Digger Indian," with all its ugly implications, from the region of the Great Salt Lake and the Humboldt Valley and applied it to the California Indians. As thus applied the term was as unjustly opprobrious as it would have been to call all Chinese "rat-eaters."

At a later date, when the Mission legend had become part of a grandiose real-estate ballyhoo, a wholly mythical "Mission Indian" was created and invested with the sentiments of a New England schoolmarm. Thus, to this day, the word "Indian" in Southern California has its sacred and profane connotations. In the flesh—in the areas where they still survive—Indians remain "Digger Indians," fabled in local folklore for their thievery, filth, and lechery. But, with each annual production of the Ramona Pageant, pictures of godlike Indians in battle-dress appear in the rotogravure sections of the Los Angeles *Times* and the Indian Love Call echoes throughout Southern California. Underlying these layers upon layers of confusion, myth, and prejudice is a substratum of fact which it is the purpose of this chapter to explore.

1. In Pre-Columbian Times

In pre-Columbian times, it is estimated that there were about 130,000 Indians in California. If this estimate is correct, then California had about 16% of the aboriginal population of the United States by comparison with 5% of its land area. Even at the minimum estimate of 130,000 (the figure has been placed as high as 700,000), the density of Indian population in California was three or four times greater than for the nation as a whole. The relative density was even greater than indicated, for the California Indians were highly concentrated in limited areas of settlement in the state. They were not distributed randomly, but clung to the main watercourses, the valleys or their edges, and the open canyon areas. Each particular Indian grouping had its area of settlement to which the members of the group were devoted as they were to nothing else in their culture.

Like the Californians of today, the California Indians were a highly heterogeneous lot. Some 22 linguistic systems and 138 different idioms have been recorded. Lacking definite tribal organizations, the Indians were scattered in small land-owning politically autonomous groups. Each group had a chief of a sort, but hereditary priests were unknown. Such social organization as existed was extremely rudimentary in character. So far as political organization was concerned, the small settlement or rancheria, made up of 130 or 150 Indians—usually of related families—was about the most comprehensive unit that existed. While the Indian settlements were scattered, they were, as Dr. S. F. Cook has pointed out, "spaced very exactly in conformity with the food supply." Despite the primitive stage of their culture, the California Indians had not been declining in numbers prior to the Spanish explorations and settlement; on the contrary, they had apparently achieved a stable relationship with their environment.

In general, the distribution of Indians in Southern California followed the pattern of population distribution today. In the region south of Tehachapi were seven groupings, some known by their native names, others by the name of the Mission with which they were later associated. The northernmost group, the Chumash, occupied three of the Santa Barbara or Channel Islands, and the coastal region of Santa Barbara. The first California Indians discovered by Cabrillo in 1542, they were the most highly developed of the Southern California groups. All of the Chumash Indians, with an estimated population of 10,000, were involved in the activities of the five Missions later established in their territory: San Buenaventura, Santa Barbara, Santa Ynez, La Purisima Concepcion, and San Luis Obispo.

Farther south were several Indian groups whose language was Shoshonean in origin: the Serrano or "those of the Sierras," located in the San Bernardino Mountains and the lowlands of the San Bernardino Valley; the Gabrielino, occupying Los Angeles County south of the Sierra Madre, half of Orange County, and two of the

Channel Islands (Santa Catalina and San Clemente); and still farther south along the coast, the Luiseno. The Serranos and the Gabrielino were associated with the Mission San Gabriel; the Luiseno with the Mission San Luis Rey. Wedged in between the Gabrielino and the Luiseno were the Juaneo Indians, named after the Mission San Juan Capistrano. In the inland basin between the San Bernardino Mountains and Mt. San Jacinto were the Cahuilla Indians, separated into three groups known as desert, pass, and mountain Cahuilla. Since they remained outside the scope of Mission activity, the Cahuilla Indians survived in larger numbers than the other Southern California groups. In the area around San Diego were the San Diegueno Indians (named after the Mission San Diego), a Yuman tribe, living in a territory bounded on the west by the ocean, on the north by the country of the Luiseno and the Cahuilla, and with no very precise eastern or southern boundary.

In pre-Spanish times, the region south of Tehachapi constituted a fairly distinct cultural province. While this southern cultural province is generally regarded by anthropologists as an offshoot of the Pueblo culture of the Southwest, some trans-Pacific influences have been noted among the Indians along the coast. For example, the cosmogony of the Luiseno and Gabrielino contained some influences regarded by Kroeber as being Polynesian in character, while the Gabrielino and the Chumash had shell fishhooks distinctly Micronesian in form.

Admittedly the culture of these Southern California Indians was primitive in character. They had no agriculture. Their calendar was extremely crude. Their art-forms were limited in number and elementary in design, with basketry being their most developed art (there was only a little pottery). Partly maritime, the Chumash Indians crossed the Santa Barbara Channel to the islands in canoes of marvelous construction, moving so swifty on the waters "that they seemed to fly." Miguel Constano, an engineer who accompanied Portola in 1769, noted that the Channel Island Indians worked "handsome trays of wood, with fine inlays of coral or bone," and commented upon their considerable mechanical ability. Money, in the form of shells and a disk bead, was known. Among the Southern California Indians, warfare was virtually unknown and slavery was not practiced. Although they had no intoxicating drink, they smoked a wild tobacco. Marriage was generally by purchase, but prostitution, as such, was unknown. The women wore a two-piece apron of buckskin, shredded bark, or other plant fiber, "while the manly fashion was to go naked."

South of Tehachapi, sandals replaced moccasins. The shelters were brush-covered or made of earth and were of the one-family type. Since they were not nomadic, the Indians were reported by the Spanish to be "docile and obedient." A universal institution was the sweat-house or temescal. The most common archaeological specimen in Southern California is the stone grinding bowl or mortar, used in grinding acorns. A simple bow and a throwing stick were the principal hunting weapons. While large game was not hunted and agriculture was unknown, an adequate food supply existed. Acorns were the staple item, but herbs, grass seeds, fish, rabbits, small game, snakes, grasshoppers, snails, and slugs were also part of the diet. A drumless region, the rattle was the principal noise-maker. Invariably referred to in the early chronicles as filthy and degraded, it is nevertheless apparent from these same records that the Southern California Indians, particularly the women, were not wholly unattractive. Jose Longinos Martinez, in his journal of 1792, wrote that the women dressed their hair with great taste. "This dressing or coiffure," he noted, "makes the women graceful in their air and neat, and gives them some attraction for the Spaniards." It is interesting to observe that the earlier the record or chronicle, the more attractively the Indian is portrayed.

The backward character of the culture of these Indians was to be explained, as Dr. Caughey has pointed out, in terms of the physical facts of the province rather than in terms of the degraded character of the Indian. California was isolated by mountain ranges and a vast stretch of desert from the more advanced Indian tribes. While its resources were unlimited, they were of such a nature that they could not be unlocked except by an advanced technology. To indicate the degree of isolation which prevailed, Dr. Caughey points out that "although the Spaniards had been settled in Mexico for 250 years and in New Mexico for 170 years, not a single Spanish culture trait seems to have penetrated to California before the coming of settlers in 1769." Prior to the coming of the colonists, the Southern California Indians lived in small islands of settlement in a region that was itself an island on the land.

In Southern Caifornia proper, that is from the Tehachapi along the northern edge of the Sierra Madre and San Bernardino ranges, south through Palm Springs and along the present San Diego-Imperial County line, there were approximately 30,000 Indians when the Franciscans arrived in 1769. Beginning with San Diego in 1769, Missions were established in the region as follows: San Gabriel, 1771; San Juan Capistrano, 1776; San Buenaventura, 1782; San Fernando, 1797; San Luis Rey, 1798; La Purísima Concepcion, 1787; and Santa Ynez, 1804. Virtually all of the Indians in the region were Mission-ized, since, in this one region of California, the areas of Mission set-tlement were coterminous with the areas of Indian occupancy. Due to this circumstance and to the fact that the Mission system was more firmly rooted in Southern California than elsewhere in the state, the practice developed, in later years, of referring to the Southern California Indians, in the aggregate, as "The Mission Indians," a practice still followed by the Bureau of Indian Affairs.

With Mission rule extending throughout most of Southern Cali-fornia, only a few Indians in the region escaped the consequences of Missionization. Since the Spanish and Mexican influence did not extend east of the San Jacinto Mountains, the Cahuillas were spared the contamination which contact with Christianity involved for the other groups. Primarily because they survived in considerable num-bers, they came to have, in later years, some military importance and were utilized by the Mexicans as a kind of auxiliary force. Although San Diego was the first Mission established in California, the Fran-ciscans made only slight headway among the Dieguenos, a people described by Kroeber as "proud, rancorous, boastful, covetous, and hard to handle." In the first year of its existence, the Mission made not a single convert, and, in the first five years of its existence, less than a hundred neophytes were enrolled. Whenever the Franciscans seemed to be making too much progress, the Diegueno chieftains would engage in overt acts of hostility or would simply move their people a greater distance from the Mission. It was not until fifty years after its establishment that the San Diego Mission succeeded in baptizing any considerable number of Dieguenos. On two occasions, they rebelled, giving as a reason their desire "to live as they did be-fore." As a consequence of their resistance, the Dieguenos survived better than the other Mission groups.

Since Southern California was the area of most intensive Mission activity among Indians, it is interesting to note the consequences of

Missionization. From a total of 30,000 in 1769, the number of Indians in Southern California declined to approximately 1,250 by 1910. The seeds of this decline were sown by the Franciscans. For the thoroughly Missionized Indians, such as the Chumash, the Gabrielino, the Luiseno, and the Juaneno are, today, wholly extinct; while the groups having the least contact with the Missions, such as the Cahuilla and the Diegueno, are the only groups to have survived even in limited numbers. In fact, the survival of Indians was in inverse ratio to their contact with the Missions. So far as the Indian was concerned, contact with the Missions meant death.

2. THE EFFECTS OF MISSIONIZATION

With the best theological intentions in the world, the Franciscan padres eliminated Indians with the effectiveness of Nazis operating concentration camps. From 1776 to 1834, they baptized 4,404 Indians in the Mission San Juan Capistrano and buried 3,227; while in the Mission Santa Ynez they did somewhat better, having baptized 757 and buried 519. In not a single Mission did the number of Indian births equal the number of Indian deaths. During the entire period of Mission rule, from 1769 to 1834, the Franciscans baptized 53,600 adult Indians and buried 37,000. The mortality rates were so high that the Missions were constantly dependent upon new conversions to maintain the neophyte population which never, at any period, exceeded the peak figure of 20,300 reached in 1805. So far as the Indians were concerned, the chain of Missions along the coast might best be described as a series of picturesque charnel houses. For it was the Mission experience, rather than any contact with Spanish culture, that produced this frightful toll of Indian life. During the same period from 1769 to 1834, the "wild" or gentile Indians did not decline in numbers. Throughout Central and South America, the Spanish system of colonization, based upon the Mission, the pueblo, and the presidio, had not worked such a catastrophic decline in native population. Why were its effects so disastrous in California?

When the Spanish system of colonization was applied in California, it had to be modified in a number of respects. Since the California Indians did not live in large and stable communities, it was impossible to bring the faith to them; they had to be brought to the faith. The process of removing the Indians from their small rancherias and herding them into well-guarded Mission compounds resulted in a complete disruption of the native culture. Once the Indians were assembled in large numbers in the Missions, they had to be strictly regimented and the problem of discipline immediately became a serious one. From the moment of conversion, the neophyte became a slave; he belonged thereafter to the particular Mission. As a slave, of course, he had to be protected from contact with the unconverted. Thus a sharp wedge was driven between "converted" or neophyte Indians and the "wild" or gentile Indians. Once baptized the neophytes immediately lost caste with their people and were denied contact with the vital sources of their native culture. As soon as they were removed into the Mission compounds, "a strange lethargy and inaction" seemed to possess them. Elsewhere in the Spanish settlements in the New World, Indian life was permitted to evolve from its established patterns; but, in California, a different policy had to be adopted. Since the California Indians had so little in the way of economic organization, it was impossible to superimpose the religious faith and the military rule of the Spaniards upon the native society. For the Indian settlements could not support the colonists. It became necessary, therefore, to transform the neophyte completely, to teach him the rudiments of civilization, to make him learn the ways of a new culture.

During the first twenty years of the Mission period, the Franciscans used little compulsion in securing converts. Indians were attracted into the Missions by gifts of food, colored beads, bits of bright cloth, and trinkets. At the same time, a skillful use was made of ceremonies, rituals, music, processions, and pageants to stimulate the curiosity of the Indians and to lure them into the Mission compounds. At first they came voluntarily, prompted in part by curiosity and in part by cupidity, from the areas within a few miles of the Missions. As the number of neophyte deaths began to increase, however, Indians developed a mortal fear of the Missions. Thus to maintain the neophyte population the area of recruitment had to be enlarged and new methods devised. "Mild, sober exposition of the beauties of Christianity," as Dr. Cook notes, "and the charms of Mission life no longer sufficed."

Conquest and impression, rather than enticement and exegesis, became established Mission practices after 1800. As long as converts came from the same village, they spoke the same language, had more or less the same background, and possessed similar cultural traits.

But, as the radius of conversion expanded, Indians were brought in from diverse and distant villages, intensifying the difficulties of administration and requiring increasingly severe methods of discipline. The greater the distance between Mission and native village, the more homesick the Indian became, with the number of fugitives and apostates increasing in direct relation to the expanding area of conversion. With the increase of fugitivism and apostasy, large-scale military expeditions had to be organized to round up the escaped neophytes. The farther these expeditions penetrated into gentile territory, the more resistance they encountered.

On occasion the Franciscans permitted neophytes to escape, or "to visit," their villages, so that an expedition might be organized to follow them; in the process of capturing the fugitives, a dozen or more new "Christians" could be rounded up. In this manner, as many as two and three hundred Indians would be captured in a single raid. "On one occasion," writes Hugo Reid, "they went as far as the present Rancho del Chino, where they tied and whipped every man, woman and child in the lodge, and drove part of them back. . . . On the road they did the same with those of the lodge at San Jose. On arriving home the men were instructed to throw their bows and arrows at the feet of the priest, and make due submission. The infants were then baptized, as were also all children under eight years of age; the former were left with their mothers, but the latter kept apart from all communication with their parents. The consequence was, first, the women consented to the rite and received it, for the love they bore their children; and finally the males gave way for the purpose of enjoying once more the society of wife and family. Marriage was then performed, and so this contaminated race, in their own sight and that of their kindred, became followers of Christ."

To understand what conversion meant to the Indian, it should be remembered that the process of Missionization necessitated a sudden transition from the settled, customary existence of the Indian in a small rancheria or village to the almost urban conditions that prevailed in the larger Mission establishments. This change, as Dr. Cook points out, must have come as a deep mental shock to the Indian. For example, the young female neophytes, who were regarded as nuns, were herded into a kind of barrack or compound, called the monjerio, where they were kept under the closest surveillance and confinement. One learns from the chronicles that the typical mon-

jerio was 17 yards long and 7 yards wide and that it was usually constructed of adobe brick, with bunks ranged around the walls. The only ventilation came from a single high window, while, in the center of the room, was an improvised sewer or latrine. The stench and filth of these barracks were noted by all observers.

From 1769 to 1833, 29,100 Indian births were recorded in the Missions of California, and 62,600 deaths, the excess of deaths over births being 33,500. Of this decline, Dr. Cook estimates that 15,250 or 45% of the population decrease was caused by disease. Two epidemics of measles, one in 1806 and the other in 1828, took a heavy toll of neophyte lives. Within the first decade of Mission rule, syphilis appeared throughout the province. Despite the injunctions of officers and priests, the scrofulous Spanish soldiery spread the disease among both the gentile and neophyte Indian women. From the outset of settlement, the military guards at the Missions, in the words of one observer, were "generously infected with disease." Another observer pointed out that the neophytes were "permeated to the marrow of their bones with venereal disease, such that many of the newly born show immediately this, the only patrimony they receive from their parents, and for which reason three-quarters of the infants die in their first or second year, and of the other quarter which survive, most fail to reach their twenty-fifth year." Syphilis became, in fact, "a totalitarian disease, universally incident" among the neophytes.

The condition of the diseased neophytes was, of course, aggravated by other factors. In the Missions, they were herded together in large groups. The sanitation was wretched; the diet inadequate. From 1776 to 1825, there was only one qualified physician in all Alta California. Most of the filthy practices which later observers noted among the Indians, were practices which they had learned or acquired in the Missions. "The unsanitary condition of the Indian Villages at some of the Missions," wrote J. M. Guinn, "was as fatal as Indian war. In his native state, the Indian could burn a village and move on; but the adobe houses that took the place of the brush hovels could not be burned to purify them."

Believing that the possession of finery had a tendency to induce the Indians to run away, the padres clothed them in a coarse frieze (*xerga*), made at the Missions, which, as Hugo Reid observed, "kept the poor wretches all the time diseased with the itch." Meals were ladled out to the neophytes, never served, and consisted of *atole* (a gruel made of boiling ground corn, wheat, or barley) for breakfast, and *pozole* (a stew of barley, beans, squash, and chili) for the other meals. Fresh vegetables, milk, and meat were not generally served the Indians, although the Franciscans provided a bounteous table for themselves and for their visitors. It has been suggested, by well-informed observers, that the neophytes were kept in a state of chronic undernourishment in order to retard the tendency to fugitivism.

During the period of Mexican rule after 1822, the governors of the province repeatedly pointed out, in their reports, that the food allotments in the Missions were insufficient to support life, much less to enable the Indians to perform the labors required of them. Although the neophytes were able to get some accessory food supplies from native sources, Dr. Cook states that "the Indians as a whole lived continuously on the verge of clinical deficiency." Certainly the materials so laboriously collected by Dr. Cook conclusively refute the impression of abundance and liberality, or an easy-going pastoral existence, which has colored most of the writing about the Missions.

While the tasks assigned the neophytes were not particularly arduous—consisting of the type of work traditionally associated with a primitive agriculture and home industry—still they can hardly be characterized as light or inconsequential. The work-day was from "six in the morning until almost sunset." Since the policy of the Franciscans was to keep the neophytes constantly occupied, the tempo of work was intentionally kept at an easy pace. The same policy has, of course, always characterized most forced-labor systems. With a limited number of soldiers on hand, the Franciscans always had difficulty in minimizing the number of fugitives, which consistently averaged about 12% of the neophyte population. As a consequence, they did not insist upon strenuous exertion. But as the range of Mission enterprises expanded, the whip began to be cracked. "If the Indian would not work," writes C. D. Willard, "he was starved and flogged. If he ran away he was pursued and brought back." If a neophyte deserted from one Mission to another, he was immediately arrested, flogged, and kept in irons until he could be returned to the Mission to which he belonged, where, on arrival, he was again flogged. "If they stowed themselves away in any of the rancherias," writes Hugo Reid, "the soldiers were monthly in the habit of visiting them; and such was the punishment upon those who attempted to conceal them, that it was rarely essayed. Being so

proscribed, the only alternative left them was to take to the mountains, where they lived as they best could, making occasional inroads
on the mission property to maintain themselves. They were styled
huidos, or runaways, and at times were rendered desperate through
pursuit, and took the lives of any suspected of being traitors."

The major abuse of the forced-labor system developed, however,
when the Franciscans began to assign neophytes to the presidios and
to farm them out as servants to the worthless Spanish soldiers. The
easy conquest of the natives had bred in these soldiers a deep contempt for the Indian. Each presidio was provided with a tract of land,
el rancho del rey, which served as a pasture for the presidio livestock
and as a source of provender for the soldiers. Theoretically the
soldiers were supposed to perform all work required for the maintenance of the King's farm, but the close proximity of the domesticated Indians effectively discouraged the idea of manual labor. At
an early date, Father Salazar reported that the soldiers and the
colonists were a set of idlers. "For them," he wrote, "the Indian is
errand-boy, vaquero, and a digger of ditches—in short, a general
factotum." Within a few years, the neophytes were doing all the
work on the presidio farm and, in addition, were serving as menials
and domestics for the soldiers. While the fiction prevailed that
neophytes were to receive wages, when farmed out to work in this
manner, it is a matter of record that no attempt was made to collect
wages for these services after 1790. It is also recorded that the neophytes performed these services "under unmitigated compulsion,"
for they loathed the soldiers and their bitterest complaints were
directed at this type of forced-labor.

While the legend still prevails that the discipline of the Franciscans was "gentle and mild," the records abound with cases where
infraction of rules occasioned the harshest punishment. Interestingly
enough, most of the offenses recorded were political in character,
such as attempts to rebel or to escape from the Mission system. In a
sample of offenses committed by the neophytes, Dr. Cook found that
70% of the offenders received corporal punishment. Numerous instances were recorded of floggings of fifty to a hundred lashes. Fet-
ters, shackles, and the stocks were commonly used as disciplinary
measures. Referring to Father Zalvidea of the Mission San Gabriel,
Hugo Reid wrote that "he must assuredly have considered whipping
as meat and drink to the Indians, for they had it morning, noon and

night." In 1783 the able Governor Fages filed a bitter complaint against Father Junipero Serra—the sainted figure of California legend—for the excessive punishment he had meted out to neophytes. On coming to California, the first impression of Governor Borica was one of "amazement and aversion" at the treatment of the neophytes.

Small wonder, then, that the Indians should have detested the Missions. On two occasions, major insurrections were attempted. Additional evidence of their hatred of the Missions is to be found in the long lists of fugitives and in the growth of the practice of abortion and infanticide. While the Indians had been known to practice abortion and infanticide before the Missions were established, both practices swiftly developed, as Dr. Cook puts it, "from occasional, sporadic cultural items into a serious, although primitive and haphazard attempt to check the population growth through birth control." So prevalent was the practice of abortion, that miscarriages were punished as criminal offenses. The penalty prescribed by Father Zalvidea for the Indian woman who had suffered a miscarriage consisted in "shaving the head, flogging for fifteen subsequent days, iron on the feet for three months, and having to appear every Sunday in church, on the steps leading up to the altar, with a hideous painted wooden child in her arms."

Not only was Mission existence a nightmare for the Indians, but it is exceedingly difficult to see how they profited by the experience to the slightest degree. While the children raised in the Missions did learn some Spanish, the adults probably never acquired more than the phrase "Amar a Dios." "The padres," wrote J. M. Guinn, "were opposed to educating the natives for the same reason that southern slaveholders were opposed to educating the Negro, namely, that an ignorant people were more easily kept in subjection." For much the same reason, the Franciscans sought to prevent equestrianism. Governor Sola, in a report of 1818, complained that "the neophytes as well as the wild Indians were becoming too expert horsemen." It was only after 1825 that a few of the specially trusted neophytes were permitted to become vaqueros. To be sure, some of the Indians did acquire skills and trades, but, in general, the Mission system failed to prepare the neophytes for existence outside their native culture and, at the same time, the native culture was systematically disorganized.

For while the neophytes were permitted to retain some of their native cultural practices, such as their songs, dances, and games, no such latitude could be tolerated in the crucial matter of religious faith. From the Franciscan point of view, as Dr. Cook points out, it was "vitally necessary to extirpate those individual beliefs and tribal customs which in any way whatever conflicted with the Christian religion." Witchcraft and shamanism were vigorously opposed as thousands of neophytes were compelled to accept, or outwardly observe, the Christian faith. Not infrequently methods of extreme compulsion were used to secure observance of the mere forms of this faith. Alfred Robinson, a reliable observer, wrote that "it is not unusual to see numbers of Indians driven along by the alcaldes, and under the whip's lash forced to the very door of the sanctuary." Hugo Reid, another excellent observer, reported that the neophytes "had no more idea that they were worshiping God than an unborn child has of astronomy." Despite the intensive moral suasion and pressure applied by the Franciscans, Dr. Cook has concluded that "the Indians retained the basic pattern of their culture intrinsically unaltered." In the matter of religious faith, they even won an adaptational success, for they proceeded to adopt the forms of Christianity while retaining the substance of their native belief.

Since the native culture conflicted so sharply with the culture which the Franciscans sought to impose upon them, it is not surprising that the neophytes developed a dual set of values. Their native notions of morality, property rights, and sexual behavior did not, of course, square with the concepts which the padres so diligently sought to cultivate. Out of this conflict came the moral ambivalence which Spaniards, Mexicans, and Americans alike attributed to innate depravity and inferiority. The proverbial "laziness" of the Indian sprang from the fact that he was used to a system of intermittent rather than regularized labor, a system premised upon the seasonal quest for food in a non-agricultural culture. Even the "filthiness" of the Indian was, in large part, a by-product of cultural conflict. For the Franciscans frowned upon the Indian's addiction to the temescal, or "sweat-house," and, in the Mission, the neophyte was not permitted to burn his dwelling, as he had long burned his brush shacks, as a sanitary measure. The shrewdest observer of Indians among the Franciscans, Father Geronimo Boscana, noted that the neophytes merely imitated the forms which they were supposed to assimilate. Their reluctance to assimilate the substance of the cultural instruction of the Franciscans was attributed, however, even by Father Boscana, to "their corrupt and natural disposition."

In the relatively brief period of Mission rule, that is, from 1769 to 1832, the number of Indians in California declined from 130,000 to 83,000: a decline of about 57,000. Occurring almost entirely in the neophyte group, this decline in population alone refutes the elaborate myth which has been so diligently cultivated in California about the Mission system, its benevolence, its social efficiency, its tutorial excellence. About all that can be said for the system, in truth, is that, over a much longer period of time, the Indian population might have been stabilized at a lower level, as immunity against disease developed and the process of acculturation became operative.

3. Secularization of the Missions (1834–1843)

Under the Spanish scheme of colonization, the Missions were never intended as permanent settlements. As originally planned, each Mission was to be converted into a civil community within a decade after its establishment, by which time, so it was reasoned, the tutelage of the Indians would have been completed. The Franciscans did not hold title to the Mission lands as grants from the Crown; they merely enjoyed a right of use and occupancy at the pleasure of the government. Theoretically they were trustees for the Indian neophytes, upon whom title to the Mission lands and properties was eventually to devolve.

Although secularization of the Missions had been contemplated as early as 1813, the first proclamation on the subject was issued by Governor Figueroa on August 9, 1834. This proclamation provided for the secularization of ten Missions (six additional Missions were secularized in 1836). By the terms of the proclamation, half of the property of the ten Missions was to be turned over to the Indians, although the neophytes were still required to work on essential community enterprises and were not allowed to alienate their interests. The scheme of secularization worked out by Figueroa—one of the ablest Mexican governors—was well conceived in theory. The Governor expressly provided that the terms of the secularization decree were to be explained to the Indians "with suavity and patience."

By 1834, however, the Missions had become exceedingly rich, their lands and holdings being valued at $78,000,000. At the peak of its activities, the Mission San Gabriel, for example, operated 17 extensive ranchos and owned 3,000 Indians, 105,000 head of cattle, 20,000 horses, and 40,000 sheep. The pressure to plunder these estates soon became much stronger than the capacity or willingness of the weak Mexican government to enforce the secularization decrees. As a consequence, the laudable scheme of secularization degenerated into a mad scramble to loot the Missions. Faced with the possibility of war with the United States, Governor Micheltorana ordered the disposal of the remaining Mission properties in 1844, by which time all semblance of adherence to the plan of secularization had been abandoned.

Angered by the secularization decrees, the Franciscans effectively sabotaged the original plan by inviting the colonists and the Indians to help themselves to the Mission properties. Thousands of head of Mission cattle were driven away, horse herds were raided, warehouses were looted. Learning in advance the date fixed for the secularization of particular Missions, the Franciscans gave orders, according to Alfred Robinson, "for the immediate slaughter of their cattle; contracts were made, with individuals, to kill the cattle and divide the proceeds with the Missions." Thousands of head of cattle were slaughtered merely for their hides, with the contractors withholding half the proceeds received from the sales. No longer responsible to the Franciscans, the Indians proceeded to take part in the general looting and plundering. Most of the plundering, however, was done by the so-called Spanish Dons. "What is most astonishing," wrote Robinson, "is why the Indian does not take example from his Mexican brethren and like them kill and plunder." In such a mad scramble for wealth and booty, it is not surprising that the theoretical right of the Indians to the Mission lands and properties, or to the proceeds, went completely by the board. Formerly slaves, they now became demoralized paupers.

With the secularization of the Missions, "the rancho period" began in California. From 1769 to 1822, the Spanish had made only about twenty large land grants in the province, but, in the period from 1833 to 1846, over 500 large grants were handed out. As the threat of American intervention became increasingly imminent, the provincial governors showered their favorites with princely grants. Many of these large grants were carved out of properties expropriated from the Missions or from the ranches operated by the Missions. In many cases, they were stocked with horses, sheep, and cattle purchased from the Missions or simply appropriated at the time of secularization. By the time the last secularization decrees had been issued, California had begun to assume a feudal aspect. By the end of 1845, all the Southern California Missions had been sold or their properties leased, and extensive ranchos, with vast herds of cattle and horses, operated by thousands of Indian retainers, had replaced the Mission establishments.

During this period of shameful fraud and pillage, the neophyte Indians began to abandon the Missions. In 1833 the Mission San Juan Capistrano had 861 neophytes, but, by 1838, only 80 remained at the Mission. Hundreds of Indians crossed over the mountain ranges and sought refuge with the "wild" tribes of the San Joaquin Valley, while others simply fled to the mountains and the desert. The bewildered neophytes lucklessly remaining in the vicinity of the Missions were promptly kidnaped by the newly rich rancheros and used as peon laborers. Cut adrift from the Missions without resources, hundreds of neophytes moved into the towns and pueblos, notably Los Angeles, where, between brief periods of employment, they gathered around the grog shops in droves. The few who remained about the Missions were eventually evicted from lands to which they had both a theoretical title and a possessory right based upon long use and occupancy. Wherever Indian settlements were included within the boundaries of a land grant, it was the duty of the courts to confirm their right of occupancy, but this duty was never performed. After the American conquest, the holders of these grants relied upon Mexican law to confirm their titles and then proceeded, in reliance upon American common law, to evict the Indian squatters. Since the Indian was neither a citizen nor an alien under American law, and was not even eligible for naturalization between 1846 and 1884, there was no means by which he could acquire title to land, and by the time an allotment policy had been adopted for Indians, all the public lands in California which were of any agricultural value had long since passed into private ownership.

Prior to the American conquest, three labor systems had existed in California: the communal forced-labor of the Missions, peonage, and, to a limited extent, free labor. After the Missions were established, a few civilian colonists were imported from Mexico to Alta California. These original colonists, the lowly *pobladores*, relied on Indian labor only to a minor extent, as their agricultural operations were extremely limited. Over a period of years, however, a class of settlers known as the *gente de razon*—the people of quality—began to appear in California. It was these settlers who imported the hacienda system from Mexico, a system which, as Dr. Cook notes, became "thoroughly impressed upon the social thought of the state." The hacienda system was, of course, explicitly premised upon the concept of peon labor.

Since most of the neophyte labor was originally employed at the Missions, settlers on the large grants were given permission to recruit wild or gentile Indians. In some cases, neophytes were farmed out to the rancheros, primarily as vaqueros and house servants, with most of the unskilled labor being performed by gentile Indians. By 1848 the kidnaping of wild Indians, for employment on the ranchos, had become a major industry in California. "Our friendly Indians," as one ranchero put it, "tilled our soil, pastured our cattle, sheared our sheep, cut our timber, built our houses, paddled our boats, made tiles for our homes, ground our grain, slaughtered our cattle, dressed their hides for market, and made unburnt bricks; while the Indian women made excellent servants, took care of our children, and made every one of our meals." By 1848, 5,000 Indians were thus employed on the great ranchos.

Paid a fathom of black, red, and white glass beads for a season's work, these Indian peons were, as Don Juan Bandini said, "the working arms which made it possible to carry out agricultural and other projects and to provide necessities." After the secularization of the Missions, the supply of Indian labor was greatly augmented, for the neophytes were regarded as part of the general plunder to be obtained. Although slavery had been abolished in Mexico in 1829, peonage continued to be practiced in California. "Before the Indian could move about," writes Dr. Varden Fuller, "he was required to have a properly signed discharge showing that he was not in debt to his employer. . . . In some instances, the Indians were encouraged to work by the promise of a given rate of wages, only to be turned away at the end of the season with no more remuneration than subsistence. . . . Thus a range of devices of varying degrees of harshness was used to assemble the Indian labor supply; and in conjunction with those of a milder nature it appears that outright seizure and force were not unimportant."

Like most social changes in California, the transition from Mission to rancho was effected with uncommon rapidity and remarkable thoroughness. By 1848 the Mission system had been completely liquidated. Later the Supreme Court ruled that the Mexican governors and the administrators appointed to take charge of the Mission properties lacked authority to dispose of the church buildings, the homes of the priests, and lands to an extent of a few acres surrounding each of the twenty-one Missions. Eventually this moiety of the Mission estate was returned to the Archbishop of California; otherwise nothing remained of the Mission system, except, perhaps, its heritage of disaster for the Indian. During the period of secularization, the Indian population of California declined from 83,000 to 72,000, a decline of about 700 a year by comparison with a decline of about 900 a year during the Mission period.

4. AFTER THE CONQUEST

While much of the damage to Indian life in California had been caused prior to the American conquest, still the relative impact of Anglo settlement was about three times as severe as that of Spanish and Mexican settlement. At the time of the conquest, there were still about 72,000 Indians in California, including the remnants of the neophyte or Mission Indians. By 1865 the total had been reduced to 23,000, and by 1880 to 15,000.

In effect, the Indians of California were ground to pieces between two invasions: the Spanish from the south up the coast, and the Anglos from the east and north across the mountains and over the desert. The two invasions were characterized by sharp differences in policy and practice. Under the Spanish system, at least in theory, the Indian was permitted to retain his primitive social institutions and customs. He could testify in the courts, his life was sacred, and he could own and acquire property. Through long association with Spaniards and Mexicans, the Indian had taken over a few items of their culture and had incorporated these items, either intact or in a modified form, into his native culture. But under the impact of the Anglo invasion which began in 1848, all that was left of his culture went to pieces at one blow. "Indian life," wrote Stephen Powers in a government report of 1877, "burst into air by the suddenness and fierceness of the attack. . . . Never before in history has a people been swept away with such terrible swiftness."

American settlers came to California with two centuries of Indian warfare behind them. The Indian had no rights that the white man was bound to respect. If the Americans had a policy, it was to extirpate Indian culture, not to transform it. The Spaniards had planned on retaining the Indian population. They had even encouraged intermarriage. But the Anglos contemplated the obliteration of the Indian. The Spanish policy was to regard the Indian as a potential economic asset, but, under American rule, he was regarded as a liability to be liquidated as rapidly as possible.

Engineered by a small caste or group, the Spanish invasion was limited in character. The entire coastal portion of California had been occupied by less than a hundred Spaniards and as late as 1846 the entire "white" population of the state did not exceed 5,000 by comparison with an Indian population of 72,000. But the Anglo invasion was not so much an invasion as an inundation. Under the period of Spanish-Mexican rule, the ratio of non-Indians to Indians was one to ten; under the American rule it quickly became ten to one. Since the Spanish invasion had been along the coast, the hinterland area had been left as a kind of Indian territory. But the Anglo invasion came from the east so that the first contact Anglos had with Indians in California was with the wild or gentile group. Thus Indians fleeing to the mountains and deserts encountered miners and mountain men coming from the east. Since there were no settled Indian tribes in California, a formal Indian frontier never existed. Invading from the east, the Anglos quickly infiltrated the areas which Indians still occupied in the state. As one early pioneer wrote, "Here we have not only Indians on our frontiers, but all among us, around us, with us. There is hardly a farm house without them. And where is the line to be drawn between those who are domesticated and the frontier savages? Nowhere—it cannot be found. Our white population pervades the entire state, and Indians are with them everywhere."

By settling along the coast, the Spaniards had not interfered greatly with the aboriginal sources of food supply. But an entirely different situation existed after the American conquest. Invading from the east, the Anglos drove the Indians from their fisheries and acorn groves, destroyed the supply of fish by muddying and polluting the rivers and creeks, and, in raids on Indian villages, destroyed food supplies which had been laboriously accumulated. The Anglo settlers wanted, of course, the fertile valleys and the rich cotton lands, and from these the Indians were promptly driven. But as the Anglo invasion spread, cattle, sheep and hogs began to make inroads on the

Indians' supply of acorns, seeds, and green plants. When the Indians retaliated with raids on cattle, they were promptly visited by punitive expeditions. In less than two years after its establishment, the new state of California had incurred an indebtedness of over one million dollars in fighting Indians. It is estimated that, in about a hundred Indian "affairs," or raids, some 15,000 Indians were killed in the period from 1848 to 1865.

Although peonage was abolished after 1848, the shrewd Anglos were quick to appreciate the merits of the system. The first California legislature proceeded, in fact, to enact three measures designed to preserve the substance, if not the form, of peonage. One of these statutes provided that Indians could not testify in court (it was not until 1872 that an Indian could even file suit in the American courts); another provided that Indians might be declared vagrants upon the petition of a white person; and a third measure established a system of "indenture apprentices," under which minors, with the "consent" of their parents, might be farmed out as apprentices for a term of years. The first of these measures created, in effect, an open season on Indians in California. An Indian could be shot for any minor infraction of the white code, such as speaking out of turn, getting in the way, or demanding payment of wages. (Dr. Cook has documented 265 cases of these so-called "social homicides.") The indentured apprentice law merely rationalized the old Spanish custom of kidnaping Indian children as peons. Between 1852 and 1867, Dr. Cook estimates that 4,000 Indian children were taken from their parents and apprenticed to various employers under this statute. "The habit of stealing Indian children and selling them to Mexican rancheros in Southern California," observed the Butte Record of May 23, 1857, "is being abused."

Under the impact of the Anglo invasion, the whole fabric of Indian life, already weakened by the Mission system, completely disintegrated. While the toll of disease had been heavy enough under Mission-Mexican rule, it became still heavier after the arrival of the Americans. American settlers invaded the remaining rancherias, or native villages, teaching the men to gamble and to steal, and teaching the women, as Hugo Reid put it, "to be worse than they were." After 1848 prostitution became an established trade for Indian women in California. The old Spanish custom of raping Indian "squaws" became an established Yankee practice. The family life of the Indians was completely disrupted. According to the indefatigable Dr. Cook, some 12,000 Indian women became the concubines of white settlers. As the half-breed population increased, the half-breeds were automatically assigned to the Indian nether world and became the objects of a special loathing and disdain. Defeated in his initial resistance, his passion for revenge frustrated, the Indian was forced back, as Dr. Cook states, "to a silent, ineradicable, suppressed animosity, against all things American which was not forgotten long after other wrongs had passed into oblivion." It was this undercurrent of resentment which precluded even the thought of assimilation.

With the breakup of the great landed estates after 1848, Indian peons were forced into the "free labor" market introduced by the Americans. While the neophytes had some preparation for this system, the gentile Indians had none. Under a free labor system, the Indian was hopelessly handicapped: he did not understand the language; he was unfamiliar with a monetary economy; and he could not understand the necessity for regularized labor. Unprepared to cope with the perils of this system, the Indian sank lower and lower in the social hierarchy of the times.

After the American conquest, hundreds of Indian peons began to leave the Indianolas, as the Indian villages on the ranchos were called, and to crowd into the towns of Southern California. All the principal towns had an Indian village known as the pueblito or little town. During the period of military conquest, these pueblitos were sinkholes of crime and the favorite resorts of dissolute characters, red and white. In 1852 there were 4,000 "whites" in Los Angeles and 3,700 "domesticated Indians." The Indians were crowded into a pueblito located near Aliso and First Streets which was later moved east of the Los Angeles River. This new village became so notorious that, after the arrival of American soldiers in 1847, it was destroyed by order of the military.

In the years from 1846 to 1870, Indians were widely employed in Southern California as domestics, as farm laborers, and for most of the unskilled jobs. "Employed," however, is scarcely the right term. "If ever an Indian was fully and honestly paid for his labor by a white settler," wrote J. Ross Browne, Inspector of Indian Affairs on the Pacific Coast, "it was not my luck to hear of it." When goldmining operations were launched in the San Gabriel Mountains in 1855, the local annals mention that the work was performed by "gangs of Indians." With the vineyards becoming profitable after 1849, Indian labor was extensively used throughout Southern California. "Much of the work connected with the grape industry," writes Harris Newmark, "was done by Indians. . . . Stripped to the skin, and wearing only loin-cloths, they tramped with ceaseless tread from morn until night, pressing from the luscious fruit of the vineyard the juice so soon to ferment into wine."

During the grape season, hundreds of Indians would troop into Los Angeles every Saturday night after they had received their pay. "During Saturday night and all day Sunday," writes Newmark, "they drank themselves into hilarity and intoxication, and this dissipation lasted until Sunday night. Then they slept off their sprees and were ready to work Monday morning. During each period of excitement, from one to three or four revelers were murdered." The three grog shops maintained at the old Mission site in San Gabriel, according to Horace Bell, "did a smashing business—these devil's workshops being surrounded by a mass of drunken, howling Indians." By common practice, most of the Indian vineyard workers were paid in aguardiente or wine brandy.

"By four o'clock on Sunday afternoon," writes Bell, "Los Angeles Street from Commercial to Nigger Alley, Aliso Street from Los Angeles to Alameda, and Nigger Alley would be crowded with a mass of drunken Indians, yelling and fighting. Men and women, boys and girls, tooth and toe nail, sometimes, and frequently with knives, but always in a manner that would strike the beholder with awe and horror. About sundown the pompous marshal, with his Indian special deputies, who had been kept in jail all day to keep them sober, would drive and drag the herd to a big corral in the rear of the Downey Block, where they would sleep away their intoxication, and in the morning they would be exposed for sale, as slaves for the week. . . . They would be sold for a week, and bought up by the vineyard men and others at prices ranging from one to three dollars, one-third of which was to be paid to the peon at the end of the week, which debt, due for well performed labor, would invariably be paid in aguardiente, and the Indian would be happy until the following Monday morning. . . . Those thousands of honest, useful people were absolutely destroyed in this way. Vineyards were of great profit in those days."

After the arrival of the Chinese in the 'seventies, the Indians were driven from the towns to the outlying communities. When Ludwig Louis Salvator visited Los Angeles in 1876, he reported that most of the Indians were to be found living "like gypsies in brush huts," on outskirts of such settlements as Riverside and San Bernardino. Throughout the Southern California countryside these small settlements could be seen, with their huts made of reeds and straw with a framework of long poles. Working throughout the region as common laborers, Salvator noted that, as always, their diet consisted largely of native foods, such as acorns, clover, grass seeds, horse chestnuts, roots, and berries.

As late as 1860 the water overseer of Los Angeles was empowered by law to take out any Indians who might be in the calaboose and use them as workmen in repairing highways and bridges. Throughout the period after the American conquest, Indians were paid, when they were paid at all, one-half the going wage. Persons employing Indians as domestics were required, by ordinance, to keep them on the premises, and "those who could not show papers from the alcalde of the pueblo were to be treated as horsethieves and enemies." By 1880 "los bravos Indios" had been virtually eliminated from the labor market. As the American settlements expanded, they were driven from the hinterland towns toward the mountains and the desert. In the census of 1860, San Bernardino reported 3,028 Indians, in 1870 none; San Diego had 3,067 in 1860, and only 28 in 1870. At the present time, 2,171 Indians are enrolled in the Mission Indian Agency of Southern California—the remnants of the 30,000 or more Indians who inhabited the region in 1769.

5. The Indian Influence

The Indian background has influenced the social structure of Southern California in a number of respects. In the first place, the presence of a large pool of Indian labor had a demoralizing effect upon the Hispanos. From 1769 to 1848, Indians performed virtually all manual labor operations in the Missions and on the ranchos. With such a large pool of cheap Indian labor at all times available, little incentive existed for the introduction of labor-saving devices or machinery. Visiting California in 1835, Markoff was impressed by the fact that there were "neither wind-mills nor water-mills." Since the Franciscans thought that the use of equipment and machinery would have a detrimental effect on the morale of the Indians, the Missions were essentially primitive in their methods and practices. Indian labor was so cheap, writes Dr. Fuller, "that it did not pay to build fences to protect the crops or to retain the livestock for they could be guarded at less expense than the fences could be built." Persons who revisited California on the eve of the American conquest noted that there had been virtually no improvement in agricultural methods during the prior two decades. The weakness of the Spanish-Mexican settlements in California consisted in their dependence on cheap Indian slave labor.

In the second place, the importation of the hacienda system to California was made possible by the presence of a large mass of Indian labor. "One is tempted," writes Dr. Cook, "to follow through the persistence of the forced-labor idea in subsequent years. It would be possible to show how the cheap labor market passed from the Indian to the Chinese and how the same rationale of peonage and compulsion was applied to the latter. One might then pass on to the new groups, each of which gradually replaced the other—the Italians of the 'eighties, the Mexicans and Filipinos of the early century, down to the 'Okies' of our time. Simultaneously, one could trace the rise of great agricultural interests, dependent upon masses of un-skilled transient workers, which utilized these groups one after an-other." Closely related to this aspect of the matter is the growth, in the mores, of an arrogant attitude toward so-called "inferior" people. In fact, vestiges of the hacienda system can be found today through-out Southern California.

Both Indians and Mexicans are dark-skinned and there is, of course, a considerable amount of Indian blood in the Mexican peo-ple. Most of the Indians who survived the Anglo invasion in South-ern California spoke some Spanish and, in any case, their command of Spanish was greater than their command of English. Most of them were nominally Catholic and remain Catholic to this day. After 1848 there was a tendency for Mexicans to be pushed down to the level of Indians and for the two statuses, the Indian and the Mexican, to merge. Momentarily the Indian had served as a buffer between Anglo and Hispano, but gradually the Anglo pressure shifted from the Indian to the Mexican as the Indians were elimi-nated. Soon the distinction, always shadowy, between Indian and Mexican was forgotten. The two terms began to be used interchange-ably or jointly, as in such frequently encountered expressions as "a

Mexican Indian woman." And as the Mexican-Indian traditions merged, the "Spanish" influence became exalted out of all relation to reality. Many of the people called "Mexican" today in Southern California are the descendants of Indian-Mexican parents. In 1876 Salvator remarked upon the number of Mexicans who had married Indian women. "The majority of present-day Californians," he wrote, and by Californians he meant Mexicans, "are the descendants of these marriages." Lost in this same general Indian-Mexican category are the half-breeds, the "cholos" and the "greasers," of the numerous Anglo-Indian alliances of the early period.

"There is no doubt," writes Dr. Cook, "that the Old Mission Indians have in their veins far more white blood than any other west-coast natives. This is due to the fact that they have been living among white people for a very long time and, second, to the fact that the particular branch of the white race with which they have been in contact, the Ibero-American, has always been socially well disposed toward miscegenation. From the earliest times, the Spanish inter-married freely and on a status of equality with the natives, and in more recent times the heavy immigration of Mexicans and other Latin Americans has provided a huge and convenient reservoir of potential spouses. One need only examine the names carried on the Mission Agency rolls and the names of the white men or women who have married Indians to appreciate the tremendous degree of racial fusion in Southern California between the Indian and the American of Spanish extraction." After all these years, therefore, a triangular fusion has taken place in the blood of the three races that first met in Southern California: the Indian, the Mexican (Spanish), and the Anglo.

"I, a Mexican?—I am Californio!"
—from *Ranchero* by Stewart Edward White

CHAPTER III

CALIFORNIOS AND MEXICANOS

FOR over a hundred years, two cultural traditions—the Spanish-Mexican and the Anglo-American—have been in conflict in Southern California. In other areas of the Southwest, Anglos, Hispanos, and Indians have long since achieved a measure of mutual respect and accommodation, but, in Southern California, the conflict has been sharp and continuous. Since it has so often assumed a furtive and clandestine design, the existence of this conflict has not always been recognized. According to the official legend, the last vestiges of Spanish influence were obliterated when the conquering gringos overran the land. Actually, the Spanish influence, although submerged for years, was never wholly extinguished, nor did the struggle for cultural accommodation cease with the American conquest. Recent pachuco riots in Los Angeles demonstrate, clearly enough, that the conflict, long covert or obscure, has once again become open and notorious.

Throughout the years, the conflict between Anglo and Hispano in California has been confined to Southern California. Generally speaking, Spanish-Mexican influences do not extend north of Tehachapi. To be sure, there are numerous Spanish place-names in the northern and central portions of the state, but the great preponderance of Spanish place-names is in the south, where the bulk of the Spanish-speaking population has always resided. The key to the survival of Spanish influences south of Tehachapi is to be found in the circum-

49

stance that the discovery of gold really divided California into two states. For three decades after 1849, while thousands of Americans were invading Northern California, taking possession of the land and establishing their institutions, Southern California remained virtually unchanged. Spanish continued to be used as the language of instruction in most communities throughout the 'sixties and 'seventies. Twenty years after the discovery of gold, Los Angeles was still a small Mexican town in which Spanish was spoken almost universally, with all official documents, including city ordinances, being published both in Spanish and in English. In the years after the gold rush, the Cow Counties remained a barren, remote, largely uninhabited portion of the state. As such, they became a haven of refuge, and later a center of resistance, for Mexicans who, driven from the gold fields, retreated before the Anglo-American invasion in the north. As a result of this time-lag in social change, Spanish-Mexican influences struck deeper roots in Southern California than elsewhere in the state, as a cursory glance at the region today will readily confirm. In fact, it was not until the great influx of the 'eighties that the Spanish influence began to decline.

1. CALIFORNIOS

The complex and novel conflict which developed between Anglo and Hispano elements in Southern California can only be understood as an outgrowth of class divisions which were implicit in the social structure of the province prior to 1848. Although there were only 5,000 non-Indians in California in 1836, and not many more in 1848, sharp class and status lines separated the "white" residents into special categories. At the top of the hierarchy were the Spanish Franciscans, the Spanish officials, and the Spanish officers of the troop garrisoned in California. Included in this category were some Mexican and Spanish soldiers and officers who did not quite rate the distinction of being *soldados distinguidos*. Some of the most prominent families in California, such as the Castros, Picos, Arguellos, Bandinis, Carrillos, Alvarados, Ortegas, Noriegas, Peraltas, Sepulvedas, Yorbas, and Lugos, belonged to this latter category.

While there were a few distinguished families among the early settlers, the number having "pure Spanish blood" was negligible. "A very small percentage," wrote Charles Dwight Willard, "were pure-blooded Spaniards, although few were ready to admit they were anything else. Cases were rare in which the whole family emigrated from Spain, or where Spanish soldiers sent back for their wives or sweethearts to come over, and the extremely small number of women from the mother country is the clearest evidence of the mixed character of the population." Despite the questionable character of their genealogies, however, these "first families" exhibited all the pretentions of a grandee class. Making a great fuss about their "pure Spanish blood" and "pure Castilian speech," it was only in rare cases that a son or daughter was permitted to marry outside the charmed circle of similarly pretentious colonists. As a consequence, most of the families were interrelated, constituting, in the aggregate, a kind of upper-class clan. While the number of families making up the clan was small, the families, as such, were frequently large. Don Cristobal Dominguez died leaving fourteen children and a hundred living descendants. Captain Noriega was also survived by a hundred or more descendants. Thus the latter-day descendants of these "first families" are more numerous than might be imagined.

These were the so-called Spanish Dons of whom one reads so much in the secondary sources and numerous historical romances devoted to the period. In a few of their homes, particularly in the presidial towns of Santa Barbara and San Diego, there existed, as Walter A. Hawley has pointed out, "the dignity, elegance, refinement, and charm of people reared in the capitals of the old world." But it must be emphasized that the number of families constituting this Spanish upper crust—the *gente de razon* of the province—was never large. In fact, they were at all times outnumbered by the lower classes in the ratio of ten to one. Among the first generation were to be found some well-educated, capable, hard-working individuals, but they were certainly a minority element. The primary duty of most of the garrison officers and provincial officials seemed to be to draw their pay. The second generation, denied an opportunity for education in the isolated province of California—demoralized by the ease with which a fair competence could be obtained by the use of Indian labor, showed much less ability and far less enterprise. Being highly conscious of their Spanish background, the *gente de razon* were almost as conservative as the ruling class in Spain and naturally tended to become strongly anti-Mexican after Mexico had achieved its independence in 1822. Their innate conservatism found expression in many curious practices, such, for example, as the habit of yoking oxen by the horns rather than by placing the weight of the yoke upon the necks, a practice stubbornly adhered to because "so it was done in Spain." It was from this element that the ranchero class was largely recruited.

Below the *gente de razon* were the Mexican troops, artisans, and colonists—the cholos of the province. Recruited from the riffraff of Sonora and Sinaloa, they were certainly a miscellaneous lot. "The Los Angeles *pobladores*," writes Dr. Caughey, "had been recruited from the most poverty stricken classes in Sinaloa. Only two could claim to be Spaniards, the rest being Indian, Negro, and mixed blood. None was literate. Presidial society looked down upon these rustic villagers, and the missionaries regarded them askance, as being likely to corrupt the neophytes. Two decades later one of the missionaries could complain that the townsfolk were 'a set of idlers, addicted to cards, song, and seduction of the Indian women.'"

Both in the towns and on the ranchos, the Mexicans were sharply set apart from the *gente de razon*. They spoke a different dialect; they were Mexican, not Spanish; and they were largely illiterate. Seldom, if ever, did they rise from their restricted status to positions of power or influence. Intermarriage between them and the *gente de razon* was simply unthinkable. Most of the men, in fact, married Indian women. Having in mind the presence of large numbers of Indians, Charles Dwight Willard's description of the pre-American social structure in California becomes particularly illuminating. This social structure, he observed, was not unlike that of the Deep South: the Indians were the slaves, the *gente de razon* were the plantation owners or "whites," and the Mexicans were the "poor whites." To emphasize the pertinency of this description, it should be noted that the *gente de razon*, in addition to being conscious of their class and status, were extremely race-conscious. They looked down upon the Mexicans and Indians as a different breed of people—darker, illiterate, churlish, incapable of progress or understanding.

To these elements must be added a unique and extremely important strain, namely, the American, British, Scottish, German, and French adventurers who had drifted into California prior to 1848. While there were only a handful of these adventurers, they came to occupy a position of crucial importance at the time of the American conquest. As John Steven McGroarty once said, "they were the ginger in the yeast." With scarcely a single exception, these curiously assorted individuals became naturalized citizens of Mexico, joined the

Catholic Church, and married daughters of the *gente de razon*. Embracing the daughters of the land, they likewise made a pretense of embracing its customs. Hispanizing their surnames, they adopted the prevailing speech and style of dress. Eager to become identified with the Spanish upper-crust, they assumed the forms of Spanish culture with cheerful alacrity. By the time a man had found his way to the far-off corner of the world that was California in the period from 1820 to 1846, he was strongly inclined to believe, as Mr. Willard pointed out, that "all churches seemed alike."

In Santa Barbara, Alpheus B. Thompson, a dealer in hides from Boston, married the daughter of Commandante Carrillo; Alfred Robinson, also of Boston, married the daughter of Captain De La Guerra; Louis F. Burton married Antonia Carrillo; in Los Angeles, B. D. Wilson married Ramona Yorba and became Don Benito Wilson; Dr. James B. Winston married Margarita Bandini; the Englishman, William E. P. Hartnell, married "a California lady"; John Temple married Dona Rafaela Cota; Abel Stearns married Dona Arcadia, the daughter of Don Juan Bandini; Michael White, a British sailor, married Maria del Rosario Guillen; Johann Groninger, a German settler, married a Miss Feliz and became Juan Domingo; William Wolfskill married Dona Magdalena Lugo; Isaac Williams married Maria de Jesus Lugo; Leon Prudhomme, a French settler, married a Tapia; John Foster, an Englishman, married a daughter of Pio Pico; Joseph Chapman married Señorita Guadalupe Ortega; and so it went. No matter what the nationality of the newcomer—French, Scottish, English, American, or German; and no matter what his social status —doctor, trader, sailor, or smuggler—he apparently had little difficulty in joining the *gente de razon*, provided he joined the Catholic Church and became a citizen of Mexico. Once affiliated with the *gente de razon* by marriage, he passed over completely into the orbit of their social life. The settlers, such as Hugo Reid, Don Luis Vignes, Nathan Tuch, and Jose Mascarel, who married Indian women, never achieved the status of *gente de razon*.

The social hierarchy of provincial California was based upon a clear division of labor. On the ranchos, the Mexicans were the artisans, vaqueros, and major-domos; in the pueblos, they were the craftsmen and *pobladores*. The *gente de razon*, with their strange assortment of sons-in-law, monopolized the government positions, constituted the officer class of the military, and owned the ranchos. While they showed a lively interest in looking after their cattle and horses (fearing to trust this task to the Indians), they were little concerned with agriculture. In the towns, on the ranchos, and in the Missions, Indians comprised the real laboring population.

Conservative and anti-Mexican, the *gente de razon* were linked to the Americans, not merely by ties of marriage, but by the profitable hide-and-tallow trade with Boston. Viewing the lower classes with disdain, they were notable for another, and somewhat related, trait. "The character of the people of California," wrote Blackmar, "differed from that of every other Spanish province. Owing to its isolated position, there was but little communication with the remainder of the Spanish dominion, and there sprang up an independent spirit not observed elsewhere in the Spanish Americas." Long restive under Mexican rule, these upper-class Mexicans, however, showed a contrary inclination. They were much closer to the Indians than they were to the *gente de razon* with whom about their only ties were the Catholic faith and the Spanish language. They were also much closer to Mother Mexico than they were to Spain, America, or the California Republic. Having ties neither of blood nor of commerce with the American settlers who had infiltrated the province, they did not follow the *gente de razon* into the camp of the American party.

Thus the initial contact between Anglo and Hispano cultures in California resulted in nothing quite as simple as fusion, absorption, or rejection, but rather in a limited upper-class alliance or amalgamation. In marrying "California ladies"—usually with an eye on Spanish land grants—the Anglo-American adventurers had merely adopted the outward forms of Spanish culture. This limited acceptance of an alien culture took place under exceptional circumstances. As a group, the adventurers were young, unmarried men who had drifted into a remote province of Mexico. Isolated from the sources of American culture, they were willing, for the time being, to pose as *hijo del pais*. But with the appearance of American women on the scene after 1846, the willingness of American men to become pseudo-Spaniards came to an abrupt end. Apropos of the amount of intermarriage that occurred between 1820 and 1846, there is much significance in J. P. Widney's observation, made in later years, that he had never known "of a Spaniard or Mexican of this section marrying an American wife." Through these marriages, most of the *gente de razon* families were permitted, for a time at least, to pass as American, or if not quite American, then as "high-class" Mexicans. To distinguish them from lower-class Mexicans, a special category of "native Californians," or Californios, was created. On the other hand, the landless Mexican, whose daughter seemed most unattractive, remained a Mexican, a cholo, a greaser. In this manner, the rift in the social structure of Spanish California was preserved after the conquest.

2. THE SONORANS

The number of Mexicans, as distinguished from Spanish and pseudo-Spanish elements in California, has always been underestimated. The estimates that have been made invariably fail to take into account the number of half-breeds who, sociologically speaking, should fall in the Mexican category. By any system of reckoning, the mixed breeds constituted a sizable group. Between 1831 and 1844, a number of New Mexico settlers arrived in Southern California, and this element would also have to be taken into consideration in computing the total number of Mexicans. In addition, one would have to add to the Mexican total, the thousands of Sonorans who came to Southern California.

The Sonoran invasion really began, according to Hugo Reid, with the secularization of the Missions. "They came flocking in," he wrote, "to assist in the general destruction, lending a hand to kill cattle on shares, which practice, when at last prohibited by government orders, they continued on their private account." "These Sonorenos," he adds, "overran the country." With the discovery of gold, a stream of Mexican migration was set in motion. While most of the Mexican forty-niners came from Sonora, there were small bands from Sinaloa, Chihuahua, and Durango. Starting from Tubac, on the borders of Sonora, they traveled over the old Anza trail to Yuma, crossed the Colorado River, and then came to Los Angeles by way of San Gorgonio Pass, en route to the mines.

In California, the Sonorans, as they were called, were treated with great contempt by both Anglos and Hispanos. Wearing cotton shirts, white pantaloons, sandals, and sombreros, they were known as *calzonaires blancos*, or "white breeches." In small groups of fifty and a hundred, they started out in the early spring, worked in the mines in the summer, and returned south in the fall. Not infrequently their families came along, riding the pack mules or burros. Between 1848 and 1850, 10,000 Sonorans passed through Los Angeles each spring on their way to the gold fields, and, in reduced numbers, the processions continued until 1854. The historian J. M. Guinn estimated that, in one year alone, 25,000 Sonorans made the journey northward to the mines. Katherine M. Bell reported that she saw hundreds of Sonorans in Santa Barbara in 1849, camped in caravans of ten, twenty, and thirty on the outskirts of the town where they made merry with much singing and dancing to the music of "violins, guitars, and flutes."

Hurrying northward after the announcement of the discovery of gold, the Sonorans were the first "foreigners" to reach the Mother Lode. Not only were the Sonorans the first claimants on the scene, but many of them were experienced miners. They introduced two new methods of mining in creek beds which made possible a rapid exploitation of the surface gold resources of California. The panning system was based upon the use of a wooden bowl, or batea, with which they were long familiar, while the dry-wash method involved the use of the arrastra, a crude piece of equipment operated by a water-wheel. Staking out important claims on the Tuolumne and Calaveras Rivers, the Sonorans, by the use of these methods, made remarkable progress before the Americans began to invade the fields. Settled by Sonorans, the towns of Sonora and Hornitos quickly became populous mining centers. The first American settlements were located north of the Sonora district, along the American, Feather, Bear, and Yuba Rivers. It was not long, however, before the American miners learned that the Sonorans were in possession of some of the best claims in the region which they were exploiting to advantage through the use of novel mining methods. Open warfare promptly followed.

"The Mexicans," writes Walter Noble Burns, "who poured into California during the gold rush, were still inflamed with the anti-American prejudices engendered during the Mexican War. Their attitude towards Americans was hostile from the first and, in return, the Americans regarded them as secret enemies and treated them with frank contempt." By 1850 most of the Sonorans had been driven from the better mining districts, but, as Guinn notes, "not all of them returned to their native land. There was a residuum left in California," more particularly, Southern California. While it is impossible to estimate the size of this residuum, it must have been large, for nearly every Southern California settlement had its "Sonoratown." So numerous was this element in the region that "Sonoran" became synonymous with Mexican. It is also important to remember that, during these years, there was really no border between the United States and Mexico. People passed back and forth across the line with more or less ease and freedom. When all of these elements are taken into consideration—the number of half-breeds, the immigration from New Mexico, and the Sonoran invasion—it is apparent that the Mexican population of Southern California, by 1850, was considerably larger than has been generally recognized.

3. DURING THE CONQUEST

At the time of the American conquest, the *gente de razon*, with few exceptions, lost little time in swinging over to the American side. Ties of marriage and bonds of commerce, as well as their conservatism, served to bring them into the American fold. Outspokenly in favor of annexation, the adventurers who had infiltrated California prior to 1846 performed a highly important role in softening up the Californios in advance of the conquest and in solidifying them behind American rule. Since so many of the *gente de razon* were anti-Mexican, they were naturally inclined to look with favor on the new dispensation. At the outset, too, the Americans in California were at some pains to distinguish between "native Californians," meaning *gente de razon*, and Mexicans, meaning "greasers" and "cholos." For it was generally recognized that the *gente de razon*, if properly cultivated, could become valuable allies in establishing American rule in the province. When the first constitutional convention was called in California, seven out of forty-eight delegates were "native Californians," that is, representative of the *gente de razon*. It goes without saying, of course, that the lower classes, the *paisanos*, were not represented at this convention.

The Mexicans, in fact, bore the brunt of the animosity born of conquest. During the days of the hide-and-tallow trade, Mexicans and Indians were known, among Americans, as greasers. For to them fell the disagreeable task of loading the grimy, tick-ridden hides on the clipper ships anchored offshore. After the conquest, greaser became a synonym for Mexican, in fact, for any dark-skinned person. The swift victory over Mexico and the easy conquest of California had bred in the Americans a contempt for all things Mexican. Race feeling was strong in the mines, and, at the outset, was "strongest against men of the Latin race," including not only Sonorans but also Chileans, Peruvians, and the few Frenchmen to be found in the gold fields.

"Nowhere else," wrote Josiah Royce, "were we Americans more affected than here, in our lives and conduct, by the feeling that we stood in the position of conquerors in a new land . . . nowhere else were we driven so hastily to improvise a government for a large body of strangers." The circumstances, indeed, were unique in our American experience: a large body of restless, adventuresome, single men had been suddenly catapulted into a new and foreign land, with the excitement of gold in the air, and with no settled government to curb their predilection for violence and direct action. Unlike the other Western states, California never had a territorial government; in fact, from 1846 to 1850, there was really no government in California. Skipping the territorial phase, California adopted a constitution on the basis of which it was directly admitted to the union. Furthermore, the hordes that poured into the state after 1849 thought of themselves as sojourners, not as settlers; as gold-seekers, not as residents. The attitude of these miners, and also of the ex-volunteers and former Frémont soldiers, toward everything Spanish or Mexican was one of supreme contempt. "The manners and actions of these men," wrote Owen H. O'Neill, "were a painful surprise to the Californians and produced a silent bitterness which was to endure for many years."

The trouble began, naturally enough, in the mines, for as Royce pointed out, "a mixed population of gold-seekers was obviously a thing to be feared." At the first session of the California legislature in 1850, a Foreign Miners' Tax Law was adopted, the purpose of which was to drive "foreigners" from the mines. Using this act as the spearhead, a systematic campaign was launched to oust the Mexicans from their claims. In 1850 a mob of 2,000 American miners descended on the Mexican mining camp of Sonora and, "firing at every Mexican in sight," proceeded to raze the town. The rioting lasted for nearly a week, with scores of murders and lynchings being reported. Following this major assault, individual Mexicans were singled out for attack. Every mysterious offense was promptly blamed on some unhappy Mexican. "We can see only indirectly," wrote Royce, "through the furious and confused reports of the Americans themselves, how much of organized and coarse brutality these Mexicans suffered from the miners' meetings." Juries would convict greasers on very moderate evidence indeed, and the number of lynchings has never been computed. On July 5, 1851, a mob of miners, in Downieville, lynched a Mexican woman who was three months pregnant. As the campaign mounted in intensity and violence, Mexicans were driven south to the Cow Counties where, in canyon and foothill hide-outs, they licked their wounds and plotted their revenge.

It was during this period, as noted by Guinn, "that a strange metamorphosis took place in the character of the *lower* classes of the native Californians. . . . Before the conquest by the Americans they were a peaceful and contented people. There were no organized bands of outlaws among them. . . . The Americans not only took possession of their country and its government, but in many cases they despoiled them of their ancestral acres and their personal property. Injustice rankles, and they were often treated by the rougher American elements as aliens and intruders, who had no right in the land of their birth. Such treatment embittered them more than the loss of property." Living in California from 1840 to 1843, the South American, Don Jose Arnaz, reported that he had heard of but one murder and one robbery during that period—"Perfect security for the person prevailed in California towns and highways." In fact, crimes of violence had been almost unknown prior to the conquest, but, as the conquest progressed, the Mexicans became increasingly disaffected and their unrest began to assume a covert or "criminal" design. It is important to note, as pointed out by Willard, that "among the lower classes of Californians the same adaptability to new conditions did not develop as among the *gente de razon*; on the contrary, the presence of the Americans, or gringos, was more and more resented, and, in the end, acting upon the bad example of the Americans themselves, a great amount of lawlessness developed."

Such was the origin of the much-discussed "Mexican banditry" of the period. In 1853 the southern counties were overrun with "Mexican bandits" and two companies of Rangers were raised to fight them. In 1855 the country between Los Angeles and Fort Miller (in the San Joaquin Valley) was reported to be infested with "California and Mexican outlaws." Bands of Mexicans raided the cattle herds being driven north to the mines and occasionally looted the mining settlements. In the main, this lawlessness represented a kind of organized resistance to American rule. Typical of the attitude of these "bandits" was the statement of Tiburcio Vasquez, a native Californian, in a last interview in 1852. "A spirit of hatred and revenge," he said, "took possession of me. I had numerous fights in defense of what I believed to be my rights and those of my countrymen. I believed we were being unjustly deprived of the social rights that belonged to us." The local annals contain numerous references to the activities of these bold and daring outlaws: Vasquez, Joaquin Murieta, Louis Bulvia, Antonio Moreno, Procopio, Soto, Juan Flores, Pancho Daniel, and many others. Called El Patrio ("The Native"), by the Mexicans, Murieta boasted that he could muster 2,000 men. Containing from eighty to a hundred men, these outlaw bands were well organized for guerrilla fighting. "The racial loyalty of the Californians," to quote from one local annal, "not to mention the entanglements of family relationships with the outlaws, plus a tacit policy of noninterference among the old American population, resulted in a negligent tolerance of these evils which within five years [after 1849] swept the local situation entirely out of hand."

The practice of lynching Mexicans soon became an outdoor sport in Southern California. In 1857 four Mexicans were lynched in El Monte, eleven in Los Angeles. A Mexican by the name of Alvitre was hanged in El Monte in 1861; on November 21, 1863, two Mexicans were lynched on Spring Street in Los Angeles, with another lynching being reported in January, 1864. In fact, the local annals for the period from 1850 to 1890 are studded with references to Mexican lynchings, the last of which was reported on August 20, 1892, when one Francisco Torres was lynched in Santa Ana. Horace Bell, who was himself once indicted for the "homicide" of a Mexican, describes any number of Mexican murders and lynchings in his *Reminiscences of a Ranger* and in a later volume entitled *On the Old West Coast*.

These repeated assaults, murders, and lynchings signified, of course, that the Mexican-American War had been resumed in California. A homicide a day was reported in Los Angeles in 1854, with most of the victims being Mexicans and Indians. Although the office paid a stipend of $10,000 a year, there was one term when the office of sheriff went begging, the two previous sheriffs having been murdered. In 1853, California had more murders than the rest of the United States, and Los Angeles had more than the rest of California. In a five-year period, 1849–1854, Californians invested $6,000,000 in bowie knives and pistols, and during this period the state reported 2,400 murders, 1,400 suicides, "10,000 other miserable deaths." My impression is that "miserable deaths" was a euphemism for "Mexicans murdered."

Considering that this unofficial, undeclared war between "lower-class" Mexicans and Anglos lasted for so many years, it is not surprising that it should have left, as a lasting heritage, a deep enmity between the two groups in Southern California. Of more importance is the fact that this continuing guerrilla warfare destroyed the conditions of tolerance under which some measure of assimilation might eventually have occurred. Quite apart from the prevailing hostility toward them, the *paisanos* faced extremely difficult problems of adjustment. Unlike the *gente de razon*, they were almost entirely Spanish-speaking and illiterate, they owned little property, they lacked sponsors in the Anglo world, and the defection of their former lords and masters had robbed them of leadership. When these difficulties are considered in light of the existing enmity, it is apparent that the framework, within which some measure of acculturation might normally have been expected to take place, simply did not exist. To this day, the bulk of the old-time Mexican residents of Southern California, and their descendants, have remained Spanish-speaking, or have retained Spanish as the language of the home.

4. THE END OF THE RANCHEROS

In the great period of the ranchos, between 1830 and 1846, some eight million acres of land in California passed into the hands of less than eight hundred grantees. Some of the great ranchos were, as Horace Bell wrote, "truly baronial in their extent and surroundings." The casa of Don Bernardo Yorba in Southern California, for example, consisted of thirty rooms, not counting the schoolrooms, harness and shoemakers' rooms, which, together with the servants' quarters, totaled twenty-one additional rooms. Among his retainers were four woolcombers, two tanners, one soapmaker, one butter-and-cheese man, a harnessmaker, two shoemakers, one jeweler, one plasterer, one carpenter, a blacksmith, a major-domo, two errand boys, one head sheepherder, one cook, one baker, two washwomen, a woman to iron, four seamstresses, one dressmaker, two gardeners, a schoolmaster, and a number of miscellaneous servants. With a continually increasing band of cattle and horses, the ranchero who ruled over one of these vast estates could, and frequently did, accumulate great wealth. Raising cattle for their hides, which were sold to the Boston merchants, the rancheros spurned agriculture and permitted many of the promising agricultural developments, started by the Franciscans, to be lost through waste and neglect. With the discovery of gold, the price of range cattle soared from $2 and $4 a head to $20 and $50, and the vineyards of Southern California became immensely profitable. With riches pouring into their hands in the form of money, the rancheros began to spend with the prodigality of princes and to gamble like lords.

Their prosperity was, however, of short duration. When stock began to be driven overland to the mines, the price of Southern California cattle quickly dropped. Later, as herds of cattle, representing much better breeds than the small scrawny Spanish steer, were established in the San Joaquin Valley, few cattle-buyers made the long trip over the Tehachapi to Southern California. In two years of ruinous drought, in 1862 and 1864, between 1,000,000 and 3,000,-000 cattle perished in the Cow Counties, the number of cattle fell by 71%, and five-sixths of the land was reported tax delinquent. Pasture lands were reduced on assessment rolls to ten cents an acre and range cattle were valued at a dollar a head. "The cattle of Los Angeles County," to quote from a local newspaper account of April, 1864, "are dying so fast in many places that the large rancheros keep their men busily employed in obtaining hides. Thousands of carcasses strew the plains in all directions, a short distance from this city, and the sight is harrowing in the extreme."

After the American conquest, the rancheros were compelled to secure confirmation of their land grants under the Land Act of 1851, a process which proved to be as disastrous as drought and the collapse of the bonanza cattle market. According to Hittell, one out of ten of the bona-fide landowners of Los Angeles County was reduced to bankruptcy by the federal land policy. At least 40% of the land owned under Mexican grants was sold, by the owners, to meet the costs and expenses involved in complying with the Act of 1851. Under the Mexican regime, taxes had not been levied on land or improvements, the sole revenue being derived from a tax on brandy and wine. Wholly unfamiliar with the Anglo-American system of land taxation and the workings of a monetary economy, the rancheros were ruinously affected by the transition to American rule.

The Rancho de los Alamitos, consisting of 26,000 acres, was advertised for sale for $152 of delinquent taxes. Lots worth two million dollars in later years were sold in 1864 for $2.50 unpaid taxes. Usurious interest rates also played an important part in the general debacle that engulfed the *gente de razon*. Interest rates of 5% a month, compounded, were not uncommon. The Rancho Santa Gertrudes, worth a million dollars, was lost for a $5,000 debt. So general was the debacle that Charles Howard Shinn could write, in 1891, that, in all California, there were only thirty *gente de razon* families who had managed to preserve much wealth or influence. "These families," he said, "were the exceptions; most of the old families sank into obscurity and it is now difficult to trace their connections." Writing in 1928, the Los Angeles banker, Jackson Graves, who was certainly in a position to know the facts, stated that the Dominguez ranch was the only grant in Los Angeles County which was still owned, in part, by descendants of the original grantees.

As the *gente de razon* lost their money and holdings, they began to be called Mexican and the old practice of referring to them as Californios or native Californians was abandoned. By 1876 Walter M. Fisher, an English journalist, reported that "the meanest runaway English sailor, escaped Sydney convict, or American rowdy, despised without distinction the bluest blood of Castile, and the half-breeds descended from the Mexican garrison soldiery, habitually designating all who spoke Spanish by the offensive name 'greasers' for whom remains only the rust and the dust of a lost power." In all Southern California today, I know of only one area, in the Santa Ynez Valley, where the former practice still prevails.

The *gente de razon* did not, however, forfeit their prestige and preferred position overnight, particularly in Southern California. Here they were concentrated in sufficient numbers to preserve, at least until the 'eighties, a measure of their power and influence. As the former rancheros came to realize that "pure Spanish blood" was no guarantee of social or political position, they began to form alliances with the Mexicans in an effort to offset the gringo dominance. In most elections in Southern California from 1849 to 1879, *hijo del pais* was pitted against newcomer. To some extent, also, the traditional fear which the underpopulated southern counties had of dominance by the northern counties, created a political situation which the Hispanos could use to advantage. The southern counties were made up of land-owning interests, and state taxes, at the time, were levied on land. In 1851, the southern counties, with a population of 6,367 and twelve representatives in the legislature, paid nearly twice as much in taxes as did twelve mining counties in the north with a population of 119,917 and forty-four representatives. This regional unity of interest served, for a time, to protect the Hispanos.

"Down to the end of the 1870's," writes O'Neill, "local politics in Southern California were complicated by a natural tendency to diverge on racial lines. Vast and complex family connections would make it impossible to trace these cleavages by any process so simple as noting Spanish names, but they were a real and potent factor which became more evident after 1865, when so many of the old Californians, once magnates of the land, were being crowded to the wall by economic misfortune." From 1860 to 1868, one notes among the legislative representatives of Santa Barbara County such names as Pablo de la Guerra, Antonio Maria de la Guerra, Romualdo Pacheco (later Lieutenant-Governor of California), and J. Y. Cota. From the south, an Estudillo and a Coronel became State Treasurers, and, in Los Angeles, a Sepulveda was elected to the bench and a Del Valle became a prominent political figure.

Incidents long buried in the local annals serve to illustrate how the Hispano element, on occasion, coalesced to win an important victory. In Santa Barbara, George Nidever, an American, shot and killed a Badillo in 1859. Public opinion in the county immediately flamed against the Americans. Peace was not restored, in fact, until state troops had been called into the county. "It was a truth," writes O'Neill, "hard for the new American element to swallow that the old Californians still held the balance of power in Southern California, and liked to use it." As late as 1870, the native Californians outnumbered the Americans in Santa Barbara County, owned more than a third of the property, and occupied numerous positions of prominence in the community. While the Hispano element was particularly strong in Santa Barbara County, somewhat similar conditions prevailed throughout Southern California.

5. DURING THE 'EIGHTIES

"I am rather lazy—somewhat of a Mexican, in fact."
—from *Hilda Strafford*, a novel, by Beatrice Harraden

With the great influx of immigrants into Southern California in the 'eighties, the Hispano element was almost completely eclipsed. "Just as the Spaniards had wrenched this country away from the aboriginal tribes," wrote Willard, "so now this overwhelming horde of new arrivals took possession of the land and proceeded to make things over to their own taste." The typically Spanish appearance of the Southern California towns changed overnight. With a truly awful swiftness of transition, they became undeniably gringo villages. As much as anything else, the transition was symbolized by the disappearance of the adobes, and the disappearance of the adobes symbolized the eclipse of the Hispano. "Death and Emigration," wrote J. P. Widney in 1886, "are removing them from the land . . . they no longer have unnumbered horses to ride and vast herds of sheep, from which one for a meal would never be missed. Their broad acres now, with few exceptions, belong to the acquisitive American . . . grinding poverty has bred recklessness and moroseness. Simple healthful amusements have in many instances given way to midnight carousals; long-continued dissipation and want are huddling them together in the most unwholesome localities in the towns."

From the local annals, one can detect at least the outlines of the process by which, through a kind of occupational erosion, the Hispanos steadily declined in influence and power. One after another, the economic functions for which they had been trained were taken from them. Excellent and well-trained vaqueros, the Mexicans lost this occupation with the collapse of the ranchero regime. Then for a decade or more they appear in the annals as deft and efficient sheep-shearers, appearing year after year at the sheep ranches, always on schedule, never summoned. "The shearers would come in," writes Sarah Bixby Smith, "a gay band of Mexicans on their prancing horses, decked with wonderful silver-trimmed bridles made of rawhide or braided horsehair, and saddles with high horns, sweeping stirrups, and wide expanse of beautiful tooled leather. The men themselves were dressed in black broadcloth, ruffled white shirts, high-heeled boots, and high-crowned, wide sombreros which were trimmed with silver-braided bands, and held securely in place by a cord under the nose. They would come in, fifty or sixty strong, stake out their caballos, put away their finery, and appear in brown overalls, red bandannas on their heads, and live and work on the ranch for more than a month, so many were the sheep to be sheared." Even before the sheep industry began to decline, however, one can note the displacement of Mexican sheep-shearers by small bands of newly arrived

Basques who came to Southern California by way of South America.

With sheep and cattle disappearing, the Mexican reappears in the annals as the farm worker and livery-stable hand of the period, a type of work in which he could still exercise his skill with horses. Long before the livery stable disappeared, and just when the demand for farm workers had begun to increase, the Chinese began to invade the Sonoratowns of Southern California, driving the Mexicans from many occupations in the towns and on the ranches. Visiting Santa Barbara in 1888, Edwards Roberts noted that "the houses of the Spanish-speaking people are being taken over by the Chinese, who have invaded the adobe cottages and utilized them for shops. . . . Chinamen are an incongruity in Spanish adobes, with their glaring red posters and smoky rooms. The Mexicans now earn a precarious living by gardening and horse-breaking, and are liberal patrons of the few saloons that have opened in the State Street adobes."

Occasionally one finds a scion of some *gente de razon* family figuring in the annals as a business man or as a doctor or lawyer, but there were only a handful of these and they had passed over completely into the Anglo world. Due to the considerable amount of intermarriage which had taken place, it is difficult to trace the descendants of the once powerful ranchero families by name. In a few cases, however, one can see what actually happened to some of these people. One of the descendants of Don Julio Verdugo became a tamale peddler in Los Angeles, while still another descendant became an automobile mechanic. It is worthy of note, however, that although the Spanish-speaking element had begun to feel the pinch of poverty, you could visit the hospitals and almshouses in the late 'eighties, as J. P. Widney observed, "and look in vain for the Mexican or the Spaniard."

When Emma H. Adams visited Southern California in 1887 she found "few Mexican families living in affluence." By that time, the term Mexican was used to embrace both native Californians and Mexicans, with no distinction being noted between the two groups. "When I first came here," wrote another visitor, "there were Mexicans everywhere . . . they lounged on doorsteps, within the presidios of their homes, in front of the shops and stores, and along the country roads. Apparently without a care, they laughed, chatted, and danced. Now, I meet a few on the streets as I go about Los Angeles, but their number seems greatly diminished." Actually the impression that they had declined in number was an optical illusion;

they had only declined in relation to the great increase in the number of Anglos.

Returning to Los Angeles after a short absence, one observer reported in 1883 that "the Spanish language is heard familiarly on all sides. Here, it appears, is the stronghold of the Mexican and Spanish people in Southern California. But the swarthy faces, under the broad-brimmed hats, now so common, and so much an object of curiosity to the tourists, are to become less and less numerous. You can hear it on every side; among real estate dealers, among merchants, among hotel keepers, and eager investors—'the Mexicans are being crowded out.'" In June of the same year, the adobe houses around the Plaza had been largely occupied by Mexicans, but, by October, many of the homes were closed. "The sententious explanation of this problem, as given by a prominent real estate dealer, is 'foreclosure.' Much of the Mexican property is mortgaged. The present rapid growth of the city and the increase of value in real estate has indicated to holders of the obligations that now is the time to take possession." It will be noted that this observation was made in 1883, on the eve of the great real-estate boom in Southern California.

By 1885, the Mexicans had become "a picturesque element," rather than a functional part, of the social life and economy of the region. Helen Hunt Jackson noted the presence in Los Angeles of "Mexican women, their heads wrapped in black shawls, and their bright eyes peering out between close-gathered folds." Much Spanish was still spoken in the streets where the Mexicans, crowded out of their former occupations, appeared with their carts as venders, selling sweets, tamales, and manzanita roots which they sawed into bricks and sold as fuel. Most of them still lived in the old Plaza section, their homes clinging precariously to the slopes of Fort Moore hill. "Wooden stair-cases and bits of terrace," wrote Mrs. Jackson, "link and loop the odd little perches together; bright green-pepper trees, sometimes tall enough to shade two or three tiers of roofs, give a graceful plumed draping at the side, and some of the steep fronts are covered with bloom, in solid curtains of geranium, sweet alyssum, heliotrope, and ivy." By the turn of the century, visitors had ceased to note the presence of Mexicans, with the exception of an occasional reference to the odd night cries of the tamale venders: "*Tamales, calientes, aqui.*" Visiting Southern California in 1899 Charles Keeler noted that "a wagon, driven by a swarthy Mexican wearing a broad sombrero and bright red neckscarf, rumbles along the streets now and then."

6. The Old Life Retreats

"Defenseless in its degeneracy, San Gabriel now boasts a motley population of low-bred Mexicans and narrow-eyed Celestials."
—from *Mariposilla*, a novel, by Mrs. Charles Stewart Daggett

With the eclipse of the Spanish-Mexican element, few visible evidences of Spanish culture could be detected in Southern California. Some Spanish words, such as adobe, cañon, tules, bonanza, vara, fandango, corral, vaquero, ranch, loco, burro, reata, caballada, paisano, zanja, arroyo, and so forth, had been incorporated into the Anglo speech of the region. Important segments of Spanish-Mexican jurisprudence had been woven into the legal fabric of California. A considerable amount of Hispano blood was flowing in the veins of local residents with names such as Travis, Kraemer, Reeves, Locke and Rowlands. While many of the Spanish street-names had been changed or Anglicized, most of the Spanish place-names had been retained. Aside from a few items which had been incorporated into the dominant cultural pattern, the Spanish influence appeared to have been completely obliterated. Certainly the dominant Anglo-American cultural pattern had not been modified except in a few minor respects.

"No one who has grown up in California," wrote Josiah Royce, "can be under an illusion as to the small extent to which the American character, as here exemplified, has been really altered by foreign intercourse, large as the foreign population has always remained. The foreign influence has never been for the American community at large, in California, more than skin-deep. One has assumed a very few and unimportant native California ways, one has freely used or abused the few [Spanish] words and phrases, one has grown well accustomed to the sight of foreigners and to business relations with them, and one's natural innocence about foreign matters has in California given place, even more frequently than elsewhere in our country, to a superficial familiarity with the appearance and the manners of numerous foreign communities. But all this in no wise renders the American life in California less distinctly native in tone . . . you cannot call a community of Americans foreign in disposition merely because its amusements have a foreign look."

The end result of the initial contact between Anglo and Hispano cultures in California was, therefore, almost a complete stalemate. Clearly dominant, the Anglo-American pattern had scarcely been modified, while the Spanish-Mexican culture, although somewhat dis-organized, still remained as a sub-culture in the region much as the Mexicans survived as a submerged element in the population. In only a few respects did the Mexicans take over or incorporate traits from the dominant culture. Those Hispanos who had not passed into the Anglo-American world remained Spanish-speaking, continued to think of themselves as alien or Mexican, and were increasingly removed from vital contact with the dominant culture. By the turn of the century it appeared—in fact, it was generally assumed—that the Mexican influence had been thoroughly exorcised.

It could not be eliminated, however, as long as thousands of Mexicans continued to reside in a region which they thought of as their home. In 1887 the number of native Californians living in Los Angeles was given as 12,000, and there were certainly 15,000 in the other Southern California communities. The presence of some 30,000 Mexicans, residing in Spanish-speaking settlements, served to keep the Spanish influence alive. As Mexican immigration steadily increased after 1900, the Spanish sub-culture began to be strengthened and revived. And then, in the decade 1920–1930, a tidal wave of Mexican immigration swept into Southern California. With this great increase in the number of Spanish-speaking residents, the long-dormant conflict of cultures was once more renewed.

What had happened in Southern California, in the period from 1849 to 1900, as J. P. Widney shrewdly observed, was that the "old life"—that is, the old Mexican life of the province—had retreated southward "along the coastal plains that reach from Los Angeles to Acapulco." Retreating before the Anglo invasion, the old life had never wholly vanished. "Whether they will or not," wrote Widney, "their future [that is, the future of the two groups] is one and together, and I think neither type of race life will destroy the other. They will merge. The tropic plains will help in the merging. Out of it will come a type, not of the north, not of the south, but the American of the semitropics." This prediction may well be confirmed. Even as sentimental Americans were performing funeral rites for the departed Mexican, the tide of Spanish influence began to sweep up the coast again. Today close to 300,000 people of Mexican descent live in Los Angeles County alone. In view of the size of this colony and its proximity to the Mexican border, it is not unlikely that, in the future, some fusion of the two cultures will occur.

Clear ring the silvery Mission bells
  Their calls to vesper and to mass;
O'er vineyard slopes, thro' fruited dells,
  The long processions pass.

The pale Franciscan lifts in air
  The cross above the kneeling throng;
Their simple world how sweet with prayer,
  With chant and matin song!
                    —Ina Coolbrith

CHAPTER IV

THE GROWTH OF A LEGEND

CONSIDERING the long dark record of Indian mistreatment in Southern California, it is difficult to account for the curious legend that has developed in the region about the well-being of the natives under Mission rule. According to this legend, the Missions were havens of happiness and contentment for the Indians, places of song, laughter, good food, beautiful languor, and mystical adoration of the Christ. What is still more astonishing is the presence in the legend of an element of masochism, with the Americans, who manufactured the legend, taking upon themselves full responsibility for the criminal mistreatment of the Indian and completely exonerating the Franciscans. "In the old and happy days of Church domination and priestly rule," writes one Protestant historian, "there had been no 'Indian question.' That came only after American 'civilization' took from the red men their lands and gave them nothing in return."

Equally baffling, at first blush, is the intense preoccupation of Southern California with its Mission-Spanish past. Actually one of the principal charms of Southern California, as Farnsworth Crowder has pointed out, is that it is not overburdened with historical distractions. "As against any European country, certain parts of the United States and even neighboring Mexico," writes Mr. Crowder, "human culture has left relatively few marks, monuments and haunts over the vast virginal face of the state. Almost any square block of London is more drenched with flavors of the past than the whole of Los Angeles. The desert areas and valleys cannot evoke any such awareness of human antiquity and the genesis of great religions and civilizations as can the borderlands of the Mediterranean. No Wordsworths, no Caesars, no Pharaohs have made their homes here. The Californian simply cannot feed upon the fruits and signs of yesterday as can a Roman, a Parisian, an Oxonian." And yet this is precisely what he attempts to do. The newness of the land itself seems, in fact, to have compelled, to have demanded, the evocation of a mythology which could give people a sense of continuity in a region long characterized by rapid social dislocations. And of course it would be a tourist, a goggle-eyed umbrella-packing tourist, who first discovered the past of Southern California and peopled it with curious creatures of her own invention.

1. "H. H."

Some day the Los Angeles Chamber of Commerce should erect a great bronze statue of Helen Hunt Jackson at the entrance to Cajon Pass. Beneath the statue should be inscribed no flowery dedication, but the simple inscription: "H. H.—In Gratitude." For little, plump, fair-skinned, blue-eyed Helen Hunt Jackson, "H. H." as she was known to every resident of Southern California, was almost solely responsible for the evocation of its Mission past, and it was she who catapulted the lowly Digger Indian of Southern California into the empyrean.

Born in Amherst on October 15, 1830, Helen Maria Fiske became a successful writer of trite romances and sentimental poems quite unlike those written by her friend and neighbor, Emily Dickinson. She was married in 1852 to Lieutenant Edward Bissell Hunt of the Coast Survey, who died a few years after the marriage. In later years, she married William Sharpless Jackson, a wealthy banker and railroad executive of Colorado Springs. It is rather ironic to note that Mrs. Jackson, who became one of the most ardent free-lance apologists for the Catholic Church in America, was a confirmed anti-Papist until she visited California. As might have been expected, she first became interested in Indians while attending a tea party in Boston. At this tea, she met Standing Bear and Bright Eyes, who were lecturing on the grievous wrongs suffered by the Poncas tribe. At the time of this meeting, Mrs. Jackson was forty-nine years of age, bubbling with enthusiasm, full of rhymes. Quick to catch the "aboriginal contagion," which had begun to spread among the writers of American romances, she immediately usurped the position of defender of the Poncas tribe and thereafter no more was heard of Standing Bear and Bright Eyes. In 1881 Harper's published her well-known work, A Century of Dishonor, which did much to arouse a new, although essentially spurious, interest in the American Indian.

In the spring of 1872, Mrs. Jackson had made a brief visit, as a tourist, to the northern part of California. Later she made three trips, as a tourist, to Southern California: in the winter of 1881–1882, the spring of 1883, and the winter, spring, and summer of 1884–1885. It scarcely needs to be emphasized that her knowledge of California, and of the Mission Indians, was essentially that of the tourist and casual visitor. Although she did prepare a valuable report on the Mission Indians, based on a field trip that she made with Abbot Kinney of Los Angeles, most of her material about Indians was second-hand and consisted, for the greater part, of odds and ends of gossip, folk tales, and Mission-inspired allegories of one kind or another.

She had originally been sent to Southern California by Century magazine to write some stories about the Missions, which, according to the illustrator who accompanied her, were to be "enveloped in the mystery and poetry of romance." In Southern California she became deliriously enamored of the Missions, then in a state of general disrepair and neglect, infested with countless swallows and pigeons, overrun by sheep and goats, and occasionally inhabited by stray dogs and wandering Indians. "In the sunny, delicious, winterless California air," these crumbling ruins, with their walled gardens and broken bells, their vast cemeteries and caved-in wells, exerted a potent romantic influence on Mrs. Jackson's highly susceptible nature. Out of these brief visits to Southern California came Ramona, the first novel written about the region, which became, after its publication in 1884, one of the most widely read American novels of the time. It was this novel which firmly established the Mission legend in Southern California.

When the book was first published, it provoked a storm of protest in the Southland. Egged on by various civic groups, the local critics denounced it as a tissue of falsehoods, a travesty on history, a damnable libel on Southern California. But the book was perfectly timed, providentially timed, to coincide with the great invasion of home-seekers and tourists to the region. As these hordes of winter tourists began to express a lively interest in visiting "Ramona's land," Southern California experienced an immediate change of attitude and, overnight, became passionately Ramona-conscious. Beginning about 1887, a Ramona promotion, of fantastic proportions, began to be organized in the region.

Picture postcards, by the tens of thousands, were published showing "the school attended by Ramona," "the original of Ramona," "the place where Ramona was married," and various shots of the "Ramona Country." Since the local chambers of commerce could not, or would not, agree upon the locale of the novel—one school of thought insisted that the Camulos rancho was the scene of the more poignant passages while still another school insisted that the Hacienda Guajome was the authentic locale—it was not long before the scenic postcards depicting the Ramona Country had come to embrace all of Southern California. In the 'eighties, the Southern Pacific tourist and excursion trains regularly stopped at Camulos, so that the wide-eyed Bostonians, guidebooks in hand, might detrain, visit the rancho, and bounce up and down on "the bed in which Ramona slept." Thousands of Ramona baskets, plaques, pincushions, pillows, and souvenirs of all sorts were sold in every curio shop in California. Few tourists left the region without having purchased a little replica of the "bells that rang when Ramona was married." To keep the tourist interest alive, local press agents for fifty years engaged in a synthetic controversy over the identities of the "originals" for the universally known characters in the novel. Some misguided Indian women began to take the promotion seriously and had themselves photographed—copyright reserved—as "the original Ramona." A bibliography of the newspaper stories, magazine articles, and pamphlets written about some aspect of the Ramona legend would fill a volume. Four husky volumes of Ramonana appeared in Southern California: *The Real Ramona* (1900), by D. A. Hufford; *Through Ramona's Country* (1908), the official, classic document, by George Wharton James; *Ramona's Homeland* (1914), by Margaret V. Allen; and *The True Story of Ramona* (1914), by C. C. Davis and W. A. Anderson.

From 1884 to date, the Los Angeles Public Library has purchased over a thousand copies of *Ramona*. Thirty years after publication, the same library had a constant waiting list for 105 circulating copies of the book. The sales to date total 601,636 copies, deriving from a Regular Edition, a Monterey Edition (in two volumes), a De Luxe Edition, a Pasadena Edition, a Tourist Edition, a Holiday Art Edition, and a Gift Edition. Hundreds of unoffending Southern California babies have been named Ramona. A townsite was named Ramona. And in San Diego thousands of people make a regular pilgrimage to "Ramona's Marriage Place," where the True Vow Keepers Clubs—made up of couples who have been married fifty years or longer—hold their annual picnics. The Native Daughters of the Golden West have named one of their "parlors," or lodges, after Ramona. The name Ramona appears in the corporate title of fifty or more businesses currently operating in Los Angeles. Two of Mrs. Jackson's articles for *Century*, "Father Junipero and His Work," and "The Present Condition of the Mission Indians of Southern California," were for years required reading in the public schools of California. Reprints of Henry Sandham's illustrations for *Ramona* are familiar items in Southern California homes, hotels, restaurants, and places of business. In 1914 one of the Ramona historians truthfully said that "Mrs. Jackson's name is familiar to almost every human being in Southern California, from the little three-year-old tot, who has her choice juvenile stories read to him, to the aged grandmother who sheds tears of sympathy for Ramona." Two generations of Southern California children could recite from memory the stanzas from Ina Coolbrith's verses to Helen Hunt Jackson, often ornately framed on the walls of Southern California homes:

> There, with her dimpled, lifted hands,
>   Parting the mustard's golden plumes,
> The dusky maid, Ramona, stands,
>   Amid the sea of blooms.

And Alessandro, type of all
His broken tribe, for evermore
An exile, hears the stranger call
Within his father's door.

Translated into all known languages, Ramona has also been dramatized. The play based on the novel was first presented at the Mason Opera House in Los Angeles on February 27, 1905, the dramatization having been written by Miss Virginia Calhoun and General Johnstone Jones. Commenting upon Miss Calhoun's performance, in the role of Ramona, the Los Angeles *Times* reported that "in the lighter parts she held a fascination that was tempered with gentleness and playfulness. Her slender figure, graceful and pliant as a willow, swayed with every light touch of feeling, and the deeper tragic climaxes she met in a way to win tears from the eyes of many." Over the years, three motion-picture versions of the novel have appeared. In 1887, George Wharton James, who did much to keep the Ramona promotion moving along, "tramped every foot of the territory covered by Mrs. Jackson," interviewing the people she had interviewed, photographing the scenes she had photographed, and "sifting the evidence" she had collected. His thick tome on the Ramona country is still a standard item in all Southern California libraries. For twenty-five years, the chambers of commerce of the Southland kept this fantastic promotion alive and flourishing. When interest seemed to be lagging, new stories were concocted. Thus on March 7, 1907, the Los Angeles *Times* featured, as a major news item, a story about "Condino, the newly discovered and only child of Ramona." In 1921 the enterprising Chamber of Commerce of Hemet, California, commissioned Garnet Holme to write a pageant about Ramona. Each year since 1921 the pageant has been produced in late April or early May in the heart of the Ramona country, by the Chamber of Commerce. At the last count, two hundred thousand people had witnessed the pageant.

The legendary quality of Mrs. Jackson's famous novel came about through the amazing way in which she made elegant pre-Raphaelite characters out of Ramona and "the half-breed Alessandro." Such Indians were surely never seen upon this earth. Furthermore, the story extolled the Franciscans in the most extravagant manner and placed the entire onus of the mistreatment of the Indians upon the noisy and vulgar gringos. At the same time, the sad plight of Ramona and Alessandro got curiously mixed up, in the telling, with the plight of the "fine old Spanish families." These fine old Spanish families, who were among the most flagrant exploiters of the Indian in Southern California, appeared in the novel as only slightly less considerate of his welfare than the Franciscans. Despite its legendary aspects, however, the Ramona version of the Indians of Southern California is now firmly implanted in the mythology of the region. It is this legend which largely accounts for the "sacred" as distinguished from the "profane" history of the Indian in Southern California.

It should be said to Mrs. Jackson's credit, however, that she did arouse a momentary flurry of interest in the Mission Indians. Her report on these Indians, which appeared in all editions of A Century of Dishonor after 1883, is still a valuable document. As a result of her work, Charles Fletcher Lummis founded the Sequoya League in Los Angeles in 1902, "to make better Indians," and, through the activities of the league, the three hundred Indians who were evicted from the Warner Ranch in 1901, were eventually relocated on lands purchased by the government. Aside from the relocation of these Indians, however, nothing much came of Mrs. Jackson's work in Southern California, for the region accepted the charming Ramona, as a folk figure, but completely rejected the Indians still living in the area. A government report of 1920 indicated that 90% of the residents of the sections in which Indians still live in Southern California were wholly ignorant about their Indian neighbors and that deep local prejudice against them still prevailed.

At the sacred level, it is the half-breed Alessandro who best symbolizes the Indian heritage of Southern California. At the secular level, however, one must turn to the local annals to select more appropriate symbols. There is, for example, the character Polonia, an Indian of great stature and strength, whose eyes had been burned out of their sockets. Clad in a tattered blanket, this blind Indian was a familiar figure on the dusty streets of Los Angeles in the 'fifties and 'sixties. And there was Viejo Cholo, or Old Half-Breed, who wore a pair of linen pantaloons and used a sheet for a mantle. His cane was a broom handle; his lunch counter, the swill basket. Viejo Cholo was succeeded, as the principal Indian eccentric of Los Angeles, by another half-breed, Pinikahti. A tiny man, Pinikahti was only four feet in height. Badly pockmarked, he had a flat nose and stubby beard. He was generally attired, notes Harris Newmark, "in a well-worn straw hat, the top of which was missing, and his long, straight hair stuck out in clumps and snarls. A woolen undershirt and a pair of overalls completed his costume, while his toes, as a rule, protruded from his enormous boots." Playing Indian tunes on a flute made out of reeds from the bed of the Los Angeles River, Pinikahti used to dance in the streets of the town for pennies, nickels, and dimes, or a glass of aguardiente. Polonia, Viejo Cholo, and Pinikahti, these are the real symbols of the Indian heritage of Southern California.

2. REDISCOVERY OF THE MISSIONS

With the great Anglo invasion of Southern California after 1880, the Spanish background of the region was, for a time, almost wholly forgotten. "For many years," wrote Harry Carr, "the traditions of Los Angeles were junked by the scorn of the conquering gringos. When I was a school boy in Los Angeles, I never heard of Ortega or Gaspar de Portola or Juan Bautista de Anza." And then with the publication of *Ramona*, the Spanish background began to be rediscovered, with the same false emphasis and from the same crass motives, that had characterized the rediscovery of the Indian. Both rediscoveries, that of the Indian and that of the Spaniard, occurred between 1883 and 1888, at precisely the period when the great real-estate promotion of Southern California was being organized.

In so far as the Spanish saga is concerned, it all began in 1888 when, as John A. Berger has written, "the romantic people of Southern California," under the leadership of Charles Fletcher Lummis, formed an Association for the Preservation of the Missions (which later became the Landmarks Club). With the gradual restoration of the Missions, a highly romantic conception of the Spanish period began to be cultivated, primarily for the benefit of the incoming tides of tourists, who were routed to the Missions much as they were routed to the mythical site of Ramona's birthplace. A flood of books began to appear about the Missions, with Mrs. Jackson's *Glimpses of California and the Missions* (1883) being the volume that inspired the whole movement. It was followed, after a few years, by George Wharton James's *In and Out of the Old Missions*, which, for a quarter of a century, was the "classic" in this field. My own guess would be that not a year has passed since 1900 without the publication of some new volume about the Missions. Not only has a library of books been written about the Missions, but each individual Mission has had its historians. Books have been written about the architecture of the Missions, about the Mission bells, about the Franciscans (notably Father Junipero Serra, a popular saint in Southern California), and about the wholly synthetic Mission furniture. In fact, the Mission-Spanish background of the region has been so strongly emphasized that, as Max Miller has written, "The past is almost as scrambled as the present, and almost as indefinite . . . the whole thing got mixed up." With each new book about the Missions came a new set of etchings and some new paintings. In 1880, William Keith painted all of the Missions of California. He was followed by the artist Ford, of Santa Barbara, who, in 1890, completed his etchings of the Franciscan establishments. Since 1890, the Missions have been painted by Jorgenson, Edward Deakin, Alexander F. Harmer, William Sparks, Gutzon Borglum, Elmer Wachtel, Minnie Tingle, and a host of other artists.

In 1902, Frank Miller, owner of the Glenwood Cottage Inn at Riverside, with funds provided by Henry Huntington, began to construct the famous Mission Inn. Designed by Myron Hunt, the Mission Inn was built wing by wing around the old adobe Glenwood Cottage, until the new structure covered an entire block. Once completed, the inn gave the initial fillip to Mission architecture, so called, and soon Missionesque and Moorish structures began to dot the Southern California landscape. It was here, in the Mission Inn, that John Steven McGroarty wrote the *Mission Play*, for which he was deservedly decorated by the Pope. The play had its premiere at San Gabriel on a warm spring evening, April 29, 1912, under the sponsorship of the Princess Lazarovic-Hrebrelanovic of Serbia, with a cast of "one hundred descendants of the Old Spanish families." On the opening night, "Queer chugging noises filled the air and the acrid smoke from burnt gasoline floated over the ancient Mission and the little adobes that nestled around it. It was the first big outpouring of automobiles that San Gabriel had ever had." The elite of Southern California turned out, en masse, for the premiere. The play, of course, was an enormous success. McGroarty boasted that it had been seen by 2,500,000 people, a world's record. During the sixteen consecutive seasons that it played at San Gabriel Mission, over 2,600 performances were recorded. Later the play was institutionalized, under official sponsorship, and became an enormous tourist attraction. A tourist who went to California and failed to see Catalina Island, Mt. Wilson, and the *Mission Play* was considered to have something wrong with his head. In recognition of his great services to Southern California, "Singing John," the songster of the green Verdugo hills, was made poet laureate of California on May 17, 1933. Needless to say, the play perpetuated the Helen Hunt Jackson version of the Indians, the Spanish Dons, and the Franciscans.

As a curious postscript to the growth of this amazing legend, it should be pointed out that the Catholic Church played virtually no role whatever in the Ramona-Mission revival in Southern California, which, from its inception, was a strictly Protestant promotion. As a matter of fact, Abbot Kinney, who took Mrs. Jackson through the Indian country in the 'eighties, later wrote that "the archbishops, bishops, and priests of those days were not, as a rule, much concerned about the condition of the Indians [theoretically still wards of the church] and the old Mission churches. Many of them were Catalans, who had little or no sympathy with the high ideals of the noble Franciscans. We actually found some of these priests, or those in higher authority, selling part of the lands that had originally been held by the Franciscans in trust for the Indians—not one foot of which belonged to the Church." With the exception of a few Irish priests, such as Father Joseph O'Keefe and Father John O'Sullivan, the Catholic Church did not figure prominently in the movement to restore the Missions. Even today the expensively restored Missions, as J. Russell Smith has pointed out, are "little more than carefully preserved historical curiosities and penny-catchers." Since McGroarty was a converted Catholic, however, it can be said that through this faithful son the Church did exert considerable influence on the formation of the Mission legend.

"Why is it," asked James L. Duff some years ago in the *Commonweal*, "that such a distinctly non-Catholic city as Los Angeles should evince such a consistent emotional preoccupation with its Catholic past?" Scrutinizing the local directory, Mr. Duff reported that the word "mission" was to be found as part of the corporate name of over a hundred business enterprises in Los Angeles. He was also surprised to find that such expressions as, "in the days of the Dons," and "in the footsteps of the padres," had become community colloquialisms in Southern California. The dominantly Catholic city of San Francisco, with its Mission Dolores, has never been greatly interested in the Missions. The incongruity is only greater by reason of the fact that Los Angeles is not merely non-Catholic; it can scarcely be called a California city, except in a geographical sense. It is a "conglomeration" of newcomers and has always had the lowest percentage of native-born Californians of any city in the state. Paradoxically, the less Catholic a community is in Southern California, the more the Mission past has been emphasized. The incongruity, however, is never noticed. Not one of the numerous Pope-baiting fundamentalist pastors of Southern California has ever objected to this community-wide adoration of the Missions. "Here," writes Mr. Duff, "is a city that is almost militantly non-Catholic, audaciously energetic, worshipping Progress, adulating the tinseled world of motion pictures, yet looking with dreaming eyes upon a day and a philosophy of life with which it has neither understanding nor communion, vaguely hoping that the emotion it is evoking is nostalgic."

Not only is Los Angeles a non-Catholic city, but, popular legend to the contrary, it is not a city of churches. Recently, the Los Angeles *Times* published an editorial under the caption: "What! No Church Bells?" The occasion was the May 13, 1945 celebration of V-E Day when, much to the astonishment of the *Times*, it was discovered that "church bells are exceedingly scarce in Los Angeles." At the present time, a movement is under way, sponsored by the *Times*, to bring church bells to Los Angeles, so that "thousands of residents of Los Angeles who formerly lived in Eastern and Midwestern states," may, "on the clear Sabbath mornings," be called to worship by the pealing of bells. "To hear that call again," comments the *Times*, "in their new home, would tend to keep them in touch with their childhood and with the simple, comforting faith with which childhood is blessed, but which sometimes is neglected and all but forgotten," particularly in Southern California.

With the rediscovery of the Catholic-Mission past, the same split occurred in the Spanish tradition of the region that had occurred in relation to its Indian background. Just as Ramona and Alessandro became the sacred symbols of the Indian past, so the Spanish Dons, rather than the Mexicano *paisanos*, became the sacred symbols of the Spanish past. A glance at almost any of the popular novels of Stewart Edward White will show, for example, how the romantic side of this tradition has been emphasized to the detriment—in fact, to the total neglect—of its realistic latter-day manifestations. Despite all the restorations, revivals, pageants, plays, paintings, museum collections, and laboriously gathered materials about this Spanish past, it was not until 1945 that a serious effort was launched to teach Spanish, as a language of the region, in the public schools.

Today there is scarcely a community in Southern California, however, that does not have its annual "Spanish fiesta," of which the Santa Barbara fiesta is the most impressive. Attending one of the early Santa Barbara fiestas, Duncan Aikman reported that "every man, woman, and child who owed any allegiance to Santa Barbara was in costume. . . . Shoe salesmen and grocery clerks served you with a bit of scarlet braid on their trouser seams. Paunchy realtors and insurance solicitors full of mental mastery dashed about town in gaudy sashes. Deacons of the total immersion sects sported, at the least, a bit of crimson frill around their hat bands. High school boys scurried by, their heads gorgeously bound in scarfs and bandanas. . . . The very street-car conductors wore Spanish epaulettes and ear-rings and a look of grievance even more bitter than usual. Women wore mantillas and an apparently official uniform in the way of a waist of yellow, black and scarlet, so universally that you could tell the outland females by their native American costumes. The Mexican population dug up its old finery and musical instruments and paraded the sidewalks with the timid air of reasserting their importance after long abeyance." Once the fiesta is over, however, the Mexicans retreat to their barrios, the costumes are carefully put away for the balance of the year, and the grotesque Spanish spoken in the streets during the fiesta is heard no more. This particular attempt to revive the Mexican "Fiesta de la Primavera," like most similar attempts in Southern California, was first launched in the mid 'twenties, its immediate motivation in Santa Barbara being the popularly sensed need to inject a note of good cheer in the Santa Barbarans after the earthquake of 1924. The Santa Barbara fiesta is often highlighted by some extraordinary antic. Some years ago, for example, Cedric Gibbons and Dolores del Rio, of the motion-picture colony, dressed in fiesta costumes, astride their handsome Palominos, were the first couple to be married on horseback, a type of marriage ceremony now a regular feature of the fiesta.

About the most incongruous ceremonial revival of this sort in Southern California is the annual ride of the *Rancheros Visitadores.* This particular revival is based on the alleged practice of the rancheros, in former years, of making the round of the ranchos in the area, paying a visit to each in turn. "In May, 1930," to quote from the *Santa Barbara Guide*, "some sixty-five riders assembled for the first cavalcade. Golden Palominos and proud Arabian thoroughbreds, carrying silver-mounted tack, brushed stirrups with shaggy mustangs from the range. Emerging from the heavy gray mist of a reluctant day, they cantered with casual grace down the old familiar trails of the Santa Ynez, to converge in Santa Barbara. . . . Here, amid the tolling of bells, the tinkling of trappings, and the whinnying of horses, the brown-robed friars blessed them and bade them 'Vayan con dios.' . . .This was the start of the first revival of the annual ride of the *Rancheros Visitadores*."

Since this auspicious beginning, the affair has steadily increased in pomp and circumstance. Nowadays it is invariably reported in the Southern California press as a major social event of the year. A careful scrutiny of the names of these fancily dressed *visitadores*—these gaily costumed Rotarians—reveals that Leo Carrillo is about the only rider whose name carries a faint echo of the past and he is about as Mexican as the ceremony is Spanish. Ostensibly a gay affair, the annual ride represents a rather grim and desperate effort to escape from the bonds of a culture that neither satisfies nor pleases. Actually there is something rather pathetic about the spectacle of these frustrated business men cantering forth in search of *ersatz* week-end romance, evoking a past that never existed to cast some glamour on an equally unreal today.

All attempted revivals of Spanish folkways in Southern California are similarly ceremonial and ritualistic, a part of the sacred rather than the profane life of the region. The 3,279 Mexicans who live in Santa Barbara are doubtless more bewildered by these annual Spanish hijinks than any other group in the community. For here is a community that generously and lavishly supports the "Old Spanish Fiesta"—and the wealth of the *rancheros visitadores* is apparent for all to see—but which consistently rejects proposals to establish a low-cost housing project for its Mexican residents. However, there is really nothing inconsistent about this attitude, for it merely reflects the manner in which the sacred aspects of the romantic past have been completely divorced from their secular connotations. The residents of Santa Barbara firmly believe, of course, that the Spanish past is dead, extinct, vanished. In their thinking, the Mexicans living in Santa Barbara have no connection with this past. They just happen to be living in Santa Barbara. To be sure, many of them have names, such as Cota or Gutierrez, that should stir memories of the *dolce far niente* period. But these names are no longer important. They belong to the profane, and happily forgotten, side of the tradition. The sacred side of this tradition, as represented in the beautifully restored Mission, is worshipped by all alike without regard to caste, class, or religious affiliation. The restored Mission is a much better, a less embarrassing, symbol of the past than the Mexican field worker or the ragamuffin *pachucos* of Los Angeles.

John Chinaman, John Chinaman,
But five short years ago,
I welcomed you from Canton, John—
But I wish I hadn't though.

CHAPTER V

CATHAY IN THE SOUTH

A LAND of rapid social change, the human scene has shifted frequently and with astonishing swiftness in Southern California. Today one can travel throughout the region, from Santa Barbara to San Diego, from San Jacinto to the sea, without detecting a vestige of Chinese influence. To be sure, there are a few Chinese in such cities as Santa Barbara and San Diego, a handful of Chinese families in some of the smaller towns, and a good-sized, although highly synthetic, Chinatown in Los Angeles. Most of the present-day Chinese of Southern California, however, are thoroughly Americanized, the second and third generation of Chinese in California. Yet not so many years ago, the Chinese influence was widespread throughout this region in the development of which Chinese immigrants, the dust of whose bones has long since been returned to China, played an exceedingly important part.

According to local tradition, the first Chinese to arrive in Southern California was a servant brought to Los Angeles by Joseph Newmark in 1854. An older tradition has it that a Chinese was one of the original colony of settlers that founded the city in 1781. In any case, the census of 1850 listed two Chinese residents of the City of Los Angeles. By 1861 the colony in Los Angeles had increased to twenty-one men and eight women; by 1879 there were 236; by 1880,

1,170; by 1890, 4,424. From this peak figure, the Chinese in the County of Los Angeles declined to 3,209 in 1900; 2,601 in 1910; 2,591 in 1920; and then increased to 4,736 by 1940. Although there were scattered settlements of Chinese throughout Southern California in the 'sixties, they did not begin to assume importance, as a group, until around 1870. In the period between 1870 and 1900, every Southern California community of any size had a fairly large and flourishing Chinatown, located in almost every case near the former Sonoratown, or Mexican town, of the community. Every ranch, it was said, had its Chinese cook, every town its Chinatown. Most of these immigrants had arrived in Southern California by way of San Francisco, after an initial experience as railroad workers on the Central Pacific construction gangs, and a season or two in the agricultural areas of Northern and Central California. In 1880 there were about twenty thousand Chinese in Southern California, and, at that time, they constituted a sizable portion of the total population.

When they first came to Southern California, they were generally employed as cooks, servants, and house-boys, on the ranches and in the towns. When the tourist hotels began to appear throughout the region in the 'seventies, Chinese were practically the only servants employed. Extraordinarily frugal and industrious, these cooks and house servants sent for friends and relatives and, in accordance with their custom, established Chinatowns in the areas in which they worked. It was not long before some of the cooks branched out as vegetable peddlers, or hucksters, pushing their carts from house to house. The hucksters worked, of course, in close alliance with the cooks, and from this operating base they soon acquired a monopoly on the retail distribution of produce, much of which was raised by Chinese. In the towns, they operated all of the hand laundries, remembered for their "chatter and odor" and the familiar sign, "Wash'ng & Iron'ng," over the door. Later they began to establish small shops, curio stores, and restaurants, and to engage in general agricultural employment. By 1895 some four thousand Chinese were producing and distributing nearly all the vegetables consumed in Los Angeles. When the Southern Pacific began to construct a line into Southern California in the 'seventies, local annals report that gangs of Chinese workmen performed most of the hard manual labor and that, in the construction of the 7,000-foot San Fernando tunnel, they sustained "heavy losses" from accidents and injuries. These first-generation immigrant Chinese formed a picturesque, and conspicuous, element in the population of Southern California. In those days, they could be seen throughout the region, around the ranch houses, in the orchards, bicycling between fields in their strange Cantonese hats with their queues flying in the breeze.

In most cases, the Chinatowns had developed around the adobe huts of Sonoratowns. The early Chinatown of Santa Barbara was described by Stewart Edward White as "a collection of battered old frame and adobe buildings that mysteriously had been lifted sheer from squalor to splendid romance by no other means than red paper, varnished ducks, rattan baskets, calico partitions, exotic smells and a brooding, spiritual atmosphere of the Orient." In San Diego, Charles Keeler in 1899 reported that the Chinese had moved in and taken over the old adobes around the Plaza, covering the windows with flaming red posters, and converting one large adobe into a joss house.

The invariable butt of a thousand bad jokes, the Chinese were heckled and harassed by old and young. By common consensus, youngsters were given free license to stone the Chinese, upset their vegetable carts and laundry wagons, and pull their queues for good measure. "American boys," wrote Ludwig Louis Salvator, "frequently hold up to scorn and ridicule these younger sons of China." With the streets echoing to the hoodlum cry, "Run, run, Chinamun," it is not surprising that the Chinese should have attempted to barricade themselves in the Chinatowns, about which, over the years, a great folklore developed. "After preparing the rolls and dessert for the family dinner," wrote Widney, "the Chinese servant spends his nights gambling in the dirty hovels of Chinatown," where, "the sickening odor of their opium pipes pervades the little rooms in which they congregate." All Chinese were supposed to be active participants in the white-slave traffic. One excited commentator reported the existence in Los Angeles of "a hundred vile opium dens, where Chinese, white prostitutes and fast young men spend night and day smoking opium." The Chinese restaurants of the time were seldom patronized by Americans, who were horrified by reports that the Chinese liked abalone, ate squirrels, and roasted chickens alive to remove the feathers. At one time an ordinance was passed in Los Angeles forbidding Chinese laundrymen "to sprinkle clothes by 'squirting' water from their mouths." Despite the legend of their universal addiction to opium and prostitutes, however, Chinese merchants were widely respected in commercial circles and their credit rating was uniformly high.

Among the great cultural contributions of the Chinese in Southern California was their development of the fishing industry. For, with the exception of the Indians, they were the first fishermen in California. During the period from 1860 to 1880, Chinese fishing villages dotted the coast from Monterey to San Diego. Large Chinese fishing junks could be seen in the waters off the Southern California coast, "with the Chinese chattering and grabbing at the fish as they bounce and dance on the deck." The appearance of such a strangely rigged Chinese fishing junk in the waters off San Pedro occasioned much excited comment in Los Angeles in 1871. Visiting Southern California in 1898, Ratcliffe Hicks reported that "Chinamen have large villages, some of them more like small cities, along the shore, whose inhabitants are wholly engaged in catching, drying, and shipping fish to China. They are sure to put in an immense amount of salt, as salt in China is monopolized by the government to raise a revenue, and millions of Chinamen are never able to get any salt, strange as it may seem, on account of the expense." In the 1890's, the Chinese had a village on the San Diego waterfront known as Stingaree Town. Their fishermen's shanties stood on stilts out over the water, "backed by irregular streets of the Chinese quarter, where John chatters with his neighbor or gravely smokes his pipe while watching the group of children, with almond eyes and dangling queues of silk, playing in the doorway." As late as 1910, there was a settlement of Chinese fishermen near the harbor on Santa Catalina Island, engaged in catching oil sharks for their livers—a Chinese delicacy—which were shipped to China. When these Chinese fishing villages were first established, there was no developed fishing industry in California, nor had any consideration been given to the possibility of such an industry. Undeniably, the Chinese were the pioneers in the development of the immensely important fishing industry of present-day Southern California.

That the Chinese knew something about fishing and liked fish was, in fact, one of the principal indictments against them in early California. Their fondness for shellfish was not only inexplicable; it was regarded as conclusive evidence that they were subhuman and had the tastes of animals. Strange as it may seem, it was the Chinese who taught the Californians the superlative merits of the abalone.

Beginning in the early 'sixties, the Chinese quickly developed a flourishing abalone industry, which involved a curious triangular traffic. Not only was abalone meat eaten by the resident Chinese; it was salted for shipment to China. At the same time, the Chinese discovered that abalone shells were attractive and, after polishing, could be used for a wide variety of purposes. For a time, quite an extensive handicraft industry existed in Los Angeles based upon the polishing, tooling, and refashioning of abalone shells for ornamental uses. The Mexicans and the Indians, in particular, seemed to like the earrings and other types of jewelry made from these shells. Abalone shells were also exported in quantities. In 1866 shells valued at $14,000 were exported from San Francisco and a year later the consignments were valued at $36,000. Still later, according to Charles Frederick Holder, the shells were sent to Austria where "in the child-labor homes and factories of Vienna, they are made into a thousand peculiar things, and sent back to Catalina and other tourist resorts for sale." This traffic in shells between Southern California and Austria lasted for several decades and involved, in the aggregate, hundreds of thousands of dollars.

By 1870 the Chinese in California were exporting $1,000,000 worth of abalone annually and a decade later their annual shipments of dried shrimp to China were valued at $3,000,000. The existence of such a thriving industry in the hands of the Chinese, could not, of course, be tolerated in California. It was not long before envious Occidental eyes began to be focused on this lucrative trade. The campaign to oust the Chinese from the fishing industry began in 1860 with a measure imposing a special tax against them. In 1864 a measure "regulating the size of small-mesh shrimp nets" was enacted which, also, was directly aimed at the Chinese. Despite these and other discriminatory measures, the Chinese fishermen continued to operate for years, for the most part, however, clandestinely, as smugglers on the seas. After 1890 they began to be driven from the industry, first by Italians, and, later, by Portuguese, Japanese, and Yugoslavs. In particular, the Japanese began to muscle in on the abalone industry. In 1890 a Japanese fishing village located two miles north of Point Fermin, which had been formerly a Chinese fishing village, collected and sold 60,000 pounds of abalone and 30,000 pounds of abalone shells. As late as 1910, however, Holder reported that Chinese abalone hunters were to be found on San Clemente Island, diving for black pearls and abalone shells.

Nor was fishing the only field in which these early Chinese immigrants contributed to the rapid growth and development of Southern California. In 1891 an American conceived the idea of growing celery in the marshlands of Orange County which, at the time, were occupied by a group of derelicts known in the local annals as "tule-rooters and swamp angels." The American soon discovered, however, that he did not possess the requisite know-how of celery raising. His first attempts being entirely unsuccessful, "he bethought himself of the Los Angeles Chinese market gardeners," to quote from the local annals, who promptly agreed to assemble a crew of experienced celery-raisers. By 1892 thousands of acres in Southern California were devoted to celery culture, and these marshlands, which had jumped in value from $15 to $400 an acre, were producing 1,200 carloads of celery annually. Thus was a new, and badly needed, industry established in the region.

When the Chinese first appeared in the celery bogs, "clad in 'slickers' and rubber boots up to their hips, working steadily all day in the soft peat and stopping now and then to roll a cigarette," their presence was keenly resented by the local residents who were soon to profit so handsomely from the new industry established in their locality. According to the local annals, "white men worried and harassed the Celestials, both in season and out of season, carrying their unreasonable resentment to the point of burning the buildings erected by the Earl Fruit Company, carrying off implements used in the cultivation, and terrorizing the Chinese employed." Armed guards had to be posted at the four corners of the field where the original experiment in celery-raising was conducted. Additional deputies were used to protect the camp of the Chinese. This picture of Chinese laborers being protected by armed guards while they established a million-dollar industry in the region is one of the most graphic illustrations of the curious cultural development of Southern California with which I am familiar. Seldom have benefactors been more grossly abused.

Chinese were also extensively used in connection with the development of the citrus industry in Southern California in the 'seventies and 'eighties. In 1870 the first group of forty families was brought to San Gabriel. Visiting Riverside in 1894, Charles Stoddard was sur-.

prised to find hundreds of Chinese, "washing and brushing and sorting oranges, chattering and laughing as they worked under the direction of an American inspector." Special crews worked at night, "rapidly seizing and wrapping and placing oranges in prepared boxes, while other Chinamen, using a simple machine, press them down and nail on the covers, and stack them for packing in the refrigerator cars." But just as they were ousted from the fishing industry, so they were driven from the citrus groves. "White men and women who desire to earn a living," to quote from the Los Angeles *Times* of August 14, 1893, "have for some time been entering quiet protests against vineyardists and packers employing Chinese in preference to whites." It was not long before the protests ceased to be quiet.

By September, 1893, the Chinese were barricaded in the packing sheds, as, in the words of one grower, "hoodlums raided the fields and drove out the Celestials." At Redlands, in the heart of the citrus belt, night raiders broke into the Chinese camps. Chinese were robbed in the streets of Redlands, driven from their Chinatown, and unmercifully harassed. A mass meeting was called to protest further lawlessness. Soon the disturbances became so acute that the National Guard was summoned and two hundred special guards were deputized. The large growers denounced the rioters as "hoodlums" and "anarchistic agitators," and swore that the only reason they employed Chinese was because they could not "afford to pay the wages demanded by the whites." On September 3, anti-Chinese raiders converged on the Chinatown in Redlands, broke into the houses, set fire to several buildings, and looted the tills of Chinese merchants. By the turn of the century, virtually all the Chinese had been driven from the citrus belt.

From meager beginnings, the citrus industry of Southern California expanded phenomenally in the years from 1880 to 1890. By 1880, 1,250,000 citrus trees had been planted in the region. At the close of the decade, 12,667 acres were devoted to oranges alone in Southern California and the production from this acreage had an annual value of $2,000,000. In the local histories, this amazing development is described as though it were merely another manifestation of Yankee ingenuity at work in the sunshine of Southern California. Actually this development would never have taken place so rapidly, requiring, as it did, an enormous capital investment, had it not been for the presence of cheap and efficient Chinese labor. As one grower put it: "Poor John spreads a dirty tent in some corner of the field near water, sleeps on the ground, works by starlight, and lives on rice of his own cooking." The rapid transition from field to orchard crops which took place during these years was certainly accelerated by the use of a labor supply that was cheap even by comparison with Negro slave labor in the South. "No capital outlay," writes Dr. Varden Fuller, "such as was needed to purchase slaves, was required. Likewise, the cost of maintaining the family unit necessary to the propagation and rearing of slaves was not involved. Chinese workers came as mature individuals, without dependents, who demanded no more in exchange for their services than a moderate cash wage. When his work was done, the Chinese moved, relieving his employer of any burden of responsibility for his welfare during the slack season. And he was always available again, on short notice, when needed."

It was not only in the fields that the Chinese were mistreated in Southern California. On October 24, 1871, one of worst race riots in American history took place in the City of Los Angeles. For on that day a mob of a thousand Angelenos, armed with pistols, knives, and ropes, descended on Chinatown. "Trembling, moaning, wounded Chinese," reported the San Francisco *Bulletin*, "were hauled from their hiding places; ropes quickly encircled their necks; they were dragged to the nearest improvised gallows. A large wagon close by had four victims hanging from its sides . . . three others dangled from an awning . . . five more were taken to the gateway and lynched. . . . Looting every nook, corner, chest, trunk, and drawer in Chinatown, the mob even robbed the victims it executed. . . . $7,000 was extracted from a box in a Chinese store." Stealing $40,000 in cash, the mob lynched nineteen Chinese. On the night of October 25, the heroes of the raid paraded the streets of the town, displayed their booty, and were acclaimed by the mob. As a result of a subsequent grand-jury investigation, 150 men were indicted for this murderous assault, but, of these, only six were sentenced and they were soon released. Still later, the American government had to pay a handsome indemnity for the losses sustained, in life and property, by the Chinese.

"Contemporary writers," wrote Horace Bell, "say that it was the underworld part of our population that took advantage of the situation to start indiscriminate killing and pillaging. But they do not state that the police force of the city furnished the leaders of the mob; that the Chief of Police of Los Angeles stationed his policemen and the deputies he had mustered in for the occasion, at all strategic points with orders to shoot to death any Chinese that might 'stick a head out or attempt to escape from the besieged buildings'; nor that one of the leading members of the City Council participated in the slaughter." Many similar incidents, although of lesser gravity, are reported in the local annals. For example, on November 6, 1885, a mob set fire to a Chinese laundry in sedate Pasadena. For forty years incidents of this kind occurred throughout the region.

A popular song of the period was the ballad "John Chinaman":

> John Chinaman, John Chinaman,
>   But five short years ago,
> I welcomed you from Canton, John—
>   But I wish I hadn't though.
>
> For then I thought you honest, John,
>   Not dreaming but you'd make
> A citizen as useful, John,
>   As any in the state.
>
> I thought you'd open wide your ports,
>   And let our merchants in,
> To barter for your crapes and teas,
>   Their wares of wood and tin.
>
> I thought you'd cut your queue off, John,
>   And don a Yankee coat,
> And a collar high you'd raise, John,
>   Around your dusky throat.
>
> I imagined that the truth, John,
>   You'd speak when under oath,
> But I find you'll lie and steal, too—
>   Yes, John, you're up to both.
>
> Oh, John, I've been deceived in you,
>   And in all your thieving clan,
> For our gold is all you're after, John,
>   To get it as you can.

To appreciate the plight of the Chinese in Southern California in these years it should be remembered that they were being constantly harassed by discriminatory legislation, that they were ineligible to citizenship, that further Chinese immigration had been barred in 1882, and that under the Geary Act they were subject to registration and possible deportation. A statute passed in California on April 16, 1850, excluded the testimony of Negroes and Indians in judicial proceedings. And, in 1854, the Supreme Court of California interpreted this ban so as also to exclude the testimony of the Chinese. A law of March 16, 1863, removed Negroes from the ban, but it was retained against Chinese and Indians until 1872.

Despite these handicaps, however, a visitor to Southern California reported in 1898 that "John Chinaman is forging ahead rapidly in this country. The Chinese are doing the servants' work in hotels, boarding houses, private families, and on the farms they are leasing land, raising an immense quantity of vegetables, and have a monopoly on the huckster business. It makes a New England man squirm to see them in lines at the banks, depositing money and handling gold in quantities as easily and intelligently as if they were Wall Street brokers. . . . They are a great feature of the life here. Their New Year commences about a week later than ours, and the devout ones do not work for a week. It is amusing to listen to the firecrackers they are continually sending off out of their fields during that week to drive off evil spirits, and bring good crops, and to notice the little sticks burning just outside their houses and near the front door for similar purposes."

Early residents of Los Angeles still recall the three joss houses of Chinatown and the theater with a large troupe of players, "including a lady star." They remember the weird music; the feasts and fortune-tellers; and the funerals where the corpse was rushed at breakneck speed to the cemetery, followed by "a spring wagon load of food," while loyal friends scattered bits of paper "to distract attention of the devil in his pursuit of the newly dead." They remember the shawls and silk handkerchiefs; the beautiful embroidery; the queer hanging baskets of flowers and fruit fashioned from feathers, silk, and tinsel; the lacquer boxes; and the ginger candies and lichee nuts.

With the turn of the century, the Chinese began to be gradually displaced by the Japanese and, later, by Mexican immigrants. As the older generation died off, Negroes and Mexicans began to replace them as domestics. As late as 1903, there were still some four hundred Chinese hucksters in Los Angeles, but they had made the mistake of renting, not purchasing, the lands on which their produce was raised. When the Japanese arrived, they began to purchase this acreage and, in a year or so, the Chinese had been pushed out of the industry. Increasingly the Chinese tended to concentrate in the large Los Angeles Chinatown, where many of them prospered as merchants. Today most of the Chinatowns of Southern California have passed from the scene and the new Los Angeles Chinatown is merely Main Street in transparent disguise.

Sun Yat-sen's Chinese Revolution was really organized in the old Los Angeles Chinatown. The story, as told by Carl Glick in *Double Ten*, is this: Returning from China with a commission as Lieutenant-General in the Chinese Imperial Reform Army, Homer Lea, who had graduated from Los Angeles High School, formed the Western Military Academy to train and drill officers for the future revolutionary army of China. By 1903, Lea and his assistants had units of a hundred or more young Chinese drilling in Los Angeles, San Francisco, Sacramento, and Fresno. When visiting Chinese dignitaries came to Los Angeles, Lea's smartly uniformed, well-drilled Chinese cadets, shorn of their queues, would be lined up at attention to greet them at the station and to escort them to their hotel. For months Lea trained these troops under the eyes of the authorities. They went on field trips to the Malibu Mountains, held their maneuvers in the hills of Hollywood, and engaged in rifle practice at Laguna Beach. Over two thousand troops, trained in this manner, were gradually smuggled out of the country, with the aid of the resident Chinese, and sent to China. Smuggled into this country on a potato boat, Dr. Sun Yat-sen was honored with a banquet in the Los Angeles Chinatown on September 30, 1905. On a later visit to California, Dr. Sun visited Homer Lea at his home and in his "headquarters" at the Lankershim Hotel in Los Angeles. When the October, 1911, revolution broke out, Lea joined Dr. Sun in England and returned with him to China. Lea died in Los Angeles in May, 1912, shortly after his return from China. This little cripple, whose book *The Valor of Ignorance* (1908) so shrewdly predicted the course of the war in the Far East, was long a familiar figure, in his handsome Chinese uniform, in the streets and hotel lobbies of Los Angeles. Long regarded as a poseur and fraud, it was not until Ansel O'Banion dictated his memoirs to Mr. Glick in 1945 that Los Angeles learned of the important role Lea, and the resident Chinese, had played in the Chinese Revolution.

With the appearance of the second generation, the Chinese of Southern California lost most of their distinguishing cultural traits and people forgot all about the "vile opium dens" of Chinatown. Although the contributions of the Chinese to the culture and development of the region have been enormously important, there is today no visible reminder of their influence. There is not a single Chinese place-name in Southern California. With the exception of the garish and synthetic Chinatown of Los Angeles, there is no evidence whatever that large numbers of Chinese once lived in the region. In July, 1937, 850 graves in the Chinese cemetery in Los Angeles were opened, the siftings of dust and bones piously disinterred, neatly packed in small containers, and shipped to Hongkong. This represented the final shipment of first-generation Chinese bones back to China. An impressionable reporter, observing the scene noted that "the sun shone brightly on the dark-skinned workers, protected by gas masks, as they swung industrious picks and scooped up quantities of black earth. A golden butterfly drifted lazily into the shadow of the pepper trees and a radio across the street grated a swing tune." The removal of the bones of the Chinese dead from the soil of Southern California aptly symbolizes the thoroughness with which the evidences of their influence have been obliterated in the region.

> *"Southern California was the first tropical land which our race has mastered and made itself at home in."*
>
> —Charles Nordhoff

CHAPTER VI

THE FOLKLORE OF CLIMATOLOGY

THE popular discovery of "semi-tropical" Southern California, which began in the 'seventies, coincided with important changes in the national economy. The frontier was rapidly vanishing, industrialism was on the march, and a new middle class had begun to appear in American life. The moment had arrived when the more fortunate elements of this new middle class had begun to reach out for wider horizons. An urge to travel was in the air. A great pent-up longing for the bizarre, the novel, the exotic clamored for release. Unlike their colleagues on the eastern seaboard, the mid-America sections of this new middle class were intimidated by the thought of the Atlantic crossing. Italy, France, and Spain seemed forbiddingly remote. They wanted an Italy nearer home—an Italy without the Italians, an Italy in which they could feel at home, an Italy in which, perhaps, they might settle and live out their days in the sun.

Representing mid-America's first contact with the exotic in environments, it is not surprising that some amazing enthusiasms, misconceptions, and exaggerations should have found reflection in the first popular impressions of Sunny California. Later these exaggerated enthusiasms were put to good use by the ingenious promoters of the region, but, at the outset, it was the newcomers, the tourists, who taught the Southern Californians the art of overstatement. These early impressions, these first imprints of the exotic upon the imagina-

96

tion of middle-class America, represent a variety of folklore that has never been thoroughly explored.

1. LAND OF THE SUNDOWN SEA

The early tourists in Southern California could never quite decide how to label the region. It was "A Mediterranean land without the marshes and malaria"; "The American Italy"; "The New Palestine"; "The New Greece"; "A geographical Pleiades"; "The Land of the Sundown Sea"; "The Land of Sunshine"; "Poppy Land"; "The Better Italy"; "Our Italy"; "The Mentone of America"; a land with a "climate of Laodicean equability." In conning the European guidebooks for references which might fit the new environment, the labeling process became curiously mixed and confused. Santa Barbara County, wrote one early tourist, was a combination of all the scenic wonders of Europe. Its mountains "were Swiss, its valleys Scottish, its bay that of Naples." Charles Loring Brace, a visitor of 1869, wrote an entire chapter to prove, by Biblical references, that Southern California was "the American Palestine." Did not the mustard grow almost as tall as a tree "for the fowls of the air to lodge under the shadow of it"? Did not the region have deserts in which "heaven was as brass, and the earth as iron"? Here were the vineyards, the fig trees, the almonds and olives of Syria. Like Palestine, Southern California had "dead seas," "saliferous vegetations," and "the hot springs of Tiberias." The bolder impressionists, on the other hand, discarded all allusions and proclaimed their belief that Southern California "manufactures its own weather and refuses to import any other."

In these early impressions one can sense the thrill of discovery, the appeal of the exotic, the gradual relaxation of frontier-taut nerves. "Immediately after passing Point Concepcion," wrote one tourist, "we realize that we have come into a Southern clime; and we almost seem to see a distinct line of demarcation separating the northern gloom from the southern glamour. Then at once we begin to see the porpoises playing about, and the flying fish springing out of the water, and looking just like rainbow gossamer as the sunlight catches them. Then we begin to have exaggerated hopes of the beauty of the country awaiting us; for all unconsciously we are filled with a sensuous delight in the genial warmth and glow and tender colouring. . . . The mountains look at their very best towards the hour of sunset and after the setting of the sun, all the crudeness and harshness of their features are tempered and softened by the tender glow and glamour." In literally hundreds of similarly lush impressions one can see the psyche of mid-America stirring faintly to new life, warming to the new environment like frostbitten hands to a beaming hearth. "I have apparently found a Paradise on Earth," wrote another tourist. "The road to it, like that to the Upper Paradise, is long and stony and tedious, but when you arrive the pain of striving is forgotten in the beatitude of possession."

The climate of this western paradise was so novel that it gave rise to a new interpretative "science" of "climatology," by which its marvelous, wonder-working propensities might be catalogued and indexed. Elsewhere in the general westward movement of settlers, "climate" was regarded as a hostile element, a fit subject for curses and wisecracks, but, in Southern California, it became a major obsession. As nearly as I can discover, the miraculous qualities of the climate were invented, not by the cynical residents of the region, but by the early tourists. To be sure, the local residents soon began to take these inventions seriously, but the inventions themselves belonged to the tourists, not to them.

After exploring Southern California at some length, Dr. William A. Edwards, an early tourist, concluded that its climate could relieve, and possibly cure, the following ailments: incipient phthisis, chronic pneumonia, tuberculosis, disease of the liver, malarial poisoning, cirrhosis of the liver, jaundice, functional female disturbances, the organic ills of advanced years, simple congestion of constipation, hepatic catarrh, scrofulous affections, insomnia, and enlarged glands. Scarlet fever and diphtheria, it was confidently reported, were unknown south of Tehachapi, and "epidemics seldom occur." The enthusiastic Charles Dudley Warner stated that "diseases of the bowels are practically unknown; children cut teeth here without trouble; and disorders of the liver and kidneys are rare." The Southern California Medical Society appointed a committee to list the ailments that could be cured by the climate and scores of booklets were published with such titles as "A Study of Riverside Climate with Suggestions as to its Adaptability to Cases of Phthisis."

So widespread was the enthusiasm for "climatology" that the enthusiasm itself was dubbed "the Southern California fever." Taking cognizance of this fever which seemed to affect every incoming tourist, a Santa Barbara editor caustically observed that "the climate of

Santa Barbara is a big thing. There is apparently nothing like it in the known world. It cures the consumption. It knocks the asthma. It is a bad thing on catarrh." In fact, throughout these early impressions the cynicism of the local residents runs as an undercurrent of skeptical comment. Asked if the climate of Southern California was good for invalids, one local editor replied: "No, sir, but I think it is a pleasant place in which to be sick, and, when my appointed time comes, an easy spot in which to die. For you die not in a pent-up Northern home begging for air, but you die in the open air, and vanish ere your friends know it." At a later date, however, the local residents began to defend the climate with greater vehemence than the tourists. Addressing the American Medical Association meeting in 1891, a Dr. Gapen of Omaha had said that "California was a cloud of dust in May." The slander did not go unchallenged, for Dr. Henry Gibbons, Jr., replied: "If his brain were as cloudless as California, he would neither live in Omaha nor permit his tongue to wag such a deceit."

To appreciate the enthusiasm of the early tourists for the climate of Southern California, it should be recalled that, in the 'sixties, 'seventies, and 'eighties, there was more incipient and chronic invalidism in America than one can possibly imagine today. Whether due to dietary deficiencies, overwork, the lack of sanitation, the low state of the medical art, or whatever causes, the fact is that the newspapers of the period give one the impression of a nation afflicted with creaking joints, rheumatic limbs, catarrhal colds, and a host of mysterious "ailments" and "afflictions." Reading lush accounts of the climate of Southern California, these ailing Middle Westerners set forth in droves for the promised land. In fact, the presence of so many invalids eventually became a source of great embarrassment.

By 1880 the whole foothill district around Sierra Madre and San Gabriel was "one vast sanatarium." As early as 1869, the City of Los Angeles had begun to complain of the cost involved in providing medical care and hospital treatment for indigent invalids. It would seem that almost one out of three of the early tourists were, as they phrased it, "run down," "consumptive," or "ailing." A character in an early novel by Mrs. Charles Steward Daggett (*Mariposilla*, 1895) observes: "We jump at the chance to dance once in a while with a man who is not delicate, who has never had a hemorrhage or organic trouble. Of course, we do have a few sound men." Enjoying the spectacle of a Southern California overrun with invalids, out-of-state newspapers developed the practice of referring to the region as "the sanitarium and fruit country." The editor of a Denver newspaper in 1885 pointed out that "the moist, warm, enervating climate of Southern California, instead of making real sanitariums, makes simply soothing death-beds for those who are beyond recovery." So famous did the "climatology" of Southern California become that Horace A. Vachell, the British novelist, who lived in the region for several years, wrote in 1904 that "in a country where sickness was once almost unknown, doctors, dentists, faith-healers, and quacks multiply and increase as the quails of yore."

That Los Angeles was not bankrupted by the burden of providing medical care for transients seems to be explained by the circumstance that so many invalid tourists died shortly after their arrival. One tourist of 1887 wrote to relatives in the East: "Should we attend the funerals of all the invalid strangers who die here, we should do little else." Slight wonder, then, that Southern California should have become a paradise for morticians or that faith-healing should still flourish in the land of the sundown sea. The same circumstance probably accounts for the ease with which the fact of death is accepted in the region. "California," wrote Mrs. Daggett, "is not the place to mourn in. The climate is opposed to dejection. The natives go to funerals in the morning and chase with the hounds in the afternoon." To this day, funerals remain rather gala occasions in Southern California.

Taking notice of the fact that so many invalids were coming to Southern California, E. P. Roe, the novelist—ironically enough, also a Christian Science practitioner in Santa Barbara—published a letter in the Chicago Inter-Ocean suggesting some of the medicinal precautions that should be observed by the wary traveler. Such a traveler, he wrote, "should always carry something with him to guard against constipation. A sedlitz powder, a tea-spoonful of Rochelle salt, or a tablespoonful of Hunyadi Janos taken before breakfast, is a simple and efficient preventive. A bottle of paregoric, a bottle of aromatic spirits of ammonia, and a flask of good whiskey are, likewise, excellent things to carry in a satchel." Once arrived in Southern California, of course, the tourist could safely discard these medicants. By 1870 climate had become a merchantable commodity in the region.

In the classic expression of the time, "we sold them the climate and threw the land in."

2. A Slight Exaggeration

In the 'eighties it began to be said that Southern Californians "irrigate, cultivate, and exaggerate." Nor was it only the climate that was reported with some slight exaggeration. In particular the products of the soil, its Brobdingnagian vegetables, loomed larger than life in the tourist reports. One reads of tomato vines nineteen feet high; of cabbage plants that grew twenty feet in the air; of strawberries so big that they could only be consumed by three large bites; of cucumbers seven feet long; of horseshoe geraniums "as big as small trees" growing in hedges six feet high; of a Gold of Ophir rosebush in Pasadena with 200,000 blossoms; of a grapevine in Santa Barbara that, in 1896, bore twelve tons of grapes; of squash that weighed three hundred pounds; of daisies that grew on bushes as large as quince trees and of lilies fourteen feet high.

"Do you suppose there is a modest daisy in Southern California?" asks a character in The Leaven of Love (1908) by Clara Burnham. "Well, I guess not. They're on a level with your eyes, and stare at you as bold as brass. Here the geraniums climb right out of the ground up to the bedrooms and snoop around the windows. In the east, we carry a palm-leaf fan to church. Here, they crackle away up in the air, big enough for a giant to use." For the benefit of his eastern readers, the ebullient George Wharton James reported: "There are calla lilies by the acre, and tall enough to be picked by a man on horseback; hedges of geraniums, fifteen feet high; rods and rods of carnations and pinks; heliotrope grown into trees, forty feet high; roses of a thousand varieties, by the million, it being no rare thing to see a hundred thousand, two hundred thousand, or more, buds and blossoms and full blown roses on a single bush at the same moment." Once the visitor to paradise has returned to his home in the East, wrote James, he will ask: "Is this the land I have left behind? Is this the land I used to know? And be contented with? Am I the same man I was? . . . Here, winter scarce seems to have stepped aside."

One story, related by Kate Sanborn, had to do with a man who was once standing on top of a California pumpkin chopping off a piece with an axe. Suddenly the axe fell in the pumpkin. The man thereupon pulled up his ladder and put it down inside the pumpkin and descended to look for his axe. While groping around, he met another man, who exclaimed: "Hello! What are you doing here?" "Looking for my axe," was the reply. "Gosh! You might as well give that up. I lost my horse and cart in here three days ago, and haven't found 'em yet." "Mustard?" said a resident in response to a tourist's question, "Why, man, people nowadays don't know what mustard is. In those days, it used to cover the plains. A man on horseback could ride out of it, and you would never see him coming. When Uncle Billy Spurgeon bought the land for the founding of Santa Ana, the mustard was so thick and high that he had to climb a sycamore tree so he could see the tract he had bought."

It was not only the size but the rapidity with which things grew in Southern California that amazed the newcomers. "If you want to pick a melon in this country," wrote Charles Dudley Warner, "you have to get on horseback." The growth of melons was supposed to be so rapid, in fact, that they were bruised on the ground as they were pulled and bumped along by the rapid growth of the vine. On the fertility of the soil, B. A. Botkin reports an interesting item. "The soil of the Southern California counties is so rich as to become an actual detriment to the farmer," observed a local resident. "In San Bernardino, a farmer, named Jones, has been forced entirely to abandon the culture of corn, because the stalks, under the influence of the genial sun, mild air, and mellow soil, shoot up into the air so fast that they draw their roots after them; when, of course, the plant dies as a rule. Cases have been known where cornstalks thus uprooted and lifted into the air, have survived for some time upon the climate alone."

Here "the rank growth of fruit and flowers," as Frank Lewis Nason pointed out in a novel (*The Vision of Elijah Berl*, 1905), "a growth roused from its fiery sleep, strove in a day to make up for ages of helpless bondage." Delayed by the long dry season, nature had to work quickly in Southern California after the rains came. The wonderful lush growth was "tenfold more wonderful because of that burnt and dried-up soil from which nothing beautiful seemed possible." In many cases, however, the size and rapidity with which things grew in Southern California conveyed a sense of unreality so overpowering as to make the visitors feel unhappy and profoundly disconcerted. "It's a fraud, a deception," complains a character in one novel.

"There's one word that ought to be written across the whole of Southern California, and that word is Humbug! Nothing really gets into your heart and soul because you know it all ain't so. All those painted palm trees and muslin roses on the stage aren't one bit more imitation than those you see here. Yes, ma'am, every sightly thing there is in this part of the world was planted here by the hand of man. It's all exaggerated and showy. . . . I never go out here without feeling as if I was play-acting."

Not only were miraculous curative qualities attributed to the climate, but Southern California was a land in which natural disasters were unknown. There were no thunderstorms or cyclones or tornadoes; no snow nor ice nor sleet; and, above all, no mud. "Here," wrote one observer, "is a climate of the tropics without its perils; here is the fertility of Egypt without its fellaheen; the fruits and flowers of Sicily without its lazzaroni; the beauty of Italy without its limited markets; the sunshine of Persia without its oppressions." "The visible wrath of God," wrote one tourist, "is not to be found here: no one ever froze or roasted to death." Sunstrokes and frozen limbs were unknown. "The blast of the wild horn of the mosquito," reported Major Ben C. Truman, "is forgotten music here." The loyalty shown this blessed land of the sun by the tourists is without precedent or parallel. While there were fogs, a fog was nothing—"merely a thin vapor." And while there was a rainy season, the Creator had providentially provided that most of the rain should fall at night so that the days would be bright and clear. In fact, the folk belief that most of the rain falls at night is still widely accepted in the region. Was the climate, perhaps, monotonous? "No," replied one tourist, "the perfect oratorio is being performed—why desire a discord to break in?" Southern California was a land where iceboxes and furnaces were unknown, where mildew never gathered, and where mad dogs did not roam the land. It was a land in which there were no traps or pitfalls, no beasts of prey, no poisonous reptiles, no loathsome pests. While the early Spanish chronicles contain numerous references to earthquakes, the very word "earthquake" disappeared from the vocabulary of the region. In much the same manner, the disappearance of the word "flea" after 1870 constitutes a major phenomenon.

For years the favorite form of greeting exchanged in Southern California was: "Have the chinches disturbed you much?" Reference to fleas appear in the diary of Father Crespi (1769) and in the journal of La Perouse (1786). The activity of the flea is reflected in several place-names in California: Alameda de las Pulgas, the Rancho de las Pulgas, and so forth. "I could not sleep," wrote Alfred Robinson; "the blankets pricked my flesh, the room was warm, and at times it would seem as if a thousand needles penetrated my legs and sides. They were fleas indeed! And it appeared to me as if they came in armies to glut their appetites with human blood! It was terrifying, for I thought they would surely suck me dry before morning." "If any sinning soul ever suffered the punishments of purgatory," wrote Edwin Bryant, "before leaving the tenement of clay, those torments were endured by myself last night." William Redmond Ryan, visiting California in 1850, wrote of "fleas of so large a growth, and of so voracious a propensity, I never wish to see, much less to feel." Bayard Taylor wrote that than the California flea "nothing is more positively real to the feelings, and nothing more elusive and intangible to the search." Carl Meyer speaks melodramatically of "these body beasts, more effective than the quintessence of Spanish pepper" and refers to "flea fever" as a common malady in California. The French traveler, Earnest de Massey, boasted that he had "slaughtered enough of the creatures to fill a large graveyard." "The California flea," wrote Frank Marryat, "is unlike both in appearance and manner, the modest flea of ordinary life, that seeks concealment as by accident it is unearthed. These insects, reared in the rough school of bullocks' hide, boldly faced as they attacked us." William Taylor, the minister, referred to the California fleas as "the third plague of Egypt. They live on the ground like little herds of wild cattle." Yet one may search the tourist letters, pamphlets, and books written after 1870 and never find a reference to the flea. After they had lived in the land for a short time, however, the tourists quickly discovered the flea. "You can go to the California beaches," it was once said, "and take up a handful of sand and the fleas will kick it all away by the time they get out."

3. The Land of Upside Down

Almost every aspect of life in Southern California possessed a delightful novelty—an element of surprise—for the tourists. They wrote to relatives, with excited wonder, of rivers that had heads but no mouths; of rivers with "their bottoms on top" which disappeared in the sands "as though ashamed of such sportive energy in a land of sacred indolence"; of rivers that seemed to disappear but which really ran underground. "Why, there's so much sand and so little water mostly, they have to sprinkle the river bed to keep it from flyin' about the landscape." They wrote of rivers so dry that "coyotes had to carry canteens when they crossed them"; or they reported that the "jack-rabbits used to carry water on their backs most of the time." To their amazement they discovered that umbrellas were useless against the drenching rains of Southern California but that they made good shade in the summer; that many of the beautifully colored flowers had no scent; that fruit ripened earlier in the northern than in the southern part of the state; that it was hot in the morning and cool at noon, or, as they said, "you roast on the sunny side and freeze on the shady side of the street"; that people went to the mountains to bore tunnels for water and dug in the valleys for greasewood to burn as fuel; and, to their complete amazement, they discovered that Reno, Nevada, was west of Los Angeles. Here, in this paradoxical land, rats lived in the trees and squirrels had their homes in the ground. "How intense everything is in Southern California!" wrote Kate Douglas Wiggin. "The fruit so immense, the cañons so deep, the trees so big, the hills so high, the rain so wet, and the drought so dry!" There were more rivers and less water, more cows and less butter, and more creed but less religion, wrote one tourist, than in any region on the face of the earth.

There was some elusive quality about the region that completely baffled them. "There seems to exist in this country," wrote Emma H. Adams, a visitor from Cincinnati, "a something which cheats the senses. Whether it be in the air, the sunshine, in the ocean breeze, I can not say. . . . There is a variety in the evenness of the weather, and a strange evenness in this variety, which throws an unreality around life, and not more, so far as I can learn, in the case of persons especially affected by climatic influences than those whose feelings do not rise and fall with the thermometer. . . . All alike walk and work in a dream. For something beguiles, deludes, plays falsely with the senses. It makes only a trifling difference how close one applies one's self, the effect is the same: there is no awareness of the passage of the day. In Cincinnati I would have sensed the going by of nine honest, substantial hours; but here I do not." The effect, she noted, was "new and peculiar and wonderful." Always uncertain about the season of the year or the time of day, she wrote, with a shrewdness rare among tourists, that her "indefinite ideas of the days and the season are due, certainly in part, to the slight change which marks the seasons, with scores upon scores of days and nights being alike as to warmth, brightness, and beauty."

Doctors and amateur climatologists were put to work, at an early date, to help the newcomer to understand the nature of fogs. For example, Dr. S. P. Ford divided Southern California fogs into two general categories: some were high and dry, others were low and wet. It was only with the latter type, frequently rare, that it became necessary "to have a little fire in the house." There were, he explained, five types of "foggy" days and it was grossly inaccurate, not to say misleading, to use a single term to characterize these variations. "A foggy morning" was one in which the fog came up during the night and disappeared before seven o'clock. If the fog continued until noon, the day should be characterized as "foggy and misty." "Cloudy foggy weather" implied that it had been more or less foggy during a part of the day. "Foggy and misty," on the other hand, implied that it had almost rained, while "dense fog in the night" meant precisely what the term implied. After a season or two, the tourists became somewhat sophisticated and told their relatives in the East that there were two seasons in Southern California: the wet season in which it may rain but seldom does, and the dry season in which it cannot rain, but sometimes does. What is rain and what is fog remains, however, a moot question in the region. Some years ago, one local weather bureau contended that .01-inch precipitation was merely "fog," while another bureau, with equal firmness, continued to report .01-inch precipitation as "rain." As I write these lines, I have before me a local newspaper with the familiar headline: "L. A. Wet Mist Will Stay."

The tourists were equally surprised by the curious assortment of people they encountered in Southern California. "Here a community of Eastern people, there one of Southern, and not remote from either a Mexican settlement, and each has its own peculiarities." The country, wrote one observer, was very much like Jacob's cattle, "ring-streaked, speckled, and spotted." It wasn't like the rest of the country; it was sui generis. After desperately attempting to explain the strange social scene in Southern California, the same observer finally abandoned the effort with the remark, "It is easy to say much about the land, but difficult to say it so as to be clearly understood."

The realization that Southern California was a paradoxical land with a tricky environment, that all was not quite as it seemed, usually began to dawn in the consciousness of the tourist about the time he had learned to discard the carriage robes, umbrellas, and overshoes he had brought across the continent. And with this realization, the tourists began to feel homesick. "I sort of miss Montana in the summer," remarks a character in Myron Brinig's novel *The Sisters*. "I never get used to California. Of course it is beautiful, but I sort of miss the seasons. Here, you never know if it's summer or winter." "They fail to get that home feeling," wrote Sidney H. Burchell, the English novelist, "and want to go back east after the novelty of Californian life has worn off. Some seem to regard existence here as camping out, and never make a real home, living in their trunks for years. Even those that have homes are making changes all the time, trading one for another, or building afresh. Yes, really, it's almost like living in a big tent, with houses instead of canvas tents."

One fear about the climate continued to haunt the tourists and immigrants: the fear of enervation. "I have heard that every one deteriorated in Southern California," wrote Julia M. Sloane in one of the tourist books. Even this fear, however, they were inclined to rationalize. It was the surpassing beauty of the land "that disarms energy." While not exactly enervating, observed Charles Dudley Warner, "the climate does produce a certain placidity which might be taken for laziness." But this feeling would somehow vanish once the energetic Yankees took firm possession of the land. One observer concluded that the climate was not really enervating but that one merely got this impression from "the low educational and moral status of the native population." "A combined immigration of Yankees," wrote Charles Loring Brace, "could easily overcome many of the moral disadvantages which result from the 'Southern' and Spanish influences."

The ever-loyal George Wharton James believed that "the energy and business acumen of the keen Yankee, the smart Middle Westerner, and the sharp Northerner here unite and commingle, aroused into new and powerful manifestations by the stimulating climatic conditions of this land of the Sun-Down Sea. Though occasionally it gets hot, there is a healthful, vigorous, stirring quality in the atmosphere that provokes to labor." One of James' most popular lectures was entitled: "The Influence of the Climate of Southern California

Upon Its Literature." Neither too hot nor too cold, he thought that "the friction of the winds, generating electricity and adding power to the health-giving ozone, bromine, chlorine, and saline of the sea," killed all noxious germs in the air. Fresh fruits were a perfect diet for the brain-worker, and the presence of great forests in the mountains purified the atmosphere. "The true Californian," he said, "is not averse to exuberant enthusiasm in spite of the fixed, crystallized, cold-blooded standard of the less climatically-favored regions of the earth."

Throughout the years, Southern California has, indeed, come in for more than its share of carping criticism. "Real progress," writes the editor of the *Argus-Leader* of Sioux Falls, "is fostered in areas where the climate changes. Such fluctuations serve to keep the body and the mind active and to prevent stagnation." "Give me," writes still another critic, "the snow, sleet, rain, fog and sunshine in season, the bigness of character, the sincerity, the straightforwardness of a man's word, of the greater part of the people of Newark, New Jersey, in preference any day to the most advertised place in the world— Los Angeles, California." When the tide of national opinion began to turn sharply against Southern California around 1920, it was always the climate that was denounced. "Under the benign sun," wrote *Life*, "the people of Southern California grow lax and almost hysterical." "California," reported the editor of the *Daily News* of Jackson, Mississippi, "is a state of mind—exaltation is in the atmosphere. Birds of gorgeous plumage flit through the trees but they have no song. Flowers astound in size, gorgeous color, and infinite variety, but they have little perfume."

While it has usually been possible to convince the tourists that they will not die of enervation, the more experienced observers have not been so easily won over. "Sooner or later," wrote Helen Hunt Jackson, "there is certain to come a slacking, a toning-down . . . this is as sure as that the sun shines for it is the sun that will bring it about." "The droning of this shoreline," writes Max Miller, "finally knocked amibition out of me . . . twenty constant years of this Southern California shoreline do something to one, all right, and clumsily we can say that they make him crazy or lazy or hazy." "At present we are a hustling crowd," wrote Charles Fletcher Lummis, "but the mañana habit is a matter not of race, nor of speech, but of climate. As sure as God made little apples, this climate will put some mañana in even the most strenuous life." Nor are these impressions lacking in scientific support. Most of the activities of Southern California, observed the geographer J. Russell Smith in 1925, "are being run by a lot of imported Yankees still running with the energy that results from their having been wound up somewhere else." Granted the existence of mechanical energy in the region, he still had a lingering doubt about the persistence of human energy. In any case, it is this feeling of enervation that most Southern Californians fight like a kind of sleeping sickness. Fear of enervation still haunts the people of the region. Usually it is closely related to still another fear: that the water resources will someday be exhausted and that the land will return to its semi-arid condition.

4. THE AUTHORITY OF THE LAND

Beautiful and blond they come, the Californians,
Holding their blond beautiful children by the hand;
They come with healthy sunlight in tall hair;
Smiling and empty they stride back over the land.

Tanned and tempting, they reverse the pioneer
And glide back to Atlantic shores from their state,
And shows on Broadway have tall, oh, very tall girls,
To replace the shorter kind we generate.

California men put airplanes on like shoes
To swoop through the air they beautifully advertise,
And the women of California are splendid women,
With nothing, nothing, nothing behind their eyes.

Oranges, movies, smiles, and rainless weather,
Delightful California, you spread to our view,
And the whitest teeth, the brownest, most strokable shoulders,
And a hateful wish to be empty and tall like you.

—Theodore Spencer

Undeniably, the climate of Southern California, coupled with the severance of old social ties and traditions and customs by migration, works a change in the people who have come to the region. "Surely human beings ought to respond as the fruits do to this climate," wrote Julia M. Sloane, "in spirit as well as in body, and become a very mellow, amiable, sweet-tempered lot of people, and I think they do. Even the 'culls' are almost as good as the rest, though they won't bear transportation. It is the land of the second chance, of dreams come true, of freshness and opportunity, of the wideness of out-of-doors." "Under the calming influences," wrote Mrs. Daggett, "my pagan intuitions grew hourly. Beneath the lights and shadows of the prophetic mountains, analytical tendencies ceased. Possibly my creeds became unorthodox, but they expanded cheerfully each day."

While one may write off these naïve impressions as so much tourist rhetoric, there is no denying the fact of physical change in the California-born generation. In studies made years ago, Dr. David Starr Jordan discovered that "California college girls, of the same age, are larger by almost every dimension than are the college girls of Massachusetts. They are taller, broader-shouldered, thicker-chested (with ten cubic inches more lung capacity), have larger biceps and calves, and a superiority of tested strength." A glance at the roster of tennis, golf, baseball, football, and track stars in America will readily confirm the fact that the Californians are an outdoor people.

That the appeal of California is so physical probably accounts for the cult of the body and the cult of the out-of-doors that have tended to become more pronounced with the years. The Southern Californian's "cult of the body," writes Farnsworth Crowder, "snubs tradition, formality and dignity. Sun-bathing, nudity, bare heads, open-neck shirts are not imposed by cranks; they are dictated by the sun. Health consciousness is extreme and is reflected in the medical profession and in the prevalence of quackery, pseudo-science and cultism. The climate is so entirely congenial to the American athletics mania that sports flourish and 'champions' are a major product. Body-awareness is, of course, heightened among women by the presence of the movies and one sees glamour attempted in the most unexpected corners and on the most improbable faces and figures, until as one draws closer and closer to Hollywood and Vine the effect becomes positively bizarre. . . . All of which might be crudely summed up by saying that there is an inevitable, intrinsic sub-tropical drive, backed by the authority of the land itself, physiologically to 'go native.' This drive, however, is just sufficiently qualified that it does not push people on to complete intellectual and moral laxity. Herein lies California's singularity, her magic, her enormous appeal to outsiders and her hold upon her residents."

The longer people live in this strip of good land, this fortunate coast walled off from the desert by the great arch of mountains, the more they are influenced by the authority of the land itself. The cult of the body, mentioned by Crowder, is most pronounced. It takes the form of an enormous interest in sports, in sports ware, in the cult of nudism (Southern California has always had more than its share of nudist colonies), in sun-bathing and surf-bathing, and in the open civic planning. Adaptation is a slow process, but nevertheless it is a visible fact. Newcomers to Southern California, sooner or later, discard hats, overcoats, umbrellas, vests; the sport coat and slacks replace the business suit; Venetian blinds take the place of heavy curtains; and, in the process, the people themselves begin to thaw out. "The lands of the sun," reads a Spanish proverb, "expand the soul."

Related to the cult of the body is the general preoccupation with the out-of-doors which amounts to a cult in itself. Sooner or later, the homes are remodeled, if clumsily, to open outward to the sun. The automobile becomes more than standard equipment; it becomes an absolute necessity. With the automobile has come, what J. B. Priestley has described, as "the brand-new busy world" that exists along the roads and highways. It is a new American world with its own inhabitants, its own peculiar bustle and stir, a life which "in its pretty frivolity of colored lights and facetious appeals," is almost wholly divorced, in the desert areas, from the "savage countryside" through which it passes. In this new mode of living, "fast, crude, vivid," a new life is breaking into being "like a crocus through the wintry crust of earth." Southern California is the home of the drive-in: the drive-in market, shopping district, motion picture theater; the center of the self-service idea, in restaurants, stores, and shops; both phenomena of the free life of the automobile. "Everywhere," wrote Michael Williams some years ago, "there are pageants, festivals, out-of-door plays and masques." With this preoccupation with the out-of-doors, the pull of the land, the new orientation outward, there has developed an informality in dress, speech, housing, and manner that makes Southern California, as Otis Ferguson remarked, "loose for comfort but no stitches dropped." In part, this ease of manner is a product of the rich abundance of the land which makes for "lassitude in plenty."

Gradually the land remolds the people, gradually the new pattern emerges. "Perhaps the varying first contacts of pioneers with the soil would be of little moment," wrote T. K. Whipple, "were it not that their experiences are passed on and linger in one way or another among their descendants and followers. The process of mutual assimilation between people and land which they begin continues so long in their successors that it is nowhere yet complete. But it does begin and go on; the land starts to remake the people as quickly as they start to remake it."

Nowadays physicians are agreed that Southern California really is a rather healthy place in which to live. My friends in the medical profession tell me that certain types of pneumonia are so rare in the region as to be almost unknown and that cases of rheumatic fever—that is, cases originating in the region—are exceedingly rare. Many types of persistent and troublesome allergies, however, are reported, due to the presence of particular pollens throughout most of the year. These same friends inform me that, in their opinion, much illness in the region may be traced to inadequate home construction. Since so much of the home construction has taken place in the months of the long summer, newcomers have not always been aware of the type of construction needed in the rainy season.

> *"Southern California has changed as no other part of the world has changed. The transition is one, not of degree, but of kind."*
>
> —Theodore Van Dyke

CHAPTER VII

YEARS OF THE BOOM

SINCE 1870 the population of Southern California has increased at a phenomenal rate. Not only has the net increase in population been exceptionally large, but the *rate of growth* has been fantastic. From 1860 to 1870, the population increased 28.4%; from 1870 to 1880, 101%; from 1880 to 1890, 212.8%; from 1890 to 1900, 51.1%; from 1900 to 1910, 147%; from 1910 to 1920, 79.3%; from 1920 to 1930, 117.2%; from 1930 to 1940, 25.2%; and from 1940 to 1943, 10.9%. During the forty-year period 1900 to 1940, the population of the region increased 1107%, while the population of Los Angeles increased 1535.7%, by comparison with an increase of 172% in San Francisco. If the population of the United States had increased at a similar rate, we would today have a national population of 571,564,774.

As will be noted, the rate of growth in Southern California has been strikingly accelerated at fairly regular intervals. Minor spurts have occurred at ten-year intervals, with major upsurges being recorded approximately every eighteen years. According to Lewis A. Maverick, who has studied the real-estate cycles, the years of peak activity have been 1887, 1906, and 1923, and, since his study was made, one could add 1943. Initially the periods of rapid growth were termed "bubbles," but, after 1887, the term "boom" had to be substituted. Neither term accurately describes the nature of the phenomena involved. Every city has had its boom, but the history of Los Angeles is the history of its booms. Actually, the growth of Southern California since 1870 should be regarded as one continuous boom punctuated at intervals by major explosions. Other American cities have gone through a boom phase and then entered upon a period of normal growth. But Los Angeles has always been a boom town, chronically unable to consolidate its gains or to integrate its new population. To appreciate the social havoc caused by these periodic upsurges—these cataclysmic expansions—it is necessary to examine the booms of the 'seventies and 'eighties.

1. "The Rose Dawn"

Southern California experienced a minor boom at the time of the gold rush, when the demand for cattle and brandy brought momentary prosperity. But by 1867 Los Angeles, San Diego, and Santa Barbara were again described as "fossil towns, down at the heels." And then, with the completion of the transcontinental line to San Francisco in 1869, and plans for the extension of this line to Southern California (not completed until September, 1876), the Cow Counties began to boom. A first flush of excitement—a rose dawn— began to creep over the land.

There was little in Southern California, in the way of tangible assets, to justify this boom. The agricultural resources of the region were virtually untapped and undeveloped. Little irrigation was practiced and suitable methods of soil cultivation had yet to be evolved. The ranchos were being broken up, but no one knew just what to do with the land, most of which was regarded as arid and worthless. Grapes and grain had been substituted for cattle and sheep, but wine was about the only item of export. "Nothing worthy of the name of orange could be seen in California in 1876," according to Van Dyke. Successful agricultural colonies existed at San Bernardino, colonized by the Mormons, at Anaheim, colonized by German settlers, and at El Monte, the terminal point of the old overland trail. Scattered throughout the foothills were the bee ranches of the period. Introduced about 1858, bee-ranching had become a type of bonanza farming by 1870. On a foothill homestead, the bee-rancher would start with a swarm of a 100 stands in October, quickly increase the swarm to 400 stands, and ship 40,000 pounds of the finest comb-honey by July. The English walnut had been introduced about 1847; a start

had been made in raising various types of fruit; and the sheep industry, replacing the cattle industry, had assumed substantial proportions. Considerable comment about the agricultural possibilities of
Southern California began to appear in the farm journals after the
exhibition of orchard products at the Atlantic state fairs in 1871.

In the limited areas where surface waters were available or where
artesian wells had been drilled (some two hundred wells were
counted in the San Gabriel and Santa Ana Valleys in 1876), delightful oases had developed. Visiting Southern California in 1872, Hittell
wrote that "the song of Mignon came vividly before me as I walked
through the gardens. Luscious fruits of many species and unnumbered varieties loaded the trees. Gentle breezes came through the
bowers. The water rippled musically through the zanjas. Delicious
odors came from all the fragrant flowers of the temperate zone."
Even along the waterless foothills, "whiffs of honey-laden air came
from the stretches of chaparral thick with wild bees." Aside from
the irrigated oases, however, little real development had occurred.

With the completion of the transcontinental to San Francisco
in 1869, some 70,000 passengers a year began to arrive on the west
coast. Within a short while, a portion of the passenger stream began
to be diverted to the southern part of the state. Two hundred newcomers, it was said, arrived in San Diego with every steamer from San
Francisco. The bolder tourists came down the coast highway to Santa
Barbara in red Concord stages and then boarded the small steamers
that plied between Santa Barbara and Santa Monica. At this time,
as Stewart Edward White has written, "the exceeding pleasantness
of Southern California was a new thing: it had not been described
and over-described and advertised and made the most of. The tourist
had the intense proselyting zeal of one who has discovered something
and has something new to tell." Amazed by the land south of Tehachapi, the tourists began to write vivid letters to the eastern and
middle western newspapers and, in many cases, these letters were
later collected and published in book form. Southern California was
then as remote from the rest of the country as a foreign land or
island, and people will believe anything, as Mr. White observed of
the land, "that is far enough away."

Boosters and boomers came with the tourists, convinced that the
completion of the Southern Pacific line to Southern California would
transform the region. Long before the line was actually completed,

the railroad boomers were on the scene. Charles Nordhoff, for whom a town was appropriately named in Southern California, published a famous book about the region in 1873. Widely distributed in England and in Canada as well as the United States, the publication of this book "had a more far reaching effect on the fortunes of Southern California than anything that has ever been put into print." Nordhoff was a professional railroad boomer, as were Major Ben C. Truman, Major William McPherson, and a number of other writers, all of whom were on the scene before the rail line was completed to Los Angeles.

By 1874 the "bubble of expectation" was full-blown. Picturesque cottages were torn down in Santa Barbara, Los Angeles, and San Diego to make way for the new buildings of the cities-to-be. Wharfs, railway terminals, hotels, warehouses, and churches began to spring up in anticipation of the boom that every one expected. Sidewalks and street lights appeared as if by magic. Old-town Santa Barbara was "bisected and torn down and almost entirely destroyed." Los Angeles, which had been described in 1867 as "a town of crooked, ungraded, unpaved streets; low, lean, rickety, adobe houses, with flat asphaltum roofs, and here and there an indolent native, hugging the inside of a blanket, or burying his head in a gigantic watermelon," had, by 1876, undergone a similar transformation. The little town of 6,000 population suddenly began to think of itself as another San Francisco. San Diego experienced its "year of awakening" in 1872, when property was reported "buoyant" and "the rising tide of excitement" was running strong. Bent upon eradicating the Mexican influence, the boomers seriously considered changing the names of the three communities. Always embarrassed by the inability of newcomers to pronounce the name correctly, Los Angeles issued a phonetic warning in verse:

> The Lady would remind you, please,
> Her name is not Lost Angie Lees—
> Nor Angie anything whatever.
> She hopes her friends will be so clever
> To share her fit historic pride
> The G shall not be jellified.
> O long, G hard, and rhyme with 'yes'—
> And all about Loce Ang-el-ess.

Entirely premonitory, based solely on great expectations, "the rose dawn" soon faded from the land. Even before the Southern Pacific line was completed, the "little boom" fizzled out when the panic of 1873 struck Southern California. Property was reported "a drug on the market"; and Santa Barbara, Los Angeles, and San Diego began to look with some embarrassment upon the unsightly structures that had been built in anticipation of a boom that was stillborn. Arriving in San Diego in 1873, Abbot Kinney reported that "everything has flattened-out." Feeling that they had been taken in by the boomers and boosters, the local residents placed a curse on the enthusiastic tourists. "Their overripe fancies," complained one Los Angeles editor, "are like the Dead Sea apples that turn into ashes with the tasting." Disillusioned by the failure of the boom, the Southern California towns lapsed into a siesta that was to last for a decade.

Following the collapse of this initial boom, Southern California experienced an interval of quiet but substantial growth. Between 1875 and 1889, the production of wine increased from 1,300,000 to 14,000,000 gallons, the citrus industry underwent a remarkable expansion, and the number of artesian wells steadily increased. "This is a veritable New California," reported the San Francisco *Bulletin*. "Any one familiar with the old style of slovenly grain farming, tumble-down houses, and general lack of thrift, cannot but welcome the change. Ten years ago, the people here struggled against every kind of drawback; and many parted with their homes for next to nothing and returned east in disgust."

These new beginnings were made possible by the ill-fated boom of the 'seventies. For the boom had brought new wealth, new energy, and a new type of settler to the region. By 1885 the two model colony settlements of Etiwanda and Ontario, and the pioneer colony of Riverside, could be pointed to as successful demonstrations of the rich agricultural promise of the region. The 6,000-acre Santa Anita ranch which Lucky Baldwin had purchased in 1875 was producing 2,000 pounds of butter a week, and 43,856 boxes of oranges and lemons, 384,460 gallons of wine, 174,750 sacks of grain, and 54,946 gallons of brandy a year. In fact, Lucky Baldwin boasted that he could raise anything in the world at the ranch but the mortgage. Laid out with "velvet lawns and gorgeous flowers," the Baldwin Ranch was still another demonstration of the rich agricultural possibilities in Southern California. A famous showplace of the region, it was visited by thousands of sightseers and tourists. Had the residents of Southern California looked at the following table, prepared by Dr. Robert Cleland, they would not have been so disappointed in the boom that failed.

	Los Angeles	San Diego	Santa Barbara
1866: Estimated population ...	8,700	2,630	5,000
Assessable wealth.......	$2,353,267	$542,825	$771,861
1872: Estimated population ...	17,400	7,359	8,400
Assessable wealth.......	$10,554,592	$2,618,928	$6,000,232

By 1885 the stage was set for the next spectacular plunge, the next boom.

2. THE BOOM OF THE 'EIGHTIES

The completion of the Santa Fe line in 1886 was the spark that ignited the real-estate explosion of the 'eighties. The withdrawal of the Santa Fe from the Transcontinental Traffic Association, upon completion of the line, was immediately construed by the Southern Pacific as a declaration of war. Previously the passenger rate from Missouri Valley points to Southern California had been approximately $125. But the rate promptly dropped to $100, when the Santa Fe entered Southern California, and continued to fall as each line undercut the other. On March 6, 1887, the Southern Pacific met the Santa Fe rate of $12. In a matter of hours, the rate dropped to $8, then to $6, then to $4. By noon on March 6, the Santa Fe was advertising a rate of $1 per passenger. "The result of this war," wrote a local historian, "was to precipitate such a flow of migration, such an avalanche rushing madly to Southern California as I believe has no parallel." In 1887 the Southern Pacific transported 120,000 people to Los Angeles, while the Santa Fe brought three and four passenger trains a day into the city.

Learning of the great boom in Southern California, the townsite sharks of the Middle West began to descend on the region in droves. They settled on Los Angeles, wrote one observer, "like flies upon a bowl of sugar." "Among the new people who came to Los Angeles during the height of the boom," wrote Willard, "the speculative and adventurous class, while not in the majority perhaps as far as numbers went, were always the most conspicuous. They lost no time in asserting themselves in all public and social matters, and for a time something like anarchy prevailed. Here were 40,000 or 50,000 people

suddenly gathered together from all parts of the union, in utter ignorance of one another's previous history. It was a golden opportunity
for the fakir and humbug and the man with the past that he wanted
forgotten."

In San Diego more than 50,000 people, from every state in the
union, roamed the streets of the little city. "Drawn together from the
adventurous classes of the world," wrote Walter Gifford Smith, "imbued as it were with excitement and far from conventional trammels,
this element contained and developed a store of profligacy and vice,
much of which found its way into official, business, and social life.
Gambling was open and flagrant; games of chance were carried on at
the curbstones; painted women paraded the town in carriages and
sent out engraved cards summoning men to their receptions and
'high teas'; the desecration of Sunday was complete, with all drinking
and gambling houses open, and with picnics, excursions, fiestas and
bullfights." Theft, murder, incendiarism, carousals, and highway robberies began to be reported throughout the region.

It took these professional boomers, noted Smith, "to touch off the
magazine." Veterans of land booms in Wichita, Kansas City, Chicago, Minneapolis, and Seattle, they knew how to attract crowds to
auction sales by brass bands, free lunches, and circus performers.
"They captured the tourist and the tenderfoot by the thousand, took
in scores of old conservative capitalists from the East, who could
talk as sensibly as anyone about 'intrinsic value' and 'business basis'
but who lost their heads as surely as they listened to the dulcet strains
of the brass band and the silver tongue of the auctioneer." Soon the
cautious natives, who had burned their fingers ten years previously,
became possessed by the same fever of speculation. "The buyers,"
notes one San Diego historian, "were mostly our own people." Everyone gambled in the frenzied real-estate market, clerks, waiters, bell-
boys, housewives, doctors, lawyers, preachers. A visitor from the East
told of attending Sunday services in a Methodist Church in Los
Angeles. When the services were over, the preacher grasped his hand,
asked if he were a newcomer, and proceeded to sell him a lot in a
newly opened subdivision. Apparently the only resident of Los Angeles who remained impervious to the excitement was the caustic
Major Horace Bell, who denounced the boom in his newspaper as
"the crime of the age." Promoters, he pointed out, were "salting"
the land much as promoters had once salted mining claims. Oranges

were stuck on Joshua trees in a desert tract advertised as the only region in Southern California in which the orange was indigenous!

Buying a slice of one of the ranchos, the promoters would build a hotel, lay out a few streets, sidewalks, and curbs, and start the construction of a local railway. With white stakes marking off the lots and tracts and subdivision flags flying in the breeze, the suckers would then be assembled for the "Grand Jubilee Auction" by the bait of "free excursions; brass bands; brilliant music. Lunch served by New York caterers with California fruits and wine for dessert. Lunch and music free as air." Typical of the lyrical advertisements announcing the auction sales is this one:

> ROASTED OX!
> SATURDAY, FEBRUARY 23RD
> There will be
> BARBECUED
> A fine Young Steer on the campus of
> SAN DIEGO COLLEGE OF LETTERS
> AT PACIFIC BEACH
> He will be carved and served to the Hungry Throng at 12 o'clock. Ladies will be served in the College Dining Hall, and the gentlemen under the shining canopy of heaven.
>
> Upon this occasion there will be a continuance of the
> IMMOLATION SALE
> of Real Estate by the San Diego College of Letters Company.
>
> CHOICE RESIDENCE AND VILLA SITES
> SPECIAL EXCURSIONS!

Between January 1, 1887, and July, 1889, over sixty new towns, embracing 79,350 acres, were laid out in Southern California. Guinn estimated that there was room in these towns for a population of 2,000,000 people. Towns appeared "like scenes conjured up by Aladdin's lamp—out of the desert, in the river wash, or a mud flat, upon a barren slope or hillside." If a town site was located in a river bottom, the promoters contended that sandy soils were the best in Southern California. If it was located on the desert, then it was being planned as a health resort; if it was located on a hillside, then it was the view that was being sold. Towns located in swamp lands near the coast were, of course, laid out as "harbor cities." Buyers arrived in the region as fast as new towns were promoted. In fact, the influx was so great that the Southern California Immigration Association disbanded in 1885. The value of real estate transactions for the year 1887 was in excess of $200,000,000.

Of more than a hundred towns platted in Los Angeles County between 1884 and 1888, sixty-two no longer exist, except as Dr. Dumke notes, as "stunted corners, farm acreage, or suburbs." Among the ghost towns left in the wake of the great boom were: Sunset, Morocco, Hyde Park, Nadeau Park, Vernondale, South Arlington, Rosecrans, Walteria, La Ballona, Seabright, Bethune, Ramona, Savannah, Huntington, Alosta, Chicago Park,. Gladstone, Rockdale, Minneapolis, Ivanhoe, Dundee, Monte Vista, Maynard (located in Antelope Valley), Border City and Manchester (which clung precariously to desert hillsides), Hesperia, Lordsburg, McPherson, Rivera, Fairview, Terracina, Gladysta, Rincon, Englewood ("no fog, no frosts, no alkali, no adobe"), and Richland. The town of Border City, Guinn remarked, "was most easily accessible by means of a balloon, and was secure from hostile invasion as the homes of the cliff-dwellers. Its principal resource was a view of the Mojave desert." Typical of the curious ghost towns which dotted Southern California was Fairview which consisted, after the boom collapsed, of an artesian well, a bathhouse, a hotel, and a wood-burning railroad that extended for a mile or two toward Santa Ana. Sixty of these towns had a total population of 2,351 after the boom had collapsed. The town of Carlton had 4,060 lots and not a single resident; Nadeau had 4,470 lots but no settlers; Manchester had 2,304 lots, but no inhabitants; Santiago had 2,110 lots, a few houses, but no occupants for the houses; Chicago Park, laid out in the wash of the San Gabriel River, had 2,289 lots and one resident; while the town of Sunset had 2,014 lots and a watchman.

By 1889 the boom had "gradually shriveled up" and Southern California was reported "dead as a herring." The County of Los Angeles estimated that $14,000,000 in property values had been wiped out in a year. Surveying the wreckage, one observer said that "everything has been wrecked by the boom and financial men have gone down by the hundreds." It should be noted, however, that while the boom had collapsed, it had left a substantial deposit of wealth and population. The population of the Cow Counties increased from 64,000 in 1860 to 201,000 in 1890. At least 137,000 "tourists of the boom" remained in Southern California, many by force of necessity. In 1886, Los Angeles was assessed, writes Dr. Dumke, at $18,000,000, but by 1889 this figure had risen to $46,000,000. Some of the boom towns soon became thriving communities, notably Alhambra, Monrovia, Azusa, and Glendale. "The banks were able to weather the crisis," reports Dr. Caughey, "and the largest losses were in anticipated profits."

During the boom, many permanent improvements were effected which laid the foundation for the rapid growth of the next decade. "There is no section," wrote L. M. Holt, "where good cement sidewalks in cities and towns begin to compare with those of Southern California. There is no other section where cities and towns have so good a supply and system of domestic water service, it frequently being found that the domestic piped water system under pressure is established before there are people to use the water. There is no other section where there are so many rapid transit motor railroads." Between 1880 and 1892, fifty-seven irrigation companies were organized in the foothill belt east of Los Angeles. Out of the boom came a number of educational institutions, well in advance of the actual settlement of the region, such as the University of Southern California, the Chaffee College of Agriculture at Ontario, Occidental College in Los Angeles, the State Normal School (now the University of California at Los Angeles), the Immaculate Heart Academy, St. Vincent's College (now Loyola University), Whittier College, La Verne College, and Redlands University (its major endowments, at least, date from the boom).

Like a kind of rocket propulsion, each boom in Southern California has set in motion a chain of circumstances which, in turn, has brought about the next boom. While the boom of the 'eighties resulted in much destruction, with good farm lands being carved up into town lots and valuable vineyards being uprooted for crazy subdivisions, still it had the effect of laying the foundations, well in advance of actual settlement, for the next great wave of migration. Visiting Southern California two years after the great boom had collapsed, Henry T. Finck, correspondent for The Nation, found the region "growing like an asparagus stalk after an April shower." Despite the fact that the street-car lines were barely paying expenses, that workmen were grumbling, and that Northern California cities were crowing, he concluded that the region had "brighter prospects than any other section" of California. On a return visit in 1893, he could scarcely recognize the land. Fruits, vegetables, trees, and flowers imported from Mexico, South America, Africa, Japan, and Australia were being "acclimated in picturesque confusion." The whole region seemed to have undergone, he noted, a profound change.

In addition to many improvements, the boom left a rich deposit of folklore in Southern California. In Los Angeles, it was said that the word "real" was synonomous with "real estate." A favorite expression by which local residents greeted each other in the 'nineties was: "Has your town recovered yet from the boom?" For years the population of the region was supposed to have survived "largely on faith, hope, and climate." "I had half a million dollars wiped out in the crash," observed one of Van Dyke's characters, "and what's worse, $500 of it was cash." With the immeasurable optimism of the period, one San Diego real-estate firm announced: "We may say that San Diego has a population of 150,000 people, only they are not all here yet." Still another San Diego firm, annoyed by the prophets of despair, declaimed: "Oh! generation of carkers and unbelievers, neither you or we shall see that day of reckoning. This is no mining boom, based upon ledges that can be pinched out or worked out. This is no oil boom, based upon a product the supply of which can readily exceed the demand. This is no boom based upon wheat deals, or pork corners, or financial deadfalls, or railway combinations, or other devices of man. This boom is based on the simple fact that hereabouts the good Lord has created conditions of climate and health and beauty such as can be found nowhere else, in this or any other land, and until every acre of this earthly paradise is occupied, the influx will continue." Not a town in Southern California would admit that it had been created by the boom: the boom was created by the town "and a few similar places." "We're not boosting California for all she's worth, because, sir, no man knows what she's worth." The tourists, it was said, were the "people who still buy anything that they have never seen before." Nathaniel C. Carter, "the great excursionist," had a halftone cut made depicting himself before and after he was cured of tuberculosis in Southern California. Entitled "Before and After Taking," he exhibited the picture wherever he went, and, when asked what the remedy was, replied, "California climate."

In the wake of the boom, wry comments appeared in the local press. "The boom has struck our town but not in the way we wished for—another saloon to deal out poison to poor weak humanity, and two restaurants have been started." Visiting Southern California in 1889, Samuel Storey, a member of Parliament, found the people "suffering from a cold fit after a fever: they had what they call a land-boom last year." It was during the boom of the 'eighties that the great rivalry between Southern California and Northern California developed. In an effort to check the flow of tourists south of Tehachapi, the San Francisco boosters issued fake circulars and maps on which all Southern California was marked as "barren hills" and "desert country." After the boom collapsed, San Franciscans designated Southern California "the land of opportunity and one dollar bills" and referred to Los Angeles as "a one-lunged tourist town."

The poets of the boom were the great auctioneers, such as Col. Tom Fitch and Ben E. Ward, men who conducted auctions "on the old-style method, wherein the public, not the owners, place the price on the property." Schooled in the land booms of the Middle West, these men knew how to handle a crowd, how to manipulate a fake bid, and how to write lush advertising copy. Col. Fitch and the bull-voiced Ward auctioned off most of Southern California, their individual daily sales not infrequently ranging as high as $150,000 and $300,000. "The silver-tongued orator of Southern California," Col. Fitch auctioned lots at Santa Monica, which he christened "the Zenith of the Sunset Sea," at San Diego, at San Fernando, and at Santa Barbara. Wearing high silk hats, white neckties, cutaway coats, and doeskin gloves, the auctioneers gave superlative performances.

Col. Fitch was probably the first poet of Southern California. When skeptics in the crowd would point to the absence of growing crops, or raise ugly questions about the water supply, Col. Fitch would answer: "I don't care if you couldn't raise a bean within forty miles of this tract, it's the climate we're selling, not the land." One of his fancier pieces of advertising copy contained this passage:

> We knew it would rain, for all day long
> A spirit with slender ropes of mist
> Was dipping the silvery buckets down
> Into the vapory amethyst.

We also knew it, because the wound which our uncle received in his back at the first battle of Bull Run (he was in Canada when the second battle of Bull Run was fought) throbbed all day Saturday. Now, if Saturday night's and Sunday night's rain shall be followed by one or more showers of equal volume, we will see our bleak mesas covered with the vernal and succulent alfileria and all the streams will be running bank-full. Then there will be—

> Sweet fields arrayed in living green
> And rivers of delight!

Then the slopes of the arroyos will be flecked with the purple violets and the pink anemones and white star flowers, and over all the wind-blown heights the scarlet poppies and big yellow buttercups will wave in the breeze like the plumes and banners of an elfin army. And when you behold the earth covered with fragrant children, born of her marriage to the clouds, and when you know that this charming effect of a few showers can be increased and perpetuated the year round with a little water from the mains and a little labor with the hoe and rake, you will be thankful to us for having called your attention to Middletown Heights Lots. Here upon Block 42, Middletown Addition, we are surrounded by a grander view than can be seen anywhere else, even in this favored land. Loma to our right, with brow of purple and feet of foam outlined against a sky of crimson; far down the southern horizon towers Table Mountain, outlined against the gathering dusk. The electric lights glint across the bay to sleeping Coronado, and San Diego buzzes and hums at our feet. BUY THESE LOTS. You pays your money and you takes your choice.

3. The Pullman-Car Migration

The land booms of the 'seventies and 'eighties in Southern California were essentially railroad promotions. Elsewhere in the West and Middle West, settlers, to some extent, promoted the railroads, but here the railroads promoted settlement. From 1876 to 1890, the Southern Pacific Company, in particular, promoted Southern California by every means at its disposal: through publicity, settlement agents, land bureaus (with branch offices in Omaha, New York, New

Orleans, London, and Hamburg), lecturers, exhibits, and inspired news stories. Agents of the company sold lots in Southern California towns to prospective settlers in Ireland before they had booked passage for America. A considerable trans-Atlantic traffic was developed, in fact, with the European prospects being routed west by way of New Orleans. Unquestionably, the railroad companies were the first all-year-round clubs, the first boosters, and the first chambers of commerce. They even operated employment agencies which, for a fee, agreed to place "farm pupils" on Southern California ranches. They sold prospective settlers so-called "land seekers' tickets," under an arrangement whereby the fare could later be applied on the purchase of railroad land. They also operated "emigrant houses" along the line of westward passage so that the settlers could be offered the bait of one week's free lodging en route to California. A number of the colony settlements were, also, railroad promotions.

Among the devices which the railroads used to attract settlers to Southern California were the excursion party and the emigrant train. Nathaniel C. Carter, of Lowell, Massachusetts, is generally credited with originating the suggestion that travel to Southern California might be organized at the source. In any case, he arrived on the coast in 1872 with the first excursion party made up of "two dozen Boston men and women." For twenty-five years, "the great excursionist" escorted parties to Southern California every winter. "Ho! for California! Excursion Party!" reads the caption of a broadside dated March 25, 1870, announcing that a "party of fifty" residents of Marshall, Michigan, had been formed to visit Southern California to select a colony site. The excursion parties were frequently made up of prospective colonists from the same Eastern or Middle Western community. The emigrant train, on the other hand, catered to the unorganized excursionists and homeseekers.

To stimulate interest in excursion parties, the railroads sent lecturers throughout the East and Middle West who extolled the climate of Southern California, distributed broadsides, and gathered the names of interested parties. Needless to say, excursion parties were given the right of way in Southern California. "Socials" were organized for their entertainment, bands greeted them at the station on their arrival, tally-ho coaches took them to the nearest hotel, and a complete itinerary was prepared for their convenience. On entering Southern California, the excursion trains made special stops to permit the tourists to visit Smiley Heights in Redlands, to lunch at the Mission Inn, and to pick poppies on the sunlit slopes of early spring. On occasion, the excursion trains were halted on the outskirts of the smaller towns, while "polite gentlemen and ládies" presented the tourists with "baskets of fruit and flowers."

In the 'seventies and 'eighties, it took five nights and days to make the trip from the Missouri River points to Southern California. Traveling at a speed of about twenty-two miles an hour, the transcontinental trains carried dining cars only as far west as Chicago; beyond the Missouri River points they stopped at roadside stations for meals. "Railroad travel," writes Stewart Edward White, "across the plains was still a good deal of an adventure, not to be lightly undertaken. People settled down for a week. They got acquainted with everybody else on the train, and visited back and forth, and even got up charades and entertainments. Every party had an elaborate hamper with tin compartments in which was a great store of bread and rolls and chicken." Three or four times a day, the emigrant trains would stop, in the middle of nowhere, to permit the passengers to get out, stroll around, and limber the kinks out of their legs. Buffalo could still be seen on the prairies as the trains came west. Nearly every special emigrant train carried a clergyman who conducted Sunday services and "a young man with a violin or a young lady with a guitar and a sweet voice" to entertain the passengers. The emigrant trains aided poor settlers by providing folding seats which could be flattened out into beds, and cooking accommodations, in the form of a stove in the rear of the coach, where a pot of coffee could be prepared or water heated to boil diapers. At one time as many as a hundred special emigrant cars were in use on the Southern Pacific line.

The railroad-inspired land booms in Southern California attracted an unusual type of settler. Unlike other western settlements, Southern California drew settlers from diverse and distant places rather than from neighboring states and territories. Since they came in Pullman cars instead of covered wagons, they came in great numbers and at a much faster rate than the pioneers of 1849. Unlike the Pike County folks who had trekked across the continent after 1850, these people came from cities as well as rural areas, and they were the type of people who could afford to purchase a railroad ticket: the merchant, the banker, the uprooted professional man, the farmer with an invalid wife. Many of these settlers were drawn west by the excitement and novelty of a train trip at cheap rates. Having built expensive lines which terminated in a desert, the railroads were naturally interested in filling up the region with settlers as rapidly as possible. But once they had achieved this initial objective, they were quite willing that others should take over the task of further promotion and development.

4. The Boom of 1906

"God made Southern California—and made it on Purpose."
—Charles Fletcher Lummis

With the collapse of the land boom of 1887, the time had come for the railroads to step aside as promotion agents. They had literally put Southern California on the map. As a result of their expensive ballyhoo campaigns, the region was known throughout the world as a "subtropical" paradise with a superb climate. In the interval that had elapsed since the railroad boomers had discovered the charms of this subtropical paradise, its agricultural potentialities had been demonstrated. It was now time for a truly systematic promotion. The task was twofold: to undertake within the region the same type of promotional activity that the railroads had used, and to work with the railroads in stimulating further migration. By their nature these tasks required organized co-operative action; they could not be undertaken by individuals. Furthermore, it was imperative that they be accomplished immediately, otherwise the momentum of the boom might be completely lost.

The decade 1890–1900 saw these tasks fulfilled. In a single decade the foundations were laid for the next great expansion. Never before, perhaps, have individual boosters co-operated so successfully in promoting a region. No single decade in the history of Los Angeles has embraced such remarkable achievements as were effected in these years. The great improvements brought about in this decade are only the more remarkable in view of the fact that the region had so few natural advantages. It was short of water, short of fuel; it lacked mineral and forest resources; and, with the exception of San Diego, there was not a single good natural harbor south of Tehachapi. The boosters of the period, however, were confronted with the imperative: expand or perish.

On October 15, 1888, the famous "new beginning" was launched in Los Angeles at an emergency meeting. It was at this meeting, on the motion of General Harrison Gray Otis, that the Los Angeles Chamber of Commerce came into existence. From its inception, the chamber was one of the most active, and for years the largest, organization of its kind in the nation. Its first project was typically grandiose: the chamber proposed that the United States should purchase the peninsula of Lower California from Mexico, annex it to Southern California, and create a new state—a proposal that precipitated a diplomatic incident between the United States and Mexico. Through organized exhibits, itinerant lecturers, and expert publicity, the chamber began to advertise the specific assets of Southern California much as the railroads had earlier advertised its climate. Having only a limited number of verifiable assets to offer, the chamber not infrequently invented advantages. In a period of three years after its formation, over 2,000,000 "pieces of literature" had been distributed throughout the United States. The chamber also organized a special train, "California on Wheels," which visited every city of consequence in the South and Middle West. Carrying choice agricultural exhibits, scenic photographs, models of California homes, and statistical charts, the train was visited by a million people during its two-year tour. Costly exhibits were organized for the Chicago Fair, the Atlanta Exposition, the Omaha Fair, and the St. Louis Fair. Dozens of associations were invited to Los Angeles and royally entertained. By 1900 Los Angeles was known as the best advertised city in America.

Lack of basic resources has always seemed to stimulate a high level of technological achievement in Southern California. A succession of three exceptionally dry seasons in 1900, 1901, and 1902 brought about such a feverish drilling of new wells and tunnels for water that, by 1903, enough new water had been developed to irrigate the state of Rhode Island. Lacking wood and coal, electricity was widely used at an early date for many purposes then considered novel. Los Angeles was the first city in America, perhaps in the world, to be completely illuminated by electric lights. The availability of electricity brought about the establishment of the famous Kite-route interurban Pacific Electric transit system founded by General M. H. Sherman and E. P. Clark, two of the great boosters of the period. Between 1900 and 1915, the Pacific Electric expanded from 601 road miles to over 1,000 track miles, providing the entire section from the beach resorts to

San Bernardino with a network of rapid interurban transit. At the time this line was built, it was properly characterized as "the most complete and comprehensive system of interurban and suburban electric communication in the nation." In the decade 1900–1910, the City of Los Angeles built its famous aqueduct to acquire Owens Valley water: enough water to meet the needs of a population of 2,000,000 people. Between 1890 and 1897, the streets of the city were, for the first time, systematically laid out, sidewalks were built, streets were paved, and an outfall sewer constructed.

The discovery of important oil deposits served to meet the critical fuel shortage. E. L. Doheny brought in the first producing oil well in Los Angeles on November 4, 1892. It was not long before he had sixty-nine wells pumping, most of them in residential districts. Black derricks sprang up among the shrubs and flowers of elaborate gardens, steel-shod mules dragged loads of oil equipment across velvet lawns, finely graded roads were rutted by the wheels of the oil tanks that surged through the streets drawn by four, six, and eight mules, sometimes four abreast. By 1909 the district north of Wilshire and west of Vermont had 160 producing wells in operation and Santa Monica Boulevard had become an oil-workers' shacktown. The discovery of oil touched off a minor oil boom, as dozens of new companies were formed and a heavy traffic in oil leases developed.

With winter tourists pouring into Southern California by the thousands—60,000 in 1901, 30,000 in 1902, 47,000 in 1903—the construction industry began to boom. Blocks of four-family flats were built for the accommodation of winter tourists. From 50,395 residents in 1890, the population of Los Angeles increased to 102,479 in 1900, and then advanced to 319,198 by 1910. The earthquake, known in California as "the fire," of 1906 seriously retarded the growth of San Francisco and attracted much outside capital to Los Angeles. San Francisco manufacturing showed only a slight increase between 1900 and 1910, while Los Angeles registered a 100% increase. Aided by these developments, the boom of 1906 was touched off by the opening of the beach towns, Hermosa Beach in 1902 and Venice in 1905.

"Venice in America," one of Southern California's fanciest promotions, was the product of Abbot Kinney's imaginative mind. Having made a fortune in the East as the manufacturer of Sweet Caporal cigarettes, Kinney was, to borrow a phrase from Morrow Mayo, a

Rich Man with Artistic Impulses. Botanical expert, former Indian Commissioner, globe-trotter, a student of art and culture, he was also a diligent pamphleteer. Among the titles of his numerous pamphlets were: "The Conquest of Death," "Task by Twilight," "Money," "Under the Shadow of the Dragon," "Protection and Free Trade," "Forestry," and "The Eucalyptus." Acquiring a 160-acre tract of sand dunes and marshes twenty-five miles from Los Angeles, Kinney proceeded to build a Venice-by-the-Sea, complete with homes, hotels, inter-connecting canals (with a fleet of gondolas and twenty-four Italian gondoliers imported from Venice), amusement halls, and a vast Chautauqua auditorium.

Just as the railroads had brought excursion trains into Los Angeles during the earlier boom, so now the Pacific Electric ran special excursions to the beach towns. In 1906 Lillian Whiting reported that there "was nothing of the dreamy, languorous old Spanish atmosphere about the place," and remarked that Los Angeles was "the most electrically up-to-date city imaginable." The beach boom of 1906 was a flash-in-the-pan affair that failed to win the approval or support of the boosters. Indicative of the new spirit of the community are these lines of comment from an editorial in the Los Angeles Times: "The fake boom created at Redondo Beach is bearing fruit today. That fake has hurt every bit of beach property on the ocean front of Southern California. Women pledged their jewels, heirlooms coming down for generations, to speculate in Redondo lots at ten times their intrinsic value. Business men went crazy for the time being, and took checks which never could be cashed, and thus tied up property which might have sold at high figures. Contracts flew from hand to hand so fast that no one knew where the chain of title ran. It only lasted a short while, but its fruits ran longer, and are still running."

The steady influx of winter tourists saved Southern California from the collapse of this highly synthetic "flash" boom. For by 1900, the "doing California" fever had really hit the Middle West. A tour of California had become, for retired Middle Westerners, what the grand tour had been for residents of the eastern seaboard at an earlier date. And a winter in California usually meant a winter in Southern California or Sunny California as it came to be called. Actually the analogy to a European tour is quite exact. Considering the length of the journey and the time consumed, the trip across the great plains and the intermountain desert was rather like an ocean crossing. People did not stop en route; they jumped across the continent to the western shore. "It is absurd," remarks a character in Lawrence Rising's novel *Proud Flesh* (1924), "to think of California as part of America. It isn't. It's a foreign country." The subtropical climate, so-called, enhanced the illusion. People published letters, articles, and books about their winter in California much in the manner that an earlier generation left memoirs of their trips to Europe. Such documents as *A Truthful Woman in Southern California* by Kate Sanborn (1894), *Tourist Tales of California* by Sara White Isaman (1907), and *Uncle Jim and Aunt Jemimy in Southern California*, published in Lincoln, Nebraska, in 1912, are certainly crude performances, but they are extremely revealing. Without realizing it, many Americans were beginning to feel the pull toward the Pacific.

During the years after the turn of the century, a miniature grand tour was organized for winter tourists in Southern California. With scarcely a single exception, the winter tourists made a trip to Venice; ascended Mt. Lowe and stayed overnight in the Alpine Inn; visited the Mission at San Gabriel (where they bought as souvenirs Mission, poppy, and poinsettia pillows); crossed the channel to Catalina Island and took a ride on the famous "glass-bottom boats"; visited the Cawston Ostrich Farm in South Pasadena and Busch's Gardens in Pasadena; lunched at the Mission Inn in Riverside; spent a day at Lucky Baldwin's Santa Anita ranch; visited Paul de Longpre's garden home in Hollywood to purchase one of his flower paintings; and attended a "Bird Recital" by the California School of Artistic Whistling at Blanchard Hall (decorated with palm trees and bird cages, Blanchard Hall was one of the prize exhibits of the period). A procession of tourists attended the weekly "complimentary musicale" sponsored by a local furniture company, where a young lady sang songs in "four different languages" and every visitor was presented with a picture postcard of Los Angeles as it looked in 1880. As minor attractions there were the alligator farm, the lion farm, and the endless winter revival meetings. A week or so before the winter tourists began to arrive, the traveling evangelists would appear on the scene. For years Southern California was their favorite wintering resort. At every turn were "stereoscopic lectures," curio stores, freak exhibits, special excursion busses, and schedules of things to do and places to visit. From 1900 to 1920, Los Angeles was essentially a tourist town. Like most tourist towns, it had its share of freaks, side-shows, novelties, and show-places. Ducks waddled along the streets with advertisements painted on their backs; six-foot-nine pituitary giants with sandwich-board signs stalked the downtown streets; while thousands of people carrying Bibles in their hands and singing hymns marched in evangelical parades. With its peep-shows, shooting galleries, curio shops, health lectures, and all-night movies, Main Street became a honky-tonk alley that never closed. During the winter months, Los Angeles was, in fact, a great circus without a tent.

As town-site promotion gave way to carefully planned subdivisions, new methods of selling real estate were rapidly perfected. Before any lots were sold in Hollywood, streets and highways were platted and trees planted along the walks. The Hollywood Hotel was built on one corner of Hollywood Boulevard and Highland and an imposing bank structure on the opposite corner. Loads of brick, sand, and lumber were hauled to the tract and dumped on vacant lots so as to give the impression that hundreds of lot-purchasers had actually started to construct homes. Almost every other lot in the tract carried a sign marked SOLD, although not a single lot had actually been disposed of. The stage being set, the new subdivision was opened with a "grand excursion" on May 3, 1903. Two special Pacific Electric cars, the Mermaid and No. 400, decorated with flags, bunting, and flowers, carried the first excursionists to the tract where they were greeted by a brass band. In a speech at the tract headquarters, General M. H. Sherman, who with Harry Chandler and E. P. Clark had organized this fancy promotion, waving his arms at the SOLD signs and the scattered piles of building material, sobbed: "Behold What God Hath Wrought!" On this subdivision, the promoters made a net profit of 60% on their investment. The technician who outlined this new-style subdivision was H. J. Whitley, a professional town-site promoter for the Rock Island and Northern Pacific Railroads. Using much the same techniques, Chandler, Sherman, and their associates later subdivided and sold more than 47,000 acres of land adjoining Los Angeles.

A key figure in the expansion of Los Angeles after 1890 was Henry Huntington. "I am a foresighted man," said Huntington, "and I believe that Los Angeles is destined to become the most important city in this country, if not in the world. It can extend in any direction as far as you like. Its front door opens on the Pacific, the ocean of the future. Europe can supply her own wants; we shall supply the wants of Asia. There is nothing that cannot be made and few things that will not grow in Southern California." Only a handful of Huntington's colleagues recognized the enormous importance of the Pacific or sensed what was implied for the future of Los Angeles by the annexation of Hawaii and the extension of American rule to the Philippines. As Benjamin Ide Wheeler pointed out, "It is the ocean that awakened California and there is no doubt that in 1898, it stood at the end of a *cul de sac*, a fine decorative end of the continent—but the road went no further." People came from the East, toured the Pacific Coast, and then returned to their homes. After 1898 the Pacific became an American highway. There is no doubt that the year 1898 separates the old Los Angeles from the new. "As nearly as anything else," wrote Harry Carr, "this earlier period was punctuated by the Spanish-American War. When it began we were still a hick town. When it ended, we began to grow into a city."

The boosters who ushered in this period of remarkable expansion made a heavy gamble on the future. Most of the improvements that they brought about were clearly in advance of present needs or immediately foreseeable requirements. When the Pacific Electric Kiteroute was first laid out, it barely paid expenses. The beach resorts were a gamble. Subdivisions were planned years in advance of population requirements. If ever a region lived and planned for the future, that region is Southern California. Not only was development consistently anticipatory, but it was, to a large extent, carefully organized, plotted, and manipulated. Boyle Workman, a local historian, has called Los Angeles "the City That Grew." Actually, Los Angeles has not grown; it has been conjured into existence. Whole cities of people have been transplanted into Los Angeles. The constant influx of people, bringing new ideas, new energy, new capital, was the hedge against which the promoters made their daring investments. It was an enormous gamble, but the boosters won. With a steadily increasing population, the construction industry expanded and payrolls mounted, new industries were established, more shops and stores were opened, and opportunities in the professions and service trades multiplied. New capital imported to the region provided the energy for expansion and improvement. Expansion became the major business of the region, its reason for existence. Had the flow of population ceased or materially diminished, the consequences would have been as disastrous as a drought.

5. THE BOOM OF THE 'TWENTIES

In the decade 1920–1930, over 2,000,000 people moved into California, 72% of whom settled in Southern California, with Los Angeles County recording a gain of 1,272,037. The migration into Southern California in this decade has been characterized as the largest internal migration in the history of the American people. Less than 4% of these newcomers settled on farms; most of them came directly to the City of Los Angeles which reported a population increase of 661,375 or a gain of 114.7% for the decade. Eight new cities were created in Los Angeles County during this ten-year period. Incorporated in 1923, South Gate had a population of 19,632 by 1930. The present communities of Bell, Lynwood, Torrance, Hawthorne, Maywood, and Tujunga all came into existence after 1920. New cities and townships added 117,089 residents to the county in this decade.

The development of transcontinental automobile travel on all-weather highways had somewhat the same relation to the boom of the 'twenties that the completion of the Santa Fe line had to the boom of the 'eighties. The great migration into Southern California from 1920 to 1930 was, as Edwin Bates has pointed out, the first migration of the automobile age. In 1923 and 1924 a one-way stream of automobiles could be seen moving westward. "Like a swarm of invading locusts," wrote Mildred Adams, "migrants crept in over all the roads. . . . For wings, they had rattletrap automobiles, their fenders tied with string, and curtains flapping in the breeze; loaded with babies, bedding, bundles, a tin tub tied on behind, a bicycle or a baby carriage balanced precariously on the top. Often they came with no funds and no prospects, apparently trusting that heaven would provide for them. . . . They camped on the outskirts of town, and their camps became new suburbs."

Oil and motion pictures were important factors in attracting this great influx to Southern California. Oil production in the state had increased from 4,000,000 barrels in 1900 to 77,000,000 barrels in 1910, from 89,000,000 barrels in 1914 to 105,000,000 barrels in 1920. Production increased so rapidly during the first World War that pipe lines could not be constructed fast enough to handle the flow. The resulting increase in oil shipments from the Port of San Pedro brought about a meteoric rise in ocean trade and a vast expansion in harbor facilities. After the war, fabulously rich oil strikes were made in Southern California: at Huntington field in 1920; at Santa Fe

Springs and Signal Hill in 1921. By 1923 these three fields were producing, respectively, 113,000, 332,000, and 244,000 barrels a day, carrying the state's production for the year to 264,000,000 barrels.

Money from motion-picture production and payrolls, from the oil strikes, and the booming tourist trade touched off the real-estate boom of the 'twenties. Most of the great increase in population for the decade occurred between 1920 and 1924. What the gold rush had been to Northern California, this real-estate-oil-and-motion-picture boom was to Southern California. The great boom of the 'eighties had been spectacular, but it had been limited to land speculation. The boom of the 'twenties, on the other hand, was a truly bonanza affair. Millions of dollars in new income poured into Los Angeles, undermining the social structure of the community, warping and twisting its institutions, and ending in a debacle that was to shake the city to its foundations. For Southern California the decade was one long drunken orgy, one protracted debauch.

The boom of the 'twenties, however, was not entirely a spontaneous affair. One winter day in 1921, a lady marched into the office of Harry Chandler, publisher of the *Times*, and complained bitterly that apartment-house owners in Los Angeles prospered in the winter but starved in the summer. Couldn't something be done about it? Ever a man of action, Mr. Chandler called some of his colleagues together at a luncheon at the Alexandria Hotel. Out of this conference came the famous All-Year Club of Southern California, one of many remarkable new institutions that have emerged in the region. A private corporation, the All-Year Club is really a civic institution. For years it has received heavy appropriations from the County of Los Angeles. Like most organizations of the kind, the All-Year Club is forever "heating up the job" to justify its claims for larger appropriations; hence its figures must always be taken with a grain of salt. Even so, the club is close to the facts when it estimates that the tourist business is nowadays worth $200,000,000 a year to Southern California.

From the outset the club decided to use "Southern California" as its trademark. Prior to 1921, eastern newspapers and magazines had always referred to the land south of Tehachapi as southern California, never capitalizing the first word. But today this practice has been almost entirely discredited. Thanks to the All-Year Club, Southern California is now handled with all the courtesy due a forty-ninth state. For example, *Time* always writes Southern California, just as it does South Dakota. In its initial campaign for summer tourists, the All-Year Club selected the states of New Mexico, Arizona, Texas, and Oklahoma as the most likely areas in which to conduct the experiment (prior to 1920 the residents of Texas and Oklahoma had not been particularly interested in Southern California). Using the slogan, "Sleep under a blanket every night all summer in Southern California," the All-Year Club was able to announce, at the end of 1924, that the number of summer tourists equaled the number of winter tourists. An actual count of tourists was attempted for the first time in 1928, when the influx was estimated at 658,594, an increase of 400,000 over 1920. Like most promotions of the sort, the All-Year Club has been too successful. Its seductive advertisements were partially responsible for the great influx of impoverished Okies and Arkies in the 'thirties. Since 1929 its advertisements carry the caption: "Warning! Come to California for a glorious vacation. Advise anyone not to come seeking employment."

Nowadays Southern California is advertised as "a place of excitement," with much emphasis being placed on the race tracks at Santa Anita, Del Mar, and Hollywood Park. The club has become so confident of its propaganda that it even indulges in understatement. "Southern California," it says, "is *not* a paradise." A super-tourist agency, the club answers such questions as: When is the best time to visit Southern California? How long does it take? What is there to do and see? What should the tourist take with him in the way of clothing? What is the cost of a trip? In 1941 the summer tourist influx was estimated at 1,147,250, the winter influx at 722,364. According to the estimate of the club, tourists paid $19,000,000 in taxes in Southern California in 1941. Southern Californians are supposed to make a living by taking in each other's laundry. But it would be closer to the facts to say that they live off people from other sections of the country. While the summer tourists now outnumber the winter tourists, they only average 17.5 days in Southern California and spend a niggardly $196.54 per person. The winter tourists, with an average age-level of 42 years, stay 44.5 days and spend $356.16 per person. Nevertheless the stimulation of the summer tourist trade was an important factor in bringing about the great influx of the 'twenties, perhaps the last migration to be stimulated by community promotion in Southern California.

> *"Culture is the agent, the natural area the medium, the cultural landscape the result."*
>
> —Carl Sauer

CHAPTER VIII

THE CULTURAL LANDSCAPE

SOUTHERN California is a sharply defined region, not merely in the geographic sense, but in the sense that it is made up of people bound together by mutual dependencies arising from common interests. Today over 4,000,000 people reside in the region. Whenever man comes into a new region, he promptly modifies the natural landscape not, as Bowman has pointed out, "in a haphazard way but according to the culture system he brings with him." To understand the cultural landscape in Southern California, therefore, it is necessary to know something about these people. Where did they come from? What brought them to the region? From what environments, social classes, and ethnic groups did they come? Who were they anyway?

1. FROM THE ENDS OF THE EARTH

In studying Southern California a good working principle to keep in mind is that here everything is upside down. Reverse almost any proposition about the settlement of Western America and you are likely to have a sound generalization about the region. The earliest settlers, for example, came the greatest distances, while the latest newcomers have come from neighboring states. Since 1870 the areas from which settlers have been drawn have moved progressively closer. Not only did the first settlers travel the greatest distances, but the distance they traveled measured their cultural deviation from the American norm. The "pioneers" of Southern California came, not from Arizona or Colorado or Utah, but from China, Germany, France, Poland, and Great Britain. I have already discussed the Chinese and the Mexicans, but other foreign elements were also involved.

One of the first successful agricultural settlements in Southern California was established at Anaheim, in Orange County, by a colony of German settlers. At one time the colony was called Campo Aleman, the name later being changed to Anaheim, from the German "heim" or home, and Ana, a proper name. French immigrants constituted an exceedingly important element in Los Angeles during the 'sixties and 'seventies. Any number of French immigrants, most of them merchants, came to Southern California on the eve of the Franco-Prussian War. The names Docommun, Marchessault, Mesmer, Brunswig, and Christopher have remained important in Los Angeles to this day. Prudent Beaudry, a French-Canadian, was one of the early subdividers of Los Angeles, the developer of Angeleno Heights and Bunker Hill. Germain Pellissier operated a two-hundred-acre farm near Wilshire and Western. Remi Nadeau's herds of sheep once roamed over the Hollywood foothills. The curious chateau overlooking Valley Boulevard in Alhambra, noted by many visitors as a landmark, was built by Sylvestre Dupuy, a French immigrant. The artist Paul de Longpre settled in Hollywood in 1889. On arriving in Hollywood, he had traded three flower paintings for three acres of land near what is now the corner of Hollywood Boulevard and Cahuenga. Around the early merchants, a prosperous French colony developed in Los Angeles after 1870. There are today some 200,000 people of French descent in Southern California.

Following the Polish insurrection of 1863, a group of intellectuals, under the leadership of Karol Bozenta Chlapowski (husband of Madame Modjeska), founded a journal of opinion in Warsaw which they called Kraj (The Country). Most of the young writers and artists who sought to rally the forces of a badly demoralized Poland contributed to this journal and made the home of Chlapowski their gathering place. Among these young writers was Henryk Sienkiewicz. One winter evening in 1875, when "the circle" had gathered at the feet of Chlapowski, someone mentioned the forthcoming Centennial Exposition in America. Modjeska, in her memoirs, describes the reaction that this chance remark excited:

Sienkiewicz, with his vivid imagination, described the unknown country in most attractive terms. Maps were brought out and California discussed. It was worth while to hear the young men's various opinions about the Golden West: "You cannot die of hunger there, that is quite sure! Rabbits, hares, and partridges are unguarded. You have only to go out and shoot them!" "Yes," said another, "and fruits, too, are plenty! Blackberries and the fruit of the wild cactus grow wild, and they say the latter is simply delicious!" "Yes, everything is extraordinary!" sounded the reply. "Fancy, coffee grows wild there! All you have to do is to pick it; also pepper and castor-oil beans, and ever so many useful plants."

Plans were launched that evening to establish a Polish utopia in Southern California. So rapidly did the plans mature, that, in the spring of 1876, Sienkiewicz and Jules Synpiewski, an educational enthusiast, sailed for California by way of Panama. Months later Synpiewski returned to Poland with "glowing accounts of the beauties of California." Anaheim had been selected as a likely region for the new settlement because it had been colonized by Germans and most of the Poles spoke German. While Synpiewski was en route to Poland, Sienkiewicz obtained a position in Jacoby's store in Los Angeles as a ribbon clerk. In July, 1876, the Polish colonists sailed for Southern California: Synpiewski, his wife, and two children; L. Paprocki, "an amateur caricaturist"; Chlapowski, his wife (Modjeska), Ralph Modjeska, and the maid, Anusia.

It would be difficult to imagine a more exotic settlement than this tiny island of Polish culture in the Southern California of the 'seventies. "We presented a curious picture," wrote Modjeska, "for when we passed through the town [Anaheim], there was not one person in the streets that did not stop to take a look at our convoy." After investing $15,000 in the project, the Poles finally wearied of utopia, quarreled among themselves, and, in 1878, decided to return to Europe. But Southern California never lost its charm for Modjeska. In later years she built her famous "Arden" cottage, designed by Stanford White, in Santa Ana Canyon, where she lived for many years. The experience in Southern California had an important influence on Sienkiewicz. "It opened new vistas of life before him and had an enduring effect upon his psychological and literary development," writes one critic. The experience itself is reflected in four charming short stories: "Memories of Mariposa," "A Comedy of Errors," "The Lighthouse Keeper," and "Orso"—a little masterpiece. In later years, he also wrote a novel, *After Bread*, about Polish immigrant life in America, and a series of articles for the *Gazeta Polska* about Southern California which, alas, have never been translated.

Paderewski was a frequent visitor at Madame Modjeska's home in Santa Ana. While staying there in 1913, he was advised by his physician to visit the hot springs at Paso Robles. It happened that the physician he consulted in Paso Robles was, also, a realtor. One day when Paderewski was in the hot springs, up to his neck in mud, the physician induced him to buy a large ranch in the vicinity, the Rancho San Ignacio. As soon as he acquired the property, he began to make extensive improvements, planting two hundred and fifty acres to almonds, pears, and walnuts. It is not without interest to note that the world-famous pianist was one of the pioneer almond growers in the district. Today the Rancho San Ignacio has some twelve thousand almond trees.

In the 'seventies, all sorts of foreign nationalities were represented in Southern California: Basque sheep-herders; peasant vineyardists from France; Germans (Kohler, Frohling, Fleur, Coll); and German-Jewish merchants and bankers, such as Newmark, Kramer, Lazard, and Hellman, names well known in the financial history of California. Among the earliest settlers of Hollywood were a Danish sailor; two Germans; an English veteran of the Crimean War; a French sailor, José Mascarel; Manuel Andrada, a Spaniard; a Basque sheep-herder; a Prussian ex-cavalryman; and the son of a Mexican general. Peter Ramau, native of Hungary, ex-officer in the Austrian Army, had a beautiful show-place in early Los Angeles: two acres of anemones, verbenas, roses, heliotropes, pinks, forget-me-nots, and "tulips as large as tea-cups." Visited by all tourists of the period, his place was also famous as the home of hundreds of mocking birds. There were, also, many English remittance men in Southern California. Horace Vachell once said that "in addition to the family fool, the Englishmen to be found on the Pacific Slope include the parson's son, the fortune-teller, the moral idiot, the remittance man, and the sportsman." El Toro, in Orange County, was an English colony, and Santa Monica was a favorite winter resort of English tourists. The European influx to Southern California was stimulated by the publication of a travel-book by Ludwig Louis Salvator in 1878, *Eine Blume aus dem Goldenen Lande oder Los Angeles*, which had numerous printings.

Many amusing items about English tourists are to be found in the local annals. "The party of English gentlemen who left Santa Barbara a few days ago," wrote a local reporter, "are reported to be riding around Los Angeles with 17 valises, 6 pocket flasks, 21 demijohns, 3 repeating rifles, 12 mosquito nets, 5 alpaca dusters, 4 ulsters, 10 trunks, 3 plug hats, 6 lunch baskets, 8 umbrellas, 5 canes, 6 pairs of blankets, 12 pairs of rubber boots, but no other baggage worth mentioning." One of the early British settlers was Horace A. Vachell, the novelist. In 1882 Vachell bought a large cattle ranch near Arroyo Grande, a ranch which he later named Tally-Ho. There, for some years, he lived an indolent existence, riding through "pastures studded with oaks, thick chaparral, sun-soaked, care-free, alive to my toes," fishing at Port Harford for king salmon, halibut, and smelt. It was Vachell who first introduced polo on the Pacific Coast. He was forever being bantered by his neighbors about his polo ponies and his polo costume. "Say, Horus," one neighbor asked, "why do you wear your drawers outside your pants?" In odd moments, he wrote stories and sketches, selling his first short story, "Tiny," a tale of the San Luis Obispo foothills, to the *Pall Mall Gazette*. Later he returned to England where, as he said, he "rubbed off some California rugosities and pared the corns off." He once wrote a "comedietta" entitled *Cupid in California*; and his books, *Life and Sport on the Pacific Coast*, *Fellow-Travellers*, and *Distant Fields* contain much interesting information about Southern California.

Long before the Iowans invaded Southern California, these exotic Polish intellectuals, British remittance men, Chinese immigrants, Basque sheep-herders, French and German peasants, and German-Jewish merchants and financiers were on the scene. While most evidences of their presence have disappeared, or cannot be traced, the diverse origins of these "pioneers" contributed much toward the brisk development that had its first beginnings in the 'seventies. When Ludwig Louis Salvator visited Los Angeles, he reported that, of approximately 16,000 residents of the county, Americans, Europeans, and Californians (meaning Mexicans) were about equally divided. Commenting on the cosmopolitan nature of the region, he said that "on the streets of Los Angeles are heard spoken English, French,

Spanish, and German." One reason for the extinction of these cosmopolitan influences, of which few visible tokens remain, is that, after 1880, Southern California was engulfed by a tidal wave of American immigrants. It was not, in fact, until after 1900 that a "foreign coloration" again became apparent with the influx of Mexicans, Japanese, Filipinos, Yugoslavs, Russians, and other groupings.

2. Tourists and Troubadours

In the cultural history of Southern California an important distinction is to be observed between newcomers and tourists. Tourists travel, of course, for pleasure or culture, not to colonize or to settle. Ordinarily tourists do not leave much of an impression on the land, but in Southern California tourists have been important cultural carriers. In other areas, tourists have been late visitors, but here they were explorers and discoverers. The early tourists were an interesting lot: Britishers and Bostonians; butterfly-catchers and collectors of flora and fauna. As a matter of fact, the expression "tourist" is supposed to have originated in Southern California. Tourists were so unlike the ordinary travelers that, as Robert J. Burdette noted, "a new name had to be applied to them, and they were called 'tourists.'" Most of them came to subtropical California out of curiosity, with notebooks in their pockets, but many traveled in search of health. Many of the early tourists who came by boat stayed on for years or became "repeaters," or, as they were called, "old regulars," who returned winter after winter. After the completion of the railroads, the "old regulars" began to be augmented, as Stewart Edward White wrote, "by the professional tourists who abandoned Europe for a season to see this newly-talked-of land." Not only did the tourists stimulate the later mass migrations, but they left an imprint on the land.

The tourist hotel was an important institution in early Southern California. By 1890 the region was honeycombed with a network of these unique hostelries, some of which became world-famous and were, in their own right, a major attraction for tourists and newcomers. In the 'seventies, the society of the towns, the ranches, and the tourist hotels was strangely intermingled. The tourist hotel gave a curious urban overtone of sophistication to a number of rural areas outside Los Angeles. Today Southern California is the most highly urbanized section of California: a third of the population of the region live within a hundred-mile radius of the City Hall in Los Angeles. But a few rural areas have retained more pronounced urban characteristics than the metropolitan center of Los Angeles, which still possesses a distinctly rural coloration.

The most famous of the early tourist hotels was the Arlington, built in Santa Barbara in 1876 by Col. W. W. Hollister. The Arlington was an elegant establishment for such a dusty, unkempt village as Santa Barbara was in 1876. Each of its ninety rooms had a fireplace and marble mantel, running water and gaslight, and the rooms connected with the office by an "annunciator," or speaking-tube. Under the management of Capt. Dixey W. Thompson, the Arlington was one of the first hotels in America to plan elaborate entertainment for its guests. The tireless "Captain Dixey," as he was known to thousands of tourists, organized picnics, tally-ho excursions, flora-and-fauna expeditions, hunting trips, surf-bathing parties, and all sorts of excursions. Located in a region which was itself separated from the rest of the country by "a zone of exotic experience," the Arlington was a rare exotic, a sport, a freak of the landscape. Around the hotel, there developed in Santa Barbara a social life that was neither fashionable nor rustic, neither rural nor urban, neither Eastern nor Western.

Equally famous was the Raymond Hotel which opened in Pasadena in 1886. For some years before the hotel was opened, Walter Raymond, of the Boston travel agency of Raymond & Whitcomb, had been bringing excursion parties to California. On land donated by the railroad, Raymond built a superb hotel in Pasadena which, for years, was operated in conjunction with the Crawford House in the White Mountains which was owned by the same agency. Since the railroad stopped opposite the entrance to the Raymond, excursion parties could be taken "directly from a snow storm in Boston, and, a few days later, find themselves in a Boston hotel in Pasadena." A palatial establishment, the Raymond was equipped with gas and electric lights, tennis courts, swings, playgrounds, bowling alleys, rustic gardens, and spacious grounds. Built on a fifty-five acre knoll tract, it could be seen, when it was first built, for a distance of twenty-five miles. Like the Arlington, it planned an elaborate round of entertainment for its guests. The well-known naturalist, Charles Frederick Holder, was retained as a guide for flora-and-fauna expeditions. For the children, there were Shetland ponies to ride; for the oldsters, carriages and tally-ho coaches; and, for old and young, a large orchestra. In the first year it was opened, the Raymond welcomed 35,000 guests. Its balls and parties were famous wherever tourists gossiped about their travels. In effect, it was a community-within-a-community. When the California season opened in October, the Raymonds moved their entire staff of several hundred employees from the White Mountains to Pasadena. Thoroughly Bostonian in atmosphere, the management of the hotel arranged for busses to drive up on Sunday morning, while the doorman announced: "Presbyterians this way; Episcopalians here; Methodists in the blue bus; Unitarians along here; Congregationalists this way."

The most beautiful of the tourist hotels, however, was the Hotel del Coronado, built on a five-acre tract on Coronado Beach, across the bay from San Diego. Designed by James W. Reid and Merritt Reid, two "railroad architects" of Evansville, Indiana, the Hotel del Coronado opened on February 19, 1888. Over three hundred employees were imported from the East to operate this luxurious establishment. According to Charles Dudley Warner, there was no hotel in the world "that so surprised at first or improved on acquaintance or that left an impression so agreeable." Every room in the hotel opened on a patio or the ocean. Its mammoth dining room, beautifully paneled in wood, covered a floor area of 10,000 feet, without pillar or post. "Airy, picturesque, and half-bizarre," writes Edmund Wilson, "it is the most magnificent example extant of the American seaside hotel as it flourished in that era on both coasts. White and ornate as a wedding-cake, clean, polished and trim as a ship, it makes a monument not unworthy to dominate the last blue concave dent in the shoreline before the United States gives way to Mexico." Shortly after the hotel was completed, it was purchased by John D. Spreckles, a major booster of San Diego. Through the years it has retained its charm and grace.

By 1900 all of Southern California was dotted with hotels of this variety: not so elegant as the Hotel del Coronado, not so comfortable as the Arlington, not so full of social activity as the Raymond; but spacious, clean, attractive hotels. Redlands had the Casa Loma; Santa Monica, the Hotel Arcadia; Riverside, the Mission Inn; Pasadena, the Pintoresca, the Green, and the Maryland (in addition to the Raymond); Monrovia, the Grand View; San Diego, the Horton House; and Sierra Madre, the Sierra Madre Villa, "the first Southern

California hotel whose fame extended to all parts of the world." There were also numerous roadside inns, country taverns, and "invalid hotels" with mineral baths and hot springs.

With the construction of the Potter House in Santa Barbara in 1901, the tourist hotel, as such, was succeeded by the modern luxury hotel. The Potter House had polo grounds, croquet grounds, tennis courts, a golf course, squash-ball courts, bowling alleys, billiard and card rooms, and a concert hall. It catered not to "tourists" but to "exclusive people." At a later date it was followed in Santa Barbara by the El Mirasol, the El Encanto, the Miramar, the Samarkand, and the Biltmore. It will be noted that most of the luxury hotels are located outside Los Angeles, but, so thoroughly integrated is the region, that these hotels are really part of the life of Los Angeles.

In large part, the early tourist influx and the tourist hotels account for the breakdown between urban and rural distinctions in the region. They account for the curiously incongruous spectacle of Shakespeare Clubs, oratorio societies, lecture forums, and academies of science in a region that was still in its frontier phase. They were responsible for the circumstance that, in Southern California, "Boston culture over-lapped the *dolce far niente* of the Mexican." At a time when roaring Tombstone was at its bawdiest, it is a little shocking to read of Professor Coe lecturing throughout Southern California on Joan of Arc, Cromwell, Queen Mary, and Haroun al Raschid, and to note the appearance, in rural areas, of societies set up to study mineralogy, geology, conchology, and archaeology. The tourist hotel is a key to this curiously mixed social scene. At the turn of the century, as Sarah Comstock has written, "Los Angeles, coupled with Pasadena, was the least 'western' community in the United States." As one woman said, "they out-East the East." Today most of the Bostonian veneer is confined to the outlying communities, but, at one time, the entire region was covered with a film of elegance. Paradoxically, Southern California's genteel period came first. The frontier phase did not develop until the decade 1920–1930 when the boys began to shoot up the town.

Just as the railroads had a hand in the establishment of the tourist hotels, so they were responsible for the first cultural expression in Southern California. They brought the troubadours to the Southland. Not only did they finance numerous art exhibits, magazines, and publications, but they subsidized artists, writers, and novelists.

The Southern Pacific brought Charles Nordhoff, then on the staff of the New York *Tribune*, to California. Made up of articles which he had previously published in *Harper's*, his book *California For Health, Pleasure and Residence* (1873) put Southern California on the map. Well known for his studies of the reconstruction period and of communistic societies in the United States, Nordhoff lived for many years in Southern California, where he died, at Coronado Beach, on July 14, 1901.

From 1879 to 1890, Major Ben C. Truman was "chief of the literary bureau of the Southern Pacific," an agency responsible for a dozen or more books about the region. The well-known writer Charles Dudley Warner was another Southern Pacific troubadour. The Southern Pacific also retained Alice M. Williamson, a popular novelist of the 'nineties, to write a novel about Southern California. En route to California, she was met by Charles Field, editor of *Sunset* magazine (owned by the Southern Pacific), and shown the various scenic spots which she was instructed to use as the locale of the novel. Apparently rather a naïve person, Mrs. Williamson wanted to include Grand Canyon in the novel, but Mr. Field reminded her that the Grand Canyon was on the route of the Santa Fe and must, therefore, be excluded. The novel in question, *Port of Adventure* (1913), is a cleverly disguised travel book, illustrated with photographs, and with most of the action taking place in the parlor cars of the Southern Pacific. Not to be outdone by the Southern Pacific, the Santa Fe brought numerous novelists and writers to Southern California and for years subsidized the work of such artists as Fernand Lungren.

Collaborating with the railroad troubadours were the public-relations personnel of the tourist hotels. Charles Frederick Holder, of Lynn, Massachusetts, the author of a life of Darwin and a life of Agassiz, was brought to Pasadena in 1885 by the Raymond Hotel. For years Holder kept up a steady stream of books, articles, and feature stories about Southern California. He organized the first Tournament of Roses in Pasadena in 1889. He was also responsible for the development of the sport of deep-sea fishing off the Southern California coast. The first man to catch a tuna with a fishing rod, he founded the Tuna Club in 1898, with headquarters on Santa Catalina Island and a membership scattered throughout the world. A first-rate naturalist, his book, *The Channel Islands of California* (1910), was a substantial contribution to the knowledge of the region.

Still another troubadour of the period was the Englishman, George Wharton James, who came to Southern California in 1881. For many years, James traveled about the region as an itinerant Methodist clergyman. But in 1889 he was involved in a personal crisis, characterized by his biographer as "more than physical," and left the church. From then until his death in 1923, he was one of the most tireless, prolific, and careless publicists the region has ever known. Over forty volumes flowed from his pen, most of them about Southern California, and no one has ever dared to list his magazine articles. He, like Holder, was a tourist-hotel troubadour, the editor of the Mt. Lowe *Echo*. In no small measure, he was responsible for the rediscovery of the Missions and the extravagant ballyhoo about Ramona. His Thursday evening soirees in Pasadena were for years a great attraction for the culture-seeking tourists.

The most fantastic troubadour of the period, however, was the scientist, Thaddeus Sobreski Coulincourt Lowe. Taking off from Cincinnati during the Civil War, in one of the first balloon ascensions in America, "Professor" Lowe drifted far off his course and landed near Charleston, South Carolina, dressed in formal evening attire. A little puzzled about this curiously dressed Man from Mars, the Confederates finally gave him a pass through their lines to the Union Army. On reaching Washington, he got President Lincoln interested in the idea of using balloons for observation work and spent the balance of the Civil War spying on the Confederate armies from the skies. Coming to Southern California in 1888, he designed and built the Mt. Lowe Railway, a cable line that ran from a point near Pasadena to the top of Mt. Lowe.

Once the line was constructed, Professor Lowe built two hotels on top the mountain: the Chalet (or Alpine Inn) and the Echo Mountain House. Not satisfied with this grandiose achievement, he proposed to build still another hotel, farther up the mountain, and to establish an institute for the study of pure science on a nearby peak. The site for the proposed hotel, which was never built, would have had to be carved out of solid granite. He also designed a plan by which he could operate a swinging cable railway from the hotels on Mt. Lowe across a vast gorge to the proposed hotel. His plans called for the excavation of an underground temple "to surpass in grandeur and impressiveness the temples of the Caves of Elephanta." These rich fancies were never realized for poor Professor Lowe got caught in the panic of 1893, but for twenty-five years, "the trip of a lifetime," up Mt. Lowe, was a major tourist attraction.

While the institute of pure science was never realized, Lowe did build an astronomical observatory which later became the present Mt. Wilson Observatory where important scientific discoveries have been recorded. A sadly neglected figure in the cultural history of the region, Lowe made one extremely important contribution. It seems fairly well authenticated that he worked out the first plans for the use of artificial ice for commercial purposes, notably for the icing of refrigerator cars. In fact, he is supposed to have designed the first refrigerator car, a development of vast importance in a region producing perishable fruits for shipment to distant markets.

Still another troubadour of the period was Charles Fletcher Lummis. Walking across the continent in 1885, he was greeted at El Monte by General Harrison Gray Otis who, in the spirit of the occasion, marched out from Los Angeles to meet him. For a period editor of the Los Angeles *Times*, Lummis took over the magazine, *The Land of Sunshine*, shortly after it was founded in 1894. For many years the magazine, another subsidized venture, was the principle medium of cultural expression in Southern California, numbering among its regular contributors David Starr Jordan, Mary Hallock Foote, John Vance Cheney, Edwin Markham, Ina Coolbrith, Mary Austin, Frederick Webb Hodge, T. S. Van Dyke, and Charles Dwight Willard. It was the Harvard-educated Lummis who discovered the Southwest for American culture. In numerous books, articles, and magazine pieces he strenuously proclaimed the doctrine that the center of American culture was destined to shift westward. Around his residence in Highland Park, the first artist colony in Southern California developed. The artist William Lees Judson, and such writers as Idah Meachan Strobidge, Mary Austin, and Will Levington Comfort lived, for a time, in this colony. Later the district became a center of dry sentiment, the only Southern California area ever to send a prohibitionist to Congress. And, for some reason, it still retains a strong Presbyterian orientation.

Unlike other areas, Southern California received its initial cultural expression from newcomers especially imported for this precise purpose. Not only were they imported for the purpose of describing the wonders of the region in print and on canvas, but many of them saw the region through glasses colored by subsidies. While some of them

did excellent work, they also succeeded in confusing the residents
of the region and a later generation of artists and writers with their
railroad and tourist-hotel impressions of the land. They were also a
factor in creating that early Bostonian atmosphere, traces of which
can still be detected in such communities as Pasadena.

3. The Rich Came First

*"Los Angeles could never have accomplished the feat of get-
ting that way by a slow and gradual growth. Rather, it is the
result of several inundations which have stratified like lava."*
—Sarah Comstock

Curiously enough, the vanguard of the great army of American settlers who began to descend on Southern California after 1880 was
made up, for the most part, of fairly well-to-do people. This was
particularly true of those who settled in the country areas outside
Los Angeles. Not only was this initial wave of migrants socially and
economically unlike the usual frontier influx, but it was sharply in
contrast with the type of settlers who had flocked to Northern California, forty years earlier, at the time of the gold rush. As Charles
Fletcher Lummis once said, the gold-rush influx represented Sheer
Adventure, while the Southern California invasion represented Reasoned Migration. The first was of men; the second, of families. Gold
lured the one group; oranges and climate the other. The early American immigrants to Southern California were, as Lummis said, "the
least heroic migration in history, but the most judicious; the least
impulsive but the most reasonable. They brought far less muscle than
their predecessors, and have developed far less, but in 'sinews' they
were far better supplied. In fact they were, by and large, by far the
most comfortable immigrants, financially, in history. . . . Instead of
by Shank's Mare, or prairie schooner, or reeking steerage, they came
on palatial trains; instead of cabins they put up beautiful homes;
instead of gophering for gold, they planted gold—and it came up in
ten-fold harvest."

Generally speaking, the first wave of American migration to the
region was made up of the well-to-do, the second of people in medium circumstances (1900–1920), the third of lower middle-class
elements (1920–1930), and the fourth of working-class people (1930
to 1945). Reversing the process of western settlement, each successive wave of migrants to Southern California has been made up,

in the main, of people less important economically and socially than the one which preceded it. And the basic explanation of this curious reversal of the pattern of migration is that people have always been attracted to Southern California for other reasons than to better their economic position.

"One noteworthy feature of the incoming population," wrote J. P. Widney in 1888, "is that it is made up almost entirely of the well-to-do—those who bring intelligence and money with them, and are prepared to improve their lands at once." The fact that so many of these people were possessed of ample means made possible a rapid development of the region and accounts for the curious circumstance that Southern California skipped the frontier phase altogether, or passed through it with such astonishing swiftness that it left few marks on the cultural landscape. "They are men with more or less means," wrote another observer in 1883, "some maybe rich, and nearly all in comfortable circumstances."

Many of these early settlers were people of enterprise, talent, intellect, and culture. "They had civic vision," writes Owen H. O'Neill, "and they brought wealth into the country to give it realization." The strata of people of means was paradoxically more noticeable in rural than in urban communities in Southern California. To these rural areas they brought, as one observer noted, "the social elements in which they were reared, their religious principles, temperance habits, education, and the refinements of civilized life." Unlike the typical Western settler, not many of the early immigrants were farmers. "Ordinarily the men who reclaim a land," to quote from a tourist book of 1883, "subdue nature, and lay the foundations of new communities are a hardy and muscular race; quite different from these were the pioneers of Southern California. The greatest number of them came from the stores, counting-houses, shops, and offices of their homes in the eastern states. Lawyers, who had fled the stifling air of the courtroom, and the dusty tomes of their libraries; physicians; and others unused to manual toil, comprised almost altogether the people who here took upon themselves the labor and privations of founding a new community."

Judge John Wesley North, who founded the town of Riverside, may be taken as an interesting example of this type of early settler. He had been chairman of the Minnesota delegation to the Republican Convention of 1860 where he first met Lincoln. Later he became a close friend of Lincoln's. In fact, Lincoln appointed him, first, Surveyor-General of Nevada, and, later, Chief Justice of the Territorial Supreme Court. Judge North presided at the constitutional convention in Nevada and is said to have written the state's constitution. An ardent anti-slavery man, he established an iron foundry in Knoxville after the war, as a means of helping the recently emancipated slaves. It was from Knoxville that he sent out the call for colonists to found the Riverside colony in 1870. Long before he came to California, however, he had founded a number of communities in Minnesota. Judge North was a man of wide experience, considerable means, and a gifted organizer.

Of this same type of settler were the famous Smiley twins, Albert Keith Smiley and Alfred Homans Smiley. Educated at Haverford College, they had remained on after their graduation in 1849 as instructors of English and Mathematics. In later years, they purchased a thousand-acre tract fronting on Lake Mohonk in New York and made over an old inn on the premises as a handsome country hotel. It was here that the well-known Lake Mohonk Conferences on Indian affairs were held for so many years. In 1879, President Hayes appointed Albert Keith Smiley to the board of Indian commissioners on which he served until his death. In fact, it was his interest in Indians that first brought him to California in 1889 as chairman of a committee to select lands for the Mission Indians. The Smiley twins were men of great wealth, national reputation, and considerable social distinction.

Deciding to make Redlands their home, they purchased a two-hundred-acre tract on a hillside back of the town overlooking San Bernardino Valley, on the one side, and San Timeteo Canyon, on the other—one of the most magnificent sites in Southern California. Then they proceeded to make Cañon Crest Park, or Smiley Heights as it was later known, into one of the great show-places of the West. The shrubs, trees, plants, and flowers in this park came from all over the world: from South America, Africa, the islands of the Pacific, Australia, Japan, India, Persia, and Ceylon. Over a thousand varieties of trees and shrubs were planted in the park: forty varieties of the eucalyptus; twenty of acacias; fifteen types of palms; and a host of exotic shrubs, flowers, "tropical plants, bamboo, and sweet-scented vines." For years the Southern Pacific Company advertised the park as one of the "scenic wonders" of Southern California. Tourist trains stopped at Redlands while parties went for a trip through Smiley Heights. At one time, an electric trolley ran between the Casa Loma Hotel, in Redlands, and Smiley Heights. To the City of Redlands, the Smileys gave a library of 10,000 volumes, a $60,000 park, and Smiley Heights itself. Today Smiley Heights has been closed to the public; the City of Redlands does not know what to do with this magnificent tract. Albert Keith Smiley, a "pioneer" settler of Redlands, was a trustee of Brown University, Bryn Mawr, and Pomona College.

Many of the communities founded by these enterprising first settlers in Southern California were laid out with streets, sidewalks, curbs, a water supply, churches, schools, and not infrequently a college, before they were opened for general settlement. Stepping from comfortable transcontinental trains, the incoming migrants were ushered into an urban existence almost as pretentious as that which they had left in the East. Redlands, for example, was colonized by wealthy Chicago families and was known as the Chicago Colony. By the turn of the century, Redlands and Santa Barbara had begun to attract millionaires rather than "people of means." An item from the Santa Barbara press (1893) laconically notes that "millionaires were pretty thick about here last Saturday and Sunday," referring to the arrival from New York, in a special train, of a party which included Cornelius Vanderbilt, Chauncey Depew, John Hone, and W. K. Vanderbilt. The next year, W. K. Vanderbilt returned in a special train of five cars, one of which was "the handsomest palace car ever built." After 1900 Montecito became a rich man's colony, with the arrival of the Bliss, Peabody, Armour, McCormick, and other families, and such chronic socialites as H. Chatfield-Taylor.

The curious distribution of millionaires in Southern California, in specialized communities as Santa Barbara, Montecito, Pasadena, and Redlands, has led even such an astute observer as J. Russell Smith into the error of believing that "social stratification" is almost nonexistent in the region. Obviously Mr. Smith has never toured the real gold coast. No more striking examples of social stratification than Santa Barbara and Redlands can be found in America. Montecito and the hillsides above Santa Barbara are known to the townspeople as "the butler belt," while in Redlands social rating is clearly marked by altitude. The heights of the town are occupied by the extremely wealthy, between the heights and the lowlands live the well-to-do townspeople, below the middle-class townspeople are the lower middle-class residents, and still farther down the slope, and across the tracks, are the Negro domestics and the Mexican field workers. "The peculiarly proud spirit of this people," wrote Harold Bell Wright of Redlands (*The Eyes of the World*, 1914), "is undoubtedly explained by this happy arrangement which enables every one to look down upon his neighbor."

4. George Chaffee and the Colony Settlements

Something of the character of these early settlers, and their characteristic institution "the colony settlement," can be illustrated by brief reference to the career of a remarkable man, George Chaffee. Born in Canada in 1848, Chaffee came to Riverside with his family in 1878. Entirely self-educated, he had shown remarkable engineering talent as a young man, having designed twenty passenger and freight ships for the Great Lakes traffic before coming to California. It was Chaffee who first made irrigation a science in Southern California and who first discovered the remarkable adaptability of the terrain to irrigation. In partnership with his brother, Chaffee purchased a 2,500-acre tract near Riverside in 1881 on which he established his first colony settlement. The colony was called Etiwanda, after an Indian chief of the Great Lakes region. Dividing the land into ten-acre blocks, Chaffee brought water to the tract in cement pipes: the first use of cement pipes in western irrigation. In connection with this same project, Chaffee installed the first dynamo (which he himself designed) for the generation of hydroelectric power in the West. He was also the first engineer in Western America to file a claim on mountain streams for electric current. Bringing this current to the tract, he used it to illuminate a great arc light, or beacon, which he had placed on the roof of his home. This light, which could be seen for miles, was the first electric light to be exhibited in California. An immediate success, Etiwanda has remained a prosperous community through the years.

It was in connection with the Etiwanda project that Chaffee, working in collaboration with L. M. Holt, a local newspaperman, devised a method by which the riparian-rights doctrine could be circumvented in California. The pattern of legal relationships which he worked out, in the form of the mutual water company, has remained a basic pattern for all subsequent irrigation developments in the West. The idea was quite simple. When the Etiwanda tract was acquired, Chaffee formed a water company incorporated under the laws of the state. To this company he then transferred all the water rights which each portion of the land possessed under the riparian-rights doctrine, together with the rights which he had acquired by appropriation. He then transferred one share of stock in the mutual water company to each purchaser. This arrangement had the important consequence of making each landowner in the tract equally interested in the conservation of water and its proper utilization. In most irrigated projects, the owners of the lands nearest the stream-head had either monopolized the flow or refused to do their share of work on irrigation laterals and canals. By first severing the water rights from the land and then collectivizing the ownership and control of the water, Chaffee had created a system which automatically insured equality of treatment and service in irrigation projects. Unquestionably the mutual water company represents one of the major social inventions of the West.

Following the success of the Etiwanda project, Chaffee acquired a 6,000-acre tract on which he proceeded to establish his famous Ontario Colony, named after his native province in Canada. From the point of view of social planning, the Ontario Colony of 1882 still remains the classic pattern for irrigation projects. In fact, it set a new standard for rural communities, not only in America, but throughout the world. All the basic improvements were installed before a single parcel of land was sold. The land was carefully divided into economical units; streets were laid out; provision was made for a community center or town to which all portions of the tract had equal access. Through the center of the tract, Chaffee laid out a great highway, eight miles long and two hundred feet wide, running up to the foothills. On each side of the highway, he planted rows of beautiful trees which are today a magnificent sight. In a parkway in the center of the highway, he installed a gravity-propelled tram or trolley car which ran the length of the tract. For the community center, Chaffee set aside 640 acres, one half of which was deeded to trustees for the endowment of the Chaffee Agricultural College (operated today as a junior college). To supplement the water supply, he tunneled under the bed of San Antonio Canyon on the theory that the dry creek-beds marked the pathway of underground streams. This was the first tunnel constructed to tap an underground flow in Southern California.

To make sure that the colonists were a thrifty and pious lot, he inserted a provision against the sale of alcoholic liquor in every deed that he issued.

Ontario was instantly a huge success. A model of the colony was exhibited at the St. Louis World's Fair in 1904. People came from all over the world to study Chaffee's methods of colonization. By 1907 the annual value of agricultural products raised on the Ontario tract had risen to $2,500,000. It should be emphasized that Ontario was a pioneer experiment in rural planning, one of the first experiments of its kind in Western America. It was the model imitated by the other colony projects. While none of the other colonies were quite as successful as Ontario, they did succeed, by studying the model, in avoiding the usual mistakes of frontier settlement.

On the invitation of a royal commission, Chaffee later established a number of colonies in Australia. In 1884 he founded the Los Angeles Electric Company, making it possible for Los Angeles to boast that it was the first city in the United States to be entirely lighted by electricity. Returning from Australia after the turn of the century, Chaffee developed the remarkable irrigation plan by which water was brought to Imperial Valley, a plan that converted 500,000 acres of desert land into one of the great truck gardens of the world. To this early generation of settlers, of which North, Chaffee, and the Smiley twins may be taken as outstanding examples, Southern California owes an enormous debt. Men of wealth and ability, they came west not to retire but to build a new land. All visitors to the region between 1880 and 1900 were impressed by its progressive, enterprising, venturesome spirit. It is impossible to detect in these impressions even an echo of the idea, so current in our time, that Southern California is peopled by idlers, oldsters, playboys, and crackpots.

5. The Boosters

The first wave of migration brought wealth, enterprise, and culture to Southern California; the next great wave brought cunning, shrewdness, and calculation. It brought the boosters and go-getters who proceeded to capitalize upon the foundations laid by the Norths, Chaffees, and Smileys. "The awakening after 1900," writes Willard, "came largely through new men, some to the manor born and some with eastern capital that they were not afraid to invest." One notes from the annals the arrival of Henry Huntington in 1891; of Eli P.

Clark in 1891; of M. H. Sherman in 1889; of William May Garland in 1890; of Harry Chandler in 1888; of John D. Spreckles in 1889; of E. L. Doheny in 1890; and of General Harrison Gray Otis in 1882. These were the men who, about 1890, began to organize Southern California as one of the greatest promotions the world has ever known. With few exceptions, these boosters were all newcomers to the region. In the local annals, it is not the Norths, Chaffees, and Smileys who are referred to as "empire builders," but rather these promoters who came in after the groundwork had been laid and reaped the harvest that others had sown. Most of the boosters arrived in Southern California shortly after the boom of 1887 had collapsed and on the eve of the boom of 1906 which they, in large measure, organized.

After 1900 the tide of immigrants to Southern California was increasingly made up of people of moderate means who came west to retire, to take it easy rather than to have a good time. As the type of immigrant changed, the character of the region itself began to change. From 1850 to 1870 Los Angeles was "the toughest town in the nation," but it became the most priggish community in America after 1900. A glacial dullness engulfed the region. Every consideration was subordinated to the paramount concern of attracting church-going Middle Westerners to Southern California. In 1896 the gambling houses were closed in Los Angeles and, a few years later, the saloons were required to close on Sundays. By 1906 the number of saloons was restricted to two hundred, and Los Angeles began to boast that it had more churches than any city of comparable size in America. In 1922 San Francisco voted against a prohibition measure by 91,000 "no" votes to 32,000 "yes" votes, but Los Angeles, the home of the vineyard industry, cast 143,000 "yes" votes and 84,000 "no" votes. Over the years, the mores of Los Angeles have undergone similarly swift changes reflecting the changing character of the immigrants to the region.

By 1913 Willard Huntington Wright could explain in *The Smart Set* that the character of Los Angeles had been formed by the "rural pietist obsessed with the spirit of village fellowship, of suburban respectability. . . . Hypocrisy, like a vast fungus, has spread over the city's surface. . . . During the early morning hours no frou-frou of silk disturbs the sepulchral silence of the streets. You will look in vain for the flashing eye, the painted cheek, the silken ankle. No yellow-haired Laises haunt the dark doorways of the down-town thoroughfares. The city's lights go out at twelve, and so does the drummer's hope. . . . The current belief in Los Angeles is that there is something inherently and inalienably indecent (or at least indelicate) in that segment of the day between 12 midnight and 5 A.M. Therefore these five hours constitute a gloomy hiatus, a funereal void, a sad and intolerable interregnum. And there is a good old medieval superstition afloat in Los Angeles that all those things which charm by their grace and beauty are wiles of the devil, and that only those things are decent which are depressing. Hence, the recent illumination and guarding of all public parks lest spooning, that lewd pastime, become prevalent. Hence, the Quakerish regulation of the public dance halls. Hence, a stupid censorship so incredibly puerile that even Boston will have to take second place. Hence, the silly legal pottering about the proper length of bathing suits at the beaches, the special election to decide whether or not one should be permitted to eat in saloons, and the fiery discussion as to the morality of displaying moving pictures of boxing matches. Los Angeles is overrun with militant moralists, connoisseurs of sin, experts of biological purity."

This development, he noted, was due to the fact that "the inhabitants of Los Angeles are culled largely from the smaller cities of the Middle West—'leading citizens' from Wichita; honorary pall-bearers from Emmetsburg; Good Templars from Sedalia; honest spinsters from Grundy Center—all commonplace people, many of them with small competencies made from the sale of farm lands or from the life-long savings of small mercantile business. These good folks brought with them a complete stock of rural beliefs, pieties, superstitions, and habits—the Middle West bed hours, the Middle West love of corned beef, the church bells, *Munsey's* magazine, union suits and missionary societies. They brought also a complacent and intransigent aversion to late dinners, malt liquors, grand opera and hussies. They still retain memories of the milk can, the newmown hay, the Chautauqua lecturers, the plush albums, the hamlet devotions, the weekly baths. There are other evidences in Los Angeles of the village spirit. There is her large and inextinguishable army of quid-nuncs. Everyone is interested in everyone else. Snooping is the popular pastime, gossiping the popular practice. Privacy is impossible. This village democracy naturally invades the social life of Los Angeles." It should be noted that this transformation occurred in the middle period in the growth of Los Angeles, a period usually marked in the growth of large cities by the rise of industry, the arrival of foreign immigrants, and the spread of tenderloin districts. But the evolution of Los Angeles has never followed the general pattern. The more it grew in population between 1900 and 1920 the more it resembled a village.

Knowing nothing of the land, these villagers brought with them, as Stewart Edward White phrased it, "the mode of existence they learned elsewhere, and have not the imagination to transcend." "They often live," wrote Charles Stoddard in 1894, "in isolated communities, continuing their own customs, languages, and religious habits and associations." In the process of settlement, they reverted to former practices and built, not a city, but a series of connecting villages. They wanted homes, not tenements, and homes meant villages. The grouping of the houses and the use of land was not determined by industrial considerations, for there was little industry. The ex-villagers gave Los Angeles its squat appearance, its flattened-out form. Fear of earthquakes had brought about, at an early date, an ordinance limiting the height of buildings, but it was really this home-owning impulse that spread Los Angeles into its present fabulous proportions. The villagers and farmers from the plains of the Middle West wanted to build their homes on the flatlands. As a consequence the march of homes after 1900 moved swiftly past the attractive hillsides and spread west and south across the plains. Beautiful sites, such as Mount Washington and the Elysian Park district, were abandoned and never revived, as the flatlanders began to arrive by the thousands.

After 1920 a new heterogeneous tide of migrants brought still further cultural changes to Los Angeles. The motion-picture industry attracted odd and freakish types: dwarfs, pygmies, one-eyed sailors, showpeople, misfits, and 50,000 wonder-struck girls. The easy money of Hollywood drew pimps, gamblers, racketeers, and confidence men. The increasing fame of Southern California lured much of the wealth of the Coolidge prosperity to the region. The settled wealth of the great packing-house, plumbing, plate-glass, automobile, and agricultural implement families descended on Pasadena and Santa Barbara, while the parvenu element built up Hollywood and Beverly Hills. While many wealthy people came with this wave of migration, a majority of the migrants were lower middle class: the *lumpenprole-*

tariat of Los Angeles, the Okies of Bell Gardens, the Arkies of Monterey Park. And the steady flow of retired Middle Westerners continued.

By 1925 Los Angeles was still, as Louis Adamic has said, "the enormous village," but it had begun to change. "The people on the top in Los Angeles, the Big Men," he wrote, "are the business men, the Babbitts. They are the promoters, who are blowing down the city's windpipe with all their might, hoping to inflate the place to a size that will be reckoned the largest city in the country—in the world. . . . These men are the high priests of the Chamber of Commerce whose religion is Climate and Profits. They are—some of them —grim, inhuman individuals with a great terrifying singleness of purpose. They see a tremendous opportunity to enrich themselves beyond anything they could have hoped for ten or even five years ago, and they mean to make the most of it. . . . And trailing after the big boys is a mob of lesser fellows . . . thousands of minor realtors, boomers, promoters, contractors, agents, salesmen, bunko-men, office-holders, lawyers, and preachers—all driven by the same motives of wealth, power, and personal glory. . . . They exploit the 'come-ons' and one another, envy the big boys, their wives gather in women's clubs, listen to swamis and yogis and English lecturers, join 'love cults' and Coue clubs in Hollywood and Pasadena, and their children jazz and drink and rush around in roadsters. Then there are the Folks. . . . they are the retired farmers, grocers, Ford agents, hardware merchants, and shoe merchants from the Middle West and other parts of the United States, thousands and tens of thousands of them. . . . They sold out their farms and businesses in the Middle West or wherever they used to live, and now they are here in California—sunny California—to rest and regain their vigor, enjoy climate, look at pretty scenery, live in little bungalows with a palm-tree or banana plant in front, and eat in cafeterias. Toil-broken and bleached out, they flock to Los Angeles, fugitives from the simple, inexorable justice of life, from hard labor and drudgery, from cold winters and blistering summers of the prairies."

With the increasing industrialization of Los Angeles after 1920, and notably after 1940, came still another tide of migrants: Negroes from the Deep South, industrial workers from the Middle West and East and Far West, sharecroppers from Oklahoma and farm-hands from Texas. They were younger, had less means, and were far more malleable than the waves of migrants who had preceded them. By 1940 Los Angeles began to assume the form and structure of a city—159 years after its founding. Migrants began to be fitted into various niches and pigeon holes, to be sorted out by the processes of an urban industrial community. The village began to disappear and the city, at long last, to emerge.

6. THE SHIFT IN ORIGIN

The changing character of the stream of migration to Southern California is, perhaps, most strikingly indicated by the gradual westward shift of the point of origin. At first New York and the New England states were heavily represented in the migration to Southern California. A great many early settlers came from Maine. The founders of the great Limoneira Company (one of the largest citrus farms in the world), N. W. Blanchard, Wallace I. Hardison, and C. C. Teague, were all born in Maine. People born in Maine, New Hampshire, Vermont, and Massachusetts represented a sizable portion of the total residents of Los Angeles in the census of 1880, 1890, and 1900. At each of these census periods, New York also represented a major place of birth for many migrants. But after 1900 the New England contingent suffered both an absolute and relative decline.

Although the states of New York, Missouri, Ohio, Illinois, and Pennsylvania had been important points of origin from an early date, they became increasingly important after 1900. By 1910 the states having the largest contingents in Los Angeles were, in the order of their importance, Illinois, Ohio, New York, Missouri, Pennsylvania, and Iowa. New York and Pennsylvania declined in relative importance as the geographical center of the movement shifted toward the Middle West. In 1920, the principal states, in the order of their importance, were Illinois, New York, Ohio, Missouri, Iowa, Pennsylvania, and Kansas, and in 1930, the largest state totals were Illinois, the state of birth for 72,933 residents of Los Angeles; Missouri, 49,590; New York, 49,337; Ohio, 42,212; and Iowa, 41,352. Until 1930 there had been little migration from the Southern or Western states to Los Angeles. But, in that year, the number of residents of Los Angeles born in such states as Texas, Colorado, Utah, Arizona, and Nebraska showed a heavy increase over prior census periods. Obviously the geographical center of the movement had shifted still further west. For California as a whole, the percentage distribution

of residents by state of birth between 1860 and 1940 has changed as
follows: persons born in New England declined from 8.5% of the
total California population to 1.9%; the Middle Atlantic states declined from 11% to 5.1%; the East North Central states increased
from 7.8% to 11%; the West North Central states from 4.4% to
12%; the South Atlantic states—never important—declined from
3.2% to 1.5%; the East South Central states declined from 3.8% to
2%; the Western states increased from 1% to 5%; the West South
Central states (Arkansas, Louisiana, Oklahoma, and Texas) increased
from 1% to 5.1%; and the Pacific Coast states from 20.6% to 36.2%.

It is extremely important to note that persons born in California
have never constituted a high percentage of the total number of
residents of the state: 20% in 1860, 30% in 1870, 37% in 1880, 39%
in 1890, 44% in 1900, 38% in 1910, 37% in 1920, and 34% in 1930.
For these same years, the percentages of persons born in California
would, of course, be much lower in Southern California and considerably higher in Northern California. It is equally important to
note that the percentage of persons born in California who have continued to remain residents of California is exceptionally high: from
1860 to 1930 it has, in fact, never been less than 90%. In view of
these figures, there can be little doubt about the westward shift of
population in America.

Statistics on "state of birth" do not reveal, however, the exact shift
in the origin of westward migration. Unfortunately there are no
figures available which show where the present residents of Southern
California were living at the time they decided to move west. It has
been estimated, for example, that several hundred thousand immigrants have moved from Iowa to Southern California. But a majority
of these people, perhaps, were born in such states as Illinois, Ohio,
and Missouri. The Iowa migration, therefore, is of much greater
significance than the census figures would indicate.

To understand the origin of the Iowa-to-Southern-California movement, it is necessary to look at the settlement of Iowa. In 1860 only
one-third of Iowa had been settled, but, after the Civil War, the
population of the state increased phenomenally. By 1890 the free
lands were gone. In the next decade, the rate of rural population
growth began to decline and, by the turn of the century, Iowa had
begun to export population. Although a comparatively new state,
the population of Iowa showed an actual decrease between 1900 and

1905. As much as anything else, farm prosperity had been responsible for the exodus from Iowa. Farm lands purchased in 1880 for $5 an acre were selling for $75 an acre in 1905. With the free lands gone, Iowa farmers began to worry about "the younger son." Had rail transportation not developed as rapidly as it did after 1880, it is quite possible that these "surplus families" would have moved merely a short distance. But Southern California began to attract national attention at precisely the time when Iowa needed to export population.

If you look west from Iowa, what do you see? Arid plains, mountains, intermountain deserts, and still more mountains. But over that final range is paradise. The Iowa migration to Southern California started about 1900, momentarily abated during the first World War, and then sharply increased from 1920 to 1930 when it has been estimated that at least 160,000 Iowans came to the coast. By 1930 one-third of the persons born in Iowa were living in some other state.

While the Iowa influx to Los Angeles is primarily to be explained by economic and social changes in Iowa that happened to coincide with the opening of Southern California, still some artificial stimulation has long been a factor in the migration. One of the earliest excursion parties was made up of Iowans recruited for settlement in the American Colony (which later became Long Beach). Throughout the 'eighties, one reads of excursion-party leaders and itinerant lecturers who toured Iowa extolling the advantages of Southern California. In 1881 an exhibit of Southern California fruits and vegetables was shown at the state capital of Iowa and the lecturer who accompanied the exhibit was invited to address a joint session of the Iowa legislature. When the California Fruit Growers Exchange decided in 1907 to experiment with national advertising, Iowa was selected as the ideal state in which to conduct the experiment. Under the slogan, "Oranges for Health—California for Wealth," a large amount of newspaper and billboard advertising was placed throughout the state. Iowa newspapers were given cartoons of a very pretty Miss Southern California giving a magnificent orange to the Iowa farmer. During the first year of this experiment, out-of-state citrus sales increased 17% but sales in Iowa showed a 50% increase. From then on, the amount which Sunkist spent on national advertising steadily increased with most of the money being spent in Iowa and the adjoining states. After 1911 the advertising campaign was spread throughout the vast Middle Western domain that lies north of Oklahoma, and north of the Arkansas and Ohio Rivers. Artificial stimulation has certainly played a part in encouraging Iowans to settle in Southern California, a region which the Iowa newspapers frequently refer to as New Iowa. While Iowa and Southern California are, of course, not contiguous, they are nevertheless joined together by an interconnecting system of waterways. In the early 'thirties, an ambitious Iowan actually traveled by boat from Iowa to Southern California, which is probably the origin of the saying that Southern California is the sea coast of Iowa.

"On the road to old L. A.,
Where the tin-can tourists play
And a sign says 'L. A. City Limits'
At Clinton, Ioway."

CHAPTER IX

"I'M A STRANGER HERE MYSELF"

IN 1890 native-born Californians constituted 25% of the residents of Los Angeles; in 1900, 27%; in 1910, 25%; in 1920, 20%; and in 1930, 20%. Visiting Los Angeles in 1930, Garet Garrett noted that "you have to begin with the singular fact that in a population of a million and a quarter, every other person you see has been there less than five years. More than nine in every ten you see have been there less than fifteen years. Practically, therefore, the whole population is immigrant, with the slowly changing sense of home peculiar to non-indigenous life. The mind is first adjusted, then the conscious feelings; but for a long time—for the rest of the immigrant's life perhaps—there will be in the cells a memory of home that was elsewhere."

An excellent statement of a major aspect of life in Southern California, this observation requires some refinement. While retaining a "memory of home," the newcomer in Southern California is not really an exile for he and his kind have always constituted a dominant majority of the population. In such a unique situation, the newcomer is generally able to find, somewhere in the vast recesses of Los Angeles, others of his kind. Association with them enables him to keep alive his memory of home. Out of this situation has been improvized a unique social institution, "the state society," which has functioned among out-of-state Americans in Southern California much as an immigrant-aid society functions in foreign-born communities. It assists the newcomer in making an adjustment by placing him in touch with others of his kind, thereby assuaging the aching loneliness—the really terrible loneliness—that for years has been so clearly apparent in the streets and parks, the boarding houses and hotels, the cafeterias and "lonely clubs" of Los Angeles. In fact, there is no more significant Southern California institution than the state society.

1. SHEPHERD OF THE LONELY

"For Southern California's balmy days,
Movie sets and palm-lined ways,
Snow-capped peaks and azure bays—
Land of fortune, land of rest—
For you alone we journeyed west."

The first state society was formed in Los Angeles on November 16, 1882, when Col. C. H. Haskins assembled the Pennsylvanians and organized a club. A tradition survives that Maine was the first state to organize, which may very probably have been the case, but I have been unable to verify the statement. In part, the state societies had their genesis in the colony system of settlement, whereby colonists were recruited from a particular region or community to form new townsites in Southern California. At the outset, the motivation was purely social, as shown by a resolution adopted by the Illinois Association at a meeting held on December 18, 1886:

Whereas we, the members of the Illinois Association, having endured the tortures inseparably connected with life in a region of ice and snow, and having fled from our beloved State to this favored land;

Resolved: That we sympathize with our friends and former fellow citizens of Illinois who still endure the ills they have, rather than fly to pleasures that they know not of;

Resolved: That in this grand country we have the tallest mountains, the biggest trees, the crookedest railroads, the dryest rivers, the loveliest flowers, the smoothest ocean, the finest fruits, the mildest lives, the softest breezes, the purest air, the heaviest pumpkins, the best schools, the most numerous stars, the most bashful real estate agents, the brightest skies, and the

most genial sunshine to be found anywhere in the United States;
Resolved: That we heartily welcome other refugees from
Illinois and will do all in our power to make them realize that
they are sojourning in a City of Angels, where their hearts will
be irrigated by the healing waters flowing from the perennial
fountains of health, happiness, and longevity.

Iowans were among the first to form a state society and the first
group to establish the practice of holding picnic meetings. A notation
in one of the annals mentions a picnic meeting in Lincoln Park on
January 1, 1887, which was attended by 408 Iowans. It was an Iowan,
C. H. Parsons, who, on April 24, 1909, sponsored the formation of
the Federation of State Societies of which he remained the guiding
influence until his death a few years ago. (The federation was not
formally incorporated until January 10, 1913, by which time a society
had been formed for every state in the union.) By the late 'twenties,
the federation boasted a membership of 500,000, representing every
state in the union and every province in Canada. Centering in Los
Angeles, the movement began to spread throughout Southern California. Branch state societies were formed in Ventura, Riverside, San
Diego, Pasadena, Long Beach, and Santa Paula (the home of the
people from Maine.) Today the Iowa Society, long the dominant
group in the federation, has branches throughout the region.

In his memoirs, Parsons tells of the first Iowa Society picnic he
attended, in Pasadena, on January 18, 1900. It was, he noted, "no
pickle and cold-coffee affair," but a real picnic. Here it was that he
first sensed the wave of the future, or, as he put it, that he first heard
"the steady oncoming tread of the dauntless Iowans, whose faces
were toward the Setting Sun." At this meeting 3,000 Iowans were present; the next year saw 6,000 on hand, then 12,000, 18,000, and, finally,
in the 'twenties, when the picnic ground had been transferred to
Bixby Park in Long Beach, 150,000 Iowans answered the roll call. In
the early 'twenties, writes Parsons, it was a thrilling experience to
hear "the tramp of Iowa's mustered hosts," as people set out for the
picnic grounds. On Iowa Day, "a singular excitement was in the air,
when, from far and near, the tribes begin to assemble . . . a sight not
to be matched in any commonwealth of the world." For years all
roads in Southern California, on Iowa Day, led to the picnic grounds.
"On the morning of the Great Reunion," wrote Parsons, "there is

wont to be a light on land and sea that must impress newcomers with the glory of the home of their adoption: a light that flashes along the purple embattlements of the Sierra Madres, touching dark canyons and scarred mountain walls, leaping along foothills that ripple to the plains; a light that brings into relief the bright green of the wide reaches thus carpeted in mid-winter, and that finally dances out and out, in elfish beauty, to caress the waves of the Pacific." On Iowa Day, the jealous Native Son found himself standing outside the picnic grounds or morbidly paced deserted streets.

This man Parsons was, perhaps, the first real sociologist in Southern California. He had an uncanny insight into the acute loneliness that haunted the region. Out of this insight, he created a social institution that perfectly answered a need sensed by thousands of residents. To be sure, the federation became, and to some extent still remains, a promotion agency, giving information to tourists and homeseekers, routing newcomers to the right real-estate offices and banks, and indirectly sponsoring the "right" candidates for public office. But, essentially, the state society was an innocent conception, a purely spontaneous folk affair.

Parsons also had a great flair for organization. Under this leadership, the Iowa Society became a thing of beauty and an object of wonder. Beginning around 1920, he broke the bulky Iowa Society down into its component parts by forming county societies within the larger state society. At the Iowa picnic, signs directed visitors to ninety-nine sacred spots in the park, each designation representing one of the counties of Iowa. Polk County, he noted, always had the largest attendance, followed by Lynn, Scott, Woodbury, and Marshall. The cost of the picnic was largely financed by the sale of ribbons, and, here again, the genius of Parsons was revealed. For the ribbons were not alike. Red ribbons, representing "the life blood that must be sold only to natives," went to those born in Iowa, blue ribbons were sold to those "who have merely lived in Iowa" (the color blue, said Parsons, symbolized "the feeling of blueness for not having been born there"), while yellow ribbons were sold to the visitors, the yellow symbolizing the "jaundice of envy" of those who were not Hawkeyes. Still later, a white ribbon was sold as a badge of glory to those haughty pioneers who had lived in Iowa for fifty years or more. The official "button" of the society, sold in vast quantities, consisted of a white background with an ear of corn in the center, bearing along its length a picture of a fat pig, with the caption: "Hog and hominy."

Not content with this masterly organizational apparatus, Parsons proceeded to form Iowa college-reunion societies so that the graduates of the thirty-five colleges in Iowa could meet beneath particular trees designated by the various college flags and pennants. So famous did these Iowa picnics become that people came from all over the world just to attend them. Notices of the meetings were, of course, mailed to all Iowans listed in Parsons' voluminous records. In addition, notices appeared in all the newspapers published south of Tehachapi, giving the time and place of the meeting, and, in later years, most of the Iowa newspapers carried notices and stories of the meetings. Mrs. Parsons informs me that Iowa families have for years made a practice of planning their winter vacation so that they could be present in Los Angeles on Iowa Day. The picnic became the established form of meeting largely because, as Parsons put it, there was no hall in all Southern California large enough to house the Iowans.

A small, modest little man, "inconspicuously dressed as a field mouse," Parsons was known as "the man who makes half a state feel at home," and, as "the man who meets a million cordially." While he could not remember all the Iowans, he knew thousands of them by name, and all of them knew him. He felt, and rightly, that the state societies had served an enormously important function in anchoring people in Southern California. As he put it, the state societies "liquidated the blues." After they had formed a state society, the Iowans, he noted, began to speak affectionately of Southern California and "settled themselves down in its warm sunshine like kittens under a kitchen range." Parsons took the keenest delight, as he wrote, in watching "the long line of Iowa's hosts swinging down the curving walk, ten, fifteen abreast, in endless serpentines." Only he knew how valuable the new social form was to these newcomers. "I've seen a lot of thrilling scenes," he wrote, "of brother meeting brother for the first time in years; of friends standing, hands clasped, tears on their cheeks, greeting each other for the first time in ten, twenty, thirty or forty years."

As loyal to California as a Native Son, Parsons always insisted that the state-society movement did not alienate the affections of the newcomers. "People don't like California less," he stoutly contended, "merely because they like to gather together and reminisce." Gifted with rare sociological insight, Parsons observed that Middle Westerners invariably identified themselves in terms of the states or counties in which they had lived, never by towns. The expression heard among them was, "I'm a Polk County man." He used to amuse himself by asking them to name the capital of the state from which they came and noted that, in most instances, they did not know the answer. On the other hand, Easterners always say "I'm from Boston," or "I'm a New Yorker."

Those who have never attended an Iowa picnic cannot possibly imagine the scene, when, the hilarity of the picnic over, gnarled old hands and beaming faces would answer the roll call of the counties. The societies were, and to some extent still are, more than one-party annual affairs. On the contrary, for twenty-five years these societies each averaged one regular monthly meeting, all announced, planned, and arranged by Parsons and his delightful wife. "For a quarter of a century," wrote Parsons, "I averaged six nights out a week attending state-society functions." Obviously these societies were a powerful integrating force, making for a sense of social solidarity and cohesiveness. In fact, I believe it fair to say that the state societies constituted *ersatz* communities, communities within a community, workable substitutes for the lack of real communities. The federation of state societies, for example, functioned, for many purposes, as a community. For many years, the federation was a major political force in Southern California, with politicians clamoring to be "introduced" at the picnics and eagerly identifying themselves with one or another of the state societies. The Iowa Society elected one of its members, Frank Merriam, governor of California and placed a number of its members on the bench.

One could make a book of the Iowa jokes heard in Southern California. It was proposed, for example, that Southern California be known as Caliowa. Long Beach has been known for years as Iowa's Sea Port. On meeting in Southern California, strangers were supposed to inquire: "What part of Iowa are you from?" The transcontinental trains were supposed to run non-stop excursions directly from Iowa to Bixby Park on Iowa Day. Whether the expression, "I'm a stranger here myself," actually originated in Los Angeles or not, it aptly expresses the reality of loneliness that was responsible for Parsons' great success. When he first began to devote full time to the federation, he did so, he said, because he had so frequently heard the expression, "If I could only run into some one I know," in the streets of Los Angeles. In Darwin Teilhet's novel, *Journey to the West*, the section on Southern California is entitled "The Iowa Coast."

2. "California, Here We Come!"

It is not by accident that the forty-eight state societies have, for so many years, held most of their meetings in the cafeterias of Los Angeles. I am convinced that the popularity of the cafeteria in Los Angeles is primarily due to the loneliness of the people. A cafeteria is a friendlier type of eating place than a restaurant. The possibility of meeting someone—just someone—is much greater in a cafeteria than in a cafe or restaurant. Furthermore, the informality of the cafeteria has always appealed to the ex-farmer and rural townsman. Essentially, a cafeteria is a sort of indoor picnic, particularly in Los Angeles, where so many cafeterias are dressed up with artificial trees, water wheels, cascading fountains, palm leaves, and all the paraphernalia of a park. Many of the early cafeterias of Los Angeles were flooded with light from skylights, bore names like "The Fern Cafeteria," and were decorated with all sorts of potted plants, ferns, vines, and flowers.

In the curious Spanish that was spoken in Los Angeles "before the gringo came," a cafeteria was, in effect, a saloon that served food. The cafeteria, as we know it today, actually had its origin in Los Angeles, where, in 1912, Boos Brothers opened the first self-service restaurant (one year before the federation of state societies was organized). Even before Boos Brothers appeared on the scene, I am informed by Clifford Clinton, one of the most successful cafeteria operators in Los Angeles, that "a little old woman had a hole-in-the-wall place on Broadway where you ran a tray along a railing and were served food." Cafeterias and state societies have always been intimately associated in Los Angeles. It may be that newcomers, unfamiliar with established eating places, are naturally drawn to cafeterias. In Los Angeles, cafeterias are quasi-public institutions around which a flourishing social life has always revolved. All sorts of groups, organizations, and associations hold their meetings in cafeterias. A cafeteria in Los Angeles is a place where you go to attend a meeting, and, perhaps, to eat. Most of the larger cafeterias have numerous meeting rooms, rest rooms, chapels, alcoves, balconies, and sell a variety of gadgets from books to gardenias, from tourist scenes to curios. Harry Leon Wilson, in 1923, was the first writer to refer to Southern California as "Sunny Cafeteria."

The state-society meetings in the cafeterias literally reek of friendliness, a jovial, spurious kind of friendliness, not the friendliness of intimates, which is usually low-pitched and often silent, but the falsetto friendliness of people pretending that they are not lonely. In effect, the state societies have always been "lonely clubs," haunted by clever old real-estate rascals in search of the "widow with means." I have not the slightest doubt that 50% of the marriages between oldsters, for which Los Angeles is proverbially famous, have grown out of meetings of the state societies in cafeterias. It is nothing for octogenarians to wed in Los Angeles; they frequently do so in teams of four and five couples at a time. At the state-society meetings, one can usually witness much aged coquettishness, much holding of hands, and much genteel cafeteria love-making. There is no free masonry in the world quite like that of the state societies. All you need to do in order to be able to attend one of these meetings is to be able to carry a tray in a cafeteria. The office of sergeant-at-arms is quite unknown. Actually I suppose that 40% of the Iowans really aren't Iowans at all. They merely pose as Iowans in order to be admitted to the charmed circle, to warm their old and withered limbs at the friendly hearth, to gabble into friendly ears. In this sense, to be an Iowan in Southern California is merely another way of confessing one's loneliness.

The straining for friendliness at the state-society meetings is indicated in the nickname used to designate the various groups. People from Arkansas are "toothpicks"; those from Connecticut are "nutmeggers"; the Coloradoans are "rovers"; people from Delaware are "the Blue Hen's chickens"; Florida is the "fly-up-the-creek state"; Georgians are "crackers" and "gauber grubbers"; the people from Illinois (Illinois once had its own club house on South Broadway, with branches in Whittier, Pomona, and Riverside) are "suckers"; the Iowans (with branches in Pasadena, Riverside, Ontario, Anaheim, Orange, Pomona, and, believe it or not, a branch in *Des Moines, Iowa*) are, of course, "hawkeyes"; Kansans are "jayhawkers"; Louisianans are "pelicans"; Nevadans are "sage hens"; New Jersey-ites are "clam catchers"; North Dakotans are "flicker tails"; Ohioans, "buckeyes"; Marylanders are "crawthumpers"; Kentuckians, "corn-crackers"; Mississippians, "tadpoles"; and so forth.

In the proceedings of the state societies, one can catch the note of exaggeration with which the exile always alludes to his homeland: "Little Delaware! In the eyes of her loyal sons, the glittering, dazzling diamond in the jeweled tiara of the states. Her citizenship is clean cut and virile as the crystalline gem. Her womanhood is pure and gentle as the zephyrs that play in the rushes of the Southland." On occasions, the federation has sponsored state carnivals at which the various state societies have been represented. Floats move through the streets of Long Beach with such captions as "Corn is King," "North Dakota: The Bread Basket of the Nation," "Minnesota: The North Star State." Most of the state societies have their own songs. I have heard the Missourians intoning, over the rattle of cafeteria dishes, "Peerless State! Our Own Missouri!" while, in another part of Clifton's Cafeteria, the Nebraska cornhuskers were singing, "There's a land with its sweet-scented meadows." Meetings of the Ohio State Society are usually closed on a note of wishful nostalgia, as the folks rise from the cafeteria tables, like members of an Elks lodge saluting departed brother Elks on New Year's Eve, and sing: "Should Old Ohio be forgot and scenes we left behind? No, wheresoever be our lot, we keep them still in mind." And so they sing:

> Then Hail the dear old Buckeye state,
>   For go where'er we will,
> Whatever be our local fate,
>   We are her children still.
> We'll give her every honor due,
>   Nor shall our love grow cold.
> However much we love the new
>   We'll not forget the old.

The crowning achievement of Parsons' career—it marked the decline of the state societies—was the establishment, in the late 'twenties, of a special Old Folks Picnic Association. He had discovered, so he wrote, that there were "at least three couples in Los Angeles who had passed the century mark, a hundred past 90, thousands past 80, and hundreds of thousands past 70, and so it is fitting that these should have a day to call their own." Let no one imagine, he said, "that it is a dull and solemn occasion. Happy laughter, jolly sociability, deep enjoyment of the good things to eat and the splendid fellowship and an enthusiastic pleasure in the formal," characterized these meetings. For the oldsters, Parsons provided card games, "hundreds of gallons of coffee with cream and sugar in abundance," and "tasty dinners." At his prompting, the aged couples would arrange themselves in special categories, such as "the over-nineties" and "the over-eighties." I seriously doubt if any other community has ever provided a special social form, of this type, for the pleasure and entertainment of the aged. Certainly Iowa never had anything remotely like the Old Folks Picnic Association to offer the aged. In their eyes, Los Angeles was Paris, New York, and Buenos Aires all rolled into one.

That Parsons should have been compelled to cater especially to the aged, however, indicated that the state-society phenomenon was on its way out. Today the federation retains its headquarters and lovely old Mrs. Parsons still carries on, but the movement has lost much of its former zip and dash. She explained the change to me in this way: "If the boys and girls were born in Iowa, and remembered it, then they didn't mind coming along with their parents to the picnic, but Iowa means nothing to the California-born grandchildren. You can't get these native-born Californians to a state-society meeting." With the passing of so many first-generation immigrants to Southern California, the state societies have begun to decline, much as the immigrant-aid societies of the foreign-born have tended to disappear with the first generation.

This is not to imply, however, that the state societies have vanished. Iowa Day will remain a major folk festival in Southern California for years to come. Despite the war, 30,000 Iowans gathered in Bixby Park for the 1944 summer picnic. Sixty-two members of the Golden Wedding Club of Iowa were introduced; thirty-one couples, married fifty years or longer, slowly paraded onto the stage; and the crowd sang "Jesus, Savior, Pilot Me" and "When You and I Were Young, Maggie." There was a move to introduce 98-year-old Eli W. McKinney, born in Iowa before it became a state and who fought with the 45th Iowa Infantry during the Civil War, but his feet weren't what they used to be, and he had gone home. There was, as usual, plenty of fried chicken and much chatter about the tall corn back home. At the 1945 picnic about 20,000 were on hand to witness the presentation of a fifty-pound birthday cake to Herbert Hoover, formerly of West Branch, Iowa, and to listen to his somber vision of things to come. The newsboys were on hand shouting the same fake headlines, "Blizzards in Iowa!" and the same crowd was there eating sandwiches, pies, doughnuts, and pickles, drinking coffee from tin cups, making bad jokes about the Iowa-California rapprochement, "having a wonderful time." The Iowa Day picnic is, indeed, likely to survive long after the feeling of estrangement, the loneliness, has vanished. For it has become, as Mark Lee Luther once pointed out, "a folkmote," a tribal festival.

Needless to say, the state-society movement never penetrated the region north of Tehachapi. For many years, the percentage of native sons in the north has been twice that in the south. Selective processes have long been at work sifting out newcomers to California, directing one type to the north, another to the south. From 1900 to 1920, those who came to Southern California were, predominantly, middle-class, middle-aged people seeking to retire, not to re-engage in business or the professions. As such they were potentially more cohesive, more like-minded, than other out-of-state migrants in California. I believe that the state-society movement has tended to accentuate regional differences in California. Through this social form, newcomers in Southern California have been knit together as compact cultural groups. By organizing the immigrants, the state societies brought into being a regional consciousness in the south which was only further emphasized by a parallel movement in the north, namely, native-son-ism.

3. THE NATIVE SONS

"When I said I was born here in Los Angeles she almost gasped, and then she flushed and said, 'Oh, really?'"
—from *Play the Game*, a novel by Ruth Comfort Mitchell

On July 4, 1869, San Francisco planned a special celebration, not merely to observe Independence Day, but to mark the completion of the continental railway. General A. M. Winn, who was not a native son, decided, as Grand Marshal of the Parade, that it would be interesting to have a group of "native sons" included in the line of march. Accordingly, he sent out a call for all "native sons" to meet at the armory. When the general arrived, the armory was a madhouse, for the only native sons to report were, of course, 'teen-age youngsters. "They were noisy, turbulent, and utterly unmanageable. The marshal, in vain, attempted to bring order out of confusion, but the noisy, whistling crowd was untamable. Finally, benches and chairs were upset, the gas turned off, and the crowd of young Americans expelled." Although the Native Sons of the Golden West was not organized until 1875, this incident was the event that brought them into existence.

Traditionally the Native Sons and Native Daughters have never been strong in Southern California. From 1890 to 1930, the native-born element has never constituted more than 27% of the population of Los Angeles, but the percentage of native-born in San Francisco was 66% in 1910 and still constituted 44% of the population in 1920. For many years, the news about the Southern California parlors of the Native Sons and Native Daughters has been carried in a small section of their magazine, well toward the last page, under the caption, "Tehachapi South Bulletin." Well organized in the north, the Native Sons dominated state politics for many years; in fact, their dominance prevailed until the middle 'twenties when, for the first time, the southern counties outstripped the northern counties in population. Thus for many years there have been two organized movements, representing in effect two cultural groups, in California: native sons in the north, state societies in the south. The existence of these two movements has tended to sharpen regional differences in California.

Just as the state societies invested their homelands with halos, so the native sons have pompously proclaimed the dazzling merits of California. The official "salute" of the Native Sons consists in the right hand shading the eyes; its password is "Truckee"; its official publication, The Grizzly Bear. For years this magazine has been stuffed with verses about "pioneers" with stanzas, such as

> Let us sing to the Mothers of men,
>   With a nation's pride of years,
> They spoke the fate of the Golden State,
>   The Mother Pioneers.

Its editorials have echoed with such bombast as "California is rightly lauded as Queen of the West. She lifts her royal head, and her serrated crown pierces the clouds. Raising her sunbeamed scepter, she accentuates her towering peaks and domes, sweeping forests, limpid lakes, rolling uplands, and stretches of plain. Her blossom-embroidered robes trail to the Golden Gate, where her waiting feet are laved by the sparkling Pacific, and her regal splendor is mirrored in the Sunset Sea." Almost every issue of this magazine since it was established in 1907 has contained poems about sunsets, poppies, grizzly bears, and pioneers: the dominating symbols of the native-son ideology. Of these symbols, however, the Pioneer is the one which strikes the most responsive chord with the native sons:

> Ah, there, above my heart, friend,
>   It's a racking, rending pain—
> My God, I never thought the thing
>   Would trouble me again.
> Just hold my hand—you true gold son—
>   I know the end is near—
> There goes the ketch—I'm done for, lad,
>   A Dying Pioneer.

On only one occasion, so far as I have been able to discover, have the Native Sons and the state societies met in joint assemblage in Southern California. The occasion was a dinner jointly sponsored by both organizations. A representative of the state societies read a poem with the stanza:

> There's a home, sweet home in Kansas, there's a grave
>   in Illinois;
> A mother's love in Old Kentucky—in Tennessee a boy.
> O God, why can't we have them here, our folks, our
>   very own,
> What are mountains, breezes, sunshine, if the heart
>   must beat alone?

Not to be outdone by this burst of song, a representative of the Native Sons read a poem with the lines:

> But our rosy California, beside the crimson sea—
> Our stately California, ah, that's the state for me.

On one occasion in the past, the native-son movement was nearly disrupted when some thoughtless member suggested that, perhaps, non-native sons might be admitted to honorary membership. This suggestion was greeted with catcalls, whistling, and much violent stamping of feet.

Always a lily-white organization, the Native Sons have exhorted themselves "to put our hearts into California; to labor earnestly and continually for her welfare and development, and, above all, TO KEEP HER A WHITE MAN'S PARADISE." Firmly believing that they alone have kept California on the upward path all these years, the Native Sons have stated that upon the outcome of "what transpires in the meeting halls of the different Parlors of the order depends the future of California." Eligibility to membership consists of (1) birth upon the sacred soil of California, (2) a good moral character, (3) belief in a Supreme Being. Unofficially another requirement has long been recognized, namely, possession of a white skin. Despite these rather vague requirements, the Native Sons have always been an extremely cohesive, closely knit clan in California, with the hypersensitivity and egocentric behavior of a minority group. As long as the northern counties were dominant, the Native Sons had great political power in California. But the election of the Iowan, Frank Merriam, as governor in the 'thirties, symbolized the emerging dominance of the south and the eclipse of the Native Sons. For a native-born movement to flourish, it is essential that the native-born constitute a minority, although a sizable minority, of the population of a state. Once the percentage of native-born has risen in California to, say, 65% or 75% of the population, nativism will no longer command a premium value and the movement will probably pass out of existence. It is likely to survive, however, somewhat longer than the state-society movement. One major accomplishment must be chalked up to the credit of the organization: it has consistently, and successfully, opposed all efforts to divide the state at the Tehachapi line. Largely due to the efforts of the Native Sons, California has remained, at least in name, a single state.

4. ALIEN PATRIMONIES

"Culture in Los Angeles is not indigenous, but rather an elaborate transmutation."
                                    Willard Huntington Wright

Newcomers in Los Angeles begin to feel at home, as Garet Garrett noted, first, through an adjustment of mind to the new environment, and then much later, through an adjustment of conscious feelings or sensibilities. There is a popular saying in Los Angeles that it takes ten years to make a native out of a newcomer. I have discovered that it takes men, on the average, about ten years to discover that a hat is superfluous in Southern California. Although newcomers come to dress like Southern Californians rather quickly, a much deeper resistance develops at a different level of behavior.

I am convinced that first-generation immigrants, particularly if they are middle class and middle-aged, never really come to feel completely at home in Southern California. I came to Southern California from Colorado in 1922, with my mother and brother. Although my mother has lived in the region since 1922, spiritually, mentally, imaginatively, she is still living in Colorado. Colorado is a real, beautiful, and vital memory to her. Her friends in Los Angeles are, without exception, former Coloradoans who have moved to Southern California. She has never felt at home in Los Angeles nor has she ever felt that she could like the place. Like a character in Mark Lee Luther's novel, she has always felt "an alien, a stranger in a foreign city whose language was mysteriously her own." Her experience is, I believe, quite typical.

It is also, as T. K. Whipple demonstrated in a brilliant essay, a typical American experience. But in Southern California this experience is accentuated, italicized, invested with new meaning. Here the "alien patrimony" is not European, but American. The nostalgia is for an America that no longer exists, for an America that former Kansans, Missourians, and Iowans literally gaze back upon, looking backward over their shoulders. The loss that the transplanted person feels in emotional relation with his natural surroundings is, as Whipple emphasized, by no means his greatest loss. "Perhaps the most important is social. He may settle among aliens—aliens to each other as well as to him; and a number of strangers, however friendly and kindly, cannot soon coalesce into a close-knit community. Even supposing a whole community migrates in a body, the communal life cannot go on; it speedily disintegrates, because it was based upon the other locality. Emigrants turn into detached individuals, like so many grains of sand—but for a man to be severed from a social organism is for him to suffer abnormal deprivation. . . . Human adaptability, astounding as it is, has its limits; there is a kind of inertia in the mind. The difficulty of taking root again is not to be underestimated, nor of forming an organic community which provides all that communal life ought to provide. The individual may make an excellent superficial adjustment and get on well; but men's feelings, their basic desires and imaginings, are the deposits of centuries of racial experience."

How much of the notorious feeling of unreality, of which newcomers complain in Southern California, is to be explained by this "abnormal deprivation"? Does a new and novel environment ever seem quite real to the middle-aged newcomer? From story after story, novel after novel, that have been written about Southern California, one can find phrases like these from *Oh, Say Can You See!* by Lewis Browne (1927): "There was something unreal about the scene: about that illumined doll's-house of a station, with its stucco arches and clambering vines; and about the tousled palms standing like sentries against the star-lit sky. It was all too neat and clean, too pretty, too much like a picture. The very night seemed unreal."

The first loyalty of many residents of Southern California has always been to their state of origin about which they know far more than they do about the region in which they live. The state-society movement has probably tended to keep old loyalties, allegiances, and attachments alive much longer than might normally be the case. Despite the tug and pull of these "ancient patrimonies," however, the old is adjusted to the new. Newcomers bring their habits, customs, manners, and religious practices to Southern California but here they quickly assume, as Charles Phelps Cushing once observed, "a milder form." Institutions imported to the region are, as Dr. Henry Harris has said, "American, yet, embodying the experiences of many homelands, these institutions in general take on a less provincial mark than those elsewhere in the nation." A character in Mark Lee Luther's novel finally concludes, despite much resistance to the idea, that "by some chemistry of her own, California was triumphantly blending the races into a single type."

With the percentage of native-born declining in the north and rising in the south, some of the cultural differences between the two regions have begun to disappear. "This is indeed a new race," wrote Lillian Symes some years ago in *Harper's*. "These are the torchbearers of that new Greek civilization arising on the southwest coast. It is a race and a civilization that have been heralded for a decade. There can be no question about it—the race, at least, is here. It is Walt Whitman's or perhaps Bernarr McFadden's—dream come true." In an interview, Bertrand Russell once told Duncan Aikman that "Los Angeles represents the ultimate segregation of the unfit." But from all these culls, misfits, and migrants from all the states and all the nations, have come, as Frank Fenton has said, "the beautiful Californians," who play with "intent seriousness and a grim passion."

In fact, it is the diverse cultural background of Southern California that accounts for its commonplaceness. "There is no Los Angeles face," wrote Garet Garrett, for whom Los Angeles was "the truest conceivable representation of the whole American face, urban, big town, little town, all together." Just as exiles become conscious of their accents, so these diverse newcomers become conscious of their speech in Los Angeles. It was James M. Cain, I believe, who first noted that the residents of Los Angeles speak quite good English. You hear few regional accents or dialects in Southern California. For here the diversity of speech mannerisms quickly cancel out. Just as the newcomers abandon their dialects, so the rigors of their Protestantism begins to assume "a milder form." Evangelical sects continue to thrive in Los Angeles, but only because migration continues. The commonplaceness of Los Angeles is the commonplaceness of America, caricatured and distorted and exaggerated. Just as America has produced a fairly commonplace type out of sons and daughters from so many varied lands, so newcomers to Los Angeles take on something of its commonplaceness of manner and appearance. "At heart," wrote Irvin S. Cobb, "Los Angeles is a vast cross-section of the Corn Belt set down incongruously in a Maxfield Parrish setting." "It is as if you tipped the United States up," wrote Frank Lloyd Wright, "so all the commonplace people slid down there into Southern California." One of the reasons for this persistent impression of commonplaceness is, of course, that the newcomers have been stripped of their natural settings: their Vermont hills, their Kansas plains, their Iowa corn-fields. Here their essential commonplaceness stands out garishly in the harsh illumination of the sun. Here every wart is revealed, every wrinkle underscored, every eccentricity emphasized.

The commonplaceness, however, is changing and will continue to change. No one has sensed this more vividly than D. H. Lawrence. In a letter to a friend, he once jotted down this note: "Los Angeles is silly—much motoring, me rather tired and vague with it. California is a queer place—in a way, it has turned its back on the world and looks into the void Pacific. It is absolutely selfish, very empty, but not false, and at least, not full of false effort. I don't want to live here, but a stay here rather amuses me. It's a sort of crazy-sensible." The "crazy" of Lawrence's note consists in the old traits incongruously retained; the "sensible" consists of the new, fresh growths. Perhaps it will always retain something of this "crazy-sensible" combination.

> *"Rain—the sweetest music to the California ear."*
> —Theodore Van Dyke

CHAPTER X

WATER! WATER! WATER!

SOUTHERN Californians are supposed to repeat the word "water" more often than Moslems say "Allah." Everyone knows, of course, that half of Los Angeles is wind, and the other half water. "God never intended Southern California to be anything but desert," a visitor once remarked. "Man has made it what it is." In a sense, the history of Southern California is the record of its eternal quest for water, and more water, and still more water. In the Los Angeles Basin of 1,400,000 acres of habitable land (6% of the state's total) reside 45% of the inhabitants of California. But this same basin has only .06% of the natural stream flow of water in the state. Water is the life-blood of Southern California. Turn off the flow of water that now reaches the region from such remote sources as Owens Valley and the Colorado River and the whole region would be bankrupt. The absence of local water resources is, indeed, the basic weakness of the region—its eternal problem.

It has always been difficult for visitors to Southern California, particularly since the turn of the century, to recognize the importance of water. Today the entire area from Santa Barbara to San Diego is an irrigated paradise. Water gurgles from irrigation pumps, water rushes along irrigation laterals and canals, and costly sprinkling systems spray a seemingly inexhaustible supply of water on elaborate lawns and gardens. Nowadays the land looks as though it had always been watered. But it is actually semi-arid. Not so long ago, it was a land of the *paisano,* or road-runner, the horned toad, the turkey buzzard; a land of dry brush and shabby-looking cactus. As late as 1870, a limited number of windmills and surface wells barely sufficed to supply water for the livestock and the irrigated gardens of the ranches.

Throughout Southern California there is not a single river, as people ordinarily understand the term, not a single natural lake, not a single creek with a year-round flow of water. Disastrous droughts have, in years past, spread desolation and ruin in the region. Yet, in this paradoxical land, flood waters have probably caused more damage and loss of life than droughts. High mountain ranges wall the region off from the Central Valley and the desert. Dropping directly to sea-level plains, these towering mountains have always reminded me of the lines from a poem by Edmund Wilson:

> *There where the waves are brought to heel,*
> *There where the Alps, no longer free,*
> *Come down like elephants to kneel*
> *Beside the glazed and azure sea.*

Southern California is the land of the freak flood. In this semi-arid region, it can rain as nowhere else in America. In fact, it neither rains nor pours; the skies simply open up and dump oceans of water on the land. Pouring down the steep mountain ranges with the speed and fury of a mill race, rain waters convert the dry creek-beds or arroyos into raging infernos and then, on reaching the sandy soils of the plains, vanish as quickly as a mirage. While nearly all the rainfall occurs between November 1 and March 1 (it has seldom rained between May 1 and October 1), nevertheless, years of heavy rainfall have alternated with years of excessive drought. Thus, while there is a clearly defined rainy season, no one knows how much it will rain in any particular season or just when the rains will come. To manage such a freakishly paradoxical environment has always required real insight into the basic character of the region, an insight difficult to cultivate in a land made up of newcomers and migrants.

1. In Search of Water

Originally good-sized perennial streams flowed out onto the coastal plain. The first agricultural settlements and towns developed along the banks of these streams, in particular along the Los Angeles, San

Gabriel, and Santa Ana Rivers. From an early date the waters from these streams were diverted for irrigation purposes. The first attempt to augment this supply of surface water took the form of drilling for artesian waters. In 1868 the first artesian well was bored near Compton, producing a seven-inch flow of water and demonstrating the existence of considerable underground sources in the Los Angeles Basin area. By 1910 approximately 1,596 artesian wells had been drilled. The entire coastal plain was at one time dotted with artesian wells that sprayed water into the air, for no pumping was then required. The first wells were drilled to a depth of from forty to no more than seventy feet, depending upon the location, but within two decades after 1868 the flow of artesian waters had begun to slacken. It then became necessary to drill new wells to a much greater depth, to conserve water by the use of cement pipes and other devices, and to apply electrically driven pumping systems.

By these and other methods, the use of underground waters was steadily increased. "One of the most noteworthy features during the past few years," wrote H. E. Brooks in 1904, "has been the utilization of an abundant subterranean water supply." Between 1899 and 1904, over 100,000 inches of water were developed from underground sources; between 1904 and 1907, 25,000 additional inches were added to the supply from the same source; and by 1910 still an additional 25,000 feet had been developed. At one time, California had 89.9% of all the farm acreage in America that is irrigated by artesian wells, and most of this acreage was located in the southern part of the state. From 140,000 acres thus irrigated in the South Coastal Basin in 1890, the number of acres increased to 342,400 by 1910. In 1905 Mendenhall estimated that two thirds of the land under irrigation in Southern California tapped underground sources (by 1938 the figure had risen to 90%). But nowadays, however, it is the annual underground flow that is being tapped, not the accumulated artesian pools or reservoirs. In fact, the water plane has been lowered to such an extent, through excessive pumping, that but little remains of the original artesian areas. The artesian water supply was wasted, as a young spendthrift might dissipate a legacy, in a single generation.

Better utilization of water, more flexible legal arrangements for its proper management (such as mutual water companies and irrigation improvement districts), and the constant expansion of pumping systems, served to keep the rural areas fairly well supplied with water from 1880 to 1910. The first real shortage was felt in the cities and towns. From the earliest date, Los Angeles had obtained its water supply from the Los Angeles River, the watershed of which embraces the entire San Fernando Valley. Water was diverted from the river by a system of *zanjas*, or open ditches, for irrigation and domestic consumption. Early residents of the city got their water, either from the *zanjas*, or from the water peddlers who roamed the town. The first attempt to conserve and to develop the available supply occurred in 1854, when the city appointed a *Zanjero*, or water commissioner, to guard the *zanjas* and to keep them repaired. From its founding in 1781 until 1886, the city owned and operated its own water system. In the latter year, the city leased its water rights to the Los Angeles City Water Company, a private corporation, for a period of thirty years. Reacquiring control of the water system in 1899, the city has since operated its own municipal system.

During this hiatus from 1868 to 1899, I. N. Van Nuys and J. B. Lankershim, and others, had acquired vast holdings in the San Fernando Valley which were nearer to the sources of the Los Angeles River than was the City of Los Angeles. Relying upon the doctrine of riparian rights, these landowners asserted a prior claim on the waters of the Los Angeles River, both surface and underground, as owners of upstream lands along the river. The only thing that saved the city from this claim was the happy circumstance, which the city had been trying to forget for several decades, that it had been the one pueblo founded by the Spanish in Southern California. Under Mexican and Spanish law, pueblos were given a prior right to all waters within the watershed for domestic uses, and to supply manufacturing establishments and to irrigate lands within the pueblo limits. In a famous law suit between the City of Los Angeles and the land barons of San Fernando Valley, the Supreme Court ruled that Los Angeles had succeeded, by virtue of the Treaty of Guadalupe Hidalgo, to all the rights which it had enjoyed as a pueblo; therefore, its claim to the waters within the watershed was prior to that of all appropriators subsequent to 1781. In the same decision, it was also held that the city might put its water supply to uses not known under Mexican law, such as sewers, artificial lakes, and ornamental fountains. This decision saved the City of Los Angeles from disaster. Never did an American city owe more to the fortuitous circumstance of Spanish settlement.

Even with its watershed right firmly established, Los Angeles began to fear a future water famine. Although the city had enough water in 1900 for a population of 102,249, it began to be disturbed by the discrepancy between the available supply and the rate of population increase. In large part, however, this fear was artificially stimulated by a group of powerful "empire builders" of the period. In 1905 and later in 1910, a syndicate financed by Harry Chandler, General Harrison Gray Otis, Joseph F. Sartori (the banker), Henry Huntington, E. H. Harriman, E. T. Earl, and M. H. Sherman acquired most of the former holdings of the Van Nuys and Lankershim families in the San Fernando Valley. In terms of what subsequently happened, it is important to note that M. H. Sherman, a member of this syndicate, was also a member of the city's water board. Eventually this group of men acquired control over 108,000 acres of land in the valley. Once in control of this vast acreage, they came to the water board of the City of Los Angeles with a typically grandiose proposal: that the city should build a 238-mile aqueduct to tap the waters of Owens Valley (located between the Sierra Nevadas and the desert); and thereby hangs a tale.

2. THE OWENS VALLEY TRAGEDY

No one has ever seriously questioned the right of the City of Los Angeles to be concerned about its water supply, or, for that matter, to obtain water from Owens Valley. The greatest good for the greatest number is, indeed, familiar American doctrine. But the Owens Valley project was conceived in iniquity. The citizens of Los Angeles knew nothing about the project, at the time it was first proposed, for the members of the San Fernando Valley land syndicate controlled the press of the community. Even the City Council was kept completely in the dark. Worse than the conspiratorial silence, however, was the fact that the project was carried out by reprehensible tactics.

In 1903, J. B. Lippincott, chief engineer of the United States Reclamation Service in California, went to Owens Valley ostensibly for the purpose of explaining to its hard-working pioneer settlers that the government was about to launch a vast reclamation project in the area. While purporting to work on this project, Lippincott acquired full information about water resources in the valley and even managed to induce many settlers to surrender priority claims on water. The following year, Fred Eaton, formerly mayor of Los Angeles, appeared in Owens Valley. Representing himself as Lippincott's agent, he began to take options on lands riparian to Owens River. In possession of Lippincott's reports, he proceeded to checkerboard the area, that is, to take options on every other ranch on each side of the irrigation canals and along the Owens River. Once in possession of a sufficient number of options, he then exercised his right to buy the land. At the same time, Lippincott announced that the government had abandoned its "reclamation project," resigned from the service, and was promptly employed by the City of Los Angeles. The trap having been sprung, the Los Angeles *Times* broke a gentlemen's agreement with the other newspapers, and, on July 29, 1905, plastered the news of the Owens Valley project on its front page. Traditionally opposed to all forms of public ownership, it is interesting to note that, in this instance, the *Times* worked hand in glove with the officials of the municipally owned water system of the City of Los Angeles.

Once the scheme was announced to the public—and for the first time to the City Council—the city agreed to float a bond issue of $25,000,000 to build the Owens Valley aqueduct. In the ensuing campaign, only one newspaperman in Los Angeles had the courage and honesty to denounce the deceit which had been practiced on the residents both of Owens Valley and of Los Angeles. This lonely journalist, the late Samuel T. Clover, paid for his honesty by forfeiting control of his little weekly newspaper. In order to secure approval of the bond issue, the project sponsors resorted to strange and devious tactics. Thousands of inches of water were clandestinely dumped into the sewer system from reservoirs and storage dams, so as to create an artificial water famine. The water supply became so scarce that, on the eve of the election, an ordinance was passed forbidding people to spray their lawns and gardens. On September 7, 1905, the citizens of Los Angeles, by a heavy vote, approved the bond issue.

The sponsors of the Owens Valley project, however, were not interested in bringing water to the parched City of Los Angeles; they were concerned about 108,000 acres of previously unirrigated land in the San Fernando Valley which they had quietly bought up at prices of five, ten, and twenty dollars an acre. At the time the aqueduct was constructed, San Fernando Valley, as its historian Frank M. Keefer has pointed out, was "the logical and *only practical place for the disposal of this surplus* water" (italics mine). To the amazement of the residents of Los Angeles, who had just assumed a $25,000,000 indebtedness, the aqueduct line was brought to the north end of San Fernando Valley, not into the City of Los Angeles, and there the terminal point still remains. With water available to irrigate the lands they had acquired in San Fernando Valley, the "men of vision" who had engineered this extraordinary deal, proceeded to sell their holdings for $500 and $1,000 an acre, making an estimated profit of $100,000,000, at the expense of the residents of Owens Valley and of Los Angeles. As late as 1930, 80,000 acre-feet of Owens Valley water were still being used to irrigate San Fernando Valley farm lands, enough water to provide each and every one of the 1,300,000 residents of Los Angeles with fifty gallons of water a day for one year.

The facts concerning this amazing project have never been denied. The whole story is told with a wealth of detail in an excellent chapter in Morrow Mayo's book about Los Angeles, and is recited, in fictional form, in Mary Austin's novel, *The Ford* (1917). As federal land agent in Owens Valley, Mrs. Austin's husband had intimate knowledge of this sordid scheme which he tried, by every means at his disposal, to prevent. There is far more to the story than I have told here. For example, to keep homesteaders out of Owens Valley, Gifford Pinchot was prevailed upon in 1906 to declare most of the desert lands of Owens Valley a federal forest district! To facilitate the acquisition of a right of way for the aqueduct line, Congress was induced to pass special legislation upon assurances from the City of Los Angeles that the water would be used only for domestic purposes. When a provision to this effect was written into the bill, Senator Frank Flint, of Los Angeles, asked President Theodore Roosevelt to have the section removed, since, as he said, some of the residents of Los Angeles might want, occasionally, to water their gardens! At a later date, the City of Los Angeles proceeded to annex most of San Fernando Valley thereby removing any question as to its right to use Owens Valley water for all purposes. What is of greater significance, however, is the fact that there existed, in Long Valley, a potential storage basin of sufficient capacity to have supplied the needs of both Los Angeles and Owens Valley. Not a single storage dam was built as part of the original aqueduct project; the waters of Owens Valley were simply funneled into the mouth of the aqueduct and piped to Los Angeles.

The acquisition of Owens Valley water by the City of Los Angeles ruined a prosperous farming community. Early in the spring of 1927, the remnants of the Owens Valley settlers published an advertisement in the Los Angeles newspapers under the heading: "We, the farming communities of Owens Valley, being about to die, salute you!" And die they did. Orchards withered, prosperous farms reverted to desert, and the blight of aridity reclaimed the valley. Failing to secure justice in their appeals to public opinion, the legislature, and the courts, the farmers of Owens Valley, in May, 1924, blew up sections of the aqueduct, opened control gates, and, for three years afterwards, conducted a gallant fight against the City of Los Angeles. The sponsors of the Owens Valley project, however, knew how to cope with such stubbornness. The resistance in the valley had been financed by two pioneer bankers who, by manipulating their books in violation of the state banking act, were able to carry delinquent mortgages. Waiting until these leaders had become deeply involved, the powers-that-be then had them indicted and sentenced to San Quentin Prison. Having broken the resistance movement, the City of Los Angeles then proceeded, in 1931, to buy up most of the remaining lands in the valley. As late as 1945, the City of Los Angeles, and the Los Angeles Times, opposed state legislation designed to provide a small measure of belated justice to the ruined farmers of Owens Valley.

To this day, according to Mr. Mayo, "ninety percent of the people of Los Angeles have no idea of the colossal swindle which was put over on them, nor do they have the slightest inkling of what was done in Owens Valley." In fact, the conspiracy of silence still prevails. The highly important role played by the late Harry Chandler in the Owens Valley affair is never mentioned or discussed in Los Angeles. Morrow Mayo's book, which contained the first complete account of the rape of Owens Valley, was greeted by the almost audible silence of the Los Angeles press. Owens Valley remains one of those topics concerning which "the less said the better." One reason for the persistence of this attitude is that, although the Owens Valley project was conceived by a group of business men, it was actually executed by the municipally owned Department of Water and Power of the City of Los Angeles. Most of the reform leaders of Los Angeles, the men who had fought valiantly for public ownership, felt compelled to remain silent or actually to endorse the project. At various points in Los Angeles, one can today observe prominent statues, plaques, and memorials that have been erected in honor of the one-time Zanjero of the Los Angeles water system, the engineer in charge of the Owens Valley project, William Mulholland. Just why the City of Los Angeles felt compelled to honor the engineer responsible for the Owens Valley fiasco, or even to mention Owens Valley, remains one of those curious examples of ambivalent civic ethics.

3. The Quest Is Pursued

Because the Owens Valley project was unsound from an engineering standpoint, the City of Los Angeles got off to a bad start in its quest for water. The alternative project, namely, the Long Valley reservoir, would have been a much sounder undertaking. Started in 1907, the Owens Valley project was not completed until 1913. Two years later the city was again in search of water. This time its engineers went to the Mono Basin, even farther from Los Angeles than Owens Valley, and acquired an additional supply of 135 cubic feet per second. And, still later, the city sponsored the Boulder Dam Act which was finally approved by Congress on December 21, 1928. Today water is brought by aqueduct from the Colorado River a distance of 242 miles to the Cajalco Reservoir near Riverside. To distribute Colorado River water, the Metropolitan Water District of Southern California was created in 1928, on the board of which thirteen Southern California cities are now represented. From the point of intake at Parker Dam, to Los Angeles, the Colorado River aqueduct actually travels a distance of 392 miles. The inadequacy of the Owens River project is indicated, not merely by the subsequent search of the City of Los Angeles for water, but by the fact that storage dams were not originally considered in connection with the Owens Valley aqueduct. Even the matter of developing hydroelectric power came about, not as a basic aspect of the project, but as a more or less accidental by-product developed after the aqueduct was constructed.

Today the Metropolitan Water District has estimated the total water supplies, from all sources, for the 1,400,000 acres in the South

Coastal Basin (which includes all the arable lands from Santa Monica to Redlands, from the coast range to the sea) as follows:

Local water supply	0.5 in depth
Owens River and Mono Basin	0.2 in depth
Colorado River	0.7 in depth
Total future available supply	1.4 in depth

As Dr. Samuel B. Morris has pointed out, a supply of 1.4 feet in depth per acre of economically productive and usable lands is a gross figure with no allowances for losses in handling or distribution. As such it is "somewhat low for either irrigation or modest residential use," and is "quite insufficient for congested and industrial districts." It is, however, all the water that is in sight for the South Coastal Basin. When Colorado River water was finally obtained, the residents of Los Angeles were assured that the supply would be adequate at least until the year 1980. But this estimate did not take into consideration the fact that World War II was destined to convert Los Angeles into a great industrial center. As I write these lines, the Los Angeles *Times* carries a story under the caption: "Water Demands on Coast Zoom." The story quotes Col. G. E. Arnold of the War Production Board to the effect that: "The curve of water consumption on the coast went up sharply after Pearl Harbor and each seasonal peak has been higher than the last. This summer's peak has brought some communities near the danger point and a dry season would create some serious shortages." Obviously, the perennial problem of water has not been solved.

To a considerable extent, the problem of water in Southern California is a cultural problem. By this I mean that newcomers to the region, who have always made up a majority of the population, have never understood the crucial importance of water. Crossing the desert, they arrive in an irrigated paradise, in which almost anything can be grown with a quickness and abundance that cannot be equaled by any other region in America. There does not *seem* to be a water problem. Nor are they told that there is such a problem, for Southern California has always been extremely reluctant to discuss its basic weakness. As a consequence, there has been a truly amazing institutional lag in the culture of the region, that is, new institutional devices for coping with the eternal water problem have only been evolved years after the case for their establishment had been known to exist. It was years after California had been admitted to the union as a state before the courts and the legislature began to evolve a body of law to cope with water problems. It was not until 1887 that the legislature passed the Wright Act, which permitted communities to form, and to bond, irrigation districts—an act which has served as the basis for practically all similar legislation in the United States. It was not until 1911 that the Irrigation District Bond Commission Law was enacted; not until 1917 that the state began to supervise all dams built by irrigation districts; not until 1921 that the state passed the Water Storage District Act; and it was not until 1921 that the state appropriated $200,000 for a systematic inventory of its water resources.

Not only has the institutional lag been pronounced, but the culture of the region has only slowly and imperfectly been adapted to the physical factors of a semi-arid environment. The development of conservancy districts, by which communities in Southern California pour surface water onto sandy soils so that it may percolate to the underground storage basins, was a comparatively late innovation. Soil practices calculated to conserve water were only evolved at a late date. A remarkable Southern Californian, William E. Smythe, tried years ago to hammer home the point that a semi-arid environment necessarily requires a new orientation of an imported culture pattern. His volume, *The Conquest of Arid America*, first published in 1899, might well be the bible of residents of Southern California. In particular, he insisted that a semi-arid environment necessarily implied extensive collective action, a subordination of private interests to the public welfare, and public ownership or control of water resources. He took a leading part in the formation of the California Water and Forest Association, around the turn of the century, only to have the "private enterprise" advocates of the period completely subvert the original purposes of the association. Some of his incidental papers, such as the essay on "The Ethics of Irrigation," raise issues basic to the economy of Western America. Like most prophets, however, Smythe was largely ignored.

That Southern California is an irrigated civilization largely accounts for the breakdown between rural and urban distinctions. Irrigated settlements naturally require a compact pattern of homes rather than scattered farmsteads. The presence of running water, bathtubs, and electricity in the early colony settlements is, in part, an aspect of irrigation development. "Rural" life has never been precisely "rural" in Southern California. Irrigation requires a heavy investment of capital and labor; it implies "co-operation of the many," through stable social organizations. It was this orientation that Smythe, with his early background in the socialist movement and his training in the principles of Fourierism, sought to develop in his "little lander" projects, through the irrigation congresses that he organized, and in his magazine, *The Irrigation Age*.

If ever a region had an important stake in co-operative organization, that region is Southern California. Co-operative action is required to develop water sources; to distribute, and to use, water efficiently; to introduce new technologies; to develop hydroelectric power. Nearly every major advance in the region has been made possible, not by greedy "men of vision,"—the so-called empire builders—but by the co-operative action of the people themselves, through mutual water companies, irrigation and conservancy districts, co-operative marketing agencies, and such instrumentalities as the Metropolitan Water District. Yet a general awareness of this fact does not exist.

4. FLOODS IN A DESERT

The general lack of cultural understanding in Southern California is strikingly shown in the neglect of forest resources, a matter intimately related to the ability of the region to husband its limited water supply. For the environment is dynamic as well as paradoxical and has always required careful management based upon accurate understanding. "No flood problems," writes Dr. Morris, "existed in primitive uninhabited California." Flood and forest problems arose in direct ratio to the increasing density of population. There is, for example, an almost perfect correlation between the number of forest fires and population increases. The damage caused by forest fires, particularly brush fires, in Southern California simply cannot be estimated. For many years, the brush fires have begun to burn each August and September. During these months, fires can usually be seen burning in a half-dozen areas of Los Angeles County. Following the first "Santa Ana" desert winds in May, similar fires frequently occur. For example, on May 17, 1945, the Los Angeles *Times* reported: "Firemen Kept Busy as Heat Again Hits 90." On this particular day, 388 grass fires were reported in the county. A glance at the scarred hillsides, in fact, is sufficient to indicate the damage caused by forest fires.

With so much of the sparse cover of the mountains having been removed by fires, it is not surprising to note a correlation between the increasing amounts spent on flood control and the number of forest fires. During the rainy season of late years, waters trumpet down the canyons and arroyos, causing extraordinary damage. In a five-day period in March, 1938, eleven inches of rain fell, flooding 30,000 square miles of land, taking a toll of 81 lives, and causing an estimated $83,000,000 in property damage. Seeing no connection between forest fires and floods, the residents of the region perennially "solve" the problem by increasing the expenditures for flood control. Flood control has, in fact, become a major political setup in Los Angeles, the basis of which is to build more cement causeways so that surface waters may be carried to the ocean as swiftly as possible and with the minimum damage to extensive property holdings which have been built in areas that should have been zoned against occupancy. Through increasingly efficient flood control measures, Los Angeles has been wasting an ever-growing volume of surface waters.

In much the same manner, the flood hazard has been increased, in the past, by the construction of badly designed water storage dams at poorly selected sites. On March 12, 1928, the St. Francis Dam in the Santa Clara Valley, designed by William Mulholland and associates, fell apart, releasing a torrent of waters. In this particular disaster 1,240 homes were destroyed and 385 lives were lost. Most of the homes destroyed were occupied by Mexican citrus workers, and most of the lives lost were Mexican, for the Mexicans, of course, were permitted to live directly in the pathway of possible floods. Some time in advance of this disaster, the City of Los Angeles had knowledge of the weakness of the St. Francis Dam, yet nothing was done to relieve the mounting pressure of rain waters on the dam. For this folly, the city paid a heavy indemnity, but retained, and continued to honor, its chief engineer.

Although always in need of more and more water, Southern Californians hate moisture like cats and are probably the world's most incompetent rain-manipulators. Always praying for rain, they are invariably embarrassed and confused when Providence answers their petitions. A major rainstorm in Los Angeles has always spelt disaster for the community. When 4,761,548,800,000 pounds of rain fell from the skies in March, 1938, one could read in the newspapers of perch being fished from downtown streets; of hail pellets the size of hen's eggs falling in the Arroyo Seco; of movie sets floating on Malibu Lake; of rowboats appearing in suburban areas; of marathon swimmers diving into the swirling waters of the proverbially "dry" Los Angeles River; of the "continuous cannonade of boulders, big as houses," rolling down from the mountains through the streets of Montrose. Cottages floated off their flimsy moorings; lots disappeared; alder and cottonwood trees bobbed in the streams; men in bathing suits rescued passengers from stalled automobiles; alligators washed out of the Lincoln Park Zoo splashed about in the streets, as elephants trumpeted, apes chattered, dogs went mad and jumped into the rivers, and birds bashed themselves to death against stone walls. The Hollywood Humane Society treated injured animals at the rate of thirty an hour, as hundreds of canaries, cats, goats, chickens, dogs, and even lions, were rushed in for treatment. Overstuffed furniture, stoves, and tin cans bobbed along "fierce chocolate tributaries"; and airplanes flew south from San Francisco with relief supplies. Catching the excitement from afar, the *London Daily Mirror* reported that "people are frantically climbing the tops of trams and crowding into skyscrapers . . . the ultra-religious are campaigning among the refugees crowded by the hundreds in schools, crying to them, 'Repent! Repent! The Floods are a Judgment.'" A few days after the flood waters had begun to recede, the County Coroner sagely pronounced, after an open hearing, that the floods had been "an act of Providence and no one person can be held responsible." (Note: there is a vivid description of this particular flood in a novel by Rupert Hughes, *City of Angels*, published in 1941.) For weeks after The Great Flood of 1938, I watched the Los Angeles newspapers carefully to see if, by chance, one of the papers might possibly run an editorial on forest fires and forest resources. Needless to say, not a single editorial of this character appeared.

5. HATFIELD THE RAINMAKER

In a semi-arid land, such as Southern California, it is not surprising that the first popular folk-hero should have been a rainmaker. Concerned by the delay of the rains, one reads that the residents of Santa

Barbara in 1833 "besought the holy father of the Missions that the Virgin, Nuestra Señora del Rosario, might be carried in procession through the town whilst prayers and supplications should be offered for her intercession with the Almighty in behalf of their distress." If the rains did not appear on schedule, wrote an observer in 1887, "all classes of business men are at a white heat of anxiety." From the earliest date, the annals contain reference to "water magicians" and "precipitators," who used hazel wands and other devices. J. W. Potts —Prophet Potts as he was called—was a famous predictor and precipitator in early-day Los Angeles. The outstanding water magician of Southern California, however, was Charles Mallory Hatfield, "Hatfield the Rainmaker," who derived his ideas about "the science of pluviculture" from a treatise written by one Edward Powers in 1871. Such was the interest that this book aroused that, in 1891, Congress instructed General Robert Dyrenforth to make an official investigation of the subject and appropriated a sizable sum for the study.

Hatfield first began to experiment with rainmaking on his father's farm in San Diego around 1902. After making some sixteen experiments, he managed to produce, as he put it, "a slight precipitation." Always a modest man, Hatfield never contended that he could make rain. "The term is too broad," he objected. "I merely assist Nature. I only persuade the moisture to come down." As an experimenter, Hatfield was far in advance of the hazel-wand variety of rainmaker. When called into a drought-ridden area in Southern California, he would erect a few large "evaporating tanks" filled with "certain chemicals the character of which must necessarily remain secret." At the appropriate time, he would remove the lid from the tanks, thereby permitting the mysterious chemical fumes to mix with the air, "overturning the atmosphere," and precipitating rainfall. In the dry season, these Hatfield evaporators were once a familiar sight throughout Southern California.

Hatfield secured his first contract "to lend Nature just a little assistance" in Los Angeles in 1903. Setting up his evaporators, he produced an inch of rainfall in five days and was given twice his fee of $50 by a grateful and astonished landowner. Thereafter his rainmaking reputation quickly spread throughout the region and his services were in great demand. Over a period of years, he conducted 500 rainmaking demonstrations in the region, for fees ranging from $50 to $10,000. For eight consecutive years, the farmers of the San

Joaquin Valley contracted with Hatfield to "make rain"; and nearly every city government in Southern California, at one time or another, signed contracts with him "to precipitate moisture." He once signed a contract to fill the reservoir of the Lake Hemet Land & Water Company for a fee of $4,000. He was so successful, on this occasion, that he precipitated a downpour of eleven inches of rain, raising the water level of the dam by twenty-two feet. In Los Angeles, during the first four months of 1905, he produced eighteen inches of rainfall.

Hatfield's most fabulous exploit, however, occurred in 1916, when he signed a contract with the City of San Diego to fill its giant reservoir by a specified date. Large crowds gathered to watch Hatfield set up his evaporators and mix his mysterious chemicals. As the date for the expiration of his contract drew near, headlines in the local press counted off the days and all of San Diego watched with bated breath to see if he would make good his agreement. With less than twenty-seven days left to run on the contract, the Great Rainmaker precipitated the mightiest downpour in the history of San Diego County. More than sixteen inches of rain fell in a two-day period. Not only did he fill the 18,000,000 gallon reservoir (it had never been more than one third filled before), but a torrent of water rushed over the dam and caused great havoc in San Diego and environs. Railroad bridges were washed away, cities and towns were flooded, and attendance at the San Diego World's Fair fell to zero. "This was a phenomenon," said Hatfield, "that I was never able to repeat." The City of San Diego, indignant over the results of his experiment, refused to pay his fee. "We told you," the City Council said, "merely to fill the reservoir: not to flood the community."

In later years, the fame of Hatfield spread from Southern California throughout the world. He received fat contracts for rain-precipitation all the way from Texas to the Klondike, from Canada to Honduras. One of his last great feats was to produce forty inches of rainfall in three hours on the Mojave Desert near Randsburg. In fact, he was so successful that Southern California municipalities became fearful of his evaporators. The belief was widespread that Hatfield could not control his own magic. "I do not doubt," said Hatfield, "that my methods would have saved all the tremendous losses of the dust bowl, had they been called into play."

At the height of his fame, Hatfield was known throughout Southern California. The stories about him rival those told about Riley, and Paul Bunyan, and Pecos Bill. When I came to Southern California in 1922, municipalities were still signing contracts with him to make rain. As the newspapers counted off the number of days left to fulfill his contracts in screaming headlines, thousands of Southern Californians, scanning the skies, would speculate on whether "Hatfield was going to make it." The belief in his magic was well-nigh universal. In 1925, David Starr Jordan of Stanford University made an investigation of Hatfield's methods for *Science* magazine. According to Dr. Jordan, Hatfield was a close student of weather charts. His usual technique was to wait until the dry season was far advanced and the people were beginning to despair of rain. Then he would appear upon the scene, sometimes as late as mid-January, and obtain a contract to produce rain within, say, thirty or sixty days. And of course he never missed. But the cruel debunking by Dr. Jordan had no effect whatever upon the popular belief, particularly prevalent among newcomers, in Hatfield's magic. It was not until the City of Los Angeles finally secured Colorado River water that the Hatfield evaporators disappeared from the Southern California landscape. As nearly as I can determine, Hatfield secured no further contracts for rainmaking after the passage of the Boulder Dam Act in 1928.

Although Southern Californians do not understand the semi-arid environment in which they live, they are haunted by a vague and nameless fear of future disaster. Mary Austin was convinced that a stern God would someday visit just retribution upon the City of the Angels for the crime it had committed in Owens Valley. The belief in some awful fate that will some day engulf the region is widespread and persistent and has a history which cannot be chronicled here. "There is something disturbing about this corner of America," wrote J. B. Priestley, "a sinister suggestion of transience. There is a quality, hostile to men in the very earth and air here. As if we were not meant to make our homes in this oddly enervating sunshine. . . . California will be a silent desert again. It is all as impermanent and brittle as a reel of film."

It is the odd combination of almost perpetual sunshine with a lush, but not indigenous, vegetation that produces this impression of impermanence. Even newcomers are vaguely aware that the region is semi-arid, that the desert is near, and that all the throbbing, bustling life of Southern California is based on a single shaky premise, namely, that the aqueduct life-lines will continue to bring an adequate supply of water to the region. The exotic has been superimposed on this semi-arid land; it is not native. "It ought to be exotic," a visitor once complained, "but somehow it really isn't exotic." The perpetual sunshine baffles, confuses, irritates, and eventually maddens the inhabitants. "This damnably monotonous sunlight," complained Denis Ireland. "Sometimes," observes a character in a novel by Carl Van Vechten, "I think I'll die if this sun don't stop shinin'. I wake up some mornings and I pull down the shades and turn on the electric lights to pretend it's rainin' outside." The hot-dry Santa Ana winds will not permit the residents to forget the nearness of the desert. "Shrieking and moaning," wrote George Randolph Chester in a novel published in 1924, "the wind swept in from the desert . . . it was one of those summer days rare to the Pacific coast, but poignant, when through the yellow sunlight there sift vague phantom shapes of impalpable dust which bite the skin and smart the eyes, and are the prickling forerunners of a three-day withering heat from out the very heart of the vast shadeless inferno up yonder in the waste places . . . a day that lowers the vitality and depresses the spirits and sets the nerves on edge. . . . No one knows what tremendous extent of folly and of tragedy may be chargeable to this same shrill, shrieking, moaning, sobbing wind from the deadly desert." Facing the ocean, Southern California is inclined to forget the desert, but the desert is always there and it haunts the imagination of the region.

6. "HORRID LITTLE SHAKY EARTHQUAKES"

It is not only the desert that haunts the imagination of Southern California; there is an abiding fear of earthquakes. While taking elaborate precautions against earthquakes (such as ordinances limiting the height of buildings), Southern California amusingly minimizes the actual dangers involved. In a Santa Barbara booster book written in 1919, Lelia Weekes Wilson wrote that "a real earthquake has not been felt here for over a hundred years, so the danger from seismic disturbances need cause little worry." On June 29, 1925, Santa Barbara was nearly shaken asunder by a major earthquake. An investor's manual, issued by a bondhouse in Los Angeles in 1939, glibly assures the investor that "California will not experience an earthquake exceeding materially the violence of that which occurred in

San Francisco in 1906." Not only are earthquakes seldom mentioned in the history books, but, when mentioned, they are usually praised:

> We have an earthquake
> Now and again
> To let the people know
> God's greater than the men.

Let some Middle-Western city be inundated by flood waters, let some Florida community be devastated by a tornado, and the Los Angeles *Times* can be relied upon to publish a pious editorial stressing the fact that, after all, earthquakes are "not so bad." In an editorial of October 2, 1933, the San Bernardino *Sun* even contended that "an earthquake never killed anyone." On one occasion when a flood in Tennessee had resulted in considerable loss of life and the wire services were carrying stories about "mangled victims being recovered from the turbulent waters," the *Times* ran a lengthy editorial pointing out that, while earthquakes do occasionally take human lives, the victims are never mangled. The editorial prompted Duncan Aikman to dash off the lines:

> The blessed dead of Tennessee
> Make blyther heads for you and me.
> Each Nashville babe in heaven that wakes
> Blows down the blurb of local quakes.
>
> This week the choicest news bears out
> That others catch it on the snout,
> And though our losses be more numerous,
> We find Confederate dead more humorous.
>
> Let storm and quake, then, leave us gory all,
> Cheer up and read our editorial:
> Tornadoes twist 'em; earthquakes mangle less
> The population near Los Angeles.

Following the disastrous earthquake of March 10, 1933, which caused $40,000,000 property damage and took many lives, the Los Angeles City Council adopted a resolution thanking the Almighty for a disaster which had demonstrated, once again, the warmhearted and generous character of the population of Southern California.

The resolution went on to emphasize that the earthquake had overcome local civic rivalries and had created new bonds of friendship between Los Angeles and Long Beach. A few weeks after this particular quake, the Coroner of Los Angeles held an official inquiry "to determine the truth concerning the causes and needs in building materials." Among those called to testify was Dr. Harry O. Wood, a distinguished seismologist from the California Institute of Technology. When asked a hopeful question as to whether Los Angeles could expect "relief" as a result of the Long Beach quake, Dr. Wood seemed reluctant to answer, stating that the question was dangerous. Ignoring this warning, the Coroner pressed for an answer and got it. Dr. Wood testified that Los Angeles, situated near three major earth rifts, might expect even more severe earthquakes in the future than in the past. According to the one newspaper that reported the hearing, "a distraught laugh, like the rattle of falling plaster, broke over the inquest room. Dr. Wood was turned off the subject and hurried through the rest of his testimony." As soon as a recess was called, the newspaper reporters were herded together and told, "Boys, we can't let this get out over the wires." So severe was the shock of this testimony that the five daily newspapers promptly buried the story. And, once the hearing was concluded, the contractors proceeded to use brick in rebuilding structures damaged or destroyed by the earthquake, despite testimony that brick store-fronts had collapsed with the first temblor.

The persistent failure of the press to report the findings of modern seismologists has resulted in an immense amount of folklore about earthquakes in Southern California. Most Southern California residents are thoroughly convinced that tall buildings are peculiarly perilous in a quake area, that earthquakes are caused by the drainage of oil from the bowels of the earth, and that earthquakes are invariably preceded by a period of what is called "earthquake weather." Despite the fact that earthquakes have occurred in summer and winter, spring and fall, the belief in earthquake weather persists. In the sense in which most residents understand the expression, "earthquake weather" refers to a close, stifling, sunless, muggy day. The belief in the oil-drainage superstition is of equal tenacity and antiquity. As a matter of fact, there is a slightly melodramatic quality, a hint of the sinister, about an oil field. The great shining storage tanks, the forest of derricks that assume fantastic shapes in mist and

cloud, light and darkness, and the ceaseless idiotic thumping of the
pumps does make for an atmosphere of doubt and misgiving.

When a major quake jars Southern California, popular fancy is
immediately quickened. After the Long Beach earthquake of 1933, I
culled the following items from the local press: a hen laid three eggs
a few moments after the first shock was felt; a woman who had been
suffering from paralysis for years was immediately cured by the vibrations of the quake and walked forth from an invalid's room without
assistance; the quake was "predicted" by "scientists" weeks before it
happened, but the information was "suppressed"; a woman, taking
a bath in Long Beach when the first shock came, was compelled to
remain in the bathroom without clothes for three days and nights
when a section of the wall fell in and blocked the doorway (she was
eventually rescued by a squad of legionnaires); sixteen boys were
killed in the Polytechnic High School in Long Beach, but were never
reported as missing and their parents were promptly "hushed up." It
also seems that, while gazing at the Los Angeles City Hall, a group
of people saw the hall sway out of sight, come back into sight, sway
out of sight in the opposite direction, and then come to rest "with
an awful jar"; that a worker in a chemical plant in Long Beach was
thrown thirty feet in the air after the first shock and that, on hitting
the ground, he bounced skyward, and was thus bounced up and down
"for three times in rapid succession"; that the earthquake was really
caused by a moving mountain near Durango, Colorado; that an automobile on a Long Beach boulevard shook so hard during the quake
that it lost all four tires; that the undertaker in Long Beach did not
charge "a single penny" for the sixty or more interments following
the quake; that the quake was the first manifestation of an awful
curse which the Rev. Robert P. Shuler had placed on Southern California, after he failed to be elected to the United States Senate; that
sailors on a vessel a mile or more offshore saw Long Beach's Signal
Hill disappear from sight; that the bootleggers of Long Beach saved
hundreds of lives by their public-spirited donation of large quantities
of alcohol; that women showed more courage than men; that men,
for some reason, simply cannot stand up to an earthquake; that the
shock of the quake caused a dozen or more miscarriages in Long
Beach and that an earthquake will often cause permanent menstrual
irregularities; that every building not damaged by the quake was
"earthquake proof"; that a cross on a Long Beach church was not

damaged although the rest of the building was destroyed; that an earthquake is much more terrifying than a cyclone, but not quite so frightful as a tornado, and just slightly less ghastly than a hurricane; that Californians should construct "earthquake cellars"; that "the first temblor is always hardest"; that, in fact, there is only one real quake, the subsequent temblors being merely "echoes" of the first; that it is extremely dangerous to rush out of doors during an earthquake; that the best place to be during an earthquake is in a doorway; that the reason the government never built a fort in California was because of the earthquake hazard; that every community which escaped serious damage was "not in the path of the fault" and was, therefore, a safe and good place to live; and that the earthquake, followed as it was by the appearance of a mighty meteor on March 24, presaged the beginning of the end.

How deeply the experience of living in an earthquake country has impressed the residents of the region is clearly shown in the novels that have been written about California. In many of these novels, one will find that the climax of the tale invariably is reached at precisely the moment when the dishes begin to rattle, the stove to bounce, and the chairs to dance. According to the novelist Lawrence Rising, there is a stillness and expectancy in California "found only in earthquake countries." Myron Brinig closed a novel about Southern California with a fantastic, perhaps prophetic, vision: "Los Angeles tobogganed with almost one continuous movement into the water, the shoreline going first, followed by the inland communities . . . the small pink and white, blue and orange houses of the shore were blown like colored sands into the tempest. All of California, from the Siskiyous to Mexico, from the eastern border to the coast, started sliding swiftly, relentlessly, into the Pacific Ocean." (See also Frank Fenton's novel, *A Place in the Sun*, pp. 182-183, where a somewhat similar impression is recorded.) As a matter of fact, the German geographer, Alfred Wegener, in a treatise written in 1924, hinted that something of this sort might actually happen. Studying his theory of the origin of continents and islands, one can readily imagine that this island-on-the-land that is Southern California, this sub-tropical paradise, might someday be severed from a continent to which it has always been capriciously attached and float gently westward into the Pacific to become, as it has always been destined to be, a charming Tahiti in some glazed and azure sea.

"He hangs in shades the orange bright,
Like golden lamps in a green night."

CHAPTER XI

THE CITRUS BELT

CLEARLY marked as a distinct region, Southern California has a number of equally well-defined climatic sub-regions not apparent from a casual inspection of the land. Within the region, for example, there is an amazing variation in rainfall. The average rainfall in San Diego is 9.7 inches, while the average for Los Angeles is 15.0 inches. On the foothill slopes, the rainfall increases, in some areas, by ten inches in a single steep mile. Riverside, with an elevation of 850 feet, has 10.8 inches of rainfall, but San Bernardino, ten miles distant, with an elevation of 1050 feet, has 16.1 inches of rainfall. On the rim of the mountains surrounding this semi-arid region, the rainfall frequently averages 30, 40, and 50 inches. Differences in temperature and the incidence of frost vary as widely, and as imperceptibly, as the amount of rainfall. Thermal belts mark the pathway of warm air currents. The areas penetrated by fog, along the river bottoms, are the areas of frost and the early freeze. Not charted on the maps, these freakish climatic sub-regions had to be discovered by a painful and costly trial-and-error process, prompting Van Dyke to observe that Southern California was "a land of solid realities and glittering frauds."

The existence of these climatic sub-regions accounts for the highly specialized character of the region's agriculture. Throughout the region today one can see a number of clearly defined belts or zones of agricultural production, the present visible tokens of invisible soil and climatic variations. Alfalfa, grain, sugar beets, and other crops not injured by frost, are planted in the lowlands; farther up the slopes appear the belts of grapes and fruit crops; still higher, and usually in the form of a dark-green horseshoe curve around the rim of the valleys, is the orange belt; and, still higher on the slopes, are the zones of lemons and avocados. In this paradoxical land, orchard crops are raised, not in the lowlands, but in the foothills. Relatively more free of frost than any area in California, Southern California is the home and center of the citrus industry. Virtually all of the lemons raised in the state come from Southern California (about 90% of the nation's production), and three-fourths of the orange production is also centered in the region. That oranges and lemons will grow in the region technically justifies its characterization as sub-tropical, otherwise a very misleading description of Southern California.

While the citrus industry extends from Santa Barbara to San Diego, it has several points of concentration. In popular parlance, the citrus belt designates the foothill orange district extending from Pasadena to San Bernardino through the orange towns of Monrovia, Azusa, Glendora, Covina, Pomona, Upland, and Ontario. This inland district, relatively frost-free, is the home of the winter-ripening Washington navel orange. Here the soil is largely decomposed granite, the drainage excellent, and the quality of the water superb. The citrus industry of Southern California had its origin in this district. Early in the present century, groves of the summer-ripening Valencia orange began to be planted in the coastal areas of Santa Barbara, Ventura, Orange, and San Diego Counties, thus providing the industry with a year-round production. In the areas of Valencia production, the soil is largely shale and sandstone, not so well drained, and likely to be injured by over-irrigation. Having a sturdier resistance to frost than the navel orange, the Valencia tree thrives in the coastal sections. The "cities of the plain," such as Whittier, Anaheim, Fullerton, Orange, and Santa Ana, are within the zone of Valencia production, while lemon production is concentrated in the areas around Santa Barbara, Carpinteria, and Santa Paula. The determining factor in citrus production is the zone of ocean-fog penetration. While citrus crops can be raised in this zone, the fruit produced is of an inferior quality.

Throughout Southern California are many similar belts: a walnut belt from Ventura to San Fernando; a walnut belt in Orange County which produces about one-third of the world's supply of English walnuts; a lima bean belt along the coast; a general farming area extending along the river bottoms from El Monte to Downey; a dairy belt; and a series of truck-farming belts. In none of these belt-areas, however, does one notice quite the same social stratification and the curious mixture of urban-rural cultures that so strikingly characterizes the citrus belt. For wherever citrus production predominates, a rather distinctive social life has long existed. This citrus belt complex of peoples, institutions, and relationships has no parallel in rural life in America and nothing quite like it exists elsewhere in California. It is neither town nor country, neither rural nor urban. It is a world of its own.

Basically the orange tree itself provides the key to an understanding of the social life of the citrus belt. For the orange, as Charles Fletcher Lummis once pointed out, is not only a fruit but a romance. The orange tree is the living symbol of richness, luxury, and elegance. With its rich black-green shade, its evergreen foliage, and its romantic fragrance, it is the millionaire of all the trees of America, the "golden apple" of the fabled Gardens of the Hesperides. The aristocrat of the orchards, it has, by a natural affinity, drawn to it the rich and the well-born, creating a unique type of rural-urban aristocracy. There is no crop in the whole range of American agriculture the growing of which confers quite the same status that is associated with ownership of an orange grove. To own a large wheat farm in Washington unquestionably gives a sense of possession and proud dominion; to own a well-stocked corn-and-hog farm in the Middle West undeniably confers a sense of solid well-being and plenty; but to own an orange grove in Southern California is to live on the real gold coast of American agriculture. It is not by chance that millionaire row in Pasadena should be called Orange Grove Avenue.

Carefully trimmed and corseted, the orange tree is like a rather plump middle-aged dowager bedizened with jewels and gems and a corsage of gardenias. The typical grove is as immaculately kept, and as orderly, as the parlor of such a dowager. Plebeian weeds are removed as rapidly as they have the impudence to intrude upon these elegant preserves. Delicate in health, the dowager-orange is carefully protected against even the mild rigors and hazards of climate in Southern California. Elaborate windbreaks of cedar, cypress, and eucalyptus protect the sacrosanct groves where the smudge pots are lighted at the first threat of frost. The water brought to the trees is examined as carefully as the diet of a diabetic patient in a Santa Barbara hospital. The armed might of California, represented by its famous highway patrol, guards the borders of the state to prevent the invasion of bugs, insects, and blight. A whole retinue of servants waits upon this perennially pregnant lady. The grove in which she lives is not a farm, but a kind of outdoor hothouse guarded as jealously as a Scottish lord's hunting park. (If you doubt this statement, try to pick an orange, sometime, in Southern California.) The dowager-orange is always well groomed, carefully manicured, and willing to receive guests—provided they remain at a distance and admire her discreetly. Like most dowagers, her perfume is heavy, rich, a little overpowering.

Today it is difficult to appreciate that Southern California was, not so many years ago, a semi-desert. It actually comes as something of a shock to find the land described, in the early chronicles, as "a wretched land, barren and bereft"; rimmed by "great mountains, uncompromisingly stern and barren of everything except stone and brush"; "a loveless land, a starved region where every green branch is dearly prized." The appearance of orange and lemon groves in such a land was as pleasing to the eye as the sight of an oasis in the desert. The ever green and fragrant belts of citrus trees tended to compensate for the dryness, the heat, the scorched earth of the long summers. "At all times of the year," wrote Beatrice Harraden in an early novel, "there was that green stretch yonder of clustering trees, nestling near the foothills, which in turn seemed to nestle up to the rugged mountains . . . that belt of green so soothing and restful to the eyes through all the months of the year." In a sprawling and unkempt land, there was something about the precise formality with which the groves were laid out that gladdened the heart almost as much as the refreshing, lustrous green of the trees. Today, when the appearance of the land has changed so much, people have lost the sense of living in a desert, but, even so, they retain a special affection for the citrus groves. Just how important the citrus belt has been in changing the physical appearance of the land can only be sensed by trying to imagine what Southern California would be like were these green belts removed. They have contributed as much, perhaps, as any single factor to the physical charm of the region.

"Of all the trees," wrote Charles Fletcher Lummis, "that man has.

corseted to uniform symmetry and fattened for his use, none other is more beautiful and none more grateful than the orange." It has certainly been the gold nugget of Southern California. Not only has it attracted fully as many people to California as did the discovery of gold, but since 1903 the annual value of the orange crop has vastly exceeded the value of gold produced. Since 1894 the citrus industry has produced over two billion dollars in income for the people of Southern California. With an annual average income, from some of the groves, of a thousand dollars an acre, it is not surprising that the orange should be a sacred tree in Southern California.

1. SUNKIST

While oranges have been raised in Southern California since an early date, the industry was really founded in 1870 when J. W. North established one of the pioneer colony settlements at Riverside. The tract of land which Judge North purchased at $3.50 an acre was regarded as desert land. Constructing a $50,000 canal to bring water to the land, the Riverside colonists demonstrated that the uplands were more desirable for citrus culture than the lowlands and that on well-drained tablelands there was less danger that the tree roots would reach the water level and drown. These discoveries were·of revolutionary import in the development of the industry.

The original orange grove in Southern California had been planted to so-called seedling stock which came from the trees about the old Franciscan Missions. Another revolutionary advance was made in the industry when the Department of Agriculture in 1873 shipped two budded trees of the Washington navel orange from Bahia, Brazil, to Mrs. L. C. Tibbetts of Riverside. The navel orange proved to be ideally adapted to the environment, producing a large seedless orange of excellent color and fine flavor. It was not long before the two imported trees were so famous that the Tibbettses had to enclose them with an extra high barbed-wire fence to guard against theft. In 1903 Lummis reported that the original trees were still growing in the backyard of the Tibbetts home in Riverside, "where an old man and his wife have been left to poverty amid the vast riches they helped to create."

From these early beginnings, the industry rapidly expanded after 1880. The completion of the Southern Pacific line to Los Angeles in 1876, the extension of this line to New Orleans in 1881, and the arrival of the Santa Fe in 1886, not only made possible a swift development of Eastern, Southern, and Middle Western markets, but attracted much badly needed capital to the region. Oranges grown at Riverside took first prizes at the Cotton Exposition of 1884 and provoked wide interest and comment. On February 14, 1886, the first special train loaded exclusively with oranges was shipped from Los Angeles.

Despite the high freight rates (at one time it cost $600 to ship a car of oranges to the Missouri River points), the completion of the rail lines really unlocked the potentialities of the industry. As cooling and refrigeration methods steadily improved, the market for Southern California oranges became nation-wide in scope. By 1900, 5,648,-714 orange and 1,493,113 lemon trees had been planted in the region, five times the number of orange, eighteen times the number of lemon trees in the area in 1890. With a great increase in the Valencia and lemon acreage, the industry represented a $200,000,000 investment by 1915, and, with improved cultural methods, production steadily increased. In 1938, a year of low prices, the returns to California citrus growers amounted approximately to $51,000,000, nearly ten per cent of the total farm income for the state.

From the outset, the nature of the citrus industry compelled a large measure of associative effort. To establish a new industry in such a tricky environment necessarily required organized effort and a pooling of resources and experience. Heavy irrigation costs, expensive cultural practices, and difficult marketing problems, all demanded co-operative action. In particular, research had to be organized on a collective basis. No other crop area in America developed, at such an early date, a comparable level of technological achievement. New methods of irrigation had to be developed; constant improvements had to be effected in the type of frost-protection devices; blight had to be fought by systematically organized research; new cooling and refrigeration processes had to be evolved; and the task of organizing a national market for this comparatively new American product had to be approached as an industry problem. The establishment of tariff barriers also required joint action. Under the circumstances, it was only natural that the citrus growers should have organized at an early date.

In 1893 the Southern California Fruit Exchange was formed to cope with the problem of a vastly expanded production which had not been accompanied by a systematic expansion of markets and distributing facilities. This early organization was succeeded in 1905 by the present-day California Fruit Growers Exchange, perhaps the most efficient marketing co-operative in the world. Long before the central exchange came into being, however, local packing and marketing associations were established throughout the area. Superimposed, from above, on 201 local packing associations and 25 district exchanges, the Sunkist colossus reigns supreme today over the entire industry.

To give a rough idea of the magnitude of its operations, the exchange shipped, in the 1941–1942 season, 65,610 cars of oranges, 3,962 cars of grapefruit, and 16,148 cars of lemons, three-fourths of the entire movement of packed citrus fruit from California and Arizona. Through subsidiary corporations, it operates important by-products plants manufacturing citrus acid, sodium citrate, lemon oil, pectin, orange oil, orange pulp, and many other products. It spends $120,000 annually in research. Operating a lumber mill in Northern California, the exchange also owns large timber properties. From the commencement of its advertising program in 1907, over $37,000,000 has been spent on national advertising. Today the famous label "Sunkist" is known throughout the world. Through a far-flung sales and marketing apparatus, it has systematically organized the market, established a reputation for its various standardized and graded products, worked steady improvements in shipping and refrigeration methods, and has stimulated the use of new cultural practices. Gradually taking over one function after another, the exchange today really manages and operates, as well as controls, the entire industry.

The tendency of the exchange to dominate all phases of production has been furthered by the circumstance that the typical orange-grove owner is a gentleman-farmer who has purchased a suburban estate as a means of acquiring status. Today the local packing associations supply all the harvesting labor for their members, furnishing picking crews, hauling facilities, and all equipment, and undertaking, upon request, to take charge of pruning and insect control. Not only is this procedure agreeable to the average grower, but it enables the exchange to rationalize production. Thus the harvesting proceeds on a carefully worked out schedule, area by area, zone by zone, as a single collective year-round operation. So thoroughly has management been divorced from ownership in the industry that, in the words of Dr. J. Eliot Coit, "there are many citrus farmers who do no manual work on their farms." If desired, the local exchange will even cultivate, irrigate, and fertilize the groves and prune the trees. Through the local exchange, the grower can purchase all of his farming supplies at wholesale rates. Within five days from the sale of his oranges in some Eastern market, he receives a check for the proceeds. The average orange-grove owner is, therefore, no more a farmer than the typical citrus-belt community is a farming center. The peculiar nature of the extensive social organization that has developed in the industry largely accounts, in fact, for the complacent, conservative, functionless character of its communities.

However, there are some real farmers in the industry. These are the "commercial growers," who operate citrus farms, not for status, but for profit, the "determined agriculturalists" who put the industry on a paying basis. Fabulously successful, these larger concerns dominate the central exchange and its local and district branches. For years the managerial talent for the central, district, and local exchanges has been recruited from the personnel of the large commercial producers. Nor can there be any doubt that these concerns dominate the industry. In 1930, 115 commercial growers, constituting 3.4% of the total number of growers, received 27.7% of the $20,000,000 income from citrus farms in Orange County. Since most of the orange-grove owners are well-to-do retired people, they are quite willing that the commercial concerns should dominate the exchanges (whose policies reflect the special interests of the commercial growers) and control the industry. The center of power in the industry, therefore, is not to be found in the elegant residences on Smiley Heights in Redlands, but in the offices of the California Fruit Growers Exchange in Los Angeles. Here is the real dynamo.

Typical of the large commercial concerns is the Limoneira Company, controlled by Charles Collins Teague, who, for years, has been the undisputed boss of the California Fruit Growers Exchange. The acquisition of the 3,250 acres of citrus land operated by the company was financed, in the past, by floating huge bond issues much in the manner of an industrial concern. On the property is a "company town" of 400 homes which house a permanent "ranch population" of 1,500 people. For the first eight months of 1943, the company's payroll averaged $72,000 per month. Judged by any standards, this is quite a "farm." The secret of the company's success, as of all similar concerns, consists in the fact, pointed out by Mr. Teague, that "the unit cost of production on the marginal grove is almost prohibitive." Up to the time of harvest, it costs as much to produce a half carload of citrus fruit as it does a carload. The greater the production, therefore, the wider the margin of net profit. With such a marked advantage over the small grove, these concerns naturally dominate the industry.

Over the years the dominance of the large commercial concerns has steadily increased as marginal groves have been gradually eliminated. Although oranges can be raised almost anywhere in Southern California, they can only be grown commercially in the various belts or zones. In the process of discovering this sad fact, hundreds of romantic settlers went bankrupt. "In all too many cases," writes Mr. Teague, "the hopes and dreams of those who thus trustfully purchased citrus ranches ended in disillusionment and tragic failure." Scores of owners were eliminated by a disastrous blight that destroyed thousands of trees until it was finally eradicated in 1888. "The great freeze of 1913" removed still more marginal operators. Since it is impossible for the novice to tell a good orange grove from a poor one, the turnover of the marginal groves was, for many years, a major real estate racket in Southern California. With the zones of production being clearly defined, the large commercial growers have nowadays firmly stabilized production.

It is difficult to emphasize sufficiently the importance of the citrus industry in the development of Southern California. In this wonderfully fertile region (Los Angeles and Orange Counties have for years been the richest agricultural counties in the nation), the citrus industry was predominant from 1890 to 1938, when, for the first time, the value of dairy and livestock products slightly exceeded the value of the citrus crop. Not only has the industry been a great producer of agricultural income, providing a fine market for consumer goods, but it has been an invaluable tourist attraction and has brought much sorely needed capital to the region. With the establishment of an industry that reported exceptional earnings of $3,000 an acre and frequent earnings of from $800 to $1,000 an acre, the value of lands suitable for citrus production rapidly increased. This increase in land values made possible the formation of land companies, irrigation companies, and development corporations with sufficient capital to undertake the huge task of converting a semi-arid region into an agricultural wonderland. The rapid expansion of the citrus industry was responsible for the fact, reported in 1902 by the State Board of Agriculture, that "the very face of nature was changed, and in a few years Southern California became one of the most important sections of the state."

2. IN CITRUS LAND

The average orange grove in Southern California represents an investment of from $1,500 to $2,000 an acre. Exclusive of the cost of buildings, a fifty-acre citrus grove represents an investment of $80,000, a ten-acre grove of $16,000. Cultural costs are, also, exceptionally high, averaging $154 an acre for oranges in 1938, exclusive of interest, depreciation, and taxes, with the cost of lemon production being still higher, approximately $244 per acre. It has required men of wealth and ability to bring these groves into production and to operate them, once established.

"The California citrus culture," writes Dr. J. Eliot Coit, "among all horticultural industries, is peculiar in that the people who have built it up have been, in many cases, retired business men or professional men from New England and the Central States," who brought to the industry "needed capital, commercial habits, and business ability." This type of person was attracted to the citrus industry by the circumstance, pointed out by F. O. Wallschlaeger, that "there is a charm to be found in the culture of citrus fruits which can not be found in other outdoor pursuits." In addition, an orange grove is the perfect setting for a handsome suburban estate. From the outset, the attractiveness of the groves as suburban homesites had a tendency to inflate land values and to select the type of person who could afford to own a grove. To the ordinary capitalization of citrus lands, based upon earned net income, there was invariably added, depending upon the location and sightliness of the grove, a capitalization based upon its attractiveness as a homesite. By appealing to the rich and discouraging the poor, this selective process has long given a homogeneous character and a unique social quality to the citrus-belt communities.

Many of the early citrus communities in Southern California, such as Pasadena, Riverside, and Ontario, were the outgrowth of colony settlements. The colony settlements naturally attracted "people of intelligence and refinement," drawn from many occupations and professions, few of whom were trained or experienced farmers. That the colony settlements were laid out as complete communities, in advance of the sale of acreage units, was a great inducement to people anxious to avoid the rigors ordinarily associated with pioneer ex: istence in a new land. Moving into a colony settlement was rather like buying a lot in an exclusive subdivision. As people of means, these colonists brought the necessary funds to develop an industry requiring a heavy initial investment.

That many of these early settlers lacked farming experience proved to be a distinct asset, for it predisposed them to look with favor upon experimentation and the use of novel methods of water preservation, irrigation, and soil cultivation. As Dr. Coit notes, the citrus industry in Southern California has always been characterized by its willingness to experiment, to improvise, to develop its own methods. European methods of cultivating, irrigating and pruning citrus trees have had virtually no influence in the development of the industry. Having made modest, and in some cases substantial, fortunes in business, many of these early citrus growers brought to the industry a wide variety of business backgrounds and experience. From its inception, the citrus industry has made a more extensive use of modern business methods, particularly in the marketing and advertising fields, than any other segment of American agriculture.

Not only were the initial growers a highly selected group to begin with, but the nature of the industry tended to make them increasingly more homogeneous. "Everybody's fruit ripens at about the same time," explains a character in Howard Baker's novel *Orange Valley* (1931), "and if everybody picks his fruit and ships it the moment that it ripens, a good part of it must go to waste, for there would be more oranges on the market than could be used. We are in a peculiar situation. We all raise the same thing, and we all have to ship our crop to the same market and across the continent. You see, we have to have some sort of system." Many of the settlers in the colony projects came from the same locality, had much the same background, and had worked together in planning the colony before they arrived in Southern California. As a consequence, the colony settlements, out of which the towns in the citrus belt developed, had a homogeneous character which they have retained through the years. The settlers who built homes in the groves, built them, in most cases, upon the highest point of ground in order to be near their wells. Thus most of the homes are similarly located. With the lands suitable for citrus culture being limited in area and running in belts or strips, settlers in the area were drawn together by the fact that they all raised the same crop, for the same market, and were members, in most cases, of the same colony, packing association, and mutual water company.

Today "the orange empire" extends from Pasadena to San Bernardino through a series of evenly spaced communities, with the whole area being almost as densely populated as a city. Many of the towns are located literally in the heart of citrus groves. In 1929 nearly 16,000 acres of orange groves were still included within the city limits of Riverside. In most cases, the groves penetrate, not to any clearly defined urban boundary, but, along the avenues and highways, right into the center of the towns. Unlike the average American farm community, the towns or colony settlements came first, and the groves developed later. It is this circumstance which accounts, in part, for the highly urbanized character of the citrus belt.

A distinction is to be noted, however, between the communities located in the inland district of the Washington navel orange and those along the coastal areas where the Valencia type predominates. The navel orange districts are older, more densely populated, and have retained the urban character of the early colony settlements. The settlements are wealthier, more urbanized, more largely made up of former city-dwellers than are the more rural communities in the Valencia district. The difference is that between Redlands and Santa Ana, hard to define, almost imperceptible to an outsider, but very real nonetheless. The cities and towns in the Valencia district are less numerous and retain an unmistakably rural coloration. Actually, these settlements are older than those in the foothill districts, but they are newer from the point of view of citrus culture. They were settled by "dirt farmers," by people more concerned with good crops than with fine homes. In the Valencia district are to be found some of the largest commercial growers.

The handsome homes that one sees throughout the foothill districts are not farm houses, they are suburban residences. The older homes are ornate and rococo, and built very much in the taste and style of urban mansions in the 'seventies and 'eighties. With good roads, telephones, electric lights, water, fine schools, power lines, and the spread of civic improvement associations, these districts have enjoyed, almost since their inception, every convenience of urban life. Since land suitable for citrus production is limited in area, the citrus-belt districts are devoted to a single crop with every available foot of land being utilized. The groves are solidly, compactly arranged, "like a cluster of plump umbrellas of dark green leather," like regiments drawn up at attention in a city square, laid out flush with the streets and highways that knife through the district. Although there are some large estates, the average grove is small in size with many of the districts being laid out like urban subdivisions.

The typical citrus-belt town is really neither a town nor a city, but a suburban shopping district. With unmistakable urban overtones, these communities frequently have many of the institutions of small cities: a college or university, an art gallery, a museum, a luxury hotel. Many of these city-towns are beautifully laid out. Riverside, Redlands, and Pasadena were the first cities in the West to adopt ordinances regulating the size, character, and arrangement of trees along the streets. Appointing a tree-warden in 1906, the City of Riverside has, over the years, planted 30,000 trees in the city limits. Pasadena, "the Crown of the Valley," was for years "the aristocratic nucleus for the surrounding towns," with few places, as one early novelist recorded, "being so rich in conditions to palliate or allay" the usual conditions of rural life. Something of the appearance and flavor of these citrus-belt towns is to be found in two otherwise uninteresting novels: *Jacob Peek: Orange Grower* (1915) by Sidney Herbert Burchell and *The Eyes of the World* (1914) by Harold Bell Wright, both of which describe Redlands, perhaps the most charming community in the district. Like the groves, the citrus-belt towns are characterized by a certain elegance and richness, an air of quiet and complacent charm.

3. Across the Tracks

"There are times when bloody murder stalks under the red sun of California, though mostly it sulks in cowardice in the dark of the scented nights that spill such riches so inequitably distributed."

—Carleton Beals

To cultivate and to harvest citrus crops in Southern California requires a vast amount of labor: a monthly average, throughout the year, of about 15,000 field workers. In addition to the field workers, about 22,000 workers are employed in the packing sheds, grading, sorting, washing, packing, wrapping, and shipping citrus fruit. It would be difficult to imagine a sharper line of social cleavage than that which separates these 40,000 workers from, first, the managerial elite who operate the large commercial properties and the various exchanges, and second, the do-nothings who own the groves.

Originally most of the labor in the groves and sheds was performed by gangs of Chinese workmen. From 1900 to 1910, the Japanese supplanted the Chinese, with the peak of Japanese employment being reached in 1909. As late as 1913, all the employees of the Limoneira Company were Japanese, with observers reporting that "the orientals who move so quickly here and there in their work" were exceptionally deft and efficient, "taking a lemon, wrapping it in its tissue covering, and placing it in the box ready for shipment in the twinkling of an eye." In 1915, there were still about 3,500 Japanese employed in the industry. While Mexicans have always worked in the groves, they did not become the dominant element in the labor supply until after 1914. Between 1914 and 1919, the number of Mexicans in the industry increased from 2,317 to 7,004 (30% of the total). Today they constitute two-thirds or more of the workers employed both in the fields and in the packing sheds. They are not migratory workers, but settled residents of the areas in which they are employed (only 17% of the labor supply is non-resident). Many of these Mexican workers have grown up with the industry, being the second and third generation to work in the groves.

While a few of the large commercial growers maintain camps for their employees, the typical citrus worker settlement is the Mexican town or, in the parlance of the region, the "jim-town." From Santa Barbara to San Diego, one can find these jim-towns, with their clusters of bizarre shacks, usually located in an out-of-the-way place on the outskirts of an established citrus-belt town. Needless to say, the settlements are always located "on the other side of the tracks." Being for the most part unincorporated settlements, the jim-towns lack governmental services; the streets are dusty unpaved lanes, the plumbing is primitive, and the water supply is usually obtained from outdoor hydrants. A good gust of wind would blow most of the shacks into eternity. Some of the older towns in the district have a Mexican section within the city limits, invariably separated from the rest of the community by a through highway or railroad right of way.

Throughout the citrus belt, the workers are Spanish-speaking, Catholic, and dark-skinned, the owners are white, Protestant, and English-speaking. The owners occupy the heights, the Mexicans the lowlands. That both groups are highly homogeneous is a circumstance that serves to widen the gulf of social distance that separates the one from the other. While the towns deny that they practice segregation, nevertheless, segregation is the rule. Since the Mexicans all live in jim-town, it has always been easy to effect residential segregation. The omnipresent Mexican school is, of course, an outgrowth of segregated residence. The swimming pools in the towns are usually reserved for "whites," with an insulting exception being noted in the designation of one day in the week as "Mexican Day," or, as it is sometimes called, "International Day." Mexicans attend separate schools and churches, occupy the balcony seats in the motion-picture theaters, and frequent separate places of amusement. Since the exchanges employ the Mexicans, the growers have little direct contact with the people who work their groves. Even the exchange officials, moreover, deal with Mexicans through a Spanish-speaking foreman or contractor, so that they, too, have only a slight and casual acquaintance with their employees. The whole system of employment, in fact, is perfectly designed to insulate workers from employers in every walk of life, from the cradle to the grave, from the church to the saloon.

Such a system, of course, has always minimized opportunities for acculturation and offered few incentives for assimilation. A variation of the hacienda system of former years, the present dispensation is one under which the Mexican worker, whether he is a citizen (as most of them are) or an alien, tends to remain Spanish-speaking, to live in an isolated Mexican-American environment, and to exist separate and apart from the main stream of community life and activity. Unorganized for social, economic, or political action, the Mexican workers have virtually no voice in community affairs. Occupying the intermediate zone between the Mexicans and the grower-manager cliques are the townspeople: the employees of the chain stores, the filling-station operators, the doctors, lawyers, teachers, shopkeepers, and clergymen. This in-between element, however, invariably adopts the grower-exchange point of view on all controversial issues, and, during periods of social tension, is quickly neutralized or goes over, en masse, to the growers.

I well remember, some years ago, my own astonishment in discovering how quickly social power could crystallize into an expression of arrogant brutality in these lovely, seemingly placid, outwardly Christian communities. The occasion was a strike of 2,500 Mexican citrus workers in Orange County. The moment the strike was called, the sheriff deputized and armed 400 special guards. Trucks loaded with food supplies for the barricaded strikers were hijacked in broad daylight on highways crowded with traffic and patrolled by the state police. I found over 200 workers, all Mexicans, in jail in Santa Ana, charged with petty traffic violations, assaults, trespass, and a wide variety of trumped-up offenses. In a single raid over 155 workers were arrested. In my presence, a justice of the peace summarily denied this batch of prisoners a jury trial. One of the attorneys for the defendants was given six tickets for alleged traffic violations in a single day, in an effort to drive him out of the community. Visitors attempting to interview the strikers at their camp were turned back by armed guards and highway patrolmen. In the courtrooms of the county, I met former classmates of mine in college, famous athletes of the University of Southern California, armed with revolvers and clubs, ordering Mexicans around as though they were prisoners in a Nazi concentration camp.

During the strike, highway patrolmen established a portable radio station, KAPA, by means of which they directed, with matchless efficiency, the reign of terror by which the strike was broken. Large sums were quickly appropriated, from public funds, to purchase tear-gas bombs and firearms. Even in the courtrooms, I saw deputies armed with sub-machine guns, shotguns, and rifles. On the morning of July 11, 1936 a workers' camp was bombed with tear gas, as men, women, and children ran for cover in all directions. A patrol of armed guards, extending over an area of forty miles, stopped cars on the highway, turned back all "suspicious" characters, and otherwise took over the function of maintaining "law and order." On July 8, the Los Angeles *Times* carried a graphic story of these thugs breaking up a strike meeting at the Mexican settlement of El Modena: "Suddenly, late in the night, three or four automobiles loaded with grim-faced men, appeared out of the darkness surrounding the little settlement. In a few seconds, tear gas bombs hissed into the small building where the asserted strikers were in conclave, and the conferees with smarting eyes broke and ran under cover of darkness and the meeting was at an end. Witnesses said they heard the mysterious automobiles and the night-riders whirring away without leaving a trace of their identity." Actually, there was no mystery about the identity of these night-riders; they were the regularly constituted law-enforcement officials of the county.

On July 7, the *Times* carried a front-page story, telling in exuberant terms, about how "old vigilante days were revived in the orchards of Orange County yesterday as one man lay near death and scores nursed injuries." On July 11, 115 strikers were taken from jail and herded into vans guarded by "men armed with sub-machine guns, tear gas bombs, pistols, and shotguns." Instead of being arraigned in a courtroom, these defendants were crowded onto a lot in the rear of the courthouse, where an *al fresco* mock-trial was staged. They were then lodged in a bull pen, or stockade, that had been constructed in Santa Ana in anticipation of the strike. All of this fury was unleashed by a demand of the field workers for an increase in wages from twenty-five cents an hour to forty cents an hour.

Throughout this affair, and it was only one of many similar incidents which have occurred in the citrus belt, the citizens of the county, with few exceptions, remained silent and raised neither voice nor hand against what amounted to an outright usurpation of the local government by private interests. The guiding intelligence behind this affair seems to have been the California Fruit Growers Exchange. From 1936 to date, the exchange has largely financed the activities of the Associated Farmers movement in Southern California.

Long frustrated in their efforts to organize, the Mexican workers of recent years have been making remarkable progress in their organizational campaigns and it is only a question of time, now, until the industry is completely organized. In 1941, 6,000 field workers in the Ventura-Santa Barbara area, most of them employees of the Limoneira Company, conducted a long, bitterly opposed, well-managed strike. While the strike was broken, as dozens of similar strikes have been broken, some important organizational gains resulted. Once they have achieved self-organization, the Mexican-Americans will begin to vote. In many areas throughout the citrus belt they could be a determining factor in local elections.

They will not succeed, however, in organizing the industry without a major battle in which class and status lines will be sharply drawn. The bitterness of the struggle will turn in part upon the question of status. For, over a long period of years, field work has come to be associated with a definite status. "The harvesting, washing, grading, and packing of fruit and vegetables," writes Mr. Teague, "requires a natural aptitude," that is, it is the kind of work that God created Mexicans to perform. A challenge to this concept of status-labor involves, of course, a threat to the social structure which has been erected upon it. In his autobiography, Mr. Teague, to find something nice to say about Mexicans, finally concludes that they are "good-natured and happy." "They have one trait," he writes, "I have always admired: they are generally willing to share what they have with their relatives when they are in need."

The tension that has developed in the citrus-belt communities of recent years is merely one evidence of approaching social change. Nowadays the children of the grove owners, oppressed by the placidity of Riverside and Redlands, have begun to leave the area and to settle in the cities. At the same time, young people from outside the area have started to move into the citrus belt as social workers, clerks, teachers, junior executives, doctors, and lawyers. The exchange of young people first became noticeable during the depression. With this infusion of new blood, something of the compact, colony-insulated, homogeneous character of the communities has begun to disappear. As the grove-owners have relinquished the reins of power and have not been succeeded by their sons, all sorts of civic positions have been filled by outsiders. Occasionally the service clubs of the district, largely made up of this newer element, have asserted themselves, on minor issues, in a manner not sanctioned by the older generation. This tendency is likely to become more pronounced in the future as the grove-owners, already divested of many of the functions ordinarily associated with ownership, are removed by death. Seemingly impervious to social change, Citrus Land has finally begun to respond to new movements of thought and opinion.

4. THE FAIREST FRUIT

Around us were trees laded with the little golden lamps of oranges, and as we moved up the foothills, scents of orange-bloom were blown to us, even from the orchards that were in fruit. We wound through the orchards up to the foothills, where one touched once more the original desert of California, a desert whose golden drought seems to have been deliberately designed by some great artist in order to enhance the deliciousness of the great globes and clusters of fruit that it bears."

—Alfred Noyes

The citrus belt, as a sharply defined segment of social life in Southern California, has three dominant symbols: the church, the orange, and the "no trespass" signs that mark all approaches to the groves. Wherever one turns, along every highway, street, and bypath of the citrus belt, the "no trespass" and other warning signs appear. To pick an orange in Southern California, unless you are an employee working under the direction of a foreman, is a perilous undertaking. If performed surreptitiously, it is likely to invite a blast from a shotgun, a jolt from an electrically charged wire fence, or a sentence in jail. Many of the larger concerns employ armed guards to police the sacred trees. According to Charles Fletcher Lummis, ferocious bulldogs were used, at an earlier time, to keep visitors out of the groves. Some years ago, a Mexican boy was killed in Los Angeles County by a blast from a shotgun which a grower, by an ingenious process, had attached to a tree in such a manner that the trigger would be pulled by a disturbance of the wire fence enclosing the grove. Almost every resident and visitor in Southern California has wanted to pick an orange; but few persons can claim the distinction of having done so.

The "no trespass" signs are symbolic of the insularity, the tight social organization, the airless vacuum-like quality of the citrus belt. Not so long ago, I spoke in Riverside on the subject of civil liberties. On the same platform was Dr. E. P. Ryland of Los Angeles who is my idea of a Christian saint, gentle, considerate, full of the milk of human kindness. The Associated Farmers of Riverside County ran a page advertisement in the local press warning the residents of Riverside to stay away from the meeting and hinting at various forms of reprisal that might be visited on those venturesome enough to attend. Present at the meeting were the sheriff, a delegation from the

Associated Farmers, and a stenographer who took complete notes. Members of the Associated Farmers delegation stood up during the meeting and "spotted" various people in the audience, dictating their names to the stenographer.

In all the citrus-belt towns, Protestant churches are much in evidence, for orthodox Protestantism is deeply rooted among the older residents, a pious and conservative lot. There is a church on each of the four corners of one downtown intersection in Redlands. Throughout the district, the Protestant churches are usually handsome and costly structures, somber and substantial, with ivy-covered walls and elegant rectories. There are no unpainted or neglected churches, such as one sees in so many rural areas in America. In fact, the citrus-belt communities are about the only regular churchgoing towns in Southern California. Some of them were founded as temperance communities, and, in almost every colony settlement, provision was made against the sale of intoxicating liquors. The proud white temperance banners of the W.C.T.U. still fly from some of the church steeples. Some of the colony settlements, in fact, were founded by particular Protestant sects, still another explanation of their homogeneous character. The colleges and universities established in the region reflect the sectarian bias of particular communities. The University of Redlands is Baptist-supported; Pomona was founded by the Congregationalists; LaVerne College by the Dunkers; while Whittier College is a Quaker institution named, as is the town of Whittier, after the poet who once dedicated a poem to the community:

> Dear town, for whom the flowers are born,
>   Stars shine, and happy song birds sing,
> What can my evening give to morn,
>   My Winter to thy Spring—
>
> A life not void of pure intent,
>   With small desert of praise or blame,
> The love I felt, the good I meant.
>   I leave thee with thy name.

Not only is it difficult to pick an orange in Southern California, but, as William Allen White once observed, it is almost impossible to get a glass of real orange juice in the region, particularly in the citrus belt. On three occasions in the last year I have been unable to obtain a glass of orange juice in the hotel in which I was staying in Redlands. Despite the absence of orange juice, however, the orange remains the dominant symbol of the region. Mountains of oranges, "the fairest fruit in the history of the human race," are exhibited at the National Orange Fair held, over a period of two weeks, in San Bernardino each February. Frequently a million oranges, lemons, and grapefruit are used in building the towering columns and curious structures of citrus fruit seen at the fair. Oranges are converted into caricatures of Donald Duck, Mickey Mouse, Minnie, Pluto, the Three Little Pigs, and the Big Bad Wolf. Even during the depression, when the local exchanges were dumping tons of "surplus" oranges into the dry river beds sprayed with oil and tar so that relief clients would not be tempted to salvage any from the decaying heaps, the orange show went on as usual.

The National Orange Fair is, indeed, as Carleton Beals has written, "a great cornucopia of golden glory." Visiting the show in 1939, Mr. Beals found "manikins of Joan Crawford and Marlene Dietrich lolling in the lawn chairs among garden paths laid out with lemons and grapefruit, and pretty-boy Clark Gable in neat white flannels and open-throat shirt under a fake orange tree glistening with two large golden globes . . . the great annual orange fair of San Bernardino showed such gorgeous taste, and yet such hybrid mixtures, that at bottom it was garish, a bit crude, lacking in pure form and subtlety, devoid of finesse, largely boosterism run amuck"—a rather good description of Southern California. Sampling some of the fruit, Mr. Beals, who had known the region in his youth, found that it had lost "a bit of its once half-wild pungency and its virile resistance; the tang has turned to juice and sugar." The fruit was too perfect, if not in taste, at least in size, uniformity, color, and visual appeal.

Once the groves were a major tourist attraction as thousands of tourists were whisked through them, a mile-a-minute, on the famous Kite-route of the Pacific Electric. Seldom did the eager tourist get more than a panoramic view of the groves, with "the flawless lines of the orange trees wheeling away like endless spokes," each grove maneuvered "like a mile-square regiment glittering in the sunlight," and a fugitive sample of the sweet fragrance of the blossoms. Today oranges are raised, not as a tourist attraction, not to provide elegant backgrounds for suburban estates, not to inflate land values, not even to provide orange juice for local residents, but as slick standardized commodities produced on an assembly-line basis for sale, and only for sale.

Unquestionably the process has been profitable, but, in some vague sense, I share Carleton Beals's apprehension that all is not well, that some vital quality of the land has been subverted. Perhaps it is, as Charles Fletcher Lummis once said, that "the life of these valleys is drawn not from the number of educated and wealthy people who settle in them; not from the golden crops they yield; not from the railroads, hotels, blocks, or all the labyrinth of enterprise—but from the granite breasts of the Sierra Madre, the Mother Range. And those breasts are going dry." The denuding of these steep slopes through forest fires and a criminal neglect of forest resources, the incessant pumping of underground waters, and the ever-expanding demand for water in large urban centers, makes one wonder just how real and enduring are these beautiful groves. Puzzling over the same question, a character in Howard Baker's novel concluded that "the people were powerless to change the desert very much," over the long reach of the years. Who was it that said that the life of an irrigated civilization was about four hundred years?

"Los Angeles was not like some Middle-Western city that sinks its roots into some strategic area of earth and goes to work there. This was a lovely makeshift city. Even the trees and plants did not belong here. They came, like the people, from far places, some familiar, some exotic, all wanderers of one sort or another seeking peace or fortune or the last frontier, or a thousand dreams of escape."

—from A Place in the Sun by Frank Fenton

CHAPTER XII

THE SOCIOLOGY OF THE BOOM

ALMOST every eccentricity of social behavior in Southern California has been attributed, at one time or another, to the climate or the physical environment. Observers have uniformly explained in terms of the climate what they have not been able to account for in other terms. But, as Franz Boas once said, "the study of the cultural history of any particular region shows clearly that geographical conditions by themselves have no creative force and are certainly no absolute determinants of culture." The volume and velocity of migration, rather than the fabled climate, account for most of the unique features of the region's cultural landscape. To understand these features, one needs a sociology of migration, or, more particularly, a sociology of the boom.

1. The Appearance of the Land

As a result of the boom-cycle phenomenon, the old and the new exist in curious juxtaposition throughout Southern California. Communities that have grown as rapidly as Los Angeles develop what Richard Neutra has called "an obsolescence praecox." Each wave of migration has brought modes of living and patterns of design that have been superimposed upon, or placed side by side with, the monuments of earlier migrations. There has been neither time nor inclination to remove the old. "In cities like New York," wrote Harry Carr, "where the area is restricted and there can be no spread, old buildings are torn down to make way for new." But Southern California has rarely bothered to remove the old.

Writing of Los Angeles in 1888, J. P. Widney said that it was both old and new: "Old, as a picturesque, sleepy, free-and-easy Spanish pueblo, but new as a thriving, progressive American city; old, as a center for an extensive grazing country—new as a distributing commercial mart; old, as a station where the solitary horseman stopped for rest and refreshment—new as a railroad center; old as a Catholic mission—new as a cosmopolitan city where a hundred Protestant churches vie with the Catholic chimes." Throughout Southern California, relics of the various booms from 1870 to 1940 clutter up the landscape: old tourist hotels converted into cow barns; slabs of cement protruding from the sands of the desert; and ugly false-front office buildings, with the date "1887" carved over the entrance, side by side with ultra-modern structures. The successive layers of cultural litter deposited by the various booms can be measured like the soil stratas in an ancient geological formation. Here, one can see, was the high tide of the boom of 1887; over there lie the unburied remains of the boom of 1906; and here, closer to view, the boom of 1920 began to recede. In the small towns of the region, one can still see relics of the booms preserved like artifacts in a museum.

Underlying this singular combination of old and new is an extremely subtle paradox, namely, that immigrant communities tend to make a fetish of the old and familiar. "In a western town or village," wrote Horace A. Vachell, "the first thing likely to catch the eye of the traveler (indeed it was invented for that purpose) is the sham front of his hotel. Upon examination he will mark that nearly all the stores and buildings are built to beguile the imagination . . . the thing is obviously sham, obviously built for show. . . . Is there not something pathetic in this? It is a sort of mild hypocrisy which, like a Scotch mist, pervades the atmosphere. The men who leave old countries for new must be profoundly conscious of the difference between the old and the new; they are forever adjusting, so far as they can, this difference. Lacking the real thing, they try to console themselves with its counterfeit presentment. And the consciousness that despite their efforts the thing is sham has a curious effect for good and evil." It makes, as Vachell shrewdly noted, "for an instinct of display which manifests itself in crude and vulgar decoration: friezes, panels, mouldings, what in short the people themselves call—frills."

In an effort to recreate the old appearance in the new land, immigrants develop a sense of the incongruous which eventually begins to take on a life of its own. The instinct for display becomes chronic. "Throughout Southern California," wrote Vachell, "where the sun shines steadily for more than three hundred days in the year, the school-houses lack awnings and broad verandahs. Economy forbids, you reply. Not so. Most of these gimcrack shanties are embellished with towers and cupolas." While the false fronts have begun to disappear in Southern California, the instinct for display manifests itself in buildings built like giant owls, derby hats, shoes, airships, teakettles, windmills, and mosques. "Imagination," writes Frank Fenton, "had run around this city like an artistic child. Somewhere it showed a pure and lovely talent. Somewhere it was crude and humorously grotesque. A man had built a little restaurant like a windmill, another like a cave." Curiously enough, however, this "onomatopoeic architecture" serves a functional purpose in an immigrant community. Patronage based upon long familiarity with an established location is entirely non-existent in a city made up of strangers. In Los Angeles a coffee pot is like a coffee pot, a restaurant called The Green Dragon looks like a dragon. As Stoyan Cristowe has observed: "No signs are necessary, and you can't make the mistake of finding yourself in the mouth of the dragon when you wish to be in the coffee pot."

There is still another finesse about this combination of the old and the new. The newest metropolitan district, Los Angeles is, in a literal sense, an old community. Of the ten largest cities in the United States in 1930, Los Angeles had next to the lowest percentage of population under twenty years of age and the highest percentage of persons forty-five years and over. Furthermore, as Dr. Constantine Panunzio has noted, the old-age segment of the population has been increasing more rapidly than in other cities of comparable size. Until 1940 the rate of natural increase (excess of births over deaths) was insufficient to sustain the level of population. There were as many people in Los Angeles in the age bracket from 65 to 69 as there were in the 35 to 39 bracket in San Francisco. "Childless people," observes Dr.

Panunzio, "are compelled to resort to dogs, cats, monkeys, parrots, or to a round on round of meaningless diversions" to satisfy their emotional hungers. The lack of balance in the age groupings merely reflects, of course, the type of migration. In the settlement of Southern California, the first waves of migrants were made up largely of the middle-aged with the more recent waves being made up of younger people. Paradoxically, the old came first and left an imprint of age on the land.

To make the paradox more striking, it should be observed that the earlier waves of migration contained many invalids, people with the odor of decay about them. It is not by chance, therefore, that Los Angeles has been a mortician's paradise. The providing of professional escorts to accompany lonely caskets back east once constituted a thriving business. Along with the intoxicating fragrance of the land, there has always been the stench of decay. Los Angeles is an *old* town, full of death, dust, and decomposition. With houses festooned with cobwebs, reeking of decay and dry rot, parts of the city are as old as the 'fifties. Like a loathsome snake sloughing off parts of its skin, sections of Los Angeles are forever dying and rotting. "In a region of so fluctuating a constitution as Los Angeles," writes Neutra, "the psychologically natural custom of speedy amortization leads to light construction and this, also, to short-term, physical depreciation." Los Angeles is the capital of all the termites in America, a place where the greedy, noisy little monsters are endlessly consuming the rotting timbers of jerry-built homes.

The symbol of the old and new, of death and life, in Los Angeles is Forest Lawn Memorial Park, the cemetery described in Aldous Huxley's novel, *After Many a Summer Dies the Swan*. In planning this unique institution back in 1917, Dr. Hubert Eaton says that he wanted to build it as "unlike other cemeteries as sunshine is unlike darkness, as Eternal Life is unlike Death." Only a community of old people could, of course, support such a palatial institution as Forest Lawn, and only a community as new as Los Angeles could dream of converting a cemetery into a park of happiness and art. The morbidity of death simply evaporates in the pseudo-Hellenic atmosphere of Southern California. Forest Lawn operates its own undertaking establishment. Its advertisements refer to "sacred services in sacred grounds," "comfort to the bereaved," "peaceful slumber rooms," and "no long funeral processions" (an important attraction in traffic-crazy Los Angeles). As many people are married in the three chapels of Forest Lawn, The Church of the Recessional, The Wee Kirk o' the Heather, and The Little Church of the Flowers, as are carried from their portals in funeral processions. While a laughing bride emerges from The Little Church of the Flowers, a funeral cortege is likely to be passing in front of the chapel. "Here," as Bruce Barton once said, "sorrow sees no ghastly monuments, but only life and hope." Strolling along the beautifully kept walks, one listens to soft music broadcast from amplifiers concealed in rose bushes. In addition to its "Mausoleum-Columbarium," Forest Lawn has a collection of "Old Masters" that is the great pride of all loyal Southern Californians. It is at once an art gallery, a Gretna-Green marriage mart, and a place where the dead can be tucked away with as little sorrow as one can bury a tin can in the backyard. A great institution in the Southland, Forest Lawn maintains a fulltime lobbyist in Sacramento to protect its vested interests. When controversial issues arise in Los Angeles, the recently bereaved widow is likely to inquire, "What does Forest Lawn say about it?"

As a community at the end of a long trail of migration, Los Angeles has become the junkyard for a continent. Every newcomer to the city has brought something with him, usually the oldest relic, the antique piece, the family heirloom. Los Angeles has been a great city for van-and-storage companies, for moving companies, for auctions and auctioneers, for antique stores, for pawnshops, for dealers in used automobiles and used furniture, for second-hand bookstores and hand-me-down clothing establishments. Auctions are sometimes reported as social affairs in the local press, particularly when some celebrity's effects are being auctioned off. It is also a great place for exchanges, trades, and what are termed "swaportunities."

There is a flourishing traffic in old and used ideas in Los Angeles as well as books and clothes. Stumble-bums in Pershing Square, "that serene isle of theory" in downtown Los Angeles, have carried on the same debate, night and day, for sixty years. "Its loungers," Mark Lee Luther once noted, "apparently enjoyed as great leisure as the pigeons which made a poultry-run of the pavement about the central fountain. They came from every section of the country and their mental luggage was as strange as their clothes." Gathered in the square, these refugees from toil "air the ancient nonsense and all the ancient fallacies." It is the Valhalla of all the faiths that man's conceit has ever invented. Listening to the endless debate, one catches faint echoes of Comte, Spencer, Winthrop Reade, Nietzsche, Schopenhauer, Mencken, Haldeman-Julius, Frank Crane, Madame Blavatsky, and Ella Wheeler Wilcox. The ideas that float about the square are as old and faded and used as the clothes worn by its favorite denizens.

"As New York is the melting-pot for the peoples of Europe," wrote Sarah Comstock, "so Los Angeles is the melting-pot for the peoples of the United States. Hither have flocked natives of every state in the Union, and they have brought not only their trunks but their tempers. Such juxtaposition of unlikes is so characteristic that it is all but impossible; like certain stories and plays, it is too real to seem true. What Los Angeles is to excess, all our cities are to some extent." But there is a difference to be noted. In New York immigrants remain tenants and find it difficult to build memorials to the old. Los Angeles, on the other hand, is a melting pot of home-owners whose varied backgrounds and traditions have found visible expression. In this land of rapid real-estate turnover and speculative building, "stylistic fashions," as Neutra has observed, have been quickly adapted to appeal to varied backgrounds; to distinguish, for advertising purposes, one subdivision from another; and to mark off the new from the old. "Precisely because of these amazing contradictions," wrote Miss Comstock, "I came to believe that no other community in America represents so fully what, to European eyes, seeing us in perspective, is so inexplicable because so incongruous."

The confused arboreal pattern of Los Angeles is directly traceable to the boom-cycle. When Hollywood was subdivided, for example, Palm Avenue was lined with palms; Magnolia Avenue (now Cherokee) with magnolias; and, of course, olive trees were planted along Olive Street and sycamores along Sycamore Avenue. The only tree to be seen in Hollywood today that was there before the booms is the pepper tree which remains, as one might expect, the most attractive tree in the area. The long avenues of palms to be seen in the older sections of Los Angeles, outrageously tall in relation to the squat bungalows, formerly marked the principal avenues of newly opened subdivisions. Visiting Los Angeles after the collapse of the 1887 boom, Mary Austin was "daunted by the wreck of the lately 'busted' boom; the jerry-built bungalows, the blameless young palms abandoned along with the avenue they had been planted to adorn. The unwatered palms had a hurt but courageous look, as of young wives when they first suspect that their marriages may be turning out badly."

Most of Los Angeles, in fact, has been built by contractors as unfamiliar with the environment as the purchasers who bought the homes. Not only are many sections of the city boom-built, but the construction is, in many cases, unintentionally incompetent. "Apart from major seismic events," writes Neutra, "frequent minor shocks in this region cause initial cracks in structural enclosures and surface shell. Termites and dry rot attack non-aerated and even ventilated wood constructions. The often overlooked peculiar differentiation of seasons, with concentration of radiation at one time and downpours at the other, causes leaks in roof skins. Regular night moisture detrimentally oxidizes corrodible metals. Hygroscopic, periodically swelling adobe soil cracks foundations and impairs integrity of floors and walls. The mild climate induces much carelessness in construction . . . the resulting dilapidation, often not balanced by proper maintenance, greatly contributes to the blight of quickly-built sections . . . simultaneously, purchasing power is again lured to a new, colorfully advertised subdivision."

"All visitors from the East," writes Edmund Wilson, "know the strange spell of unreality which seems to make human experience on the Coast as hollow as the life of a troll-nest where everything is out in the open instead of being underground. . . . This is partly no doubt a matter of climate: the empty sun and the incessant rains; and of landscape; the dry mountains and the vast void of Pacific space; the hypnotic rhythms of day and night that revolve with unblurred uniformity, and of the surf that seems to roll up the beach with a purposeless expressionless beat after the moody assault of the Atlantic." But I wonder to what extent this impression is really traceable to the climate? It can be more accurately explained, perhaps, in terms of highly imperfect cultural adaptation, the general unrelatedness of things, the ever-present incongruity, and the odd sense of display. The impermanence of much of the construction in itself conveys an impression of unreality. "Towns do not develop here," wrote Sarah Comstock, "they are instantly created, synthetic communities of a strangely artificial world. Plant a few yellow and green stucco bungalows, a few shops, a real estate office, a church, a soda fountain, a school, a movie theater, a cafeteria, and a filling station, and there you are. Another satellite. Another demonstration of growth."

2. The Eunuchoid Giant

"Los Angeles is a community of annexed parts as loosely joined as an eunuchoid giant."
—Dr. Henry Harris

The sprawling, centrifugal form of Los Angeles is still another product of the boom-cycle. Within the County of Los Angeles are 45 incorporated and 60 unincorporated communities, ranging in size from Los Angeles with a 1940 population of 1,504,277 to West Covina with a population of 850. Most cities have grown outward from a central district, but, in Los Angeles, the volume and velocity of migration has spilled over, breaking economic, geographical, and political dikes. This overflowing process has been made possible, of course, by geographical considerations: a vast expanse of land unbroken by rivers, mountains, or other barriers. It is in part cultural, in the sense that so many of the newcomers have been flatlanders addicted to openness, horizontally minded, chronic and eternal villagers who have repeated the village pattern in a metropolitan environment. Political considerations have also influenced the form of settlement. Los Angeles has never been able to evolve adequate governmental forms to cope with the influx. Nuclear settlements, new towns and cities, have sprung up almost before the city and county officials were even aware of their existence.

With real-estate companies fostering the centrifugal movement, Los Angeles became a city without a center. Population density in Los Angeles is quite low for a city of its size, about 3,400 people per square mile by comparison with an average of ninety-six large cities of 8,228. As a result of the centrifugal tendency, however, the density outside the central portion of the city is high, 1,045 per square mile as compared with an average of 529 for other metropolitan areas. As Dr. Panunzio notes, this general tendency has made for "space both within and without the city." In 1940 there were 175 square miles of vacant, subdivided land in the County of Los Angeles with over 250,000 vacant lots. The cost of maintaining 2,222 miles of streets bordering these empty lots amounted to $1,450,000, to which should be added $66,500,000 for interest, taxes, and assessments. The preference for single-family residences, encouraged by the boosters and made possible by a combination of circumstances, has made Los Angeles a collection of suburbs in search of a city.

In an effort to exert some measure of control over the new cities and towns that began to spring up around its borders, Los Angeles used its monopolistic control of the water supply to bring about annexations and consolidations. Starting with an area of 28 square miles in 1850, the city increased to 100.72 square miles by 1910. Then San Fernando was annexed, adding 169.89 square miles. Between 1915 and 1925, 44 annexations and 3 consolidations were effected, increasing the area to 410.19 square miles. By July 1, 1930, 11 more annexations and 3 consolidations occurred, bringing the area up to 441.69 square miles. This process, however, did not obliterate the communities annexed or consolidated. They continued to function, and still function, as communities within a community.

Within the city limits of Los Angeles today are numerous areas that have many of the characteristics of distinct communities: definite boundaries, a common business or service district, and specific population characteristics, such as age levels, sex distribution, and so forth. There are also numerous ethnic colonies or communities. But the problem has always been to define the larger unit to which these communities are theoretically related. Where does all this bustling life center? Even in these communities-within-a-community there is often lacking a true sense of community as well as any feeling of being related to a larger unit. The people living on the same side of the same street in the same block in the same neighborhood are often complete strangers. Furthermore, they remain strangers, since migration within the area is of about the same velocity as migration into the area. While these various communities can be classified on socio-economic lines, the pattern of social stratification is confused, i.e., a poor community is often found sandwiched in between two rich communities.

Small in relation to Los Angeles, the outlying communities have never achieved much social self-sufficiency. The communities which possess the most form, as communities, for example, Pasadena and Beverly Hills, are those which by reason of wealth have been able to offset the strength of Los Angeles and to escape annexation. Most of the smaller communities are as obviously lacking in a focal point as Los Angeles itself. That so many residents of Los Angeles have their cultural roots elsewhere accounts, in Dr. Panunzio's opinion, for the fact that the city resembles a series of sprawling real-estate subdivisions over which population has been made to jump like grasshoppers. It is the basic influence of migration, however, rather than cultural alienage as such, that has given Los Angeles its curious form. The citrus-belt communities are also made up of outsiders, but, not having been periodically inundated by new migrants, they have managed to retain a degree of homogeneity and compactness.

Since the period of its most spectacular growth coincided with the rise of the automobile age, Los Angeles has always been a city on wheels, an automobile metropolis. In the ownership and use of automobiles, Los Angeles stands unchallenged among the counties of the nation. In 1940 Los Angeles residents owned 1,076,000 automobiles, five automobiles for every four families, more cars than were to be found in all but six states of the union. Wage-earners in Los Angeles spend more on their cars than they do on clothes. Eighty per cent of all passenger miles of travel are by automobile. Los Angeles has more policemen detailed to traffic work than there are policemen in San Francisco. In a five-year period ending in August, 1934, 225,000 people were killed or injured in automobile accidents in California, and 50% of these casualties occurred in Los Angeles. Widespread use of the automobile has aborted all efforts to develop other types of transportation and has given an enormous impetus to the tendency of the city to expand along "strips," or highways radiating in all directions. The open character of settlement created opportunities for parking lots not available in other cities, thereby encouraging the use of automobiles. Furthermore the "fluctuating employment geography" of non-industrial Los Angeles, as well as the climate, catered to the motoring impulse. As a consequence of these factors, an amazing crisscross pattern of auto transit has developed, with literally no relation existing between place of employment and place of residence.

While the rapid expansion of Los Angeles has stimulated agricultural and industrial production, population has always increased more rapidly than employment opportunities. "It struck me as an odd thing," wrote Morris Markey in 1938, "that here, alone of all the cities in America, there was no plausible answer to the question, 'Why did a town spring up here and why has it grown so big?'" The richest agricultural county in America, Los Angeles had little diversified industry until after 1920. In the absence of industrial employment, the number of clerical, domestic, and personal service employees increased by 90% during the 1920's. In no city in America has there been such a proliferation of wasteful and meaningless service occupations. "The thing simply won't add up," complained James Cain in 1933. "Life takes on a dreadful vacuity here. I don't know what I miss." And then, as an afterthought, he added that perhaps it was "the piddling occupations to which the people dedicate their lives" that was responsible for this feeling. "Of what electric importance can be felt in a peddler of orange peelers? or of a dozen ripe avocados, just plucked that morning? or a confector of Bar-B-Q? or the proprietor of a goldfish farm? or a breeder of rabbit fryers? They give me no kick at all. They give themselves no kick." On the main highways leading into Los Angeles, the roadside signs tell the story of the city's improvised economy: canary farms, artificial pools for trout fishing, rabbit fryers, dogs at stud, grass-shack eating huts, psychic mediums, real-estate offices, filling stations, vacant-lot circuses, more rabbit farms, roadside peddlers, hobby shops, hemstitching store-front evangelists, bicycles to rent, and frogs for sale. The lack of meaningful social and economic functions has contributed to the rootless character of the population, enhanced the impression of unreality that the community has always given, and emphasized its incongruous appearance.

Los Angeles has the largest number, and the best-equipped, dog-and-cat hospitals of any city in America. It boasts dog training schools, dog rest homes, special dog-food stores, dog equipment shops, dog resorts in the mountains to which pets can be sent for a vacation, and magnificent dog-and-cat cemeteries. The Hollywood Pet Cemetery might well be regarded as a monument to the lack of industry in Los Angeles prior to 1940. In this thirty-acre, elegantly kept cemetery lie the remains of countless dogs, cats, canaries, parrots, horses, and pet turtles. Bill Bounce, the horse, lies buried here in a $2,000 metal casket, side by side with Kabar, a Doberman Pinscher owned by the late Rudolph Valentino; Puzzums, Mack Sennett's talented cat; John Gilbert's Topsy; Miriam Hopkins' Jerry; Corinne Griffith's Bozo; Dolores Del Rio's Da Da; and Dumpsie who once acted with Eddie Cantor. A Hollywood concern specializes in manufacturing caskets for animals. Some years ago, a Dog's Beauty Shop was opened, "a service that has been seriously and thoughtfully undertaken for the expert and skilful treatment of your pet's coat and condition." A short while later, the Foxie Dog Restaurant was opened as "a de luxe canine cafe." The Tailwaggers Foundation, founded to protect the rights of dogs and dog-owners, is an important Southern California institution. In addition to dog service trades, there are trout farms, snake farms, ostrich farms, lion farms, and there is a concern in Hollywood that rents moths, flies, butterflies, and birds to the motion-picture studios. More schools to teach trades, and more service occupations, are represented in Los Angeles than in any city in America.

Industrial cities tend to develop an integrated, hierarchial structure. The formlessness that most observers have noted in Los Angeles is not due to "lassitude induced by the climate"; it reflects the curious spectacle of a large metropolitan city without an industrial base. The lag in industrial employment also accounts for the retarded character of the trade-union movement. San Francisco, with 363,000 gainfully employed workers in 1940, had proportionately twice as many trade unionists as Los Angeles with 727,000 gainfully employed. "The constant influx of new workers to be assimilated in the social and economic structure of a community," writes Dr. Paul Dodd, "even where there are no differences in language or racial stock, makes for lags in labor organization. This alone would account for the failure of the labor movement to develop strength in a community which has multiplied its urban population as rapidly as did Los Angeles before 1929." Incessant migration also accounts for the loose social organization of Los Angeles, the lack of social integration, and the notorious lag in institutional development. In Los Angeles, as Dr. W. Lloyd Warner has said, "the original social system and its carriers have been destroyed," not once, but at repeated intervals, as a result of continuous migration. Other communities have also had to assimilate newcomers, but newcomers have been a "continually perpetuated majority" in Los Angeles. Not only because so many of them are newcomers, but also because of the sprawling character of the community itself, the residents of Los Angeles are not integrated to their jobs, their neighborhoods, or their social institutions. A less than normal circulation of leadership, brought about by the same cause, has contributed to the confused social scene.

Incessant migration has made Los Angeles a vast drama of maladjustment: social, familial, civic, and personal. The divorce rate of the county is more than twice as high as the average for the nation: 38.6 divorces per 100 marriages by comparison with 17.0. Los Angeles has always had a high suicide rate: 25.1 per 100,000 population as compared with 18.8 for all cities and 15.6 for the nation as a whole. "A childless city," it has always had a somewhat abnormal population pyramid. It should be noted, however, that newcomers and Native Sons make up two rather distinct cultural groups when indexes of this sort are applied. For example, the population pyramid for the native-born has a substantial younger-age bracket and is, in no wise, abnormal. The suicide rate for the native-born is 15 per 100,000 as compared with 24 per 100,000 for the state. This is not to imply that there is some mysterious elan associated with birth in California, but rather that migration spells maladjustment.

Ideas grow as rank, coarse, and odorless as geraniums in the freakish environment of Southern California. When so many people have nothing meaningful to do with their time, nothing real with which to occupy their minds, they indulge in fantasy, in silly daydreams, in perversions, and, occasionally, in monstrous crimes. Social neuroticism is a distinct phenomenon in Los Angeles. It is not by chance that the celebrated crimes of Hickman, Clara Phillips, and Winnie Judd should have been committed in Los Angeles. Los Angeles is the kind of place where perversion is perverted and prostitution prostituted. As Myron Brinig once said, "Los Angeles is a middle-aged obese woman from somewhere in the Middle-West, lying naked in the sun. As she sips from a glass of buttermilk and bites off chunks of a hamburger sandwich, she reads Tagore to the music of Carrie Jacobs-Bond." There can be no doubt that Los Angeles has paid a high price for its rapid growth. The price is indicated in the pathology rates in many categories: suicides, divorces, crime, juvenile delinquency, bankruptcies, narcotic addiction, and so forth. In a community made up largely of newcomers, as Charles N. Reynolds has pointed out, "social control agencies such as the opinion of neighbors, friends or relatives are weakened or absent and the law itself fails to function as it should."

The boom-cycle largely accounts for the curious lack of social continuity in Southern California. Projects begun in the enthusiasm of boom years have collapsed with the particular boom or have been abandoned like a wagon wheel in the desert. Reform movements inaugurated during short periods of comparative stability, when the population has begun to take stock of its environment, have been quickly disrupted by new avalanches of population. People who have lived in the region long enough to become interested in its history, background, and traditions, find themselves isolated from neighbors who arrived the day before yesterday. The collectors of Californiana are passionately interested in the history of the state, but they have become recluses, almost a sect, because others neither share nor understand their enthusiasm. The traditions of the region have, accordingly, become twisted, contorted, and confused. Even its history has become a crazy-quilt of misconceptions, misrepresentations, and mistakes. Seeking desperately to find an explanation for the simplest phenomenon, the newcomer may live next door to the man who was responsible for it or who can explain its meaning.

"The rapid technological, economic, and social changes," writes Lloyd Warner, "combined with conflicting cultural backgrounds of people from the South, Midwest, and Far West have," in Southern California, "kept the status system in flux. . . . All the elements of class are presented except social stability and maturity." Unlike San Francisco, Los Angeles has really never had a coterie of "first families." The first families exist, but they do not perform a vital social function. The reason, of course, is that pointed out by Willard when he wrote that "startling uncertainties" began to develop in the social life of Los Angeles in the 'eighties. How can a community, which has grown so rapidly, even prepare a Who's Who much less a Social Register? The average resident has not the most remote idea as to the identity of the first families of Los Angeles, much less as to their comparative rating in social distinction. In 1945, Los Angeles gave an enormous civic welcome to General George Patton. In preparing the reception, the city discovered, almost as if by accident, that General Patton is not only a Native Son, but that he belongs to one of the early first families. It is not surprising that the social system of the community is, like the community itself, jumbled, chaotic, and confused.

While each boom has brought its quota of people of wealth, enterprise, and ability, it has also brought its quotas of fakirs, humbugs, and frauds. Common types in Los Angeles are the "widower" with undivorced wives in Shreveport, Pittsburgh, and Albany, the business man wanted in Columbus for mail fraud, the clergyman from Cincinnati who ran off with the collection plate or the other man's wife. Referring to the boom of the 'eighties, Willard wrote that "the list of swindlers, embezzlers, and confidence men of that time would be a long one, if anybody should undertake to set it forth." He tells of the well-known local preacher who won a large following but who, it later developed, was wanted for polygamy in the East; of the successful "booster" who had served, it was discovered, two prison terms before arriving in Southern California; of the man who came within a few votes of being selected chief of police but who was exposed as a person with a long criminal record (he was later sentenced to San Quentin Prison). The main qualification for public office in Los Angeles has been a pleasant and easily remembered name. In such an environment, the respected civic leader has hardly any advantage over the newcomer. As late as 1944, the liberal-progressive forces of Hollywood nominated for Congress a man who was exposed as a former member and active leader of the K.K.K. In such an environment, social life is disorganized, institutional development is erratic, and great family and personal disorganization is to be expected.

Business methods and practices are tolerated in such an environment, which would be abhorrent in a more stable community. It is not surprising that California should be one of the first states to regulate the activity of real-estate agents. After the boom of the 'eighties, wrote Willard, a new society formed, but it was "a little colder," a little more wary and distrustful. Years of experience have made the older residents of Los Angeles a cynical and suspicious lot. "The easy flow of capital," writes Dr. Dumke, "encouraged fraud and corruption." Each boom has underscored the same traits. Today Los Angeles is one of the most difficult communities in America in which to cash a check. Amusingly enough, it is distrustful to the point of credulity. The perfect sucker, of course, is "the wise guy" who, believing in nothing, will believe anything. "I have an uneasy suspicion," wrote Harry Carr, "that our pueblo has always been a sucker town. It is an environment so new and strange to the people who come here that miracles seem to be in the air . . . the old-timers in Los Angeles are mostly poverty-stricken." While legitimate business ventures have always had difficulty in securing adequate financing, a complete stranger, like the late C. C. Julian, could breeze into town and, overnight, raise fabulous sums from seasoned financiers on Spring Street.

The succession of booms has bred in the people of Los Angeles a rather easy code of commercial ethics. To put it bluntly, the booms have periodically corrupted the civic virtue of the body politic. I have no doubt whatever that more actions for fraud have been filed in the courts of Los Angeles County than in all the other counties of the state. The lack of commercial ethics is paralleled by an appallingly low standard of political conduct, particularly in the past, and a general lack of social responsibility. Most tourist towns have shown a similar willingness to gyp the newcomer, "to get out from under," to pass on the termite-ridden apartment house to the next sucker. Los Angeles has always been the city of phony business opportunities, the city of swaps and trades, the city of auctions. The jerry-built character of so many structures has inclined many newcomers to believe that Los Angeles is one vast conspiracy of crooked real-estate agents.

3. THE JULIAN FIASCO

"Southern California—where good men go wrong
and wise people lose their money."

Not only have newcomers brought a vast amount of capital to the region for speculation and investment, but great riches have been developed, in oil, in motion pictures, in the tourist trade. In the early 'twenties it was estimated that 125,000 visitors were spending $300,000,000 a year in Southern California. In the bonanza years from 1920 to 1930, Los Angeles had all the giddiness, the parvenu showiness, and the crazy prosperity of a gold-rush town. The social history of the decade is to be found in a single episode: the Julian fiasco. What the failure of W. C. Ralston was to San Francisco after the gold rush, the Julian fiasco was to Los Angeles: the event that shocked a community into some semblance of sanity after a decade of lunacy.

The principal figure in this fiasco was Chauncey C. Julian—"C. C." as he was known to millions. Born in Canada, Julian had worked as a rigger in the oil fields of Texas before drifting to the Santa Fe Springs and Signal Hill fields. When he arrived in Southern California, he was in his early 'forties, a happy-go-lucky gambler without a dime. He soon began to speculate in oil leases, and, from the start, his luck was phenomenal. As a successful independent operator, he developed the grandiose notion of forming a production, refining, and distributing company to compete with the major oil companies. Out of this ambition came the Julian Petroleum Company. With so much easy money floating around, it was not difficult to sell stock in Julian "Pete."

Julian had an extraordinary flair for publicity and was as skillful a showman as Aimee Semple McPherson, whose career, in so many respects, paralleled his own. "C. C." and Aimee, in fact, discovered the "folks" of Southern California at about the same time. As breezy as a circus barker, Julian knew how to appeal to the folks. "Come on in, folks, you'll never make a thin dime just lookin' on. . . . I've got a sure-fire winner this time, a thousand to one shot. . . . We just can't lose. . . .We're all out here in California where the gushers are and we just ought to clean up. . . . Come on, folks, get aboard for the big ride. . . . I'm not kiddin', folks, you're looking opportunity in the eye." It was not long before 40,000 of the folks had invested $11,000,000 in the stock of Julian Petroleum. Julian's appeals for funds were, in fact, so successful that one particular stock issue was oversubscribed by $75,000.

During the years from 1920 to 1925, Julian was a legendary figure in Southern California. A dapper, flashy fellow, his exploits were the talk of the town and his prodigality as famous as Paul Bunyan's strength. He is supposed, on one occasion, to have given a cab driver a $1,500 tip. On a visit to New York, he entered a cab and said to the driver, "You be the fare—I'll drive." With Julian at the wheel, the cab careened around corners, shot through traffic signals, jumped over curbs, and finally smashed into an automat. He later boasted that this particular spree had cost him $25,000. He gave a Cadillac sedan to a girl that he met in a night club, and once raised $1,500,000 in a few hours on Spring Street. Always good for a touch, he showered money wherever he went; fought with Charles Chaplin in a Hollywood night club; barricaded himself in a Los Angeles hotel against process servers and finally drove them off by brandishing a Colt revolver in the air; maintained four homes in Los Angeles and apartments in New York and Oklahoma City; and bedazzled the Los Angeles press with a series of spectacular stunts and exploits. After the crash, when his personal effects were auctioned off in Los Angeles, his creditors discovered, among other fancy items, a gold-lined bathtub.

Arriving in Los Angeles at the same time and under similar circumstances, Julian and Aimee McPherson both began to get into trouble about 1925. When he first started out, the major oil companies had not taken Julian any more seriously than the fundamentalist ministers had taken Mrs. McPherson. But by 1925 they had decided to close in. Various pressures began to be applied: on the Corporation Commissioner to restrict his stock issues; on the newspapers to refuse his advertisements; and on the refineries not to handle his oil. To escape from these tentacles, Julian needed vast sums of money. Unable to raise the funds required, despite the showing he had made he resigned in April, 1925, when a Price-Waterhouse audit showed that the company had $11,000,000 in assets and only owed about $200,000 in debts. Under his rather eccentric management, the company had rapidly expanded and had paid large cash and stock dividends.

When he resigned, Julian relinquished control to S. C. Lewis, against whom a federal indictment was then pending in Texas for stock manipulations, and Jacob Berman, known to Los Angeles investors as Jack Bennett, an experienced bucket-shop operator. At the time these dubious characters acquired control of the company, they were both broke and had borrowed money to pay their hotel bill in Los Angeles. Seeking to negotiate a merger with one of the larger concerns, they managed to keep the company alive, for a time, by negotiating short-term loans. As it became apparent, however, that the merger would not be concluded, they began to raise, through various stock pools, a vast amount of money at exorbitant interest rates. When they ran out of legitimately issued shares of stock to pledge as collateral for these loans, they began to forge stock certificates. Before the mad spree was over, they had issued 3,000,015 shares of fraudulently issued stock involving more than $150,000,000. Long before the bubble burst, rumors of an over-issue were widespread on Spring Street, yet nothing was done to remove the stock from the market.

The various pools that were formed to take part in this crazy financing interestingly reflect the social chaos of Los Angeles. At the top was a so-called bankers' pool, to which only the elite of the financial hierarchy were admitted. The members of this pool were old-time residents, pillars of the community, most of whom were Shriners and Scottish Rite Masons. This pool had a slightly anti-Semitic tinge, although a few motion-picture executives of Jewish origin were permitted to participate. At a lower level, was a so-called Jewish pool, made up entirely of rich Jewish stockbrokers, merchants, and bankers. And, below these, was the Tia Juana pool, made up of gamblers, confidence men, race-track operators, and other curious characters. Among the members of the bankers' pool were Harry M. Halderman, founder of the Better American Federation; Senator Frank Flint and his brother Motley Flint, a socialite banker; the socially prominent realtor, W. I. Hollingsworth; William Rhodes Hervey, the banker; and Henry M. Robinson, a close friend and associate of Herbert Hoover's. Not only did the members of these various pools demand exorbitant interest rates, but they received fantastic cash and stock bonuses.

May 7, 1927, was a black day in the history of Los Angeles, for on that day further traffic in Julian Petroleum stock was stopped and 40,000 investors awoke to the realization that they had been fleeced, by someone, of $150,000,000. And then began the long and sordid aftermath, involving jury-fixing, bribery, and murder. Although various indictments were returned against the members of the pools, and against the officials of the company, *not a single malefactor was ever convicted* in the state courts. In connection with this case the District Attorney of Los Angeles was sentenced to San Quentin for bribery, the Corporation Commissioner of California was arrested, and Motley Flint was murdered in a Los Angeles courtroom by an investor in Julian stock who, at the time of the murder, had precisely ten cents in his pocket. Long after the crash, portions of the loot turned up in the most surprising places and continued to motivate still additional crimes of bribery, murder, and embezzlement. A double murder committed on May 20, 1931, was motivated by a fight over some of the spoils of the Julian case. The debacle spread a path of crime, violence, and social devastation as complex and as destructive as though a cyclone had struck the community.

Curiously enough, the only sympathetic character who emerges from the black pages of the case is Julian himself (just as Mrs. Mc Pherson was a far more sympathetic character than her critics and enemies). Not only was the company solvent when he resigned, but there is no evidence that he profited by the debacle. It is true that he later became involved with the law in Oklahoma, was indicted for stock manipulations, jumped his bail, and fled to China, but his record in the case associated with his name in Los Angeles is good. On March 25, 1934, he committed suicide, by taking poison, "during a glittering dinner party with a woman in the Astor House Hotel in

Shanghai." Unnamed Americans in Shanghai raised $46 to provide a pauper's burial. The only asset he possessed, at his death, was an autobiographical manuscript entitled, "What Price Fugitive."

The Julian fiasco was merely the prelude to the devastation that came after 1929. When the Richfield Oil Company went into receivership in 1931, an audit revealed an operating loss of $54,000,000. Officials of the company had been maintaining a suite of rooms at a Los Angeles hotel at an annual rental of $50,000, and had been spending company funds, at the rate of $50,000 a month, for entertainment. Certain of these officials were indebted to the company for sums ranging from five to five hundred thousand dollars. Items such as alimony, purchases of jewelry, "repair of speedboat," and so forth, had been blithely charged to the company. One official had given a yacht party off Catalina Island for some motion-picture stars. Late at night, an airplane, specially chartered, flew low over the yacht and showered his guests with gardenias.

Then the Guaranty Building and Loan Association failed (its president, "a leading citizen," had embezzled $8,000,000); then the American Mortgage Company failed for $18,000,000; then the Harold G. Ferguson Company failed for $8,000,000 and its president was sent to San Quentin. As the crazily inflated boom-economy of Los Angeles came crashing down, financiers jumped from office buildings, blew their brains out, and took poison. Nearly every major financial debacle involved some political figure: a judge, a public official, or some well-known fixer.

It was not only the bankers and stockbrokers who began to jump to their miserable deaths during these years; the folks could not jump from offices conveniently located in tall buildings, but they began to jump from the handsome bridge across the Arroyo Seco in Pasadena. In the early 'thirties, 79 people jumped to their death from "Suicide Bridge." The City of Pasadena spent $20,000 a year for a detail of policemen to guard the bridge, but the folks managed to elude them. Owners of the lovely residences overlooking the arroyo complained that $15,000,000 in property values was being jeopardized by the plummeting bodies of suicides. William Randolph Hearst then decided that something must be done about the bridge, and, at the insistence of his papers, the city finally placed a high barbed-wire fence along the sides of the bridge and the wave of suicides subsided.

A Pasadena cobbler, during the excitement over the bridge, inserted these lines of doggerel in one of his advertisements:

I will not jump off the Colorado bridge
To escape from being in the ditch,
With California's sunshine, mountain view, wine and beer,
The temptation is too great for me to live right here.
I am content and happy without booze,
And all I want is to Repair Your Shoes.

On August 19, 1931, the Los Angeles *Express* reported that the law enforcement officials had under investigation business fraud cases involving 75,000 victims. During the years 1931 and 1932, the Corporation Commissioner turned up fraud cases in Los Angeles involving an estimated loss of $200,000,000. In the early 'thirties, it would have been possible to have assembled, in the prison yard of San Quentin, a group of former "civic leaders," "empire builders," "captains of industry," and "outstanding public officials" from Southern California. In earlier booms, investors had bought "lots" which, however inflated the price, were still "real," but in the 'twenties they bought pieces of paper, forged Julian stock certificates, handsomely embossed building and loan certificates, fancy trust indentures, and oil royalties. The collapse of this boom, coinciding with the onslaught of the depression, pauperized at least 500,000 "folks" in Southern California. In 1930 the region led the nation in the number of bankruptcies and in the amount of net losses in bankruptcy proceedings.

Los Angeles had grown so rapidly in the 'twenties that the always tenuous ties which held its social structure together suddenly snapped and the whole fabric of society fell apart. Surveying the wreckage in retrospect, it is apparent that mass migration and easy money had corrupted the community. Almost every resident of the area was *particeps criminis* and all, without exception, were victims. The debacle also revealed the truth for which Josiah Royce had always contended, namely, that California had never achieved integration as a society, that its government was a hastily improvised affair, and that the gambling spirit had bred a reckless social irresponsibility in its residents. During the 'twenties, Los Angeles led the nation in the number of suicides, the number of embezzlements, the number of bank robberies, in the rate of narcotic addiction, and in the fancy character of its sensational murders. To those who want to know what Los Angeles was really like in the 'twenties and 'thirties, I recommend two volumes: an anonymous tract entitled *Sunshine and Grief in Southern California* (1931), published by "an old promoter with forty years in the field of real estate," and *Me, Detective* (1936) by Leslie T. White, the former Los Angeles police officer and detective who, under Lincoln Steffens' influence, decided to initiate the residents of Los Angeles into the secrets of their community.

At the impressionistic level, I would also recommend these lines from a piece by Austin F. Cross, which appeared in the *Evening Citizen* of Ottawa, Canada, during the 'thirties:

> Los Angeles has now replaced Buffalo in my list as the worst city in the United States. Its people sprawl all over the sidewalks—its buildings sprawl all over the countryside. Los Angeles is a one-story town that's got on in the world, a place that numbers its population in seven figures but still thinks as if it were three.
>
> Los Angeles is a big, bad-mannered hick town filled with rude people, a roosting place for bums, a harvest field for quacks, and the shrine of fakers.
>
> Los Angeles is an overgrown Des Moines, a sunny, concentrated, semi-paralyzed edition of the Corn Belt. Disease, cold and sloth brought these people here, and they loll around like lizards and alligators in the sun. Los Angeles' people crawl along. Awkward, gangling, rude, these creatures hanging on to one lung and one dollar under this wonderful sun, are in no hurry to go anywhere. One day is as good as the next, what you can't finish in April you can get done in November, and thus you have these splay-footed, limping, clumsy, bad-mannered, gawking people, ugly to look at, disagreeable to talk to, kind it is true individually but boors en masse, sliding slowly like molasses along the overcrowded sidewalks of this big, but not great, city.
>
> I never saw worse women. They come right out of beauty parlors with the curlers still in their hair, and go shopping. You see them shopping in bedroom slippers. I saw women that looked like men and men that looked like women.
>
> Ever wake up and feel as if you had slept with sawdust in your mouth all night? That's the taste that Los Angeles gives you.

Is it true what they say about Los Angeles, that Los Angeles
is erratic,
That in the sweet national symphony of common sense Los
Angeles is static?
Yes, it is true. Los Angeles is not only erratic, not only erotic;
Los Angeles is crotchety, centrifugal, vertiginous, esoteric and
exotic.
Many people blame the movies and the movie-makers for Los
Angeles' emotional rumpus,
But they are mistaken; it is the compass.
Certainly Los Angeles is a cloudburst of non-sequiturs, and of
logic a drouth,
But what can you expect of a city that is laid out east and
west, instead of north and south?

—from "Don't Shoot Los Angeles" by Ogden Nash

CHAPTER XIII

"DON'T SHOOT LOS ANGELES"

NO SINGLE aspect of Southern California has attracted more
attention than its fabled addiction to cults and cultists. "I am
told," said Mrs. Charles Steward Daggett in 1895, "that the millen-
nium has already begun in Pasadena, and that even now there are
more sanctified cranks to the acre than in any other town in America." Writing in 1921, John Steven McGroarty said that "Los Angeles is the most celebrated of all incubators of new creeds, codes of
ethics, philosophies—no day passes without the birth of something
of this nature never heard of before. It is a breeding place and a
rendezvous of freak religions. But this is because its winters are mild,
thus luring the pale people of thought to its sunny gates, within
which man can give himself over to meditation without being com-

pelled to interrupt himself in that interesting occupation to put on his overcoat or keep the fire going." "Los Angeles is full of people with queer quirks," observed Julia M. Sloane in 1925, "and they aren't confined to gardeners. I haven't had a hairdresser who wasn't occult or psychic or something." "Every religion, freakish or orthodox, that the world ever knew is flourishing today in Los Angeles," wrote Hoffman Birney in 1930. "This lovely place, cuckoo land," wrote the editors of *Life*, "is corrupted with an odd community giddiness . . . nowhere else do eccentrics flourish in such close abundance. Nowhere do spiritual or economic panaceas grow so lushly. Nowhere is undisciplined gullibility so widespread." "Here," wrote Bruce Bliven in 1935, "is the world's prize collection of cranks, semi-cranks, placid creatures whose bovine expression shows that each of them is studying, without much hope of success, to be a high-grade moron, angry or ecstatic exponents of food fads, sun-bathing, ancient Greek costumes, diaphragm breathing and the imminent second coming of Christ." Uniformly, these aberrant tendencies have been attributed to the climate. But are there other, and less hackneyed explanations?

The first eccentric of Southern California was a Scotsman by the name of William Money, who arrived in Los Angeles around 1841. Married to a Mexican woman, Money was a quack doctor, an economic theorist, and the founder of the first cult in the region. Known to local residents as "Professor Money," "Doctor Money," and "Bishop Money," he had been born, so he contended, with four teeth and "the likeness of a rainbow in the eye." It is significant that Money should have been the first person to write and to publish a book in the region, *The Reform of the New Testament Church*. Later, in 1858, he issued a dissertation in Spanish entitled, *A Treatise on the Mysteries of the Physical System and the Methods of Treating Diseases by Proper Remedies*. Of the 5,000 patients he had treated, only four, he said, had died. The cult that he founded was called "The Reformed New Testament Church of the Faith of Jesus Christ" and was pretty largely made up of "native Californians." He once prepared a map of the world entitled "William Money's Discovery of the Ocean." On this map San Francisco, a community that he detested, was shown poised on a portion of the earth that he predicted would soon collapse, precipitating the city into the fiery regions. Living in a weird oval structure in San Gabriel, the approaches to which were guarded by two octagonal edifices built of wood and adobe, Money was the leading Los Angeles eccentric from 1841 until his death in 1880. He died with "an image of the Holy Virgin above his head, an articulated skeleton at his feet, and a well-worn copy of some Greek classic within reach of his hand."

Bishop Money was a typical Southern California eccentric: he was born elsewhere, he came to the region in middle life, his aberrations were multiform, and he founded a cult. As an eccentric, however, he was in advance of his time, an exceptional figure. Southern California evidenced few manifestations of cultism between 1850 and 1900. The hordes of newcomers who came after 1880 were a god-fearing, highly respectable, conservative lot. In 1894 a visitor reported that 2,000 Easterners were spending their winters in Pasadena, that they were all regular church communicants, and that there was "not a grog shop in town." The publication of the W.C.T.U., *The White Ribbon*, was issued in Pasadena, where, as throughout Southern California, the dry sentiment was exceedingly strong. When J. W. Shawham started a "wet" newspaper in Pasadena in 1888, the local historian laconically notes that "he was a drinking fellow: he didn't last long." In 1888 the Pasadena *Standard* published a battle song of the W.C.T.U.:

> *Rise, Pasadena! march and drill*
> *To this your bugle rally—*
> *A Church or school on every hill,*
> *AND NO SALOON IN THE VALLEY.*
>
> *Stand firm in rank, but do not boast*
> *Too soon your victory's tally;*
> *You 'hold the fort' for all the coast*
> *FOR NO SALOON IN THE VALLEY.*
>
> *The seige is on, the bombs aflight!*
> *Let no true soldier dally;*
> *For truth and right, for HOME we fight,*
> *AND NO SALOON IN THE VALLEY.*

The truth of the matter was well expressed by Charles Frederick Holder when he described Pasadena in 1889 as "a city built rapidly yet without a vestige of the rough element that is to be found in the new cities of the inter-oceanic region. This is due to the fact that Pasadena has been built up by wealthy, refined, and cultivated people from the great cities of the East; and, while without maturity in years, she possesses all that time can bring, especially as regards the social ties that bind and mould communities." As long as the tide of migration was made up of such people, there was no opportunity for the visionary or the faith-healer or the mystic. But, as the region grew in wealth and fame, it began to attract some strange characters.

1. THE PURPLE MOTHER

The first major prophetess of the region was unquestionably Katherine Tingley. Born in New England in 1847, three times married, Mrs. Tingley lived in almost total obscurity for the first forty years of her life. When she was forty, she moved to New York, where, through her interest in spiritualism, she came to know the theosophist William Quan Judge, over whom she soon acquired an extraordinary influence. Much talk began to be heard in theosophical circles about the emergence of a mysterious disciple, referred to by Judge as "The Promise," "The Veiled Mahatma," "The Light of the Ledge," and "The Purple Mother." Shortly after Judge's death, Katherine Tingley was revealed as The Purple Mother. Although she had never been west, Mrs. Tingley had, since childhood, dreamed of "building a White City in a Land of Gold beside a Sunset Sea." Raising a considerable sum of money in the East, she established the Point Loma Theosophical Community near San Diego in 1900.

The community was an extraordinary apparition to appear in the complacent middle-class village of San Diego. It consisted of forty buildings, with "a harmonious blending of architectural lines, partly Moorish, partly Egyptian, with something belonging to neither." One of the main structures, called The Homestead, had ninety rooms and a great dome of opalescent green. Still another building, The Aryan Temple, had an amethyst Egyptian gateway. When visitors approached the colony, a bugler hidden behind the Egyptian gates sounded the note of their arrival. It was not long before some 300 bizarre devotees, representing 25 different nationalities, had taken up residence in the colony. When a person entered the colony it was customary to present Mrs. Tingley with a sizable "love offering." The Purple Mother ruled the colony with the utmost despotism. "From changing the milk-bottles of the newest baby to laying the last shingle on a bungalow," wrote one observer, "her desire equals a Czar's edict."

On the lovely 500-acre Point Loma tract soon appeared a School of Antiquity, a Theosophical University, a Greek Theater, a Raja Yoga College, and the Iris Temple of Art, Music, and Drama. Still later an opera house was acquired in San Diego, where the Point Loma yogis, appearing in Grecian costumes, lectured the natives on the subtle dialectics of theosophy. In its early years, Point Loma possessed an atmosphere described as "like ozone—like poppy-scented champagne." Wearing strange costumes, the residents of the colony raised chickens, vegetables, and fruits, and cultivated silkworms. During the years of Mrs. Tingley's residence, Point Loma was the headquarters for the branch of the theosophical movement which she headed and which claimed a membership of 100,000 followers scattered throughout the world. Not only did theosophists from all over the world visit Point Loma, but the emphasis placed on music attracted visitors from far and wide. Madame Modjeska, visiting the colony, called it "a second Bayreuth."

Needless to say, the appearance of this exotic colony in Southern California greatly disturbed the boosters of the period who regarded it as "bad advertising." General Harrison Gray Otis was convinced that weird orgies were being enacted at Point Loma. He was particularly incensed by stories of a sacred dog, called Spot, who was supposed to be the reincarnation of one of Mrs. Tingley's deceased husbands. Under such headlines as "Outrages at Point Loma Exposed by an 'Escape,'" "Startling Tales From Tingley," sensational stories began to appear in the Los Angeles *Times*. General Otis contended that Point Loma was a "spookery"; that Mrs. Tingley exercised a hypnotic influence on the colonists and fed the children so skimpily that they became "ethereal"; that "the most incredible things happen in that lair"; that purple robes were worn by the women and khaki uniforms by the men; and that, at midnight, the pilgrims "in their nightrobes, each holding a torch," went to a sacred spot on the Point Loma peninsula where "gross immoralities were practiced by the disciples of spookism." For once, however, General Otis had met his weight in wildcats. Mrs. Tingley promptly sued the *Times* for libel, and, after years of litigation, eventually collected a handsome judgment.

It was through Point Loma that the yogi influence reached Southern California. Attracting thousands of visitors to the region, some of whom purchased real estate, the colony soon ceased to be regarded as heretical. Unfortunately Mrs. Tingley became involved in a serious scandal in 1923, as a result of which she abandoned Point Loma and went to Europe. One of the first couples to settle at Point Loma, Dr. and Mrs. George F. Mohn lived for some years in the Homestead before Mrs. Mohn first suspected that the Purple Mother was exerting a powerful influence on her husband. Whatever the nature of the influence, it was unquestionably persuasive; Dr. Mohn contributed $300,000 to the colony. Mrs. Mohn thereupon sued Mrs. Tingley for alienation of affections and a jury returned a verdict in her favor for $75,000.

After Mrs. Tingley's appearance in Southern California, the region acquired a reputation as an occult land and theosophists began to converge upon it from the four corners of the earth. One of these early colonists was Albert Powell Warrington, a retired lawyer from Norfolk, Virginia, who arrived in Los Angeles in 1911. Purchasing a fifteen-acre tract in what is now the center of Hollywood, he established Krotona, "the place of promise." The particular site had been selected, according to Warrington, because "not only does the prevailing breeze from off the nearby Pacific give physical tone to the surroundings, but a spiritual urge seems to be peculiar to all this section." The hills and groves around Krotona were, it seems, "magnetically impregnated."

At its heyday, Krotona boasted an Occult Temple, a psychic lotus pond, a vegetarian cafeteria, several small tabernacles, a large metaphysical library, and a Greek Theater. Grouped around the central buildings, were the dwellings of the colonists, described as a people whose faces had "a consciously sanctified look." Krotona was the headquarters of the Esoteric School, the Order of the Star of the East, and the Temple of the Rosy Cross. Under the direction of Dr. F. F. Strong of Tufts College and W. Scott Lewis of Los Angeles, research was conducted "in the subtler fields of physics and chemistry, psychology and psychic phenomena." Like Point Loma, the architecture was Moorish-Egyptian. At one time, Warrington rented a hall on Hollywood Boulevard where courses were given in Esperanto, the Esoteric Interpretation of Music and Drama, and the Human Aura. Krotona, in fact, "became a considerable factor in the commercial life of Hollywood."

At Krotona lived the mystic Phil Thompson who founded the science of "stereometry," a science of nature based upon a three-dimensional geometric alphabet. Thompson demonstrated the science by a form on which he had worked for fifteen years. The form was made up of more than a million pieces of wood which he had fitted together. More than three tons of good redwood lumber went into the creation of this singular contraption. A charming man from County Down, Thompson was the author of *The Great Weaver* and *Letters of a Lunatic to Passing Shadows*. At one time his work attracted the attention of Albert Einstein and Dr. Robert Millikan. He died a few years ago at the Hondo "poor farm" in Los Angeles. Another resident of Krotona for many years was the writer Will Levington Comfort. "Krotona," writes his daughter, "in its circle of hills above Hollywood, was like some mystical birthplace of his soul and it welcomed him like a prodigal son." At Krotona, also, lived a remarkable woman, Wilhelmina L. Armstrong, who, under the pen-name of Zamin ki Dost, wrote eighteen of the superb stories collected in Mr. Comfort's *Son of Power*. Miss Armstrong, who spent many years in India, was the author of *Incense of Sandalwood* (1904), a rare collector's item.

The story of Krotona has been well told, in novel form, by Jane Levington Comfort (*From These Beginnings*, 1937). While most residents of Hollywood have never heard of the place, Krotona left a definite cultural imprint on Southern California. It was at Krotona in 1918 that Christine Wetherill Stevenson, a wealthy Philadelphian, sponsored an outdoor production of Sir Edwin Arnold's *The Light of Asia* which ran for thirty-five nights. It was this production which led to the creation of the Theater Arts Alliance in 1919, out of which eventually came the Hollywood Bowl concerts of today. Mrs. Stevenson was also responsible for the production of the *Pilgrimage Play* in 1920, long since institutionalized by the boosters as one of the major tourist attractions of Los Angeles.

By 1920 Hollywood had begun to encroach upon Krotona and Dr. Warrington decided to lead the faithful to Ojai Valley, a section of Southern California thoroughly impregnated with occult and psychic influences. It is the home of Edgar Holloway, the Man from Lemuria, who claims to have flown to Ojai some years ago in a great flying fish. The real genesis of Ojai as an occult center, however, may be traced to the publication in the early 'twenties of a magazine article by Dr. Hrdlicka predicting the rise of "a new sixth sub-race." It seems that psychological tests given in California schools had revealed the existence of a surprising number of child prodigies; ergo, California was the home of the new sub-race. Once this revelation was made, writes the biographer of Annie Besant, "theosophists all over the world turned their eyes toward California" as the Atlantis of the Western Sea. Among those who came to California was Mrs. Besant, who, "acting on orders of her Master," purchased 465 acres in the Ojai Valley as a home for the new sixth sub-race. And to Ojai, she brought Krishnamurti, "the new Messiah." Throughout the 'twenties, the annual encampments in Ojai were widely reported in the Southern California press, as thousands of people, mostly elderly neurotic women, trouped to Ojai to worship the Messiah. Ojai is, today, the center of all esoteric influences in the region. The Ojai Valley theosophists, however, do not get along well with those of Point Loma. Bitter enmity existed between Annie Besant and Katherine Tingley, the former referring to the latter as "a professional psychic and medium" and "a clever opportunist."

2. NEW THOUGHT AND KINDRED INFLUENCES

"Some one made the careless remark before we came, that there wasn't any religion in Los Angeles, and we hadn't been here a week before the Persian who rents a room opposite us asked Uncle Jim if he were a Christian, and when we were on the car going to Whittier, a lady handed each of us a leaflet with a solemn question on it, and afterwards asked him if he'd read it, and if he were a Christian; now, if that isn't religion I don't know what is."
—from Uncle Jim and Aunt Jemimy in Southern California (1912)

Just as theosophy migrated to Southern California, so other strange faiths have been imported. Originally the New Thought movement was centered in New England; in fact, it was called "the Boston craze." But, like all metaphysical and religious movements, New Thought traveled westward. From Boston it moved to Hartford, then to New York, and finally spread westward to Chicago, Kansas City, and St. Louis. First appearing on the west coast in San Francisco, it did not reach Los Angeles until after the World's Fair in 1915. A day at the San Francisco Fair was given over to New Thought, and George Wharton James, the omnipresent, delivered a lecture on "California—the Natural Home of New Thought."

Following the fair, the New Thought leaders began to arrive in Los Angeles: Annie Rix Militz, who established the University of Christ; Fenwicke Holmes, who founded the Southern California Metaphysical Institute; and Eleanor M. Reesberg, who organized the Metaphysical Library. During these years, New Thought studio-lecture rooms sprang up throughout the city and the Metaphysicians' May Day Festival became an annual civic event. Among the pioneers of the movement was the Rev. Benjamin Fay Mills. Under his leadership, the Los Angeles Fellowship was a flourishing institution from 1904 to 1911, with over 1,000 members, a large organizational apparatus, and its own orchestra, schools, and magazine. In 1915, alas! Reverend Mills abandoned New Thought, left California, and died, a few years later, in Grand Rapids, a sound Presbyterian.

These two imported movements, theosophy and New Thought, constitute the stuff from which most of the later creeds and cults have been evolved. Since Southern California was the world center of both movements—theosophy from 1900; New Thought since 1915—it not only attracted adherents of these creeds from all over the world, but it became a publishing center from which issued a steady flow of magazines, newspapers, and books devoted to mysticism, practical and esoteric. The mystical ingredients came from Point Loma, the practical money-mindedness from the New Thought leaders. Of nearly a hundred books catalogued in the Los Angeles Public Library under the heading "New Thought," over half have been published in Southern California. I once attempted to examine these items, but abandoned the effort after a try at the first volume indexed: *Scientific Air Possibilities With the Human* by Zabelle Abdalian, "Doctor of Airbodiedness."

On meeting in Southern California, strangers are supposed to inquire, first, "Where are you from?" and, second, "How do you feel?" Invalidism and transiency have certainly been important factors stimulating cultism in the region. In Los Angeles, wrote Mark Lee Luther, "a vast amount of therapeutic lore was to be had for nothing in Westlake Park. The elderly men and women, hailing chiefly from the Mississippi watershed, who made this pleasance their daily rendezvous, were walking encyclopedias of medical knowledge. They seemed to have experienced all ailments, tried all cures. Allopathy, homeopathy, osteopathy, chiropractic, faith-healing and Christian

Science, vegetarianism and unfried food, the *bacillus bulgaricus* and the internal bath had each its disciples and propagandists." The number of food and body cults in Southern California has never been reckoned. In the early 'thirties, there were over 1,000 practicing nudists in Los Angeles, and three large nudist camps: Fraternity Elysia; the Land of Moo, over the entrance to which appeared the saucy slogan, "In All the World, No Strip Like This"; and, in the hills of Calabasas, a mysterious retreat called Shangri-la. The existence of a large number of transients and visitors has always stimulated the cult-making tendency. It should be remembered that, for the last twenty-five years, Los Angeles has had, on an average, about 200,000 temporary residents.

More than invalidism, however, underlies the widespread belief in faith-healing and magic cures. As a result of intensive migration, the growth of medical science has been retarded in Southern California. Much of the early medicine of the region was a combination of folk-healing, quackery, and superstition. Chinese herb doctors still did a lively business when I first arrived in Los Angeles in 1922. For years all the institutions of medical learning and most of the hospitals were concentrated in the northern part of the state. As late as 1870, Southern California had only one doctor in attendance at the annual meeting of the State Medical Society, and a local society was not formed until 1888. The vacuum created in the medical art was filled by Chinese herb doctors, faith-healers, quacks, and a miscellaneous assortment of practitioners. As a consequence, the unorthodox medical sciences got an early foothold in Southern California. Of eight schools of osteopathy in the United States in 1909, two were located in Los Angeles. Today, of 1,580 osteopaths in the state, all but 500 are in Los Angeles; of 3,655 licensed chiropractors, 2,052 are in Los Angeles. Osteopaths, chiropractors, and naturopaths were so powerful by 1922 that they were able to carry an initiative measure under which they have their own regulatory setup. Anti-vivisection, and similar initiative measures, always get a heavy vote in Southern California, a region that, to this day, lacks a real school of medicine. In such an environment it was, of course, foreordained, that a Messiah would some day emerge. The first local Messiah was a poor, uneducated, desperately ambitious widow by the name of Aimee Semple McPherson.

3. SISTER AIMEE

Aimee, who was "not so much a woman as a scintillant assault," first appeared in California at San Diego in 1918. There she began to attract attention by scattering religious tracts from an airplane and holding revival meetings in a boxing arena. That Mrs. McPherson's first appearance should have been in San Diego is, in itself, highly significant. In San Diego she unquestionably heard of Katherine Tingley, from whom she probably got the idea of founding a new religious movement on the coast and from whom she certainly got many of her ideas about uniforms, pageantry, and showmanship.

Furthermore, San Diego has always been, as Edmund Wilson once said, "a jumping-off place." Since 1911 the suicide rate of San Diego has been the highest in the nation; between 1911 and 1927, over 500 people killed themselves in San Diego. A haven for invalids, the rate of sickness in San Diego in 1931 was 24% of the population, whereas for the whole country the sick rate was only 6%. Chronic invalids have always been advised to go to California, and, once there, they drift to San Diego. From San Diego there is no place else to go; you either jump into the Pacific or disappear into Mexico. Seventy per cent of the suicides of San Diego have been put down to "despondency and depression over ill health." Curiously enough, Southern California has always attracted victims of so-called "ideational" diseases like asthma, diseases which are partly psychological and that have, as Wilson pointed out, a tendency to keep their victims moving away from places under the illusion that they are leaving the disease behind. But once they acquire "a place in the sun" in California, they are permanently marooned.

From San Diego, Mrs. McPherson came to Los Angeles in 1922 with her Four Square Gospel: conversion, physical healing, the second coming, and redemption. She arrived in Los Angeles with two minor children, an old battered automobile, and $100 in cash. By the end of 1925, she had collected more than $1,000,000 and owned property worth $250,000. In the early 'twenties, as Nancy Barr Mavity has pointed out (in an excellent biography of Mrs. McPherson), "Los Angeles was the happy hunting ground for the physically disabled and the mentally inexacting . . . no other large city contains so many transplanted villagers who retain the stamp of their indigenous soil. . . . Most cities absorb the disparate elements that gravitate to them, but Los Angeles remains a city of migrants," a mixture, not a compound.

Here she built Angelus Temple at a cost of $1,500,000. The Temple has an auditorium with 5,000 seats; a $75,000 broadcasting station; the classrooms of a university which once graduated 500 young evangelists a year; and, as Morrow Mayo pointed out, "a brass band bigger and louder than Sousa's, an organ worthy of any movie cathedral, a female choir bigger and more beautiful than the Metropolitan chorus, and a costume wardrobe comparable to Ziegfeld's." Founding a magazine, The Bridal Call, Mrs. McPherson established 240 "lighthouses," or local churches, affiliated with Angelus Temple. By 1929 she had a following of 12,000 devoted members in Los Angeles and 30,000 in the outlying communities. From the platform of Angelus Temple, Sister Aimee gave the Angelenos the fanciest theological entertainment they have ever enjoyed. I have seen her drive an ugly Devil around the platform with a pitchfork, enact the drama of Valley Forge in George Washington's uniform, and take the lead in a dramatized sermon called "Sodom and Gomorrah." Adjutants have been praying, night and day, for thirteen years in the Temple. One group has been praying for 118,260 hours. While Mrs. McPherson never contended that she could heal the sick, she was always willing to pray for them and she was widely known as a faith-healer. A magnificent sense of showmanship enabled her to give the Angelus Temple throngs a sense of drama, and a feeling of release, that probably did have some therapeutic value. On state occasions, she always appeared in the costume of an admiral-of-the-fleet while the lay members of her entourage wore natty nautical uniforms.

On May 18, 1926, Sister Aimee disappeared. Last seen in a bathing suit on the beach near Ocean Park, she had apparently drowned in the Pacific. While Los Angeles went wild with excitement, thousands of templites gathered on the beach to pray for her deliverance and return. A specially chartered airplane flew over the beach and dropped flowers on the waters. On May 23, an overly enthusiastic disciple drowned in the Pacific while attempting to find her body. A few days later, a great memorial meeting was held for Sister at Angelus Temple, at which $35,000 was collected. Three days later, the mysterious Aimee reappeared at Agua Prieta, across the border from Douglas, Arizona.

Her entrance into Los Angeles was a major triumph. Flooded with requests from all over the world, the local newspapers and wire services filed 95,000 words of copy in a single day. Airplanes showered thousands of blossoms upon the coach that brought Sister back to Los Angeles. Stepping from the train, she walked out of the station on a carpet of roses. A hundred thousand people cheered while she paraded through the streets of the city, accompanied by a white-robed silver band, an escort of twenty cowboys, and squads of police-men. The crowd that greeted her has been estimated to be the largest ever to welcome a public personage in the history of the city. As she stepped on the platform at Angelus Temple, the people in the crowded auditorium were chanting:

> Coming back, back, back,
> Coming back, back, back,
> Our sister in the Lord is coming back.
> There is shouting all around,
> For our sister has been found;
> There is nothing now of joy or peace we lack.

The jubilation, however, did not last long. Working hard on the case, the newspapers soon proved that the kidnaping story, which she had told on her return, was highly fictitious. In sensational stories, they proceeded to trace her movements from the time she disap-peared, through a "love cottage" interlude at Carmel with a former radio operator of the Temple, to her reappearance in Arizona. Fol-lowing these disclosures, she was arrested, charged with having given false information designed to interfere with the orderly processes of the law, and placed on trial. Later the charges against her were dropped. During the trial, thousands of her followers gathered daily in the Temple and shouted:

> Identifications may come,
> Identifications may go;
> Goggles may come,
> Goggles may go;
> But are we downhearted?
> No! No! No!

Sister's trial was really a lynching bee. For she had long been a thorn in the side of the orthodox Protestant clergy who stoked the fires of persecution with memorials, petitions, and resolutions clamoring for her conviction. No one bothered to inquire what crime, if any, she had committed (actually she had not committed any crime). It was the fabulous ability with which she carried off the kidnaping hoax that so infuriated the respectable middle-class residents of Los Angeles. Miss Mavity writes that, in her opinion, it is "improbable that Aimee ever deliberately sought to harm another human being." Although I heard her speak many times, at the Temple and on the radio, I never heard her attack any individual or any group and I am thoroughly convinced that her followers always felt that they had received full value in exchange for their liberal donations. She made migrants feel at home in Los Angeles, she gave them a chance to meet other people, and she exorcised the nameless fears which so many of them had acquired from the fire-and-brimstone theology of the Middle West.

Although she managed to maintain a fairly constant following until her death in 1945 from an overdose of sleeping powder, she never recovered from the vicious campaign that had been directed against her in 1926. The old enthusiasm was gone; the old fervor had vanished. She was no longer "Sister McPherson" in Los Angeles, but merely "Aimee." In many respects, her career parallels that of Katherine Tingley: both were highly gifted women with a great talent for showmanship, both had lived in poverty and obscurity until middle-age, both founded cults, and both were ruined by scandal. In 1936 the Four Square Gospel had 204 branch organizations and a total membership of 16,000. More than 80% of her followers were city residents, mostly lower-middle-class people—small shopkeepers, barbers, beauty-parlor operators, small-fry realtors, and the owners of hamburger joints. Never appealing to the working class, as such, she had an enormous fascination for the uprooted, unhappy, dispirited lumpenproletariat. Over the years, many of her followers moved into the area around Angelus Temple, where they still reside.

4. MIGHTY I AM

The outstanding cult movement in Southern California in the 'twenties, the Four Square Gospel was succeeded by still fancier cults in the 'thirties. By any standard of the conceivable, the I AM cult is the weirdest mystical concoction that has ever issued from the region.

It is a witch's cauldron of the inconceivable, the incredible, and the fantastic. Stated in objective terms, the tenets of the cult constitute a hideous phantasm. Originating in Los Angeles, the cult spread across the nation, with centers in Chicago, New York, West Palm Beach, Washington, Philadelphia, Boston, Cleveland, Denver, Salt Lake City, Fort Worth, and Dallas; enrolled 350,000 converts; and deposited in the hands of its creators the rather tidy sum of $3,000,000.

The creators of the cult, Guy W. Ballard and his wife Edna Ballard, came to Los Angeles from Chicago around 1932. Paperhanger, stock salesman, and promoter, Ballard had been obsessed, since his childhood in Newton, Kansas, with visions of gold and jewels. Indicted in Illinois in 1929, for a gold-mine promotion, he had fled westward. A professional medium, his wife had edited a spiritualist magazine, The Diamond, in Chicago. After coming to Los Angeles, Ballard, under the nom de plume of Godfrey Ray King, published a treatise in 1934 entitled Unveiled Mysteries, which sets forth the doctrine of the Mighty I AM Presence.

The deity of the cult, it seems, is the Ascended Master Saint Germain. While on a hiking trip near Mt. Shasta in Northern California, Ballard relates that Saint Germain, appearing out of the void, tapped him on the shoulder and offered him a cup filled with "pure electronic essence." After drinking the essence and eating a tiny wafer of "concentrated energy," Ballard felt himself surrounded by "a White Flame which formed a circle about fifty feet in diameter." Enveloped in the flame, he and Saint Germain set forth on a trip around the world in the stratosphere, visiting "the buried cities of the Amazon," France, Egypt, Karnak, Luxor, the fabled Inca cities of antiquity, the Royal Tetons, and Yellowstone National Park. Wherever they journeyed, they found rich treasures: jewels of all kinds, Spanish pirate gold, rubies, pearls, diamonds, emeralds, amethysts, gold bullion, casks of silver, the plunder of antiquity. Fantastic as this revelation may sound, Unveiled Mysteries began to sell like hot cakes at $2.50 a copy. Soon the Ballards were able to secure radio time. The "love gifts" poured in so rapidly, that they took over a large rambling tabernacle from the top of which a blazing neon light flashed word to all Los Angeles of the Mighty I AM Presence.

And then the Ballards began to sell things: a monthly magazine called The Voice of the I AM; various books, The Magic Presence, the *I AM Discourses*, the *I AM Adorations, Affirmations*, and *De-crees*, and the *Ascended Master Discourses*. Photographs of Ballard, "our beloved messenger," sold for $2.50; phonograph records, which recorded "the music of the spheres" and lectures of Ballard, sold for $3; a "Chart of the Magic Presence" brought $12, a steel engraving of the "Cosmic Being, Orion, better known as the Old Man of the Hills," retailed for $2; the "Special I AM Decree binder" was listed at $1.25; I AM rings at $12; a special electrical device, equipped with colored lights, called "Flame in Action," sold, in varying sizes, for $50 and $200; and, finally, a "New Age Cold Cream" preparation was available for the faithful. When Mrs. Ballard was later convicted in the federal court in Los Angeles, an audit of the books revealed that over $3,000,000 had been collected in sales, contributions, and "love offerings."

The meetings of this cult were unlike anything of the sort I have witnessed in Los Angeles. Buxom middle-aged usherettes, clad in flowing evening gowns, with handsome corsages of orchids and gar-denias, bustled around at the morning services in a tabernacle that literally steamed with perfume. Although sex is taboo in the I AM creed—it tends to divert "divine energy"—it would be difficult to imagine a ritual in which sexual symbolism figured as prominently as it does in Master Saint Germain's revelation. Basically the cult has two symbols, wealth and energy. Great emphasis is placed on words such as "energy," "wealth," "jewels," "riches," and "power." The faithful are promised power by which they can acquire wealth, gold, radios, hotels, automobiles, jewels, and innumerable luxuries. A key word in the affirmations, chants, and adorations is "blasted" by the dynamic energy of Saint Germain's "purple light" and the "atomic accelerator." A talented appropriator, Ballard had lifted ideas at ran-dom from a dozen sources in putting this strange creed together (the sources are documented in an interesting volume: *Psychic Dictator-ship in America* by Gerald B. Bryan, published in Los Angeles in 1940). One of the sources that Ballard used was a series of articles which William Dudley Pelley had published in 1929, entitled "Seven Minutes in Eternity," written while Pelley was a resident of Sierra Madre, near Pasadena. It is not by chance, therefore, that the I AM cult has Hitlerian overtones, with such auxiliary organizations as "the Minute Men of Saint Germain" and "the Daughters of Light." By the time an I AM audience repeat a chant the fourth time, they are shouting with all the frenzy of a mob of Nazis yelling *Sieg Heil!* Will some future historian regard this Buck Rogers phantasy as the first cult of the atomic age?

5. Mankind United

In 1875, a group of men, whose names must be forever unknown, succeeded in establishing contact with a superhuman race of little men with metallic heads who dwell in the center of the earth. With the aid of these supermen, The Sponsors propose to eradicate war and poverty from the earth. Such is the basic revelation of Mankind United, a cult movement launched by Arthur Bell in 1934. Once 200,000,000 people have joined the organization, Mankind United will be in a position to insure that no mortal will have to work more than 4 hours a day, 4 days a week, 8 months a year, to earn a salary of not less than $3,000 a year. Pensions of $250 a month will be paid all who have worked 11,000 hours or have reached the age of sixty. Bell promised each of his followers a $25,000 home, equipped with radio, television, unlimited motion pictures, and an "automatic vocal-type correspondence machine." The homes were also to be equipped with automatic news and telephone recording equipment; automatic air-conditioning; with fruit trees, vegetable gardens, hot houses, athletic courts, swimming pools, fountains, shrubbery, and miniature waterfalls. While traveling some years before the war in China and Japan, "and certain countries in Europe," Bell had discovered 100,000,000 gardeners who were anxious to spend the rest of their lives gardening in America for Mankind United.

In exchange for these promised luxuries, members were asked to surrender their worldly possessions on joining the secret order. Throughout a network of affiliated organizations—the Universal Service Corporation, the International Institute of Universal Research, and the International Legion of Vigilantes—the leaders of Mankind United received $97,500 in 1939 from the sale of Arthur Bell's revelation. Between 1934 and 1941, more than 14,000 Californians joined the cult, most of whom were "either elderly persons or individuals who had suffered severe economic losses." Arthur Bell claimed to have possession of a ray machine so powerful that its beams, once released, would knock out the eyesockets of people thousands of miles distant (a notion based upon an article which Dr. R. M. Langer, of the California Institute of Technology had contributed to

Collier's in 1940). Using the principle of the ray machine, power plants would be created capable of exterminating 1,000,000 people at a single blast (the atomic bomb killed 100,000 at Hiroshima). Claiming to be omnipotent, Bell told a California legislative committee that, if he wished, he could go into a trance and be whisked off to the far corners of the earth. On one occasion he went to sleep in San Francisco and woke up aboard a British merchant vessel in mid-Atlantic. Shortly after the attack on Pearl Harbor, the leaders of the cult, most of whom were anti-war, were convicted of violating the sedition statutes.

Certain basic themes appear in both the I AM and Mankind United cults. In both movements there is a marked emphasis upon energy and power: symbolized by the ray machine in Mankind United and by the "mystic purple light" of the I AM cult. Both cults reflect a psychoneurotic preoccupation with the symbols of material wealth, luxury, and ease of living. Splendor and release, power and wealth, are to come, in both cases, through the intervention of a Messiah who possesses the magic formula. There are villains in both cults: hidden rulers, destructive forces, static elements that must be blasted into eternity. Sired by Buck Rogers and Superman, they are nevertheless profoundly symptomatic of the unrest, the suppressed fury, and the preoccupation with violence and power of certain classes in our society. The revelation of Arthur Bell contains this significant passage:

> The middle classes of people, who have always constituted the backbone of every nation, have been held in bondage throughout the centuries, primarily because of the fact that they have been penny wise and pound foolish in devoting their full time to performing the world's work, and in taking so little time for ascertaining the reasons for their ceaseless bondage.

The character, Tod, in the late Nathanael West's brilliant novel, *The Day of the Locust*, spends his nights at the different Hollywood churches, drawing their worshipers:

> He visited the "Church of Christ, Physical," where holiness was attained through the constant use of chest-weights and spring grips; the "Church Invisible" where fortunes were told

and the dead made to find lost objects; the "Tabernacle of the Third Coming," where a woman in male clothing preached the "Crusade Against Salt"; and the "Temple Modern" under whose glass and chromium roof, "Brain-Breathing," the Secret of the Aztecs, was taught. As he watched these people writhe on the hard seats of their churches, he thought of how well Alessandro Magnasco would dramatize the contrast between their drained-out, feeble bodies and their wild, disordered minds. He would not satirize them as Hogarth or Daumier might, nor would he pity them. He would paint their fury with respect, appreciating its awful, anarchic power and aware that they had it in them to destroy civilization.

One Friday night in the "Tabernacle of the Third Coming," a man near Tod stood up to speak. Although his name most likely was Thompson or Johnson and his home town Sioux City, he had the same counter-sunk eyes, like the heads of burnished spikes, that a monk by Magnasco might have. He was probably just in from one of the colonies in the desert near Soboba Hot Springs where he had been conning over his soul on a diet of raw fruits and nuts. He was very angry. The message he had brought to the city was one that an illiterate anchorite might have given decadent Rome. It was a crazy jumble of dietary rules, economics and Biblical threats. He claimed to have seen the Tiger of Wrath stalking the walls of the citadel and the Jackal of Lust skulking in the shrubbery, and he connected these omens with "thirty dollars every Thursday and meat eating." Tod didn't laugh at the man's rhetoric. He knew it was unimportant. What mattered were his hearers. They sprang to their feet, shaking their fists and shouting. On the altar someone began to beat a bass drum and soon the entire congregation was singing "Onward Christian Soldiers."

In Los Angeles, I have attended the services of the Agabeg Occult Church, where the woman pastor who presided had violet hair (to match her name) and green-painted eyelids (to emphasize their mystical insight); of the Great White Brotherhood, whose yellow-robed followers celebrate the full moon of May with a special ritual; of the Ancient Mystical Order of Melchizedek; of the Temple of the Jewelled Cross; of Sanford, "food scientist, psychologist, and health lec-

turer"; of the Baha'i World Faith Center; of the Crusade of the
New Civilization; of the Self-Realization Fellowship of America,
which proposes to construct a Golden Lotus Yoga Dream Hermitage
near Encinitas at a cost of $400,000; and the lectures of Dr. Horton
Held, who believes that California is an unusually healthy place to
live since "so many flowers find it possible to grow in this vicinity.
The flowers, cultivated or wild, give out certain chemicals which
beneficially affect the human body." Los Angeles is the home of the
Maz-daz-lan cult of Otoman Bar-Azusht Ra'nish (real name Otto
Ranisch), whose followers chant:

> *I am all in One individually and one in All collectively;*
> *I am present individually and omnipresent collectively;*
> *I am knowing individually and omniscient collectively;*
> *I am potent individually and omnipotent collectively.*
> *I am Maz-daz-lan and recognize the Eternal Designs of*
> *   Humata, Huhata, Hu-varashta*
> *A-shem Vo-hu, A-shem Vo-hu, A-shem Vo-hu.*

It is the home of the Philosophical Research Society, Incorporated;
of Manly Palmer Hall, "America's Greatest Philosopher"; the center
of Zoroastrianism in America; and the headquarters of the American
Association for the Advancement of Atheism. In a single office build-
ing in the heart of Los Angeles, Thomas Sugrue found the following
listed as tenants: "Spiritual Mystic Astrologer; Spiritual Psychic
Science Church, number 450, Service Daily, Message circles, Trum-
pets Thursday; Circle of Truth Church; Spiritual Psychic Science
Church; First Church of Divine Love and Wisdom; Reverend Eva
Coram, Giving Her Wonderful Cosmic Readings, Divine Healing
Daily; Spiritual Science Church of the Master, Special Rose Light
Circle, Nothing Impossible." Southern California, wrote Michael
Williams, is a "vertiginous confusion of modern idolatry and sorcery
and superstition," which is finding philosophical justification as a
"new paganism, made up of Theosophists, Rosicrucians, Christian
Mysticism, Hermeticism, and New Thought." It will be noted that
most of the movements described in this chapter represent cultic
phenomena, that is, they are not sects which have split off from some
established faith; they are new cults.

6. CITY OF HERETICS

"This was a city of heretics. A themeless city with every theme. Chicago, St. Louis and Denver had each been different; each had its own sordidness and strength and fury. Each was lusty and titanic in its own way, joyful and somber in its own way, and each was indubitably American. But not this Los Angeles. It had an air of not belonging to America, though all its motley ways were American. It was a city of refugees from America; it was purely itself in a banishment partly dreamed and partly real. It rested on a crust of earth at the edge of a sea that ended a world."
—from *A Place in the Sun* by Frank Fenton (italics mine)

Migration is the basic explanation for the growth of cults in Southern California. "History is replete," writes Dr. William W. Sweet, "with instances of corruption of religion among migrating people." In the process of moving westward, the customs, practices, and religious habits of the people have undergone important changes. Old ties have been loosened; old allegiances weakened. The leaders of the orthodox faith have repeatedly complained, with the exception of those of the Catholic Church, that established church practices and procedures have undergone various mutations in Southern California. For example, entombment in mausoleums and the practice of cremation are much more common here than elsewhere in the nation. Bishop Stevens of the Episcopal Church has said "that people in Southern California jump from one ism to another. It doesn't make much difference if one changes the labels on these empty bottles, and Southern California is full of empty bottles." A church survey made in Los Angeles points up the real problem. "For the most part," it states, "the newly developing religious teachers are sincerely trying to serve their followers, and prove to be strong influences because *traditional habits do not reach the people in this community.* Even the older-type churches have been adopting measures unsanctioned in other parts of the country for a more effective hold upon their people."

In a lesser measure, the cultic aberrations of Southern California are an accidental by-product of its geographical location. Dr. Lee R. Steiner, in her study of quacks and fakirs, has pointed out that, when difficulty besets the quack, "he usually flees to Los Angeles," not so much because it is a haven, as because it is the first metropolitan center west of Chicago. Cult movements have moved westward in America and Los Angeles is the last stop. The cultism of Los Angeles appeared highly exceptional, when it first became pronounced in the early 'twenties, because most other American cities had forgotten that they, too, had passed through a similar phase years ago. For example, San Francisco was the home and center of west-coast cults and fakery from 1860 to 1890. The geography of Los Angeles is important in another respect; it faces the East. "Every migrant," writes Dr. Horace Kallen, "is a cultural carrier." That Los Angeles faces the East accounts for the fact, pointed out some years ago by Dr. Herbert W. Schneider, that every existing religion in the world is represented by branches in Los Angeles. Some idea of the heterogeneous religious scene may be illustrated by the fact that, of 1,833 houses of worship in Los Angeles, 147 are Roman Catholic and 836 are orthodox Protestant; but what are the remaining 850 churches?

Despite the number of churches, many of which cannot be classified under familiar labels, Los Angeles does not show a high average church attendance. "When a city like Los Angeles," complained the Rev. S. H. Bailes in 1933, "with more than 1,000,000 population, can report only 100,000 persons in its churches on an average Sunday morning, it is time for the nation to come back to God." California ranks seventeenth among the states in the number of churches; while Los Angeles ranks ninth, among the cities, in number of churches, and, in 1936, had 427,348 church members. So far as the orthodox faiths are concerned, it is rather interesting to note that the Roman Catholic faith is the largest single denomination in every county in Southern California and that it has shown an increase of 134.8% in membership since 1906. Throughout Los Angeles, as Aldous Huxley observed, one can see "primitive Methodist churches built, surprisingly enough, in the style of Cartuja at Granada, Catholic churches like Canterbury Cathedral, synagogues disguised as Hagi Sophia, and Christian Science churches with pillars and pediments, like banks." Paradoxical in all things, Southern California is a land of exaggerated religiosity and also of careless skepticism, where old faiths die and new cults are born.

While the folk-belief that new religious movements always arise in desert areas is certainly naive, nevertheless there is something about Los Angeles—its proximity to the desert, its geographical position (facing east and west), its history of rapid social change through migration—that leads me to believe that some new religious movement is brewing here. Admittedly the evidence is circumstantial, but I would point to some curiously interesting details recently unearthed by Dr. William York Tindall (see *The Asian Legacy and American Life*, 1945, pp. 175-193.)

When William Butler Yeats and his wife visited California, Mrs. Yeats, a medium, had a series of occult experiences in Los Angeles. For several successive nights, her husband took notes on the daemonic or occult communications which she received. These notes constitute the strange stuff from which his extraordinary volume, *A Vision* (1925), was woven. While visiting in Los Angeles, D. H. Lawrence frequently consulted Lewis Spence, a Rosicrucian, and an authority on the Atlantis legend. Much of the mysticism of his novel, *The Plumed Serpent*, is based on materials acquired from Spence. According to Dr. Tindall, the account of the *chakras*, which appeared in Lawrence's *Psychoanalysis and the Unconscious*, is based upon a book entitled *The Apocalypse Unsealed* (1910), written by James M. Pryse of Los Angeles. In 1937, Aldous Huxley accompanied his friend Gerald Heard to America. After "investigating telepathy in Carolina and Quakerism in Pennsylvania," in search of collaboration for their burgeoning metaphysical beliefs, they settled in Los Angeles. In *After Many a Summer Dies the Swan* (1939), Huxley gives an account of Heard's (the Mr. Propter of the novel) attempt to found a new cult in Southern California. At first a skeptic, Huxley has, within the last two years, become a convert to Indian mysticism. Nowadays he regularly attends the meetings of the Vedanta Society in Hollywood and frequently consults Swami Prabhavananda of the Ramakrishna Mission, editor of *Vedanta and the West*. Still another migrant to be converted in Los Angeles is the brilliant young English writer, Christopher Isherwood. "Soon after his arrival in Los Angeles," writes Dr. Tindall, "Isherwood fell under the power of Heard's Swami, renounced literature, the movies, and the world, and proceeded to meditate in the convenient desert whence he emerges occasionally to assist the Swami in public devotions."

There is, about all this, as Dr. Tindall notes, "the strange recurrence of Los Angeles. To that city Heard, Huxley, and James M. Pryse, *contriving to go East and West at once*, retired to meditate, and it was there that Mrs. Yeats received the daemons. The attraction of this place for spiritual men and even for spirits is plain. But I am not sure that I know what it means" (italics mine). Nor do I know what it means. (See also: *The Mystery of the Buried Crosses* by Hamlin Garland, (1937); and *The Doomsday Men* (1938) by J. B. Priestley.) Emma Harding, in her history of spiritualism, said that cults thrived on the Pacific coast because of the wonderful transparency of the atmosphere, the heavy charges of mineral magnetism from the gold mines which set up favorable vibrations, and the notably strong passions of the forty-niners which had created "unusual magnetic emanations"!

Odd—and Utopian

"This, in a way, would be exceeding odd
And almost justify man's ways to God—
If, by the healing of these hills, the blind
Receive an inner sight, and leave behind
Their narrow greed, their numbing fears, and fare
Forth with new souls to breathe the honest air;

If rich man, poor man, lawyer, merchant, thief
Declare with one accord that they'd as lief
Laugh and forget, and make a gracious truce
With sea and mountain; learn again the use
Of Earth and sky and ocean-ranging breeze,
And dance, and dance, beneath the pepper trees."

—James Rorty

CHAPTER XIV

THE POLITICS OF UTOPIA

SINCE the abuse of Los Angeles has become a national pastime, no phase of its social life has attracted more attention than its utopian politics, its flair for the new and the untried—a tendency dismissed by all observers as "crackpotism," still another vagary of the climate, a by-product of the eternal sunshine. With so much attention being focused upon the socio-political phenomena of the region, it is amazing that the roots of this tendency should have been so consistently ignored. In the bulky writing about political crackpotism in Los Angeles, for example, I find not a single reference to the Julian debacle and all that this debacle implied to the residents of the region. Judging from articles in the national press, it would appear that the impression is widespread that, about 1934, Southern California became politically insane. Westbrook Pegler even suggested that a guardian should be appointed and the region declared incompetent. Here, again, the lack of continuity in the traditions of the region is strikingly apparent. For the Utopian Society and the Epic Movement did not spring miraculously into being overnight; both movements had their roots in the past; they were growths, not immaculate conceptions.

1. ECONOMICS OF THE OPEN SHOP

Following the collapse of the "great real-estate boom of 1886," the population of Los Angeles declined at the rate of nearly 1,000 a month during 1888 and 1889. The construction industry was brought to a standstill, business declined, many houses were vacant, and the railroads ran empty cars. "A critical moment," in the words of Charles Dwight Willard, "had arrived in the history of Los Angeles." At this juncture a group of men, all newcomers to the region, decided that they would take over, that they would create an agricultural-industrial empire out of the wreckage of the boom. The famous "new beginning" was launched at a meeting called on October 15, 1888, when Col. Harrison Gray Otis presented the motion which resulted in the formation of the Los Angeles Chamber of Commerce.

Born in Marietta, Ohio, February 10, 1837, Otis had come to Santa Barbara in 1876, a veteran of the Civil War, a man without resources, a typical drifter of the period. For a number of years, he edited the Santa Barbara *Press*, but, with the failure of this venture, he received an appointment as special agent for the Treasury Department in Alaska, where he served from 1879 to 1881. Returning to Los Angeles, he became editor of the *Times* in 1882, on the eve of the boom. The paper made a great deal of money during the boom, enabling Otis to acquire full control by 1886. Belligerent, choleric, opinionated, the colonel quickly developed the fixed idea that he owned Los Angeles, in fee simple, and that he alone was destined to lead it to greatness. In retrospect, it is easy to understand how this notion came to dominate his thinking. For here was a unique situation: a small group of men, under the leadership of Otis, had not merely "grown up with" a community, in the usual American pattern, they had conjured that community into existence. Having taken over at a moment of great crisis, when the older residents had suffered a failure of nerve, they felt that not only had they "saved" Los

Angeles, but that it belonged to them as a matter of right. Over the years, this notion became a major obsession with General Otis (he was breveted Major-General for "meritorious conduct in action at Calocan" during the campaign in the Philippines).

The hatred that Otis came to inspire in those who did not share his fixation is epitomized, for all time, in Hiram Johnson's characterization of the man (delivered in a speech in Los Angeles). "In the City of San Francisco," said Johnson, "we have drunk to the very dregs of infamy; we have had vile officials; we have had rotten newspapers. But we have nothing so vile, nothing so low, nothing so debased, nothing so infamous in San Francisco as Harrison Gray Otis. He sits there in senile dementia with gangrene heart and rotting brain, grimacing at every reform, chattering impotently at all things that are decent, frothing, fuming, violently gibbering, going down to his grave in snarling infamy. He is one thing that all California looks at when, in looking at Southern California, they see anything that is disgraceful, depraved, corrupt, crooked and putrescent—that is Harrison Gray Otis."

During the "hard times" which followed the collapse of the boom, the *Times* announced a 20% reduction in wages. Prior to this announcement, most of the employees in the mechanical department were union members; Otis himself carried a card in the union. When the *Times* refused to negotiate or to discuss the reduction with the union, a strike was called on August 3, 1890, which, in effect, was to continue until October 1, 1910. The calling of this strike really marks the beginning of social and industrial conflict in Southern California. While the other newspapers quickly adjusted their differences with the union, the *Times* remained adamant and began to import strikebreakers from the Printers' Protective Fraternity of Kansas City. As the union continued to seek a settlement, primarily by the use of the boycott, Otis began to organize the community in defense of the open shop. "Thus by the decision of this one man," writes Irving Stone, "Los Angeles became immersed in a half century of bloodshed, violence, hatred, class war, oppression, injustice and a destruction of civil liberties which was to turn it into the low spot of American culture and democracy."

To personalize the issue in this manner, however, is to overlook a basic consideration. Long the center of wealth and population in the state, San Francisco by 1890 had a forty-year handicap on Los

Angeles. Not only had San Francisco acquired undisputed industrial leadership as a result of this headstart, but, unlike Los Angeles, it possessed conspicuous natural advantages: one of the finest harbors in the world, a rich agricultural and mining hinterland, superb river communications, and the accumulated wealth of the bonanza period. Otis and his colleagues were quick to realize that the only chance to establish Los Angeles as an industrial center was to undercut the high wage structure of San Francisco, long a strongly unionized town, and, at the same time, and by the same process, to attract needed capital to the region.

The major asset of Los Angeles in 1890 consisted in the annual winter influx of tourists and homeseekers. It should be noted that this annual influx embraced two distinct currents, people of means or "tourists," and workers or "homeseekers." Both currents were of equal importance, the tourists to provide the capital and revenue, the homeseekers to provide a pool of cheap labor. They were, in fact, the heads and the tails of a single coin. Just as the tourist influx was artificially stimulated by various devices, so the flow of homeseekers was encouraged. During the winter months, special "homeseekers' excursion trains" brought thousands of workers to the region at cut rates. Having land to burn, the Southland dangled the bait of "cheap homes" before the eyes of the prospective homeseekers. "While wages are low," the argument went, "homes are cheap."

At first, as Dr. Ira Cross has pointed out, "the mild climate attracted invalids, many of whom were able to work at light jobs. Others who had small incomes or small savings and who were therefore willing to sell their services for almost any wage, also arrived in great numbers. Husbands and fathers, wives and mothers, came with their sick ones and made their contributions to the local labor supply." The homeseeker element, as one observer said, did not belong to the "limited class who came here to die"; on the contrary, they came to Southern California to work.

From early beginnings around 1900, the homeseeker influx was gradually increased by systematic recruitment and advertising. By 1910 the annual winter influx of homeseekers was estimated at thirty thousand and the excursion trains, starting in October, arrived at the rate of one a week. So great was the influx that, by Christmas of each season, an acute relief problem had developed. On numerous occasions, the City Council of Los Angeles protested against the practice of inserting "homeseeker excursion" ads in the Eastern and Middle Western newspapers, but the protests were ignored.

Naturally such a situation created a highly competitive labor market in Los Angeles, a market characterized by an extraordinarily high turnover. From 1890 to 1910, wages were from twenty to thirty, and in some categories, even forty per cent lower than in San Francisco. It was precisely this margin that enabled Los Angeles to grow as an industrial center. Thus the maintenance of a cheap labor pool became an indispensable cog in the curious economics of the region. For the system to work, however, the labor market had to remain unorganized; otherwise it would become impossible to exploit the homeseeker element. The system required—it absolutely demanded— a non-union open-shop setup. It was this basic requirement, rather than the ferocity of General Otis, that really created the open-shop movement in Los Angeles.

Once lured to the region and saddled with an equity in a cheap home, most of the homeseekers had no means of escape. Just as the open-shop principle was essential to the functioning of the cheap labor market, so the continued influx of homeseekers made possible the retention of the open shop. If the influx had ever stopped, the workers stranded in the region might have organized, but they could never organize so long as the surplus existed. In effect, the system was self-generating and self-perpetuating; once started, it could not be abandoned. Like a narcotic addict, the system required increasingly large shots of the same poison. Needless to say, this hopping-up process was inherently dangerous to the civic health of the community, nor was it long before some symptoms of the acuteness of the malady became apparent.

2. OTISTOWN: THE BLOODY ARENA

"It is somehow absurd but nevertheless true that for forty years the smiling, booming sunshine City of the Angels has been the bloodiest arena in the Western World!"

—Morrow Mayo

The depression of 1893, coming so shortly after "the new beginning" had been inaugurated, had serious repercussions in Southern California. Low prices for farm products ruined scores of farmers and their failure, in turn, resulted in a run on the local banks. In June,

1893, six banks closed their doors. Then the mechanics on the Santa Fe line went on strike. Hundreds of unemployed workers were enrolled in pick-and-shovel brigades, while others joined the Southern California contingent of Coxey's Army. Those who enlisted in Coxey's Army, however, did not get farther east than Colton, California, where two hundred of the marchers were arrested for disturbing the peace and sentenced to four months in jail.

When the employees of the Pullman Company walked out, on May 11, 1894, the American Railway Union tied up eleven rail lines running out of Chicago. By June 27, California was completely cut off from the rest of the country. With large shipments of perishable fruit accumulating in Los Angeles, the strike quickly assumed major proportions. Since the *Times* represented the spearhead of the antiunion movement, the railroad workers directed most of their activities against this bastion of reaction. "Daily a cordon of strikers," reported the *Times*, in a retrospective account, "would gather about the Times Building, forcibly take the bundles of papers from the emerging route men and carriers and litter the surrounding streets for blocks with tattered fragments of newsprint." Large demonstrations in support of the railroad strikers were held throughout the city. A sweeping injunction against picketing was promptly obtained from Judge Erskine M. Ross of the Federal District Court. When the injunction failed to break the strike, two companies of the First Regiment, United States Infantry, were ordered into Los Angeles. By July 15 the rail lines were able to resume service and the strike was broken. As part of the aftermath of the strike, the Los Angeles leaders of the American Railway Union were indicted, tried before Judge Ross, convicted, and given long prison sentences which were later upheld by the United States Supreme Court.

Known in local annals as the Debs Rebellion, the railroad strike marshaled the fruit growers, who had suffered substantial losses, and the local merchants, who shared the same losses, in support of the *Times'* anti-union campaign. A Merchants' Association had been formed in 1894, the year of the strike, to promote La Fiesta de Los Angeles, a gaudy tourist ballyhoo. The following year a Manufacturers' Association was formed, and, in 1896, the two groups merged, under the leadership of the *Times*, as the Merchants and Manufacturers Association, which quickly became, in the words of Peter Clark

MacFarlane, "the greatest closed shop organization this country has ever known."

One of the first acts of the newly formed M. & M. was to raise $25,000 by subscription for the purpose of "rounding up the large army of idle men in the city and putting them to work." Emboldened by a number of similarly easy victories, the M. & M. and the *Times* decided to make Los Angeles an open-shop town and to spread the fight on a nation-wide basis. Up to this time, the labor movement in San Francisco had largely ignored Los Angeles, but, with the issue being so sharply drawn, a campaign was finally launched to organize the City of the Angels. At the request of the International Typographical Union, the American Federation of Labor decided in 1907 that the Otistown threat must be met. For by 1907 it had become apparent that, at the rate industry was growing in Los Angeles, it was only a question of time until the city would be in a position to challenge the industrial supremacy of San Francisco, thereby endangering organized labor's great Western stronghold. A local newspaper, the *News*, was purchased, its name was changed to the *Citizen*, and the great battle was on.

From 1907 to 1910, a state of war existed in Los Angeles, with the community being torn apart by industrial strife. Realizing that the outcome of the fight might be decisive, not only of local, but of regional and national phases of the same issue, both sides poured thousands of dollars into Los Angeles. With the eyes of the nation riveted on Los Angeles, neither side could afford to call a truce. It is altogether likely that the *Times* might have succumbed, during this period, had it not been for the continuing support it received from sources outside the state and from the incoming tide of Middle Western farmers who were strongly inclined toward the anti-labor position. The culmination of this bitter three-year struggle—vividly described in an excellent chapter in Morrow Mayo's book about Los Angeles—occurred on the fateful night of October 1, 1910, when the plant of the Los Angeles *Times* was dynamited.

In the spring of 1910, a series of strikes had occurred in Los Angeles, first of brewery workers, later of metal workers. Called after a general lockout had been ordered, the metal-workers' strike was the issue that led directly to the dynamiting of the *Times*. As soon as the strike was called, the various companies involved obtained injunctions which prohibited all types of picketing. Instead of breaking the strike, the injunctions only further infuriated the workers and the picket lines became increasingly militant. Sensing that a real crisis existed, the M. & M. proceeded to draft, and to dictate the adoption on July 16, 1910, of an anti-picketing ordinance. One of the most sweeping ordinances of the kind ever enacted in this country, the Los Angeles ordinance is famous in labor history as the original anti-picketing ordinance later used as a model by various employer groups across the nation. Within a few weeks after its adoption, 470 workers had been arrested in Los Angeles.

So far as the workers of Los Angeles were concerned, the enactment of this ordinance was the straw that broke the camel's back. Smarting under the accumulated resentments and humiliations of two decades of industrial conflict, they decided to smash the coalition of open-shop forces in the community. The strike had been regarded as another industrial dispute, but the ordinance raised a major political issue. Juries began to release defendants charged with violating the ordinance almost as fast as they were arrested. Over 20,000 copies of Clarence Darrow's pamphlet, *The Open Shop*, were distributed in Los Angeles; the circulation of the socialist publication, *The Appeal to Reason*, jumped to 40,000 a week; and membership in the Socialist Party doubled overnight. A Union Labor Political Club was formed, delegates from which sat on the county central committee of the Socialist Party, and the headquarters of the party were transferred to the Labor Temple.

Long before this crisis, the people of Los Angeles had given indication of a tendency to depart from traditional norms of political behavior. Charlette Perkins Gilman, in her autobiography, has given an interesting account of the social enthusiasm rife in Southern California in the 'eighties. "California," she wrote, "is a state peculiarly addicted to swift enthusiasms. It is a seed-bed of all manner of cults and theories, taken up, and dropped with equal speed." A major enthusiasm of the 'eighties had been Edward Bellamy. For several years Mrs. Gilman had managed to earn a living by lecturing on everything from "Human Nature" to "Social Economics" to the various Nationalist or Bellamy clubs with which Southern California was honeycombed. Under the leadership of the brilliant trade-union lawyer, Job Harriman, the Socialist Party had succeeded in capturing much of this early social enthusiasm. But it was the anti-picketing ordinance that suddenly converted a movement of social idealism into a fighting political force.

Still another development led up to, and was a factor in precipitating, the crisis of 1910. This development was largely a result of the work of the pioneer liberal and reformer, Dr. John R. Haynes. Settling in Los Angeles in 1887, Dr. Haynes had made a large fortune in real estate. Just where he derived his reforming social impulses I do not know, but he became one of the earliest advocates of the initiative, referendum, and recall in the United States. Almost entirely due to his efforts, the City of Los Angeles was one of the first cities in the nation to adopt these measures as part of its charter in 1902. The recall measure was first used in 1904, to recall a councilman who had voted to give the city's legal advertising to the Los Angeles *Times* despite the fact that its bid was $15,000 higher than the lowest bid. In the years of 1900 to 1910, a strong Good Government movement had developed in Los Angeles around men like Dr. Haynes, a movement which was, needless to say, anathema to General Otis and associates. Not long prior to the dynamiting of the *Times*, the Good Government League had recalled a corrupt mayor, one of the earliest uses of the recall to oust a mayor in American political history. At the recall election, the league had elected George Alexander as mayor against the vigorous opposition of the *Times*. Thus at the time the metal-workers' strike occurred, the conservative elements of the community were divided.

With the conservative forces divided, the Socialist Party, functioning as the political arm of the trade-union movement, began to record striking gains. In a series of parades organized by the party, as many as ten and twenty thousand workers marched through the streets of Los Angeles singing, shouting, and chanting the slogans of the early Socialist movement. Against this background, the labor fight assumed the character, as Mr. MacFarlane pointed out in *Collier's*, "of the most desperate battle against the incoming or upgrowing of labor unions that any American city has ever witnessed." In effect, this tense situation existed in Los Angeles for seventeen months prior to the dynamiting of the *Times*. With the dreadful explosion of October 1, 1910, in which twenty men lost their lives, a reign of unmitigated political terror was unleashed in Los Angeles. Importing scores of thugs, professional gunmen, and private detectives, the M. & M. sought to use the prosecution of the McNamaras—active in the organization of the metal workers—as a means of breaking the popular rebellion that had developed.

While the case was pending in the courts, Los Angeles began to prepare for a city election. At the primary, Job Harriman, running on the Socialist ticket, polled 58,000 votes for the office of mayor, a plurality of several thousand votes over the other candidates. Both the Otis-men and the "goo-goos" (supporters of Good Government) were filled with fear and trembling by this amazing vote which, be it remembered, was recorded *after* the dynamiting of the *Times*. The outcome of the final election involved more than the fate of the McNamaras (it was currently assumed that if Harriman won, they would probably be acquitted) and the control of the city government; it involved the very future of Los Angeles. For it happened that the city faced a serious financial crisis at the time. Of $23,000,000 in bonds which the city had authorized for the Owens Valley aqueduct, only $17,000,000 had been sold in 1911. In the meantime, the city had authorized still another bond issue of $3,000,000 for the construction of a hydroelectric plant and no portion of this issue had been sold. Furthermore, a bond issue of $10,000,000 had been proposed for harbor improvements at San Pedro of which $3,000,000 had been authorized but not sold. Thus the interesting question arose: Could this largely non-industrial city of 300,000 population sell $17,000,000 in bonds if it proceeded to elect a Socialist as mayor?

To give this question added poignancy, Harriman had been campaigning on a platform which called for graduated taxes, complete ownership of all public utilities, including ice and laundry companies, and other major social reforms. That he stood a good chance of being elected was generally conceded. The "goo-goos" were backing Mayor Alexander for re-election; the *Times*, whose candidate had "failed badly in the primaries," loathed and detested Alexander; and both the *Express* and the *Examiner* had their own candidates for the office. When Harriman led the ticket at the primaries, all these elements finally decided to back Mayor Alexander. General Otis announced that he would support Alexander whether the so-and-so liked the idea or not. Seemingly assured of victory, Harriman had closed the campaign with a series of parades, demonstrations, and meetings of such magnitude that even the *Times* was moved to express its sense of "awe" and "wonder."

In the meantime, Lincoln Steffens had succeeded in negotiating a deal with General Otis, the essence of which was that the Mc-Namaras would plead guilty on the eve of the election and receive prison sentences. These negotiations were handled with the utmost secrecy; for example, Harriman, I am convinced, did not know that a deal was pending. On December 1, 1911, four days before the final election, the McNamaras entered a plea of guilty to the charge. The news that such a plea had been entered came as a stunning, paralyzing blow to the labor movement, not only in Los Angeles, but throughout the nation (see, for example, Louis Adamic's vivid account of the aftermath of the case in *Dynamite*). The next day the streets of Los Angeles, which had been echoing with Socialist battle-cries, were littered with Harriman buttons and badges. Clarence Darrow, en route to his headquarters, was hissed and booed by a crowd of erstwhile supporters. Needless to say, Harriman was defeated.

The dynamiting of the *Times*, more particularly, the plea of guilty entered by the McNamaras, aborted the labor movement in Los Angeles. It set back by twenty years a movement which, even in 1911, was dangerously retarded in relation to the growth of the community. The serious consequences of this abortion largely account for the subsequent political pathology of Los Angeles. Areas such as Los Angeles, where opposition to trade unions has assumed, in the words of a report of the LaFollette Committee, "a conspiratorial pattern of malfeasance," become "a haven of would-be exploiters and those who would preach radical political and economic doctrines. They are breeding grounds for strange nostrums. They are subject to a continuing unhealthy unbalance of economic power and position, often accompanied by occasional outbursts of class violence and a constant undercurrent of class hostility. They frequently provide a reason for the location of industry at sub-standard levels and thereby stimulate counteraction in other urban areas where real estate, banking, and service business are drawn into a circle of vicious competition. Where there are large tributary areas, a whole state or section of the state, may be dominated by the attitudes of industrial autocracy that prevail in the urban center. . . . Such areas are likely to be vulnerable to the economic, social, and political evils that democracy must meet and vanquish if it is to survive. Our society has judged them not the 'white spots' but the cancer areas."

3. "Bread and Hyacinths"

Job Harriman, the key figure in the fight to unionize Los Angeles, was an interesting person. Like General Otis and Dr. John R. Haynes, he had come to Southern California in the 'eighties (1886 to be exact), and like them he had been attracted by the tourist ballyhoo. Opening a law office, he practiced some years in Los Angeles, left for a short period, and finally returned in 1903. A prominent figure in the early Socialist movement, he was once the nominee of the party for the vice-presidency. After the McNamara debacle, Harriman came to the conclusion that a Socialist movement could never be based directly on trade-union organization implemented by political action. "I was so impressed," he wrote in *Communities of the Past and Present* (1924), "with the fact that the movement must have an economic foundation that I turned my attention to the study of means by which we could lay some such foundation, even though it be a small one as well as an experimental one. After two or three years, I decided to try to establish a co-operative colony."

Much as General Otis and his colleagues had decided to make a "new beginning" out of the wreckage of the land boom, so Harriman decided to launch a brave new world out of the wreckage of the labor-Socialist movement in Los Angeles. If Otis could build a city out of almost nothing, it did not seem too far-fetched to believe that another, and very different, kind of community might be established in this strange land in which so many things that seemed impossible of achievement had actually been realized. It is significant that the motivation of Harriman's utopianism stemmed directly from the defeat of the trade-union movement, a defeat which he rationalized, not in terms of the economics of the region, but as the outgrowth of a basic ideological weakness. In essence the idea of the project—"a retreat to the desert"—represented Harriman's violent reaction to the tragic events in which he had been involved.

In the name of the Llano del Rio Company (formed under the laws of Nevada with a capitalization of $2,000,000), Harriman acquired a tract of land in Antelope Valley, ninety miles by road from Los Angeles, located near the mouth of Big Rock Canyon which had been known to the Spanish as Rio del Llano. The tract had originally been laid out as a temperance colony by the Mescal Land & Water Company. There the temperance advocates had formed an irrigation improvement district, issued bonds, and constructed a mile-long tunnel for water. Later the project had been abandoned when the company defaulted under the bond issue. Buying up these bonds for a nominal sum, Harriman was able to secure control of the entire tract for the Llano del Rio Company. In May, 1914, the first group of five families moved to the project.

Harriman's conception of the structure of this utopian community is of considerable historical interest and importance. He had decided to use the private corporation as the legal instrument by which the colony was to be established. Although a private corporation, the Llano del Rio Company was, in effect, a collective farm, a workers' soviet. Colonists purchased stock in the company and received back an agreement from the corporation to employ them at wages of $4 a day payable out of the net earnings. Since only settlers were permitted to purchase stock, it followed that they would also own all the assets of the company. While settlers were eventually drawn from many different localities, the original colonists were persons who had long been associated with Harriman in the Socialist-labor movement in Los Angeles. Among these pioneer colonists were Frank E. Wolfe, editor of a labor paper (he made a motion picture about the Tom Mooney case in 1916 entitled "From Dusk to Dawn" in which Harriman and Clarence Darrow appeared); W. A. Engle, chairman of the Central Labor Council of Los Angeles; and Frank P. Mc-Mahon, who had formerly been an official of the Brick Layers' Union.

Today Antelope Valley is a prosperous farming community in which alfalfa is raised for the dairy farms of Los Angeles, but, in 1914, it was a desert. On this desert, the Llano colonists labored with incredible tenacity to demonstrate the workability of the socialist ideal. On the project, they constructed barns and silos, an office building, a community of homes, a cannery, two hotels, and many other structures. Completing the tunnel for water, they removed the Joshua trees, sagebrush, and greasewood of the desert, and planted 240 acres to alfalfa, 200 acres to orchard crops, and a hundred acres to garden produce. They lined the irrigation ditches with cobblestone, drew up plans for the construction of a sawmill, and took out a permit to cut timber in the mountains. Functioning as part of the project were a print shop, a shoe-repair shop, a laundry, a clothes-cleaning establishment, a warehouse, a rug-making shop, a swimming pool, an art studio, a library, and a rabbit farm. Here, at Llano, was established one of the first Montessori schools in California. In 1917 the cannery produced two carloads of canned tomatoes.

During the time the project was in existence, over 2,000 people visited Llano annually. One of these visitors reported that the social life of the colony "possessed a charm which held its members when the hardships of subjugating the desert nearly overwhelmed them." While Southern California has long been noted for the number of privately controlled co-operative enterprises, Llano represented the first real production co-operative in the region, and, as such, it attracted intense local interest and widespread national comment. On May Day the colonists, dressed in their best clothes, marched through the streets of the settlement, with their own band and a red flag flying at the head of the parade. "If you have two loaves of bread," they said, "sell one and buy a hyacinth to feed your soul."

Considering the background of the project, Harriman's insistence on proving the feasibility of Socialism cannot be dismissed as quixotic. The Soviet Union was not in existence in 1914. Here on the desert of Southern California, on the eve of the first World War, he had determined to build an island of Socialism, not only to establish the soundness of the socialist ideal, but to wipe out the memory of a disastrous defeat. The significance of the experiment was quickly recognized by its opponents. From the beginning, the Llano project was invested with an army of stool pigeons, informers, and agents provocateurs. Every difference of opinion which arose among the colonists was fanned into a flame by these internal enemies. Sensational news stories in the Los Angeles press heralded each squabble in the project as certain proof of the unsoundness of this utopia-on-the-desert. With colonists being encouraged by outside elements to file lawsuits against the company, the court records were soon littered with litigation. Harriman, the guiding intelligence of the project, was forced to spend most of his time in court defending one or another of the dozens of trumped-up lawsuits filed against the company.

Despite these difficulties, however, the project would probably have survived had it not been for the fact that a survey made in 1917 indicated that the water supply, when fully developed, would not be sufficient to meet the growing requirements of the colony. In 1917 Harriman made a trip to Louisiana, secured an option on 20,000 acres of cut-over timber land, and determined to move the entire colony to New Llano. In December, 1917, Llano del Rio was abandoned and, in a special train, the remaining colonists left for their new home in Louisiana. From 1917 to date, they have struggled to maintain themselves in their new location where, with characteristic energy, they have built still another community, with stores, hotels, homes, and a lumber mill. While a receiver was appointed for the project some years ago, some of the original colonists are still living on the property. The story of these colonists who, for over a quarter of a century, have struggled to establish the feasibility of the Socialist ideal is one of the moving episodes in the history of social movements in America. Over the years, I have come to know some of the colonists who eventually abandoned New Llano and returned to Los Angeles. Although a few of them are rather disillusioned, the enthusiasm of most of them has not abated. They still speak of those early days at Llano-on-the-desert with an elation which has survived through the years. Certain of these colonists have been active leaders in the self-help co-operative movement in Southern California. A former Llano colonist, Walter Millsap, founded the United Cooperative Industries in Los Angeles in 1923.

4. SAN DIEGO VIGNETTE

After the McNamara tragedy, the liberal movement in Southern California was reborn, not in Los Angeles, but, of all places, in San Diego. While the rebirth occurred in San Diego, Los Angeles was really the midwife. In 1909 the City of the Angels, in response to pressure from the M. & M., had enacted an ordinance restricting the right of free speech. Once the constitutionality of this ordinance was upheld in the courts, San Diego decided to adopt a similar measure. Unlike Los Angeles, San Diego had long enjoyed a considerable latitude in the matter of free speech. As a health and tourist resort, with little industry, it had remained an oasis of civil liberties in Southern California. When San Diego copied the Los Angeles ordinance in 1912, the I.W.W. announced that they would continue to fight for free speech "if it takes 20,000 members and twenty years to win."

Overnight hundreds of Wobblies began to converge on San Diego from all parts of the country, traveling in box cars, on the bumpers, and on the roofs of trains. Inviting arrest, they would mount soapboxes at different points in the downtown section of the city and start to deliver militant speeches. Within a week, 84 men and women were in jail. Those arrested immediately demanded separate jury trials. As fast as one group was convicted, another appeared on the scene. For nearly a year, the jails of San Diego bulged with Wobbly prisoners. So effective were their tactics that, early in 1912, the city was compelled to resort to extra-legal methods to enforce the or-dinance. In the traditional California style, a vigilante committee was formed to rid the city of the Wobbly menace.

One night an army of police officers, plainclothesmen, and armed thugs rounded up the remaining Wobblies and drove them to the little settlement of Sorrento. There, in front of a flagpole that had been erected on an improvised platform, the prisoners were forced to kneel and kiss the flag. Then they were lined up, single file, and told to march. As the march started, a man would, from time to time, break rank and start to run. The fugitives were promptly shot down. After marching the men around for eighteen hours, they were then rounded up, and, in groups of five and six, were made to run the gauntlet. "As they ran between a double line of so-called vigilantes," reads an official state report, "they were belabored with clubs and black-snake whips. Then the flag-kissing episode was repeated, after which they were told 'to hike up' the track for Los Angeles and not to return." One of the victims of the mob, Joseph Mikolasek, died in jail on May 7, 1912, and scores were injured. A local editor who denounced the vigilantes was kidnaped and threatened with a lynch-ing if he did not cease supporting the free-speech fight.

During the week following the Sorrento episode, Emma Goldman and Ben Reitman came to San Diego to organize a protest meeting. Shortly after their arrival, Reitman was kidnaped from his room in the U. S. Grant Hotel, severely beaten, and held incommunicado for several days. Once the mob had seized Reitman, "Red Emma" was escorted to the station and placed aboard a train en route to Los Angeles. In her autobiography, Miss Goldman reported that she found California "seething with discontent" in 1912. "The Mexican Revolution and the McNamara case had aroused labor on the Pacific Coast to a high pitch." Following this incident, large protest meet-ings were held throughout California. In Los Angeles, in particular, "the tide of sympathy rose very high," with unusually large crowds attending the meetings. Before the month was over, Emma Goldman had spoken at forty mass rallies in the state.

Among the individuals who had gathered in San Diego to hear Emma Goldman was a young girl, then quite unknown, by the name of Agnes Smedley. The "free speech" fight was her baptism in social conflict. "I knew little of theory of any kind," she later wrote in her autobiography, "but I listened. The opponents of free speech were like the land speculators I had known. . . . I heard my friends called unspeakable names, saw them imprisoned and beaten, and streams of water from fire hoses turned upon their meetings. I escaped arrest, but the fight released much of the energy dammed up within me. . . . It was in this struggle that I felt the touch of a policeman for the first time. Before me in a small group, two policemen walked deliberately pushing against a working man who walked peacefully with his hands in his pockets. One of the policemen shoved him until he was hurled against the other policeman; the second policeman then grasped him by the collar and, shouting that he was attacking an officer of the law, knocked him to the pavement. 'That's a lie!' I screamed, horrified, thinking they would listen to me. 'That policeman shoved him . . . I saw him . . . the man had his hands in his pockets.' The policemen were already upon the man. Blow after blow they beat into his upturned face, and I saw blood spurt from his eyes." Thus are liberals made and liberal movements born.

Merely as a postscript, it should be noted that the free-speech fight was won in San Diego. In June of 1915, Miss Goldman revisited San Diego lecturing on Ibsen, Nietzsche, Birth Control, Anarchism, and various other topics at a number of meetings throughout the city and no disturbances were reported. Uniformly, strong liberal movements have developed in precisely those areas in Southern California where the most severe repressive measures have been invoked to strangle the right of free speech. If I were asked to name the organization largely responsible for the so-called "utopian crackpot" politics of Southern California, I would name the Merchants and Manufacturers Association of Los Angeles.

5. "The White Spot"

Some years after the armistice, three thousand longshoremen went on strike at San Pedro. The rebirth of the labor movement in Los Angeles, after the great disaster of 1910, really dates from the call for this strike. As soon as the strike was called, the M. & M. promptly intervened. "Black Jack" Jerome, a notorious strikebreaker of the period, and scores of professional gunmen were sent into the harbor district to smash the strike. Not only were strikers arrested for the offense of merely being on strike, but any one who showed the slightest sympathy for the strike was likely to be arrested. An Episcopalian clergyman was arrested in the streets of San Pedro when he asked a policeman to direct him to the strike headquarters. The owner of a restaurant was jailed for the offense of having fed some of the strikers. Employed at the time by the Los Angeles *Times*, I used to watch the screaming Black Marias of Police Chief Louis Oaks roll up to the First Street Station loaded with strikers. At the height of the strike, over 600 strikers were in jail in Los Angeles.

In 1915 Upton Sinclair, then at the pinnacle of his fame, had come to live in Pasadena. Learning of the disturbances at San Pedro, Mr. Sinclair announced that he intended to speak at Liberty Hill, on a small tract of privately owned land which had been rented for the occasion. On the night of the meeting, Liberty Hill was black with the massed figures of the strikers. Mounting a platform illuminated by a lantern, Mr. Sinclair proceeded to read Article One of the Constitution of the United States and was promptly arrested. Hunter Kimbrough then mounted the platform and started to read the Declaration of Independence, and was promptly arrested. Prince Hopkins then stepped on the platform and stated, "We have not come here to incite to violence," and was immediately arrested. Hugh Hardyman then followed Hopkins and cheerfully announced, "This is a most delightful climate," and was promptly arrested. For eighteen hours these four men were held incommunicado while their lawyer, John Beardsley, now a judge of the Superior Court of Los Angeles County, tried frantically to discover where they were being held. He finally succeeded in serving a writ of habeas corpus and the next day they were all released. A few days later, all but 28 of the 600 strikers in jail were released and, in effect, the strike had been won.

Disturbed by this resurgence of protest, the *Times*, the M. & M., and their allies, determined to make Los Angeles "the white spot" of the nation. From 1920 to 1934, they ruled Southern California with an iron hand. From its enactment in 1919 to 1924, 531 men were indicted in California for violation of the Criminal Syndicalism Act.

Of those arrested, 264 were tried, 164 convicted, and 128 were sentenced to San Quentin Prison for terms of from one to fourteen years. A large part of these prosecutions arose in Southern California. In 1920 the Better America Federation was formed in Los Angeles with funds largely provided by the various private utilities. The wages and expenses of three professional informers who were used in virtually all of the criminal syndicalism prosecutions were paid by this organization. In response to its demand, The Nation and The New Republic were removed from reading lists in the Los Angeles schools. Teachers who advocated public ownership of utilities were denounced as bolsheviks. It was the Better America Federation that forced the City of Los Angeles to establish a "Red Squad" under the leadership of the well-known Capt. William ("Red") Hynes. For fifteen years, this squad made a mockery of the right of free speech in Los Angeles. Conducting a perennial witch-hunt for "reds" and "pinks" in all walks of life, the Red Squad drove numberless teachers and clergymen from their posts and presided, like an S.S. Elite Guard, over the City of Los Angeles. I have watched the members of this squad break up meetings in halls and public parks with a generous use of tear-gas bombs and clubs. Throughout these years, as the reports of the LaFollette Committee abundantly demonstrate, the City of Los Angeles, the Better America Federation, and the M. & M., employed a host of spies, stool pigeons, and informers to disrupt trade unions, to provoke violence, and to ferret out the "reds." Strikes of agricultural workers were broken in the very backyard of Los Angeles with a brutality and violence remarkable even in California.

For twenty years, a well-known clubwoman of Los Angeles was paid by these employer organizations to spy upon the activities of various liberal and progressive groups. Even her dues in these organizations were paid by her employers. She sat on the board of directors of virtually every liberal organization in the city and regularly reported to the police and to her employers. During the years when Los Angeles was being advertised as "the white spot" of the nation, the entire civic life of the community was honeycombed with these informers. Typical of these years is a little boxed story that appeared in the Los Angeles press: "This will be 'shove Tuesday' for the Los Angeles police. The communists plan to stage another demonstration today, according to Capt. Wm. Hynes, which means that 500 police will be held in readiness. If the communists demonstrate, the policemen will shove and keep on shoving until the parade is disrupted." The "shove days" were of regular occurrence in Los Angeles.

"Unemployment is a crime in Sunny California," wrote Louis Adamic of the decade 1920–1930. "The state is advertised as a paradise, and when 'come-ons' come and fail to get work they are jailed. Shabby-looking men are stopped in the streets, dragged out of flophouses, asked if they have work; and if they answer in the negative, are arrested for vagrancy. . . . Few persons in Los Angeles know about these things. The press of course is mum on the subject; for the tourists must not get the idea that anything is wrong with Los Angeles. Then, too, who cares about a lot of bums and reds? Folks are so busy enjoying themselves that a good-natured banker in town recently seriously announced a new 'service' his institution had just started, to relieve his clients of the 'hardship' of clipping their coupons!" The police statistics of the city amply substantiated this statement; in 1927–1928, 12,202 arrests were made in Los Angeles for "vagrancy."

"Is California civilized?" asked Robert Whitaker in *The Nation* (April, 1931). "Yes, California is civilized. That is what is the matter with it; its civilization, economically considered, is the legal, political, and disciplinary ascendancy of a ruling class which lives by the exploitation of labor, and especially of unskilled labor. . . . It will be forty-three years in August of this year since I first saw California, after a long ride through the desert. . . . For more than four decades I have been privileged to live in one of the fairest and kindliest of all the regions of the earth. California is, indeed, a marvelous land, beyond anything the passing tourist can ever know, and many of its people are among the choicest fruits of human evolution. All of this only accentuates the bewilderment and bitter disappointment which must be felt by any thinking man at the social barbarism of California, provided he has any knowledge beyond what the pitiful public press gives of our ignorance, our intolerance, and above all our complacent social inertia."

It is this long background of terrorism and police brutality that the latter-day commentators on Los Angeles crackpotism so completely ignore. It was not the climate or the sunshine of Southern California that developed a strong undercurrent of liberal-radical thought in the community, but rather the extraordinarily short-sighted and stupid activities of the power-drunk tycoons who ruled the city. "Red" Hynes made a dozen radicals in Los Angeles for every arrest he ever made. Studying the "Cossackism" of the Los Angeles police in 1931, Ernest Jerome Hopkins correctly reported that radicalism had flourished under the lash of persecution which, for twenty-five years, had been so consistently applied in the community. The sensational mass political movements that developed in Southern California in the 'thirties did not "just happen." To a great extent, they represented the inevitable expression of political aspirations that had been maturing for a quarter of a century and which, during this period, had been brutally and systematically suppressed.

It should be emphasized that the trade-union movement did not begin to develop real strength in Southern California until 1937. Throughout the period from 1890 to 1937, Los Angeles was the "last citadel of the open shop," "the white spot" of the nation, the paradise of the professional patriot and the red-baiter. The mass political movements of the 'thirties were not inspired by the trade-union movement. They were popular, largely spontaneous, political movements, based upon the prior political experience of the community, the inevitable reaction to twenty-five years of irresponsible boosterism. When the depression swelled the ranks of the dispossessed with the numberless victims of land-swindles and business frauds, the situation was ripe for demagogic political movements. Just as the physical peculiarities of the region had compelled early settlers to devise new social forms to cope with their problems, so this novel combination of circumstances prompted the creation of new and untried political techniques. Unanchored to a strong trade-union movement, having few roots in the community, the dispossessed masses of Los Angeles were quick to invent new forms of action and new forms for the expression of social discontent. Much as the region had been built by boosterism and propaganda, so the mass movements, many of which were led by ex-realtors and ex-promoters and ex-clergymen, began to use the techniques of business to foster new political promotions.

Los Angeles itself is a kind of utopia: a vast metropolitan community built in a semi-arid region, a city based upon improvisation, words, propaganda, boosterism. If a city could be created by such methods, it did not seem incredible, to these hordes of the dispossessed, that a new society might be evoked, by a process of incantation, a society in which the benefits of the machine age would be shared by all alike, old and young, rich and poor. However naive the expression of this belief may have been, and the following sections will show that it was very naive indeed, it cannot be dismissed as mere crackpotism. The real crackpots of Los Angeles in the 'thirties were the individuals who ordered tons of oranges and vegetables dumped in the bed of the Los Angeles River, while thousands of people were unemployed, hungry, and homeless.

6. PLENTY-FOR-ALL

"Utopias are often only premature truths."
—Lamartine

Technocracy was the first major social enthusiasm, the initial manifestation of utopianism, to find expression in Southern California after the stock-market crash of 1929. While the movement was not spawned in Los Angeles, it is significant that no other community in the nation responded so quickly or so enthusiastically to the new dispensation. In part, the feverish interest which Technocracy aroused in Los Angeles was due to the energetic promotion given the new movement by Mr. Manchester Boddy, publisher of the *Daily News*.

In December, 1932, the *Daily News* ran a sensational series of front-page stories about Technocracy, based on a series of articles which Wayne Parrish had contributed to the *New Outlook*. "While this series of daily articles was appearing," write Whiteman and Lewis in their study of Southern California mass movements (*Glory Roads*, 1936), "crowds congregated around the door of the press-room as publication hour approached. When the first copies, ink scarcely dry, were off the press, the excitement rose to fever pitch. Men fought and scrambled. Dollar bills in the rear were often waved over the heads of those in front. Edition after edition would be sold out." Plenty-for-All Clubs began to mushroom into existence throughout Los Angeles and, up in the lonely sand dunes of Pismo Beach (a section that has long nourished various mysticisms), E. L. Pratt founded a technocratic newspaper. For approximately three months, Technocracy was a universal topic of conversation and discussion south of Tehachapi.

Although Technocracy proved to be a "flash in the pan" (interest in the movement collapsed almost as suddenly as it arose), the quickness with which the idea of Plenty-for-All caught on in Southern

California was a harbinger of things to come. It was unquestionably the fountainhead from which flowed most of the ideas that were embodied in subsequent mass movements in the region. The mentality that embraced these ideas so avidly was essentially utopian as distinguished from ideological. "A state of mind is utopian," writes Karl Mannheim, "where it is incongruous with the state of reality within which it occurs." Ideologies, on the other hand, while they may "transcend the situation," in Mannheimian terms, are nevertheless a reflection of reality. In terms of existing social realities in Southern California, nothing could have been more utopian, in this sense, than the social order envisaged by the Technocrats. Torn apart by internal dissension, the Technocrats failed to organize the enthusiasm which their ideas had evoked, but it was not long before the new vision of abundance began to be systematically organized.

Although formally incorporated on February 20, 1934, the Utopian Society came into existence in the summer of 1933. The society was founded by Eugene J. Reed, a former bond salesman; W. G. Rousseau, a former promoter; and Merritt Kennedy, a former stock salesman for the Julian Petroleum Company. As a social movement, the Utopian Society had two novel features: it utilized the chain-letter technique of business to recruit members, and, both in ritual and in structure, the organization was patterned after the American secret society or fraternal group. So effective was its secret fraternal character, that the organization had acquired a membership running into the thousands before the press of Los Angeles even knew of its existence. By midsummer, 1934, the society had a membership of at least 500,000, with as many as 250 meetings being held every night in Los Angeles. In fact, the Better America Federation estimated that a maximum of 1,063 neighborhood meetings were held one evening during the summer. The first public meeting of the society, held in Hollywood Bowl on June 23, was attended by 25,000 people.

The essence of the movement's appeal consisted in its secret ritual designed to give the uninitiated a glimpse of "the new economic order" and to acquaint them with the arithmetic of plenty. Not only did the secrecy of the movement enable it to gain considerable headway in Southern California before the big guns of reaction were leveled against it, but its rituals fascinated thousands of ex-middle-class Americans for whom the secret fraternity was, perhaps, the social form with which they were most thoroughly familiar. In a community made up overwhelmingly of outsiders or newcomers, it had the great merit of bringing people together, in small groups, in particular neighborhoods or localities, and of uniting them by a mystic bond. A significant feature of the society was its marked emphasis upon purely social activities. In this sense, it was a kind of colossal "Lonesome Club."

I wrote the first article to appear in the national press about the society (*The New Republic*, July 18, 1934), and watched its meteoric rise and fall at close range. The membership of the society was made up overwhelmingly of white-collar lower middle-class elements. At one of the initiation meetings which I was permitted to attend, although I was not a member of the society, the neophytes consisted of a woman physician, an employee of a public-utility company, the owner of a small business, the manager of a lumber yard, a marine engineer, a garage mechanic, two city employees, a carpenter, and a barber. Politically inhibited and organizationally frustrated by the despotic dominance of reaction in Southern California, these elements saw, in the secret character of the Utopian Society, a means by which they might articulate their unrest and discontent. At the fourth-cycle initiations of the society, which were usually held at the Shrine Auditorium, the 7,000 seats would be filled hours before the ritual began and literally thousands of people would be milling about in the streets seeking to gain admission. The promoters of the society were completely surprised by its success and never did seem to know just what to do with, or how to direct, the phenomenal enthusiasm they had aroused. Once all the neophytes had been taken through the four cycles of the ritual, there didn't seem to be anything else to do with them, and, early in 1935, the movement fell apart. Between 1933 and 1935, however, it furnished the reactionaries of the community with the biggest fright of their lives.

Unnoticed by the press, Upton Sinclair had, in September of 1933, changed his political registration from the Socialist to the Democratic Party. A few months later, he announced that he would be a candidate for the Democratic nomination for Governor of California in the 1934 election. The announcement was greeted with mild ridicule. In explaining how he happened to become a candidate, Sinclair later said: "I saw old people dying of slow starvation, and children by the tens of thousand growing up stunted by the diseases of malnutrition —the very schoolteachers dipping into their slender purses to provide milk for pupils who came to school without breakfast. I saw hundreds of thousands of persons driven from their homes; the sweep of an economic process which had turned most of California over to moneylenders and banks. I saw one colossal swindle after another perpetrated upon the public; and for every official who was sent to jail I knew that a thousand were hiding with their loot." Launching his campaign with a pamphlet on how to End Poverty in California, Mr. Sinclair was soon speaking from one end of the state to another. Months before the August, 1934, primaries, it was clearly apparent that he would win the Democratic nomination, for, as Charles W. Van Devander has pointed out, "the desperation of the times had coalesced all the dissident elements of the state into one great surging political movement."

Los Angeles County was the center, the home, of the Epic Movement. By June, 1934, 300,000 people were unemployed in Los Angeles. Commenting on the situation in the county, the monthly bulletin of the State Relief Administration for June, 1934, pointed out: "Unemployment due to depressions is distorted and prolonged in Los Angeles by the deficiency of productive industries. . . . It is believed that the oil boom of the early 1920's, the motion pictures, and real estate booms, the stimulations of tourist trade and migrations by the local chambers of commerce, have over-populated the county with white collar workers. Permanent jobs do not exist for them within the basic industries of the county. The population is over 85% urban, concentrated in 29 cities, most of which cluster around Los Angeles. Since 1920, the population has more than doubled. The proportion of white collar workers to all gainfully employed workers has become almost double that of the United States as a whole. . . . The productive industries do not appear large enough to justify the size of the white collar class . . . less than one out of twenty gainful workers is employed normally in agriculture, against one out of five for the United States." Since the groups most severely affected by the depression in Los Angeles were white-collar lower middle-class elements, it is not surprising that the expression of their discontent assumed novel forms. Essentially, Technocracy, the Utopian Society, and the Epic movement represented, therefore, an upsurge of lower middle-class white-collar elements.

Nothing quite like the Epic campaign of 1934 had ever occurred in American politics. It was distinctly a grass-roots affair, organized, directed, and financed by "the little people" under the extraordinarily skillful leadership of Mr. Sinclair. By the close of the campaign, over 800 Epic clubs had been formed in the state, with most of them being located, however, south of Tehachapi. Close to a million copies of Mr. Sinclair's original Epic pamphlet and his book, *I, Governor of California*, were sold to raise funds for the campaign. When the reactionary elements of the state realized that not only had Sinclair won the Democratic nomination but that he stood an excellent chance of being elected governor, they unleashed a campaign of unparalleled vilification, misrepresentation, slander, and abuse. According to Mr. Van Devander, over $10,000,000 was spent to defeat Sinclair. The motion-picture companies, drawing upon their prize collection of villainous types, made fake news-reel interviews with "bums en route to California," which were shown in every motion-picture theater in the state. Intimidating notes were inserted in payroll envelopes, employees were directly threatened by their employers with discharge if they voted for Sinclair, and the best advertising brains in California were put to work culling scare-quotes from Mr. Sinclair's voluminous writings. In the final election, the ex-Iowan Frank Merriam was elected, the vote being Merriam, 1,138,000, Sinclair, 879,000, and Haight, 302,000. If the fight had been directly between Merriam and Sinclair, it is altogether probable that Sinclair would have been elected. As a matter of fact, it is altogether possible, as Mr. Van Devander explains, that Sinclair actually *was* elected governor, for there were many circumstantial indications that the count at the polls was fraudulent.

Although Mr. Sinclair was defeated, the Epic campaign was one of the most successful experiments in mass education ever performed in this country. Throughout the campaign, Mr. Sinclair expounded the economics of capitalism from one end of the state to the other with matchless skill, lucidity, and brilliance. While not a great orator, he is the peerless expositor, the great popularizer, the unexcelled pamphleteer. Years after the campaign was over, I used to see, in my travels about the state as Commissioner of Housing and Immigration, New Economy barber shops, Epic cafes, and Plenty-for-All stores in the most remote and inaccessible communities in California. I have seen the slogans of the Epic campaign painted on rocks in the desert, carved on trees in the forests, and scrawled on the walls of labor camps in the San Joaquin Valley. So swiftly had the depression engulfed thousands upon thousands of middle-class elements in California, that people thought nothing of enlisting in the campaign of an internationally famous Socialist, selling his pamphlets and books, and preaching the doctrine of "production for use." Five years previously, these same people, as Walter Davenport pointed out, would no more have voted for Sinclair than they would have voted for Satan himself. While the movement was widespread throughout the state, its greatest strength was recorded in the areas of heaviest migration, notably in Los Angeles County and the East Bay District of Northern California.

7. THE GOOD DOCTOR

The sensational rise of the Utopian Society stimulated dreams of abundance in many minds in Southern California and provoked a great outpouring of utopian plans and panaceas. One of the most significant of these subsequent revelations was that conjured up by Dr. Francis Townsend. The "tall, lean, and gentle-voiced sexagenarian" had come to Long Beach from South Dakota in the great migration of the 'twenties. Failing to establish himself in the practice of medicine, he had organized a company to manufacture "dry ice" and, upon the failure of the company, had entered the real-estate office of R. Earl Clements. While loafing in the real-estate office one day, "the good doctor" came upon a paper written by Stewart McCord of Seattle which expounded the ideas, based upon technocratic economics, of "retiring oldsters upon a monthly annuity the spending of which was compulsory." Since real estate was not moving very rapidly at the time, the doctor proceeded to dress up McCord's idea a bit and to open a new office in 1934 with funds provided by R. Earl Clements, realtor. Thus was O.A.R.P., Ltd. (Old Age Revolving Pensions), born.

It is significant that this particular movement should have been launched in Long Beach, famous in local wisecracks as "a cemetery with lights." From its founding as a temperance colony, Long Beach has always attracted a disproportionate number of oldsters. Without the honkytonk atmosphere of most beach resorts, it has long been a paradise for the aged. With some 40,000 Iowans residing in the city, Bixby Park has for years been the favorite picnic ground for the various state societies. All one needs to do in order to understand the popularity of a utopian pension scheme in Long Beach is to glance at the population statistics for the city. The age-level of Long Beach residents has always been somewhat higher than the average for other Southern California communities and definitely higher than the average for the state. The horseshoe pitching tournaments of California are invariably held in Long Beach with its

> Water and land and sky and sand
> And oil beneath the ground,
> Where Iowans meet and sharpers cheat
> And nary a native is found.

It is also significant that the founders of OARP should have been an elderly physician without a practice and a shrewd real-estate promoter. As part of the pension-plan promotion, "the good doctor" and his associate Clements established the *Townsend Weekly*, famous for its patent-medicine and gland-renovating advertisements, which soon had a weekly circulation of 100,000 copies. Governor Frank Merriam, a resident of Long Beach, a former Iowan, being sorely pressed by Mr. Sinclair in the gubernatorial campaign of 1934, endorsed the Townsend Plan as did Kathleen Norris, who, a short time previously, had announced that high taxes were driving her from California. By the end of 1934, the Townsend Plan had a state and national following that ran into the hundreds of thousands. Among those who joined up in the crusade "which only God could stop," was John Steven McGroarty, favorite columnist of the Los Angeles *Times*, poet laureate of California, who was elected to Congress on a Townsend Plan platform and who sponsored the plan in Congress.

Originating in Southern California, the Townsend Plan won thousands of followers in Oregon, Montana, Colorado, and began to spread throughout the Middle West and East. With thousands of oldsters across the nation chanting:

> Two hundred dollars a month,
> Youth for work, age for leisure,
> Two hundred for the oldsters,
> To be spent in ceaseless pleasure.

the movement gained steady momentum. As sole owners of the *Townsend Weekly*, with a circulation of 150,000 copies a week, Dr.

Townsend and Realtor Clements began to split a weekly net revenue estimated at $2,000. During 1935, OARP collected, largely in nickels and dimes, around $600,000 and in the peak year of 1936, collections totaled $950,000. In a congressional investigation in 1936, it was revealed that Townsend and Clements had each received $79,000 from the various subsidiary corporations which they had formed in connection with the pension-plan movement. One day in 1935 Dr. Townsend addressed a crowd of 35,000 in Northern California and, flying south, spoke to an audience of 50,000 pensionites assembled in Tujunga Canyon. In 1936 "the good doctor," in company with Gerald L. K. Smith and Father Charles Coughlin, formed the Union Party which nominated William Lemke for President. The same year marked the peak of the movement, for with the re-election of Franklin D. Roosevelt and the passage of the social-security program, the various pension-plan schemes lost much of their national significance, although still another chapter was to be written in California.

8. THE CO-OPERATIVES

During 1933 and 1934 new social movements were being born so rapidly in Southern California that I found it impossible, at the time, even to list them. Symptomatic of the times was an advertisement in the Los Angeles *Times* announcing a lecture on "Roosevelt, the Man of Destiny. Aura Symbols. Analysis of New Deal." The file in which I tossed the various schemes and proposals that came to my attention, includes pamphlets on the Americanist Plan by Horace Lackey; the New Exchange Tax System, spawned in Santa Monica; Tradex; Syncrotax; Dated Money; New America; Plentocracy; and the Universal Research Foundation. This latter group, according to its organizer, originated with "the Fifth Monarchy Men of the Seventeenth Century (which organization was largely instrumental in the incorporation of the then unprecedented ideals of human equality and justice in the Declaration of Independence and the Constitution of the United States), the foundation's ultimate aims being the establishment of a world wide theocratic state, the intermingling and absorption of races, the development of a common tongue, the eradication of artificial national boundaries, the harmonious reconciliation of religion, art, and science with its motive, the social and assimilative state under a transcendental administration, and the emancipation of all industrial and financial bondage"—all as set forth in a letter written to me by the "Vector" of the organization dated September 24, 1934.

While much of the ferment of these years was syphoned off by these fantastic promotions, some of it was directed into the creation of soundly conceived "self-help" co-operatives. With 700,000 people unemployed in California in 1932 (over half of these being in Los Angeles County), it is not surprising that the self-help idea should have spread so rapidly throughout the state. As a matter of fact, Los Angeles County was the national center of the self-help movement. By December, 1934, the county had nearly 45% of all the self-help units in the United States and about one-tenth of the entire national membership. By March, 1936, some 200 self-help units were functioning in the state and, in Southern California, 50,000 people were represented in five associations made up of self-help units. Of 160 co-operatives which received federal grants in the early period of the New Deal, more than half were located in California.

By way of explaining the extraordinary concentration of self-help co-operatives in Los Angeles County, Dr. Constantine Panunzio has listed six major factors: the presence at all times in Los Angeles County of a large surplus of perishable foods, especially fruits and vegetables; the high proportion in the county of persons of relatively advanced years (the average age of the co-operators was 52.4 years); the large number of small property owners who, by reason of the fact that they did own real property, were ineligible for relief; the presence of many needy people from rural sections of the Middle West who were reluctant to apply for relief (two-thirds of the co-operators came to Southern California from the Central states); the favor shown the self-help idea by city, county, state, and federal governments anxious to minimize the relief load; and, finally, the fact that "the self-help co-operatives in Los Angeles County commanded especially aggressive leadership."

As much as anything else, however, the tendency toward unorthodox economic and political programs in Southern California is to be explained, and can only be understood, in relation to the richness of California. There is something about this wonderfully rich and prodigiously fertile state, in which all crops can be raised with a quickness and abundance unknown elsewhere in America, that stimulates the notion of abundance, of richness, of leisure. One simply cannot imagine such grandiose notions as $30-Every-Thursday having their origin in South Dakota or Mississippi or Vermont. Lord Bryce shrewdly pointed out that the sandlot riots of the 'seventies in San Francisco were largely a reaction to the openly displayed riches and luxurious establishments of the bonanza kings of the Comstock Lode and Virginia City. In the presence of great wealth and natural abundance, poverty becomes absurd, anachronistic, insane. In accounting for the rise of the self-help co-operatives in California, Dr. Clark Kerr and Dr. Paul S. Taylor call attention, for example, to the following unharvested surpluses in 1932: tomatoes, 696,000 lugs; onions, 608,000 bushels; summer celery, 277,000 crates; cling peaches, 181,000 tons; pears, 178,000 tons. In the midst of such opulence, people will never starve. Their rudimentary common sense tells them that the destruction of such surpluses when people are starving represents the original, biblical conception of wickedness itself.

Invariably the various new-economy proposals have won the widest following in areas of heavy recent migration. Lacking traditional ties, associations, and restraints, feeling that their residence in the region is perhaps temporary in character, these newcomers are willing to take a chance—on stamp money or dated currency or barter tickets, and to buy in on Utopia. Their position being as precarious as it was in the depression years, with not even the smoke of industry on the horizon, why should the Westbrook Peglers think them insane because they took a chance? After all, if their pet plan were adopted and later failed, they could always return to Sioux Falls or Tulsa or Denver. People marooned on a tropical island have always had the wit to crack open the coconuts, build grass huts, admire the parakeets, and make themselves at home until a sail appears on the horizon. No one ever thought of calling Robinson Crusoe a crackpot.

9. HAM AND EGGS

During periods of great social stress in industrial communities, the dispossessed are likely to smash factory windows, or to conduct hunger marches, or to dramatize their desperation in some concrete manner. But in an area without smokestacks where the sale of real estate has been the major industry, there are no visible symbols upon which the distressed masses can vent their fury. To the extent that their discontent can personalize a victim, it is likely to be the "money-lender," or the "big banker." Their hatred is inclined to be expressed in abstract form; their dreams to be dominated by abstract symbols, "money," "riches," "jewels," "wealth." Consequently, when they dream of Utopia, it is not of a well-planned, perfectly governed garden city, but of a perfect scheme or get-rich-quick system. Their archangel is not Sir Thomas More or Patrick Geddes, but the promoter who promises to deliver, the salesman with enticing phrases, the business magician.

The early mass political movements in Southern California, characterized by marked social inventiveness, were a healthy manifestation of a people's impulse to do something for themselves. Continued frustration of this impulse, however, soon began to produce rank and unhealthy social growths. Of all these latter-day growths, the Ham and Eggs movement is, by all odds, the most fantastic, incredible, and dangerous. The story of this movement which follows is largely based upon an interesting document by Winston and Marian Moore, entitled *Out of the Frying Pan*, published in Los Angeles in 1939. Incredible as they may sound, the facts set forth in this document, which I have summarized, have never been disputed or denied.

The story starts with the arrival in Los Angeles of Robert Noble, a neurotic but plausible rabble-rouser, young in years, attractive in appearance, dynamic in manner. He first appears as a platform and radio speaker in the Epic campaign of 1934. Shortly after the Epic campaign, he began to make a name for himself as a radio commentator on Station KMTR, attracting a large following by his attacks on an unpopular city administration. Observing the rapidity with which the Townsend Plan had spread throughout the region, he decided to conjure up a pension plan of his own based upon an article which he had read by Professor Irving Fisher on "stamp" money. Without bothering to prepare a plan, he simply began to speak on the air about a scheme that would pay the oldsters $25-Every-Monday. The slogan was excellent, the promise attractive, and soon the flow of nickels, dimes, and quarters began to increase in volume.

In the Hollywood building where Noble made his headquarters was also located the office of the Cinema Advertising Agency, operated by two brothers, Willis and Lawrence Allen, both talented promoters. Shortly before they had formed the Cinema Advertising Agency, Willis Allen had been involved in some promotional fancywork in connection with Grey Gone, a hair tonic. In need of assistance, Noble induced the Cinema Advertising Agency to manage his program and to negotiate, in the name of the agency, a contract for radio time on Station KMTR. As Noble's attacks on the city administration became increasingly violent and vitriolic, Capt. Earl Kynette was assigned the task of devising ways and means to take him off the air. After making a cursory inspection of the situation, Kynette decided to kill two birds with one stone: to get Noble off the air and to get in on the pension scheme himself. Suggesting that Noble was not the man to head the movement, Kynette made a cash loan to the Allen brothers which enabled them to carry off a clever *putsch*.

A "rump" meeting of the pensionites was accordingly held in September, 1937, in Clifton's Cafeteria, where many plots of the sort have been staged and where many movements have been born. The meeting adopted articles of incorporation prepared by the Allens and then proceeded to elect an Allen-controlled board of directors. When Noble next appeared at Station KMTR, he found Willis Allen seated behind the microphone. And, when he called a meeting of the faithful to discuss this shrewdly executed maneuver, the meeting was disrupted by policemen making excellent use of stench bombs and tear gas. In desperation, Noble then attempted to throw a picket line around Station KMTR, but Capt. Kynette was again on hand with the "boys," and the picket line melted away like snow in the sun. In a final effort to regain control of the movement, Noble filed papers with the Secretary of State in which he sought to protect the slogan $25-Every-Monday. Not the kind of operators to be thwarted by such a ruse, the Allens immediately adopted the slogan $30-Every-Thursday which was more pleasing to the ear and more attractive to the purse. Noble was out. And soon the interesting Capt. Kynette was also "out" for, shortly after the Noble *putsch* was effected, he clumsily planted a time-bomb in the automobile of an investigator who was probing the city administration, was caught, tried, and sentenced to San Quentin Prison.

Left in undisputed control of $30-Every-Thursday, the Allen brothers did not know quite what to do with the movement. They needed, first of all, an effective spellbinder. The orator was soon discovered in the person of Sherman Bainbridge, whose voice has long echoed in the cafeteria meeting rooms of Los Angeles. It was Bainbridge who coined the invaluable slogan "Ham and Eggs" which the pensionites shout with the frenzy of storm-troopers yelling *Sieg Heil!* All meetings of the Payroll Guarantee Association are opened with the shouted salutation "Ham and Eggs" and each speaker who appears on the platform must preface his remarks with the salutation. If he neglects to do so, the crowd will shout "Ham and Eggs" until he does. The Allens also needed a plan. Incredible as it may sound, they had been in control of the movement for eighteen months, conducting an intensive campaign by radio, newspaper, and open meetings, before so much as a line or a sentence had been placed on paper. They got the "plan" from Roy Owens, who for years had been an enthusiastic disciple of Father Divine. The plan contemplates the establishment of a state bank and the issuance of phony money to finance pension payments. They also needed "a situation," a springboard, from which they could really take off, and fate soon provided an occasion.

In San Diego—it would be San Diego—64-year-old Archie Price walked into a newspaper office one day and announced that, since he was too old to work and not old enough to qualify for a pension, he intended to commit suicide. The editor of the newspaper, a veteran in Southern California, scoffed at the suggestion. The next day Price committed suicide and was buried in a pauper's grave. Recognizing that Providence had provided them with the occasion for a spectacular mass demonstration, the Allens organized a march on San Diego. "Less than a month after the death of Archie Price," write the Moores, "Sherman Bainbridge led a funeral cortege of thousands of cars from Los Angeles to San Diego, where Archie Price was exhumed and re-interred amid an avalanche of gorgeous bloom, to the sound of lovely music and surrounded by a multitude of mourners which would have done justice to a monarch. Sheridan Downey, later United States Senator from California, assisted Bainbridge in speaking at the ceremony and everything was very beautiful and impressive—and a little pitiful, because poor lonely Archie Price was so very dead." Poor lonely Archie Price became the Horst Wessel of the Ham and Eggs movement.

So rapidly did the Ham and Eggs movement grow after this incident that, in 1938, its sponsors presented the Secretary of State with a petition signed by more than 750,000 residents of California asking that the $30-Every-Thursday proposal be submitted to the voters as an initiative measure. If enacted, the proposal would have involved the issuance of $30,000,000 in warrants a week or an annual turnover of $1,560,000,000 in warrant money. As soon as the politicians were informed of the number of signatures on the petition (789,000 to be exact: 25% of the registered voters of the state), they all began to shout "Ham and Eggs" in a deafening chorus, one notable exception being Robert Walker Kenny. So effectively had the Allens tended to the organizational details that, by simply sending out a call for letters, they could inundate any state official with from 25,000 to 30,000 letters in forty-eight hours. Whatever they asked their followers to do was promptly done. If they were asked to give money, they gave money; if asked to write letters, they wrote letters; if asked to march, they marched; if asked to demonstrate, they demonstrated. From the beginning of the movement to the present time, it has been characterized by the conspicuous absence of rank-and-file democratic controls. On the eve of the 1938 election, the organization thus dictatorially controlled by the Allen brothers had a regular dues-paying membership of 200,000 and the organization itself was collecting an estimated $2,000 a day in contributions. All of the advertising and radio material of the Ham and Eggs movement has, of course, always been handled through the Cinema Advertising Agency which is owned by Willis and Lawrence Allen.

This fantastic proposal came within an ace of being adopted in November, 1938, being defeated by a vote of 1,398,000 opposed to 1,143,000 in favor of the proposal. Shortly after Culbert L. Olson took office in 1938, he was presented with a petition signed by 1,103,-000 residents of California calling for a special election on the Ham and Eggs proposal. Once again the proposal received a staggering vote, but not enough to win. After the 1939 election, the movement began to decline, as the increasing prosperity of the defense program began to develop in California. When Governor Olson came up for re-election in 1942, he was defeated by his Republican opponent, Earl Warren, who was mysteriously in possession of the pension vote.

Today the movement languishes. In an effort to inject some new life into the movement, the Allen brothers have been collaborating with Gerald L. K. Smith, who was introduced at a meeting of the Payroll Guarantee Association by Willis Allen as "one of the greatest citizens of the United States." This venture is not surprising, for there has always been an undercurrent of anti-Semitism in the Ham and Eggs movement. It should be emphasized that $30-Every-Thursday, unlike the Utopian Society, the self-help co-operatives, and the

Epic movement, is not a product of the depression. It really dates from 1938.

10. THE MESSIANIC NOTE

In a confused, distorted, half-crazy manner, these mass political movements represent a dim foreshadowing of the future. Certainly one cannot but be impressed by the recurrent Messianic note which echoes in these movements and in the various cult movements with which they are closely related. Several of the cultists, such as Ballard, Bell, and Joe Jeffers, have actually proclaimed themselves Messiahs. The framed picture of Dr. Francis E. Townsend is to be found enshrined, like that of a patron saint, in many Southern California households. During the Epic campaign, Upton Sinclair was a Messiah, a Leader, a Prophet. In an effort to alienate his following, the opposition drafted the Rev. Martin Luther Thomas, leader of the Christian American Crusade, to attack Mr. Sinclair for his "anti-religious" tracts. Roy Anstey replied to these attacks with a poem:

> The people have awakened,
>   And agree with one accord,
> That he who standeth for the POOR
>   Is fighting for the LORD.
> The evil forces grew alarmed,
>   The devil heard their prayer,
> And sent them spouting THOMAS
>   To rant against SINCLAIR.
>
> Oh, God! that he should fall so low
>   As to use YOUR HOLY HOUSE,
> To crucify the leader
>   Of a cause we all espouse.
> When SINCLAIR writes his final book,
>   And his soul floats to the skies,
> We'll still hear spouting Thomases
>   As they spew their Judas lies.

No man is more dangerous than the man who has caught a glimpse of a great idea, who has feverishly seized upon a fragment of truth and gone forth to battle chanting the slogans of a Messiah. I know of no one who has caught this undercurrent of crazy fury in Southern California quite as well as did the late Nathanael West in his novel *The Day of the Locust:*

> It was a mistake to think them harmless curiosity seekers. They were savage and bitter, especially the middle-aged and the old, and had been made so by boredom and disappointment. All their lives they had slaved at some kind of dull, heavy labor, behind desks and counters, in the fields and at tedious machines of all sorts, saving their pennies and dreaming of the leisure that would be theirs when they had enough. Finally that day came. They could draw a weekly income of ten or fifteen dollars. Where else should they go but California, the land of sunshine and oranges?
>
> Once there, they discovered that sunshine isn't enough. They get tired of oranges, even of avocado pears and passion fruit. Nothing happens. They don't know what to do with their time. They haven't the mental equipment for pleasure. Did they slave so long just to go to an occasional Iowa picnic? What else is there? They watch the waves come in at Venice. There wasn't any ocean where most of them came from, but after you've seen one wave, you've seen them all. The same is true of the airplanes at Glendale. If only a plane would crash once in a while so they could watch the passengers being consumed in a "holocaust of flame," as the newspapers put it. But the planes never crash.
>
> Their boredom became more and more terrible. They realize that they've been tricked and burn with resentment. Every day of their lives they read the newspapers and went to the movies. Both fed them on lynchings, murder, sex crimes, explosions, wrecks, love nests, fires, miracles, revolutions, wars. This daily diet made sophisticates of them. The sun is a joke. Oranges can't titillate their jaded palates. Nothing can ever be violent enough to make taut their slack minds and bodies. They have been cheated and betrayed. They have slaved and saved for nothing.

In a final passage of this remarkable novel appears a scene in which all these people, armed with clubs and baseball bats, following lighted torches, decide they will march. "All those poor devils who can only be stirred by the promise of miracles and then only to violence . . .

a super 'Dr. Know-All-Pierce-All' had made the necessary promise and they were marching behind his banner in a great united front of screwballs and screwboxes to purify the land. No longer bored, they sang and danced joyously in the red light of the flames." Frankly, it is a vision that has sometimes worried me, for I have seen the light that blazes in their eyes, I have heard the deafening "Ham and Eggs" chant, and I have listened to the anti-Semites addressing large crowds in the Embassy Auditorium.

Of course, the state of mind, the utopian mentality, so vividly described by West, is a national, not a local phenomenon. "We have developed a going understanding," writes Max Lerner in PM (June, 1945), "that the advertisers don't have to be truthful and we don't have to believe them. It is all a sort of play in which it is one man's role to lie and the other's to be skeptical. Ours is a culture in which salesmanship continues to have a throbbing life of its own even when cut off from substance and truth, like the legs of a frog still quivering after being severed from the body . . . a curious combination of qualities: Nineveh and Sparta, luxury and violence. . . . The reason is that we are a frontier nation that has moved, more swiftly than any in history, from hardihood to wealth, from timberlands to the big money. Our living standards are higher than in any other country in the world, but there is also a greater gap between lowest and highest than anywhere else. Ours is the land of success, but for every successful man there are hundreds unsuccessful. We have deep psychic hungers, all of us—hungers for money or power or dazzling beauty or acclaim."

As an embodiment of all these frustrations and fantasies, Southern California has become one of the most interesting and important regions of the nation. For here the swiftness of transition from rural to urban, from hardihood to wealth, has been most pronounced, here the social neuroticism produced by such a transition is most widespread, and here the extremes between "lowest" and "highest" are most patent and glaring. Here the movie-rich and the oil-rich are newcomers, lacking the sense of stability and the occasional sense of responsibility that wealth long-possessed sometimes confers. Social discontent in Los Angeles has been fanned to a white heat by sensational newspaper stories of elaborate Hollywood parties, of oil tycoons giving $5,000 cocktail parties, of banquet halls banked with roses and gardenias. Such anti-Semitic clichés as international bankers and money-lenders take on a horrible reality in the minds of the 40,000 people who purchased forged Julian stock certificates with the hard-earned savings of a lifetime of work and effort, stock certificates which fluttered throughout Southern California like the torn fragments of telephone books in a city parade. Here the defeat of the American Dream has been most recent in point of time, most widely sensed, most sharply experienced. It was to this region that F. Scott Fitzgerald came to write *The Last Tycoon*. "If ever there was anything resembling communism or fascism in America," a Californian told R. L. Duffus in June, 1945, "California would be the first to have it," and it would probably originate in the region south of Tehachapi.

It should be observed that the ferment of the depression years in Southern California, and the various movements which came out of this ferment, had a profound influence on the course of events not only in California but throughout the nation. Although Mr. Sinclair was defeated, some twenty-nine Epic-sponsored candidates were elected to the state legislature; the Epic movement sent Culbert L. Olson to the state senate in 1934 on his way to the governorship in 1938; it elected Ben Lindsey to public office in Los Angeles; it sent Sheridan Downey to the United States Senate; and it sent such a hard-working public servant as Jerry Voorhis to Congress. The spectacular pension-plan movements of Southern California certainly played a part in securing the early adoption of the social-security program. Out of the ferment of these years has today emerged a strong liberal and progressive movement in Southern California which, today, is allied with a powerful trade-union movement. Los Angeles ceased to be "the white spot" of the open shop in 1940 and, in recent years, the voters have repeatedly demonstrated that the hold of the old-guard reactionaries, the Better America Federation tycoons, has been broken. Today the "Red Squad" is no more and democratic currents of thought and expression can, at long last, find free expression. With the trade-union and political-organization vacuum being filled, at long last, it is unlikely that demagogic movements could sweep the field as they did in years past. Above all, Los Angeles today has a real industrial foundation to support its inflated population.

Retiring from political life in 1934, Upton Sinclair now lives the life of a recluse in Monrovia, perennially engaged in writing the

Lanny Budd novels. A remarkable man, this Upton Sinclair. During the Epic campaign, I interviewed him one insufferably hot August afternoon with a brush fire burning furiously in the hills back of Pasadena. We sat in a darkened room, the blinds pulled, our eyes smarting with smoke from the fires. While he failed to convince me that the Epic plan was feasible, he thoroughly convinced me that poverty and want could be banished from the earth. On another occasion, in 1927, I had lunch with him in Long Beach, on the day Sacco and Vanzetti were executed. I well remember what he had to say about the Sacco-Vanzetti case, the light that it shed on our culture and what it portended for the future. Looking back on that occasion today, I can only say that his prophecy of the horrors and chaos to come grossly underestimated the reality.

11. POLITICAL ISLAND

It is the Southern California vote, now dominant in California politics, that has given the state its reputation for independent political thinking. It was the plurality of 3,806 votes which he received in California that re-elected Woodrow Wilson. In 1924, LaFollette, running as an independent, polled 424,649 votes in California, by comparison with 733,250 votes for Coolidge and 105,514 votes for John W. Davis. Franklin D. Roosevelt received California's electoral votes in each of his four campaigns for the presidency. Although both political extremes are well developed, California is, and has always been, fundamentally liberal-progressive, and notably independent. Since Hiram Johnson defeated the Southern Pacific machine, there have been few political machines in California, and none, I should say, in Southern California. The nearest thing to a political machine in the state today is Bill Malone's Democratic organization in San Francisco. The really big bosses of the state, as Mr. Van Devander has pointed out, are the lobbyists and pay-off men in Sacramento.

Not only are there no political machines, as such, in Los Angeles, but it is politically one of the most progressive communities in the United States. The city itself is honeycombed with small neighborhood grass-roots political clubs and discussion groups and, despite the crackpot fringe and the apostles of utopia, the general level of political intelligence is exceptionally high. Southern Californians care very little for party labels, candidates frequently cross-file in both parties, and no punches are pulled in political campaigns. "The level of political feeling," wrote Samuel Grafton from Los Angeles on October 7, 1943, "seems higher to me here than it is in most places. The old guard is more sturdily Republican, and the pro-Roosevelts are more hotly for Mr. Roosevelt than in New York. . . . There is a simplicity and almost a quality of primitiveness about political fights here which are not seen in the East. It has been possible for such men as the previously unknown George Outland and Will Rogers, Jr., to barge into congressional campaigns and get themselves elected, simply on the basis of their liberal beliefs. . . . The air is fresh here, but the real twang in it is the foretaste of coming change. That really makes men's nostrils flare, and their eyes look round."

In politics as in other things, California is an island, the right hand of the continent. Political developments in the other Western states have virtually no repercussions here. Not one Californian in a hundred could name the governors, or the party in power, in the states of Montana, Idaho, Utah, Nevada, Wyoming, Colorado, Arizona, and New Mexico, although some correct answers might be given for Washington and Oregon. Sociologically detached from the rest of the country, and notably from the rest of the West, California functions in its own right, has its own patterns of political behavior, and exists as a kind of sovereign empire by the western shore. "When I am in California," said Theodore Roosevelt in a speech delivered in Southern California in 1905, "I am not in the West. I am West of the West."

> "Southern California is made up of groups who often live
> in isolated communities, continuing their own customs, lan-
> guage, and religious habits and associations."
>
> —Charles A. Stoddard (1894)

CHAPTER XV

THE LOS ANGELES ARCHIPELAGO

THROUGHOUT Southern California, social lines do not run across or bisect communities; on the contrary, they circle around and sequester entire communities. The arrangement of social classes in horizontal clusters, rather than by vertical categories, is, indeed, a striking characteristic of the region. "Migration," wrote Dr. Robert E. Park, "has had a marked effect upon the social structure of California society . . . a large part of the population, which comes from such *diverse and distant places*, lives in more or less *closed communities*, in intimate economic dependence, but in more or less complete cultural independence of the world about them [italics mine]." Migration has segregated social classes by communities which run the gamut from lower-lower to upper-upper rather than in tiers within a monolithic structure. When people ascend the social ladder, they do not move into a better home in the same community, they simply move into another community. Thus Southern California is an archipelago of social and ethnic islands, economically interrelated but culturally disparate.

In distinguishing between Northern and Southern California, most observers have repeated the trite notion that San Francisco is cosmopolitan, Los Angeles provincial; the one "foreign," the other "native." "The foreign population of Southern California," writes Lillian

Symes, "has always been small. The large Italian, Portuguese, and Spanish influx and the smaller group of French immigrants, settled farther north among a people friendlier to vino and alien ways. They gave to the northern valleys and to the wind-swept San Francisco district, a distinctly Latin flavor . . . while the south drew its Nordic residents from every state in the union." This general distinction, however, overlooks a basic reality. In the compact social structure of San Francisco, foreign elements function as an integral part of the community (such names as Rossi, a former mayor, and the Giannini banking family, symbolize this relationship). San Francisco is a seaport, a city whose land-area is restricted. In San Francisco foreign elements have been brought into intimate cultural juxtaposition with each other and with the dominant group. The Jewish community, for example, is quite unlike any other Jewish community in America. The Jewish first families of San Francisco have always constituted an important element in the city's social elite.

But in Los Angeles, whose harbor is a remote appendage and whose land-spread is proverbial, foreign elements exist in isolation. There is also this further difference in the pattern: there are many foreign or racial elements in San Francisco, few in Los Angeles. But the groups represented in Los Angeles are present in large blocks or aggregates, and, for this reason, are likely to exert a much more far-reaching influence on the city than the same and other groups have exerted in San Francisco. Cultural heterogeneity has produced in San Francisco a colorful, if somewhat superficial, cosmopolitanism, but the large "foreign" colonies of Los Angeles, although fewer in number, have always remained, as Miss Symes notes, "helot classes," devoid of influence or social standing. They are present, however, in such numbers, and with such a degree of concentration, that they cannot be assimilated without basic modification of the social pattern. San Francisco is a cosmopolitan, while Los Angeles is a racial and cultural rectangle: White, Negro, Mexican, and Oriental.

1. The Mexicans Return

Largely written off as a "vanquished" element, the Mexican population of Southern California began to increase after the turn of the century. In 1900 the Southern Pacific Company reported that it was employing 4,500 Mexicans on its lines in the southern part of the state. During the year 1906, the Southern Pacific and the Santa Fe began to import two and three carloads of "cholos," that is, Mexican peons, a week. As thousands of Mexicans were imported, principally from the states of Chihuahua, Durango, Jalisco, Sonora, and Zacatecas, the number employed in the citrus industry, in the desert mines and chemical plants, and in the cement and clay-products plants, steadily increased. The rapid extension of the Pacific Electric system after 1900 also attracted thousands of Mexicans to Southern California. Instead of spreading over the entire state, most of the Mexican immigrants settled in the south; in 1910 and in 1920 the southern counties had 78% of the entire Mexican population. The number of persons born in Mexico but living in California increased from 8,086 in 1900 to 33,694 in 1910 and then soared to 88,771 in 1920. Another enumeration, which included "all persons born in Mexico, or having parents born in Mexico," gave the total as 121,176 for 1920 and 368,013 for 1930. To this total would have to be added, of course, the number of "native Californians," or long-resident Mexicans, a category that has never been estimated. Today there are probably 400,000 "Mexicans," citizens and aliens, in Southern California.

In the years from 1920 to 1930, Mexican immigrants constituted the dominant element in the great migratory labor pool in California. Following the crops throughout the southern and central portions of the state, they would usually be stranded in the San Joaquin Valley at the end of the season. To get them out of the valley, the townspeople would provide just enough gasoline to enable their jalopies to get over the Ridge Route and back to Southern California. Theoretically, the Mexican immigrant was supposed to be a "homing pigeon" who worked in California in the summer and wintered in Mexico. Actually most of the immigrants "wintered" in Los Angeles County. Constituting 7% of the population of Los Angeles in 1925, Mexicans made up 27% of the relief cases and 54% of the general hospital cases. During the depression, Mexicans lost their dominant position in the migratory labor pool and began to settle permanently in Los Angeles. Today Los Angeles has the largest urban Mexican population of any community in the world, with the exception of Mexico City itself. The lowest estimate of the number of persons of Mexican descent in the county has been placed at 211,709, while 300,000 would, perhaps, be a more realistic estimate.

During the depression, the County of Los Angeles repatriated thousands of Mexicans on relief. Arrangements were made with the

Southern Pacific Company (which had imported most of the immigrants in the first place) to ship them back to Mexico at a wholesale per capita rate of $14.70. I watched the first consignment leave Los Angeles in February, 1931. The loading process began at six o'clock in the morning, when the *repatriados* began to arrive by the truckload: men, women, and children; dogs, cats and goats; loaded down with suitcases wired together, rolls of bedding, and lunch baskets. It cost the county $77,249.29 to repatriate one shipment of 6,024, but the savings in relief amounted to $347,468.41 for the year. In 1932 alone over 11,000 Mexicans were repatriated from Los Angeles. Repatriation was a tragicomic affair: tragic in the hardships occasioned; comic because most of the Mexicans eventually returned to Los Angeles, having had a trip to Mexico at the expense of the county.

From 1907 to 1940 "the Mexican problem" was a hardy perennial in Southern California. Every winter the business interests of the region worked themselves into a lather of excitement over the cost of Mexican relief, hospitalization, and medical care. With the return of the crop cycle in the spring, however, "the Mexican problem" always somehow vanished or was succeeded by the problem of "an acute labor shortage." The immigrant Mexicans were admirable workers, docile and obliging, seldom venturing into the downtown sections, spending their hard-earned wages as fast as they were paid off, difficult to organize because of the language barrier and the prejudice against them. For a variety of reasons, the immigrant generation has clung tenaciously to the imported pattern of Mexican folk-culture. Living so close to the border has made it possible for them to make frequent trips to Mexico and to retain a vivid sense of their Mexican nationality. The vestiges of Spanish influence which have survived in the region and its Mexican background have made it a second homeland in the eyes of the immigrants. Separated from the dominant groups by language, religion, and numerous cultural traits, they have keenly resented the discrimination they have encountered and have rejected the dominant culture as alien and hostile.

By 1940 a large second-generation group had reached the threshold of maturity, American-born children of the immigrants who had crossed the border after 1920. By no means so docile and tractable as their parents, the second-generation Mexicans are typical cultural hybrids. To the usual disadvantages experienced by second-generation immigrant groups, however, is added, in this instance, the deep-seated anti-Mexican prejudice of the region which the Mexican-Americans have inherited. While most of them belong, of course, to the same racial group as the dominant element, they are nevertheless regarded as though they were a racial, as well as an ethnic, minority. By 1904 there were 36,000 "Mexican" youngsters in Los Angeles between the ages of 6 and 17, 98% of whom were American-born.

Concentrated in large Mexican settlements, set apart from other second-generation groups by their dark skins, these youngsters have shown every indication of profound social unrest. Coming from Spanish-speaking homes and communities, they have experienced special difficulties in the schools in some of which they are a dominant element. Caught in a sharp cultural conflict, it is impossible for them to reconcile the values emphasized in the schools with those admired in the home. Unlike other Catholic immigrant groups, only a negligible number attend parochial schools since their parents cannot afford even the nominal fees required. Separated from their children by a wide cultural cleavage, the parents often use harsh disciplinary measures to impose standards of conduct and patterns of behavior which the children cannot reconcile with what they are taught, what they observe, and what they discover for themselves in the streets and alleys of the east side.

As the imported Mexican folk-culture has disintegrated under the impact of a highly urbanized environment, the Mexican home and the Mexican community have shown a corresponding disorganization which, in turn, is reflected in the disaffection of the second generation. Despite these handicaps, however, the second generation would have adjusted as quickly as other immigrant groups had it not been for the persistent prejudice they have encountered. Rebuffed in the schools and in the community, they have been made to feel that they do not belong, that they are "Mexican," not American, and that they will never be accepted as equals. Under the circumstances, it is not surprising that this generation should be profoundly disaffected or that it should feel a deep hostility toward the dominant group and its culture.

Following the lead of the Hearst press, the newspapers of Los Angeles launched a violent campaign against "Mexican" juvenile delinquency and "Mexican" crime in the spring of 1942. Featuring every story involving the arrest of a Mexican, they soon had the public clamoring, in semi-hysterical fashion, for "action" and "strong methods." Actually the increase in juvenile delinquency among Mexicans was less than the average increase for the community and below that for one or two other special groups. Mounting in daily intensity and violence, the newspaper campaign culminated in the well-known Sleepy Lagoon case in August, 1942.

Looking for an excuse to execute a well-planned program against the Mexican community, the police seized upon the murder of a man by the name of Diaz to make a series of dragnet raids and mass arrests. The murder of Diaz took place near a mudhole on the east side of Los Angeles which Mexican youngsters had long used for a swimming pool and which they had christened "Sleepy Lagoon." Over 300 Mexican youngsters, and only Mexicans were arrested, in these mass raids. Later, twenty-three Mexican boys were indicted and placed on trial for first-degree murder, most of the defendants being minors. At the same time, the Sheriff of Los Angeles released a report on "Mexican Crime," devoted to the novel thesis that persons of Mexican descent have a biological predisposition to criminal behavior. In an atmosphere weighed with prejudice, a jury convicted seventeen of the defendants of varying degrees of responsibility for the murder of Diaz. Eighteen months later, an appellate court reversed the convictions and severely castigated the trial judge and the prosecution for the methods which had been used to secure the verdict. The case had widespread repercussions in the community and represented the first major attempt that the Mexican community had made in the direction of self-organization for the defense of their rights. On the day the defendants were finally released, hundreds of Mexicans gathered about the entrance to the Hall of Justice, packed the corridors, and lined the streets.

For a few months after the jury had returned its verdict in the Sleepy Lagoon case, the newspapers modified their campaign. But by January, 1943, the attack had been resumed. Now the newspapers were careful to avoid the use of the word Mexican. Complying with suggestions made by the OWI, the newspapers dropped the word Mexican from their vocabulary; they substituted the word "pachuco" or "zoot-suit." This renewed campaign resulted in the zoot-suit race riots which occurred in Los Angeles in June, 1943. Roaming the downtown streets, a mob of 3,000 hoodlums dragged Mexicans, Filipinos, and Negroes from motion-picture theaters and street cars, beat them on the streets and sidewalks, and, in many cases, stripped them of their clothing. During the rioting, policemen watched the violence, made no attempt to intervene, and arrested the victims of the mob after the mob had finally abandoned them. Instead of doing public penance for their instigation of the riot, the newspapers left-handedly condoned the violence and placed responsibility for its occurrence on the Mexican community.

Since the Sleepy Lagoon case and the zoot-suit riots, open warfare has existed between the police and the Mexican boy and girl pachucos in Los Angeles. For the last two years, Mexican youngsters have not been allowed on the streets after curfew hour, although the curfew has not been enforced against other groups, and the number of arrests has reached fantastic proportions. I know of one case in which a Mexican youngster has been arrested 46 times, without a formal charge ever having been filed. The continuance of these absurd police tactics has, of course, crystallized the hostility of the pachucos and solidified their "gang" organizations. The last of this conflict has, by no means, been heard; in fact, it will echo in Los Angeles for years to come. For basically the recent disturbances symbolize the maturity of the American-born generation and their determination to cast off the whole pattern of discrimination and its invidious implications.

Responding to new currents of thought, the Mexican communities have begun to show an inclination toward self-organization and to come of age politically. Thousands of Mexican boys have been called into the services (one township on the east side of Los Angeles has sent 3,000 into the services), and when these soldiers return, an entirely new leadership element will be injected into the Mexican communities. Dormant for decades, the Mexican issue has once again become a dominant consideration in Southern California and the age-old Anglo-Hispano conflict of cultures has been resumed. This conflict is likely to continue until some fusion of the two cultures takes place. For the Mexicans of the Southwest will never "assimilate" in quite the same sense that other immigrant groups have been assimilated. They are really not immigrants; they belong to the Southwest in which important vestiges of their culture have survived through the years. While the conditions under which such a fusion might be expected to occur have improved of recent years, they have not improved sufficiently to relax the current tensions. These tensions will persist until the dominant group is prepared to accept the concept of bi-culturality, that is, until it is willing to let the Mexican alone, to treat him with respect, to recognize his equality, and to sanction the free use of the Spanish language and whatever other cultural traits may survive. Despite the long history of cultural conflict between Anglo and Hispano in Southern California, it was not until 1944 that the public schools of Los Angeles launched a concerted effort to teach Spanish as a second language of the region.

2. THE JAPANESE

In all Southern California there were only 58 Japanese in 1880, but, after 1900, the number steadily increased: from 481 in 1900 to 13,068 in 1910; from 25,597 in 1920 to 44,554 in 1940. Over the years, the Japanese in Southern California have tended to concentrate in Los Angeles County which, by 1940, had a Japanese population of 36,866. In fact, the Little Tokyo community in Los Angeles was the center of Japanese life on the west coast. From the railroads, the Japanese moved into the citrus industry which they dominated for a time to the exclusion of the Chinese and the Mexicans. As late as 1913, the Limoneira Company employed only Japanese workmen.

Not content to remain farm laborers, the Japanese began to buy up the produce lands, which the Chinese had rented for years, and to organize the industry on a highly efficient basis. As they moved from the citrus to the produce industry, they were gradually replaced, in the citrus groves, by resident and immigrant Mexicans (the number of Mexicans employed in the citrus industry increased from 2,317 to 7,004 between 1915 and 1919). By 1940 the Japanese were farming 26,045 acres of Los Angeles County and controlled 90% of the truck crops, such as, asparagus, lima beans, carrots, and cauliflower. Based upon their control of the produce industry, Little Tokyo developed into a more or less self-contained community, an island within an island.

As an immigrant group, the Japanese made remarkable progress in Los Angeles. It would take a book to detail their contributions to the culture and the economy of the region, notably in the produce, floral, and nursery industries. Much of the best landscape gardening in Southern California has been done by skilled Japanese gardeners. In March, 1901, twelve Japanese immigrants, all fishermen, visited

San Pedro in search of employment. On this first trip, one of the men happened to turn over a boulder, near the beach, and, to his astonishment, found an abalone. By November of the same year, the Japanese had laid the foundations for the present-day amazingly profitable fish-canning industry of Southern California. In 1944 over 500,000,000 pounds of fish were brought to the harbor canneries, making the San Pedro-Wilmington district the fish capital of the United States. From 1901 to 1940, the Japanese fishing village on Terminal Island, made up of around 500 fishermen, 150 merchants, and 450 women and children, was one of the most interesting ethnic settlements in Southern California. Pioneered by the Chinese and the Japanese, the fishing industry has attracted other immigrant groups —Italians, Mexicans, and Yugoslavs, who, today, are the dominant group (there are approximately 50,000 Yugoslavs in Southern California). In 1942 the Japanese, of course, were evacuated from the west coast; they began to return in 1945. Despite the manifold difficulties and barriers which they have encountered, the Japanese will unquestionably regain something of their former importance in Los Angeles County, where there is less prejudice against them than in any other portion of the region or the state.

3. THE EAST SIDE

The east side of Los Angeles has always been the area of first settlement for immigrant groups in Southern California: Russians, Armenians, Russian-Armenians, Poles, Mexicans, and Jews, particularly Russian-Jewish groups. As late as 1880, Boyle Heights, on the east side, was a fashionable residential district, but, particularly after 1908, it began to be taken over by immigrant groups. It is, in effect, an incubator which retains the immigrant groups until the influence of the first generation has begun to decline and the second generation has matured. From the east side, the Jewish second generation has jumped over downtown Los Angeles and relocated far to the west in an apartment-house district bounded by Santa Monica and Wilshire Boulevards, from Fairfax to La Cienga, which is nowadays a major area of secondary settlement. The east-side Jewish districts are Yiddish and radical; the west-side elements are prosperous and liberal. Today the Jewish community of Los Angeles County numbers approximately 175,000 members.

To the east side of Los Angeles in the year 1905, came the Russian

Molokans, peasants and pacificists who had left Russia on the eve of the Russo-Japanese War. A milk-drinking sect, the Molokans are, perhaps, the one group of newcomers which was not welcomed by the Chamber of Commerce and which had not been enticed to Southern California. They came to Los Angeles by way of Hamburg and Bremen, landing in New York and Galveston, and then making their way westward. "One bright morning in the winter of 1905," wrote Dana Bartlett, "as I was walking along the street near Bethlehem Institute, I perceived many new and strange people, Russian peasants, who, in a short time, converted the district around Vignes and First Streets into a veritable Russian Village." By the end of 1905, more than 5,000 Molokans had settled on "the flats," in a district surrounded by large Mexican, Armenian, Japanese, and Jewish neighborhoods.

Although they do not believe in churches, as such, the Molokans are a religious sect or brotherhood, held together by strong traditional ties and rigid social controls. Despite the homogeneous nature of the colony, however, the imported cultural pattern soon began to disintegrate. For years the bearded "elders" of the community clung tenaciously to their native costumes, customs, language, and institutions, but, with the appearance of the second generation, the usual schism developed. As Molokanism began to disintegrate, the Molokan-American hybrid type appeared and Los Angeles faced one of many similar "problems"—of juvenile delinquency, gang behavior, and the like. By 1929 the Molokan boy-gangs of "the flats" had the social workers busy making studies, charts, and graphs. But, by the mid-thirties, the older peasants had largely disappeared, most of the youngsters had married outside the group, and Los Angeles had forgotten all about its Molokan problem.

Around 1917 a group of 500 White Russians, all self-styled aristocrats, settled in Hollywood. Refugees from the Russian Revolution, they came by way of China, across the Pacific to San Francisco, and then to Hollywood. To this group of aristocrats and officers was later added about a thousand non-aristocrats, students, artists, engineers, and professional people. From this colony came the Russian Orthodox Church, the Russian Officers Club, and the Russian cafes of the early 'twenties: the Double-Headed Eagle, the Russian Bear, the Moscow Inn, and the well-known Boublichki night club on Sunset "strip." The Filmarte Theater in Hollywood was founded by a member of this refugee group. Lacking internal cohesion, the colony soon disintegrated and is today non-existent. For a time, these Russians emigrés published an interesting quarterly, *The Land of Columbus*.

4. THE NEGROES

Sympathetic to the cause of the Confederacy, Los Angeles was for years a "bad town" for Negroes. In this respect, however, it merely reflected the tone of opinion in California. California enacted a fugitive-slave statute, refused to accept the testimony of Negroes in judicial proceedings until 1863, and, in 1869, rejected ratification of the Fifteenth Amendment to the federal constitution. A comment in the Los Angeles News of January 25, 1867, indicates the general temper of community opinion toward Negroes, "The soul of the Negro is as black and as putrid as his body. Should such a creature vote? He has no more capacity for reason than his native hyena or crocodile." The early day journals not infrequently carried such doggerel as:

> Oh, I'm a darky genuine,
> But this I know full well,
> Beside the dif'rence in de color
> Der's a dif'rence in de smell.

In fact, it was not until after 1880 that Negroes began to migrate to Los Angeles. From 188 Negroes in the county in 1880, the number increased to 1,817 in 1890; to 2,841 in 1900; to 7,599 in 1910; to 18,738 in 1920; to 30,893 in 1930; and to 75,209 in 1940. In its beginnings, the Negro community was a typical "Pullman Car" colony, made up almost entirely of railroad employees. With most of the newcomers to Southern California being Republicans from the East and Middle West, Los Angeles by 1900 had outgrown most of its early hostility toward Negroes. A tradition survives that Los Angeles was one of the first, if not the first, city in America to employ Negro firemen and policemen. As the community developed a reputation of being a good town for Negroes, migrants from Negro communities in the Middle West began to arrive in a slow but steady stream. Some early Negro fortunes were made in Los Angeles, in real estate, scrap iron, hog-farming, and so forth. According to Arna Bontemps and Jack Conroy, Negro migrants have made perhaps a better adjust-ment in Los Angeles than in any other American city (*They Seek a City*, p. 205), a circumstance they explain by suggesting that the Japanese and the Mexicans "drew off much of the racial hostility which otherwise might have been concentrated on the Negroes."

After 1916 a sizable Negro community developed in Mud Town, or Watts, on the outskirts of Los Angeles, made up largely of mi-grants from rural areas in Mississippi, Georgia, and Alabama. Another colony sprang up on Temple Street, near an abandoned oil field. Most of the Temple Street Negro families were from rural areas in Tennessee and Georgia. Still later a settlement of Middle Western urban Negroes came into existence in what is now known as the Budlong district, or, in popular parlance, "the green-lawn section." It was not until 1912, however, that there were sufficient Negroes in Los Angeles to constitute a real colony. Originally located near First and Los Angeles Streets, the center of the colony, in response to the pressure of a rapidly expanding non-Negro population, gradually moved further south along Central Avenue. After 1920 thousands of Negroes, most of them from rural sections of Texas, Louisiana, Ar-kansas, Georgia, and Alabama, began to flock westward to Central Avenue, now one of the most famous Negro thoroughfares in America. (Note: The story of the Watts community is recounted in Arna Bontemps' novel, *God Sends Sunday* (1931), while the rise of Central Avenue is the subject of *Sweet Man*, a novel written by Gilmore Millen in 1932.)

Early in 1942, the railroads began to import thousands of Negroes, for maintenance-of-way work, from such states as Texas, Louisiana, and Oklahoma, thereby setting in motion a mass exodus of Negroes from the Deep South. Since 1940 about 250,000 Negroes have, in fact, moved to the west coast and the Negro community of Los Angeles now totals around 150,000 people. Pouring into Los Angeles by the thousands, as many as 5,000 a month, Negro migrants pre-empted the former Little Tokyo section, vacated by the Japanese, and rechristened it Bronzeville. Today there can be no question that Los Angeles is destined to be one of the great centers of Negro life in America.

With a combined population of nearly 500,000, Negroes and Mexi-cans will have a profound influence on the future of Los Angeles. Although the two groups overlap in a few sections of the city, they live for the most part in separate districts and, to date, there has been relatively little collaboration between them. Once they began to collaborate on political, social, and economic issues, they will constitute a significant balance-of-power element in the population. The Negro community of Los Angeles is already represented on the bench and in the legislature. Although they outnumber the Negroes, the Mexicans have not yet succeeded in winning similar recognition. If they were as well organized as the Negroes, the Mexicans could elect a congressman, several legislators, and a number of councilmen. In a number of outlying communities, they could be a decisive political factor. Of the various racial and ethnic groups in Los Angeles, these two, the Mexicans and the Negroes, are by far the most important.

From the foregoing sections, it will be noted that the important minority groups in Southern California are concentrated in Los Angeles; that they consist of three principal groups, Mexican, Oriental, and Negro; and that each of these groups became an important element in the life of the community at about the same date, for the most part after 1900. As comparative newcomers to the region, their full importance has not as yet been recognized. European immigrant groups, as such, have not constituted an important element in the population since 1870. It should also be noted that the three minorities in question have inherited, in each instance, a particular prejudice: anti-Mexican, anti-Oriental, anti-Negro. In the population of Los Angeles today are represented important elements of every racial strain that has gone into the making of the American people. The city has become, therefore, one of the most interesting racial melting pots in the nation.

5. CROWN OF THE VALLEY

In California, as Dr. Park has pointed out, "the disposition of racial and cultural minorities to settle in colonies and to cherish, in the seclusion and security of their own communities, different traditions and peculiar folkways is true of other sections of the population which are also, in some sense, alien, alien at least to those who count everyone a foreigner who was not born in the state." Southern California is famous for its residential suburbs, cities like Santa Barbara and Pasadena ("Crown of the Valley"), where the rich and retired live in a seclusion so complete and so silent that in some of the residential hotels, it is said, one scarcely hears anything but the ticking of the clock or the hardening of one's arteries. According to Dr. Thorndike, Pasadena ranks first among the 295 American cities included in his study, in the ratio of radios, telephones, bathtubs, and dentists to population. In 1929 the assessed wealth of Pasadena was fixed at $186,000,000, high for a city of its size. Tax assessors have estimated that fully 75% of the wealth of Pasadena is owned by women. In 1930 Pasadena had the highest percentage of widows of any city in America: 18.2% against a national average of 11.1% (6,481 widows, 1,059 divorced women). Compelled to remain single by the prevalence of non-remarriage clauses in trusts and wills, the widows of Pasadena have attracted scores of playboys, amateur actors, amateur playwrights, amateur musicians, and amateur writers. "Practically every other house in the scenic Oak Knoll, San Marino and South Orange Grove Avenue sections of the town," observed a writer in Ken magazine some years ago, "is occupied by a lonesome widow who still entertains the notion that life has cheated her."

There is a saying in Los Angeles that "rich people who move to Southern California do not go to Pasadena to live unless they have had money for at least two decades." There are no nouveaux riches in Pasadena, no motion-picture celebrities, no oil field tycoons. Pasadena shows the rather liberal streak, in matters of free speech, and the like, that communities of settled wealth are likely to manifest. It is the wealth of Pasadena that has sustained such institutions as the California Institute of Technology, the Pasadena Playhouse, and the Huntington Library. By their location in Pasadena, these institutions could hardly be more carefully insulated from the rest of Los Angeles if they were surrounded by Chinese walls. Now and again Pasadena scandalizes the rest of Southern California by one of those scandals typical of wealth possessed long enough to have induced decadence. Some years ago a leading citizen of Pasadena was arrested on the morning of the day when he was to have received an honorary degree from a local college. Along with seven or eight other leading lights of Pasadena, all men of advanced years, he was charged with having engaged in a charming assortment of sexual perversions with school-age youngsters. He later committed suicide. The prompt and efficient manner in which this particular scandal was buried under an avalanche of dense silence remains one of the most remarkable accomplishments of the remarkable Los Angeles press.

Whatever your status, income level, or racial stock, you can find a community in metropolitan Los Angeles made up almost exclusively of people who belong in the same socio-economic or racial niche. Pasadena is an upper-class island of inherited wealth; Long Beach is predominantly middle class, made up of retired Middle Westerners; Glendale is lily-white and white-collar, made up of middle-class and lower-middle-class elements; South Pasadena is middle class proper; Bell Gardens is lower-lower and Okie; Beverly Hills is upper middle class, *nouveaux riches*; while Bel-Air is definitely upper-upper. Indeed, all Southern California is, as Dr. Park said, "a congeries of cultural insulated communities," an archipelago of ethnic, cultural, racial, and socio-economic islands.

Today these various elements exist in relative cultural isolation, but in a mutually interacting relationship. This is merely another way of saying, of course, that the culture of the region has not yet even begun to achieve integration. When integration is achieved, however, the culture of the region will represent literally all America, every racial strain, every state of the union, every socio-economic class, and every ethnic group. Of the American cities, writes J. P. Priestley, Los Angeles is "the newest and strangest of them all, a vast conglomeration, and gayly-colored higgledy-piggledy of unending boulevards, vacant lots, oil derricks, cardboard bungalows, retired farmers, fortune-tellers, real estate dealers, film stars, false prophets, affluent pimps, women in pajamas turning on victrolas, radio men lunching on aspirin and Alka-Seltzer, Middle-Western grandmothers, Chinese grandfathers, Mexican uncles and Filipino cousins." Yvor Winters, the Stanford poet, some years ago wrote a poem entitled "See Los Angeles First," which suggests the hobbledehoy character of the city:

> Rosyfingered cocklehouses
> burst from burning
> rock red plaster hollyhocks
> spit crackling mamas
> tickled pink.
>
>   **on tiptoe**
> yawn into the dewy dawn
> dark wettish plushy lawn

MIZPAH
> The Temple glittergates

Ask God He Knows
> O Pyramid of Sunoil Dates

The mockingbird is singing eighty
languages a minute
swinging by his toes from
highpower
> jagged geometric currents

roar along aluminum gashed
Out of gulleys rending
night to one blind
> halo for your cold

Concrete Egyptian nakedness
 O Waterpower of cleanliness.

"You can't explain Hollywood. There isn't any such place. It's just the dream suburb of Los Angeles."
—Rachel Field in *To See Ourselves*

CHAPTER XVI

THE ISLAND OF HOLLYWOOD

HOLLYWOOD, as Katherine Fullerton Gerould pointed out years ago, exists only as a state of mind, not as a geographical entity. One of the most famous place-names in the world, Hollywood is neither a town nor a city; it is an integral part of Los Angeles. Despite its nebulous geographical status, however, Hollywood does exist as a community, but a community that must be defined in industrial rather than geographical terms. The concentration of the motion-picture industry in Los Angeles is what gives Hollywood its real identity. As Jerome Beatty once said, Hollywood exists as "a kingless kingdom within a kingdom," an island within an island.

The most highly publicized industry in the world, Hollywood has been reported, for many years, by a corps of some 400 newspapermen, columnists, and feature writers. "Only Washington," writes Leo Rosten, "the matrix of our political life, and New York, the nerve-center of our economic system, possess larger press corps." Every phase of the industry and every facet of Hollywood life has been thoroughly reported. In fact, there is only one aspect of Hollywood that is germane to the perspectives of this book, namely, the relation between Hollywood and Los Angeles. Is there an interacting influence between these communities? Where and how does the one community impinge upon the other?

1. THE COLONY PHASE

Originally the motion-picture colony was located in the Edendale district of Los Angeles, not in the suburb of Hollywood. The first motion-picture producers were attracted to Los Angeles, according to local tradition, by reports of the wide varieties of scenery to be found in the region. While producing motion pictures in New York, David Horsley is supposed to have read John Steven McGroarty's roseate descriptions of scenic Southern California and to have concluded that there was the place to make pictures. In point of fact, however, the first producers who came to Los Angeles were fugitives —from process servers and the patent trust. Seeking to evade injunctions, they wanted to be as far from New York and as close to the Mexican border as possible. It is true that once located in Los Angeles they found the climate ideally adapted to the making of motion pictures. For within a two-hundred-mile radius of Los Angeles was to be found every variety of natural scenery from the Sahara Desert to the Khyber Pass. There was also available in Los Angeles an abundant supply of cheap labor. But these discoveries were accidental by-products of the main purpose which was to elude the patent trust.

Always looking over their shoulders for process servers, the first motion-picture "people" did not live in Los Angeles; they merely camped in the community, prepared, like Arabs, to fold their tents and steal away in the night. An impudent, troublesome, harum-scarum lot, they were regarded in Los Angeles as an unmitigated nuisance. In the period from 1908 to 1912, Los Angeles was still in its sedate and stuffy phase, a self-righteous and pious community. From the day that Colonel William N. Selig started shooting *The Count of Monte Cristo* in 1908, Los Angeles took an aggressively hostile attitude toward the new nickelodeon and peepshow industry. As Gene Fowler has pointed out, Colonel Selig's cowboys were hired on their ability to whoop as well as to ride. "The whooping put them in the proper mood. They also whooped while off the set and did some shooting at bar fixtures and in the palm-lined lanes. The citizens didn't like this racket and were sure the good Colonel Selig had cloven hooves and that his men wore tall sombreros to make room for horns." The churchgoing townspeople of Los Angeles spoke of the studios as "camps" and the motion-picture people as "the movie colony."

During the camp phase of the industry, cameramen shot scenes wherever and whenever they wished: in Westlake Park, on street corners, in residential districts. Never bothering to build sets, the producers improvised the background and setting, and made up the stories as they went along. Housewives were constantly infuriated by the ringing of doorbells and traffic was forever being snarled up by the shooting of street scenes. The curiously assorted characters who made up the colony were segregated like lepers in Los Angeles. "Over no decent threshold," writes Cedric Belfrage, "were they allowed to step. They were unfit to mingle with respectable citizens." Apartment houses and four-family flats soon carried signs reading: "No Dogs or Actors Allowed." Living in out-of-the-way rooming houses and hotels, they spent their leisure hours at the Vernon Night Club and other alcoholic oases in the outlying districts. When they began to invade Hollywood, "the most beautiful suburb of America," they were similarly ostracized.

From the Edendale section near Elysian Park, the colony moved to Hollywood in 1911, when Al Christie, and David and Bill Horsley rented the old Blondeau Tavern at Gower and Sunset one day and began shooting a film the next. Just why Hollywood should have been chosen remains something of a mystery. Founded by Horace W. Wilcox, a Kansas prohibitionist, Hollywood was incorporated in 1903 with an adult population of 166 residents. On the eve of its invasion by the motion-picture industry, Hollywood had surrendered its legal status, "but not its well-earned identity," by voting, in 1910, to join the City of Los Angeles. "An obscure and dusty suburb," it had a population of 4,000 in 1911 and a reputation as a center of piety and respectability. Resenting the motion-picture invasion, the residents of Hollywood finally succeeded, in 1919, in forcing the City of Los Angeles to enact zoning ordinances which restricted studios to seven prescribed areas. In fact, Hollywood was up in arms against the invading gypsy bands from 1911 until the opening of *The Birth of a Nation*, the first great premiere at Clune's Auditorium in Los Angeles on February 8, 1915.

After 1915 both Hollywood and Los Angeles began to experience a change of attitude toward the motion-picture industry. From a suburb of 4,000 population, Hollywood had grown to a community of 36,000 by 1920 (and to 235,000 by 1930). Mary Pickford was earning $1,000 a week in 1913; Jesse Lasky and Cecil B. De Mille had arrived the same year; and Charles Chaplin had gone to work at the Keystone lot for $150 a week, and, within two years, was earning $10,000 a week. With an annual payroll of $20,000,000 in 1915, the movies had arrived. Hollywood began to accept the colony and even to regard a few of its members, such as Cecil and William De Mille, Mary Pickford, Douglas Fairbanks, and Theodore Roberts, as among its leading citizens. The strenuous effort which the motion-picture people put forth in support of the war, in the years from 1916 to 1918, helped to bridge the gap between the industry and the community.

As the movies passed from their colony phase to their purple period, however, a series of events served to widen the breach. The Fatty Arbuckle case, the murder of William Desmond Taylor, the death of Wallace Reid, the murder (?) of Thomas Ince, and the shooting of Courtland Dines by the chauffeur of Mabel Normand (whose name had figured so prominently in the Taylor case), momentarily crystallized the earlier opposition and the movies were, once again, on the defensive. Forming the Motion Picture Producers Association, the producers retained Will ("Deacon") Hays to launch a clean-up campaign. A morals clause was written in all actors' contracts, detectives were hired to scrutinize the private lives of the stars, and the purple period came to an abrupt end.

The circus-and-carnival atmosphere completely vanished, when sound was first introduced in 1925. Tourists and visitors were not welcome in the new double-walled, soundproof studios. Location trips were reduced to a minimum and the movies became an indoor industry. Before sound was introduced, well-known actors and actresses could be seen throughout the city, on the streets and on location. But after 1925 guides began to put up signs along the boulevards offering to take tourists on a tour of the studios and to point out the homes of the stars. The carnival atmosphere survived only in the gaudy premieres with their blazing klieg lights. At about the same time, the stars began to scatter to the Hollywood hills, to Bel-Air, to Beverly Hills, and, somewhat later, to San Fernando Valley. By 1930 there was not a single star or director of the first rank living in Hollywood. The exodus of the studios had begun even earlier, in 1922. Today there are only three studios in the Hollywood area. Acquiring social respectability with the introduction of sound, the movies proceeded to wall the industry off from the rest of the community. Once the retreat to the lots had been made, the earlier, tenuous, and always troubled relation between "Hollywood" and the rest of Los Angeles was terminated and a new relationship began to develop.

2. So Near and Yet So Far

The geographical area known as Hollywood extends from the summit of the Hollywood hills on the north to Beverly Boulevard on the south; from Hoover Street on the east, to Doheny Drive on the west. When other communities have threatened to appropriate the name Hollywood, the merchants and business men in this district have always raised an enormous rumpus and promptly threatened lawsuits. This is Hollywood, the suburb; Hollywood, the business and residential district. No longer the center of the motion-picture industry for any purpose, it is nevertheless a distinct community. A district of apartment houses and hotels, it has perhaps the highest occupancy turnover of any section of mobile Los Angeles. With relatively few old people and children, the population pyramid for the district is narrow at both extremes. According to the editor of Dog World, Hollywood is the "doggiest area" in California, which, in turn, is "the doggiest state in the union." Here, as Rachel Field observed, the residents belong "to an unchartered free-masonry, whose badge is the leash and stick, and whose password is a word or look of mutual admiration." Here "dog status has been elevated to a high plane," with "a marked canine class distinction being everywhere apparent." Here live the hangers-on of the industry; its carpenters, painters, and machinists; its hordes of extras. Hollywood is, as Horace McCoy once said, perhaps the most "terrifying town" in America: lonely, insecure, full of marginal personalities, people just barely able to make ends meet; a place of opportunists and confidence men, petty chiselers and racketeers, bookies and race-track touts; of people desperately on the make. Once the main thoroughfare of the motion-picture colony, Hollywood Boulevard is today a rather run-down tourist alley, lined with curio shops, used bookstores, hobby shops, motion-picture theaters, and mediocre stores. The center of the district is Hollywood and Vine, where, of course, you are almost sure to meet some one you know. When visiting British novelists, no longer on contract with the industry, denounce and revile Hollywood, it is this abandoned center of the industry—this geographical entity—that they usually have in mind. It is, indeed, as James Rorty once observed, a place of careerism and sycophancy, whose favorite word is phony, a place that suggests "the meretricious, derivative eloquence of the mocking birds" that haunt the ragged dusty palms of its bungalow courts.

But this district is not Hollywood. The community of Hollywood is made up of the people engaged in the production of motion pictures, few of whom live in this area. Where motion pictures are made, there is Hollywood. For undeniably there is a Hollywood community in the sense that the people engaged in the production of pictures have the center, the focus, of their lives in the industry and are bound together by the nature of the industry itself. Living over wide areas of Los Angeles, "picture people," and the phrase indicates their group-identity, constitute their own community, separate and distinct from the neighborhoods in which they reside and quite apart from Los Angeles proper. The relationship between this Hollywood and the rest of Los Angeles is, therefore, essentially symbiotic. When a resident of Los Angeles enters the motion-picture industry, he *disappears* almost as completely as though he had moved across the continent. "The world of movie stars," writes Frank Fenton, "was only across the hills and yet it was as far as the sun."

A world within a world, Hollywood-the-social-entity is a rigidly stratified community. The elite of the industry is made up of three strata: the two hundred or more individuals who make in excess of $75,000 a year, the junior elite who make from $25,000 to $50,000 a year, and the lesser elite who make from $10,000 to $15,000 a year. Beneath the elite are the "workers" of the industry: the craftsmen, the white-collar office workers, the skilled and unskilled laborers. The elite live outside Hollywood in Beverly Hills, Brentwood, Bel-Air, Santa Monica, the Hollywood Hills, and San Fernando Valley. Following the hierarchical structure of the industry itself, the communities in which picture people live have been perfectly zoned, as Scott Fitzgerald noted, "so you know exactly what kind of people economically live in each section, from executives and directors, through technicians in their bungalows, right down to the extras." Social rank in the industry is precisely graded in relation to income and fluctuates, as quickly and as sensitively as a barometer, with each change in earning capacity. The social barometer, however, only records changes within the industry. Once a person's relation with the industry is severed, he is automatically excluded from the Hollywood community, with rare exceptions, regardless of his income or the size of his fortune.

Highly stratified internally, Hollywood is nonetheless still a community. For the people who make up the industry, from the lowliest extra to Louis B. Mayer, all identify themselves with Hollywood and belong to a world of their own. However widely they may be separated on the social ladder of the industry, picture people still possess a strong sense of group-identity. Set apart from their fellow citizens of Los Angeles, even from those of a similar or comparable social rating, they think of themselves as a part of Hollywood. To be in pictures, in whatever capacity, denotes a vague and indefinable status, but one which is universally recognized.

This sense of community identification may be variously illustrated. The motion-picture industry has always had its own employer organizations, separate and apart from the Merchants and Manufacturers Association and Southern Californians, Incorporated. While most of the Hollywood trade unions are affiliated with the A. F. of L. and have representatives on the Los Angeles Central Labor Council, they have always felt more closely identified with Hollywood than with Los Angeles. The present-day Conference of Studio Unions is, in effect, a kind of Hollywood Central Labor Council. Such organizations as the Studio Club and the Motion Picture Relief Association also indicate the existence of a separate institutional life. Both the employers and the employees of the industry have their own separate political organizations. When Hollywood contributes to China Relief or Russian War Relief or to the Red Cross, it does so as Hollywood, that is, as the motion-picture industry.

The main studio lots are walled towns, each with its principal thoroughfares, sidestreets, and alleys. On the lot people work together, live together, eat together. With from two to three thousand employees, each lot is a community in itself. Occupying from thirty to forty acres of land, each lot has its own office buildings; its factories (the stages); its theaters and projection rooms; its laboratories, dressmaking shops, blacksmith shops, machine shops, wardrobes, restaurants, dressing rooms, lumber sheds; greenhouses; scene docks; electrical plant; garages; and planing mills. No one has ever precisely defined a motion-picture lot. It is neither a factory nor a business establishment nor yet a company town. Rather it is more in the nature of a community, a beehive, or, as Otis Ferguson said, "fairy-land on a production line." The analogy to a factory is destroyed by the bewildering variety of crafts and skills, the ever-changing personnel, and the fact that, while the production process is always the same, each "production" is separately organized and is, to some extent, a separate product. To call an industry which, in 1939, made only 376 major products, or feature pictures, a mass-production factory is to ignore a basic distinction. Each production involves a different cast, not merely of actors, but of directors, producers, and, to some extent, even of business executives and office and lot employees. Unlike the typical mass-production factory, production lacks continuity and employment lacks stability. People are constantly "in" and "out" of pictures. While personnel shifts from lot to lot and from studio to studio, picture people, however, continue to work in the same industry, in the same community.

On and off the lots, picture people associate with picture people: the elite with the elite, the junior elite with the junior elite, the craftsmen with the craftsmen, and even the office employees with other office employees in the same industry. It could even be shown that a surprisingly large number of picture people have married within the industry. Living in different sections of the city, the three elite categories, and, to some extent, even the lower-bracket employees, frequent the same shopping districts and seldom come to Los Angeles. A friend of mine, a writer, boasts that he has not been east of Western Avenue for fifteen years except to catch a train. The elite elements employ Hollywood business agents, retain Hollywood lawyers, and consult Hollywood physicians. They are protected, not merely by studio walls, but by a cordon of secretaries, managers, and agents from the rest of the community. They deal with Los Angeles, in fact, through these representatives, having few primary contacts with the outside world. Motion-picture people frequent the same mountain, beach, or desert resorts. Once a particular resort has been invaded by non-picture people, the movie folk promptly shift their patronage elsewhere. They are always just one step ahead of the Angelenos. When it becomes difficult to protect themselves from the rest of Southern California, they will even form their own corporations to acquire a particular mountain resort or desert hotel for their exclusive patronage. Some years ago, for example, the upper-bracket elite toyed with the idea of forming an

Inner Circle Club as a means of segregating themselves from "the assistant directors and the $300-a-week writers." A special mezzanine was to have been provided where the elite, as the brochure announcing the project stated, "could be a part of, but still removed from, the crowd."

Motion-picture people even use, as Otis Ferguson reported, the same "clipped and extravagant speech." They patronize the same tailors and the same golf courses, attend the fights only on "movie night," and are always seen at the same cafes, night clubs, and restaurants. "The Trocadero was the place to be seen that season," observes a character in Budd Schulberg's novel, *What Makes Sammy Run?* and another character comments, "What always amazes me is that with all the turn-over in Hollywood from year to year, almost from month to month, the faces never seem to change." Picture people exhibit many similar affectations, use the same idioms, and, even in playing poker and betting on the races, show the same remarkable clannishness. While *Variety* and *The Reporter* are avidly read, the local press is ignored except for the gossip columns and the special Hollywood "society" sections. To some extent this clannishness is largely defensive, a means of protection against salesmen, bores, and bums seeking to make a touch. But it also indicates the centripetal force of the industry itself. "Everyone belonged to the films," observed Vicki Baum, "or was non-existent." "Out here," wrote Ward Morehouse in 1942, "you're sucked into a community life you have no feeling for."

In large part, the notorious cleavage between Hollywood and Los Angeles may be traced to the absorbing nature of employment in the motion-picture industry. A writer who is currently receiving $1,000 a week, who has made a down-payment on a $25,000 home, and whose option is about to expire, is about as engrossed with motion pictures as it is possible for a person to be with any single topic. He lives, breathes, and talks nothing but picture ideas. He may not like his work, he may loathe his particular assignment, but concentration on his work precludes the likelihood of his being interested in people who do not share a similar preoccupation. Instinctively, he turns in his leisure moments, such as they are, to people in the same or a similar predicament, who speak the same language, laugh at the same jokes, and appreciate the same personal anecdotes. Although his net earnings over a period of time may not be great, his scale of pay, while he is working, is such as to place him in a different category from those with whom he formerly associated. A man who is earning $750 or $1,000 a week, although he may only be employed for six or eight weeks in the year, lives a very different life from a man who regularly makes $6,000 a year. It should be noted, however, that to be in pictures can mean that one merely occupies a marginal relation to the industry, for example, the favorite bootlegger in prohibition days, a book salesman, or a well-known bookie or poker player. Referring to one of the characters in his novel, Scott Fitzgerald wrote that "she was of the movies but not in them." (Italics mine.)

The symbiotic relation between the two communities has been of great value to both. For Hollywood it has created a set of special prestige values long expertly exploited; for Los Angeles it has invested the proximity to Hollywood, the tantalizing "so near and yet so far" relationship, with a commercial value that can be weighed, measured, and capitalized. For example, if the motion-picture industry had merged with the rest of the community, it would long ago have become impossible to place a special premium on motion-picture patronage. But, under the existing relationship, Hollywood patronage of a particular shop or cafe or hotel or bar or art gallery can be made to pay dividends. Having the industry sequestered from the rest of the community has made possible the world-wide exploitation of the name Hollywood, which, in turn, has drawn thousands of people and vast sums of money to the region. To vulgarize the concept, it has made possible the distillation of a pure essence, Hollywood, used to sell clothes, real estate, ideas, books, jewelry, furniture, cold creams, deodorants, and perfume.

3. AN ISLAND INDUSTRY

God has always smiled on Southern California; a special halo has always encircled this island on the land. Consider, for example, the extraordinary good luck in having the motion-picture industry concentrated in Los Angeles. The leading industry of Los Angeles from 1920 to 1940, motion pictures were made to fit the economic requirements and physical limitations of the region like a glove. Here was one industry, perhaps the only industry in America, that required no raw materials, for which discriminatory freight rates were meaningless, and which, at the same time, possessed an enormous payroll. Employing from thirty to forty thousand workers, the industry in

1939 spent about $190,000,000 in the manufacture of films and of this total $89,884,841 represented salaries, $41,096,226, wages, and only $31,118,277 was spent on such supplies as film, fuel and energy, and miscellaneous items. Today Los Angeles is an industrial community, but it was only beginning to become industrialized when the movies appeared as a providential dispensation. To this island community of the West, motion pictures have attracted perhaps more people than they have ever employed and more capital than they have ever invested. They provided the community with precisely what it needed, payrolls, purchasing power—a simulated industrial base. Like the region itself, this key industry is premised upon improvisation, a matter of make-believe, a synthesis of air and wind and water. To J. B. Priestley, Southern California was "impermanent and brittle as a reel of film" and to Rupert Hughes the mountains rimming the region are "as unreal as flats of stage scenery, stage pieces." Approached from any point of view, there is an extraordinary affinity between the industry and its Southern California setting.

Not only was the industry precisely of the character that the community needed and made to meet its basic weaknesses, but it has always been essentially monopolistic in the twofold sense, first, that it is monopolistically controlled, and, second, that it is concentrated in the region. Just as the region itself is separated from the rest of the nation by a wall of mountains and desert, so the industry is barricaded against competition. Ninety per cent of all the films produced in the United States are made in Hollywood. While this circumstance has probably militated against a proper circulation of competitive ideas in the making of motion pictures, it has been a godsend to Southern California. For it has anchored in the region an industry partially protected against the ups and the downs of the business cycle. Movies are apparently a necessary luxury, slow to feel cuts in the family budget, for they continued to attract large patronage throughout the depression. The advertising value of the industry to the region simply cannot be estimated. It has certainly advertised Los Angeles more effectively than the All-Year Club of Southern California, an organization that has spent millions on exploitation. What could be more desirable than a monopolistic non-seasonal industry with 50,000,000 customers, an industry without soot or grime, without blast furnaces or dynamos, an industry whose production shows peaks but few valleys?

Motion pictures have also stimulated the development of literally hundreds of subsidiary, if minor, industries. According to Mae D. Huettig's study, Warner Brothers Pictures, Inc., lists 108 subsidiaries, including a film laboratory, Brunswick Radio Corporation, a lithographing concern, a concern that makes theater accessories, ten music publishing houses, real-estate companies, booking agencies, several broadcasting corporations, a cellulose products company, a television company, recording studios, and dozens of additional corporations. Not all of these subsidiary concerns, of course, are located in Southern California, but most of them are located here. Motion pictures have stimulated the expansion of service trades, the clerical categories, and the professions. If the figures were available, it could be easily demonstrated that a staggering amount of motion-picture money has been invested in a wide variety of enterprises in Southern California. The location of the film industry in Los Angeles has, in turn, resulted in a somewhat similar concentration of radio broadcasting. Today more than twenty-five national radio shows originate in Hollywood. In 1938 the six Hollywood radio stations spent more than $18,000,000 and paid out, to 600 film stars, more than $5,000,-000. If ever an industry played the Fairy Prince to an impoverished Cinderella, it has been the motion-picture industry in relation to Los Angeles.

Here was an industry insulated against competition; requiring no raw materials other than film, a little lumber, a little grease paint, and a considerable amount of electrical energy; an industry whose product, a roll of film, could be shipped anywhere in the world for almost nothing; but which, at the same time, poured forth an enormous sum in payrolls and expenditures. In 1938 motion pictures ranked fourteenth among American industries by volume of business and eleventh in total assets. Ironically enough, it is the one industry that has not been lured to Los Angeles and that has had to fight for its right to exist in the community. No one can possibly appraise the value of this industry to Los Angeles. Only of recent years has Los Angeles become an important furniture and clothes-manufacturing center. In the manufacture of sportswear, it already occupies an unrivaled position. In both instances, the location of the film industry was an important accelerating factor. Hollywood is an all-important dateline and an equally important trademark.

4. SMOKED GLASSES AND FUR COATS

When the industry first came to Southern California, its camps or colonies were scattered about the region. Pictures were made in San Diego, Santa Barbara, Santa Monica, and Inceville, an abandoned colony located north of Santa Monica. While climatic considerations account for the location of the industry in Southern California, they do not account for its concentration in Los Angeles. Santa Barbara, for example, enjoys a slightly improved variety of the same climate as Los Angeles, while San Diego has more sunshine than any community in the region. How did it happen, therefore, that, within such a short time, all of the companies were concentrated in Los Angeles?

In part the explanation is functional; the manufacture of films is essentially the business of an industry rather than of any particular company. Unquestionably many conveniences result from the concentration of the industry within a fifteen-mile radius of Hollywood. But there is a more basic explanation, suggested by Ross Wills when he observed that Hollywood "is not America at all, but it is all America. It is Bangor, Maine, in intimate embrace with San Diego, California." An industry that must somehow reflect and appeal to all America must also be tied to its customers by some social and psychological nexus. Movies were drawn to "the enormous village" of Los Angeles as pieces of metal to a magnet. For here was the great domestic melting pot, a place which, as Morris Markey has said, "manifests in many ways a remarkable exaggeration of all those things which we are wont to call typically American." Here, in fact, was all America, America in flight from itself, America on an island. And here, of course, was the logical place to raise the big tent of the institutionalized circus which is the motion-picture industry.

Here, too, were to be found the variety of types, the loose social controls, the bigness of the city with the sucker-mindedness of the village; here in short was the kind of community in which a circus industry could take root. If one will momentarily forget climatic considerations, it becomes extremely difficult to imagine the growth of the motion-picture industry in Pittsburgh (too highly industrialized); or in New England (too much out of the main stream of American life); or in the South (too provincial, too backward). The industry required a location in which it could develop and function independently of community controls. In order to provide mass entertainment, the movies had to have social elbow-room, a factor best appraised in light of the strenuous opposition they encountered even in Los Angeles. What the industry required, in the way of mores, was a frontier town forever booming; a community kept currently typical-American by constant migration. The industry could easily have been stifled by a rigid social strait jacket. And, in this connection, it is quite beside the point to urge that the industry might have profited, in the long run, by being located in a half-dozen different cities, or to bewail the fact that it became concentrated in such a socially irresponsible community as Los Angeles.

By its partially self-imposed, partially externally coerced, isolation in Los Angeles, the motion-picture industry has profoundly influenced the culture of the region. Having said as much, however, I hasten to add that it is not always an easy task to trace this influence or to isolate the factors involved. One encounters the same difficulty here that others have faced in trying to define the influence of the movies on American culture. But there is this difference: Los Angeles is not only a moviegoing community, but a community in which movies are made. Outside Los Angeles, as Lillian Symes has pointed out, the influence of Hollywood "is diluted by the intenser realities of everyday experience. The rest of the world gets the shadow, not the essence of Hollywood."

In the field of manners and morals, Hollywood has certainly liberated Los Angeles from the sillier rituals of middle-class life. The Los Angeles that I first knew in 1922 has, in these respects, undergone a complete transformation. As late as 1922, Los Angeles was a center of Comstockism and Fundamentalism. During the 'twenties, the Rev. Robert P. Shuler, born in a log cabin in the Blue Ridge Mountains, a graduate of Elm Creek Academy, rose to great power in Southern California, the "boss" of its ethics, politics, and morals. At one time his radio audience was estimated to be the largest religious radio audience in the world. Zealot and fanatic, he unseated a mayor, a district attorney, and numerous police chiefs and was himself nearly elected to the United States Senate. Annoyed by the scientists at the California Institute of Technology, Reverend Shuler once organized a revival meeting in Pasadena, at which the Rev. Arthur I. Brown spoke on "Men, Monkeys, and Missing Links"; the Rev. Harry Rimmer on "Evolution Unmasked"; and Dr. Gerald B.

Winrod, the native fascist of later years, "The Mark of the Beast." Three weeks after this meeting, the people of Southern California, by a vote of three to one, ordered the King James version of the Bible placed in the public schools of California (the measure was, however, defeated by the upstate vote). Today Shuler, now in the camp of Gerald L. K. Smith, is just another "preacher" and it would be utterly impossible to stampede the people of the region in the direction of Comstockism. How much of this change can be attributed to motion pictures, I do not know, but the movies have certainly been a major influence.

The movies have unquestionably affected the appearance of the region. "They may be blamed," writes Richard Neutra, "for many phenomena in this landscape such as: half-timbered English peasant cottages, French provincial and 'mission-bell' type adobes, Arabian minarets, Georgian mansions on 50 by 120 foot lots with 'Mexican Ranchos' adjoining them on sites of the same size." The interiors reflect the same movie-inspired eclectic confusion: modernistically patterned wallpaper, adzed and exposed ceiling beams, Norman fireplaces, machine-made Persian rugs, cheap Chippendale imitations, and an array of "pickings and tidbits from all historical and geographical latitudes and longitudes." These buildings are not constructed as they appear to be, but are built like sets, with two by fours covered with black paper, chickenwire, and brittle plaster or occasionally brick veneer, and are covered with "a multitude of synthetically colored roofing materials." Much of the construction resembles, or actually copies, the type of construction used in the making of sets, that is, buildings are built for a momentary effect and completely lack a sense of time or permanence. Nearly every visitor to the region has commented on its resemblance to a motion-picture set. "The city seems," writes Paul Schrecker, "not like a real city resulting from natural growth, but like an agglomeration of many variegated movie sets, which stand alongside one another but have no connection with one another." "Hollywood," writes Aldous Huxley, "always seems like a movie set. Everything is very pretty but the houses, which I think are charming, look impermanent, as though they might be torn down at any moment and something else put up." "It is all made of papier-maché," complained Morris Markey, "everything—the filling stations, the studios, the mansions, and even the churches with their Neon signs gleaming among Gothic turrets. It's all just a movie set."

To appreciate the influence of Hollywood on Los Angeles it is important to note the timing: motion pictures arrived just when the community was beginning to assume the dimensions of a city. Had the movies arrived at an earlier, or even at a later date, it is doubtful if their influence would have been so pronounced. Coming when they did, as Lillian Symes has pointed out, "the Hollywood sophistication was painlessly absorbed because it was, after all, little more than Iowa-on-the-loose." Lacking socially prominent first families or deeply rooted social traditions, Los Angeles quickly adopted the motion-picture elite as its arbiters of taste and style. Although the movie elite moved in a world of their own, this world was all the more conspicuous for having the spotlight riveted on its isolated, stage-like gyrations. Hence the movies came to set the tone of opinion in style and taste, manner of living, and attitudes. In other words, Los Angeles imitated Hollywood.

Elsewhere in America, the nouveaux riches have generally been under some mild restraint of settled custom, inherited wealth, or social tradition. But in the Los Angeles of the 'twenties, the extravagant, child-like tastes of the motion-picture elite were imitated at a dozen different socio-economic levels. The Cinderella attraction that the industry has exerted on all America has been greatly magnified in Los Angeles. To employ some dreadful terms, much of the "beauty consciousness" of the industry, its preoccupation with aesthetic effect (however hideous the result), its "glamour," its "slickness," have, to some extent, permeated the rest of the community. Motion-picture techniques of advertising have been widely copied; for example, produce markets are opened with a display of klieg lights and all the pomp and circumstance of a premiere. Attendants in drive-in restaurants dress like usherettes in movie theaters. The immodesty of the industry is reflected in a hundred different ways and nuances, impossible to document but easily recognizable. Los Angeles has imitated the speech mannerisms of Hollywood, its slapstick humor, its informality of existence, and its eccentricity of manner and speech, dress, and mode of living. Here, as Jerome Beatty pointed out, "the signs are bigger and redder, the shops look like moving picture sets, the automobiles run more to nickel trimmings and cream-colored bodies, the girls are more beautiful, and there are more goofy-looking men. Hollywood Boulevard blares at you, and nearly every other person seems to be trying to make himself conspicuous. Beauty shops ballyhoo a jar of cold cream as though it were a behemoth. The average grocer would rather be known as a 'showman' than as a man who knows his groceries." The "conscious factitiousness" of Hollywood has ever been imitated by the churches and temples of the region. Something of the same influence, of course, can be noticed across the nation, but in Los Angeles it stands forth in bold relief.

5. HOLLYWOOD CASE HISTORY

He lived in a fashionable apartment on Sunset Boulevard and over his boulevard shop appeared the caption "Paul Wharton, Couturier." No one knew much about him. He liked to propagate conflicting stories about his parentage. On occasion, he liked to imagine himself the son of fabulously wealthy Montana people, or again he would announce that his parents were Chinese, or, to others, he would say that his parents had gone down on the *Titanic*. He was born, however, in Billings, Montana, in 1909. Reporters described him, at the time of his death, as "a fragile, dark-haired youth, with dark, heavy-lidded, amative eyes, almost Oriental in quality." In 1926 this strange creature, so like a character out of Firbank or Van Vechten, began his Los Angeles career as a designer of pageants at Angelus Temple. Later, he moved westward along the boulevard and became a fashionable designer. At one time he was arrested for narcotic addiction and was released at the behest of Mrs. McPherson. The sharp cleavage in his mental life was revealed in his eccentric behavior. Once, while having tea in Beverly Hills, he casually slipped a diamond ring of his hostess on his finger, and, despite her protests, walked off with it. The next day he announced that the ring had been stolen. And for this affair he was again arrested. On an April night, in the year 1935, he was found murdered in his apartment. He had been reading, during the evening, two detective stories, *The Killing of Judge McFarland* and *The Second Shot*. At the time his murder was widely reported, no one seemed to notice that his career was thoroughly typical of the period, 1926–1935, and of the place, Hollywood. One could fill an encyclopedia with biographies of the Paul Whartons of Hollywood.

6. The Breach Narrows

With the introduction of sound, the amount of capital invested in the motion-picture industry rapidly increased; between 1926 and 1933 the capital investment doubled. Hollywood became Big Business almost overnight. Eight major producing companies swiftly came to dominate the industry and five of these companies are today fully integrated, that is, they make, distribute, and exhibit motion pictures. Of the 92 companies engaged in the production of films in 1939, the eight "majors" released 396 or 82% of the 483 full-length feature films and received 53% of the gross income. The five integrated companies now own 2,600 theaters or 16% of the total. Through their control of these deluxe first-run theaters, they exercise a dominating influence in the distribution field. With more capital required, the major film companies became affiliated with or were financed by such concerns as the Western Electric Company, the American Telephone and Telegraph Company, the Chase National Bank, the House of Morgan, and the Radio Corporation of America.

The year sound was introduced, the Central Casting Corporation was formed to rationalize the employment of extras. Previously extras had applied for work at the rate of 4,000 an hour, but, by 1936, the extra work was divided among 22,937 employees and the number continued to decline: 15,936 in 1937; 8,887 in 1938; 7,007 in 1940. With the introduction of sound, a sharp wedge was driven between the actors and the extras. The average annual earnings of technicians, which was $2,463 in 1929, dropped to $1,767 in 1935, while in 1937 studio painters, carpenters, and plasterers were averaging $1,500 a year. With industrial maturity, came internal division on class lines. At the same time, sections of the Hollywood labor movement began to identify themselves with the Los Angeles labor movement and the schism between the two communities began to narrow.

Efforts to organize the industry date from 1916, but it was not until November 29, 1926, that the first basic studio agreement was executed. With the New Deal program, the writers, actors, publicists, story analysts, directors, and the other crafts and skills, quickly organized. Today Hollywood is a union labor town, from the miscellaneous service employees to the highest paid writers, actors, and directors. Organization has not been achieved, however, without a long and bitter struggle. It took the Screen Writers Guild five years to secure a contract after they had organized. For the tycoons who rule the industry have "grown up" with motion pictures and, like similar industrialists in other fields, have a fixed notion that the industry is theirs to boss and to rule as they see fit. Resourceful strategists, they have fought the unionization of the industry by every trick and stratagem known to American employers. The Hollywood guilds and unions have long had to contend with more than the usual number of employer "stooges" and "yes men," the individuals who in 1935 formed the Hollywood Hussars (see my article in *The Nation*, May 29, 1935) and who today control the Motion Picture Alliance.

The beginning of a conscious rapprochement between Hollywood and Los Angeles dates from the formation of the Hollywood Anti-Nazi League in 1936 and the formation, in May, 1938, of the Studio Committee for Democratic Political Action. The impetus for the latter movement came from within the industry itself. At the time of the Epic campaign in 1934, the politically unorganized employees of the industry were caught off guard. Using undisguised compulsion, the tycoons of the industry forced these employees to contribute to the Republican Party campaign fund. But in 1938 the employees took the initiative, formed their own political organization, and were an important factor in the election of Governor Olson. Since 1938 the political importance of Hollywood has increased with every election.

Through their anti-fascist, trade-union, and political activities, the employees of the industry have now been brought into intimate collaboration with the people of Los Angeles. Nowadays no committee is complete which does not include representatives from the Hollywood arts and crafts, and Hollywood is included, as a matter of course, in all social and political projects of a liberal nature. This general leftward tendency of the Hollywoodians has been luridly reported by Martin Dies and John Rankin and clumsily satirized by professional informers, notorious renegades, and the usual witnesses who appeared before the Dies Committee. Much fun has been poked at high-salaried stars occupying "box seats at the barricades" and at the spectacle of "Stalin Over Hollywood." While the influx of liberal ideas has not been without its amusing sidelights, it would be a grave mistake, indeed, to write off this ferment as a mere fashion of the moment or as another manifestation of the exhibitionism of a community of actors. Hollywood will never again be a big happy family. The tensions which have developed in the industry, briefly noted in this section, were clearly outlined in Scott Fitzgerald's novel, *The Last Tycoon*, which, if he had lived to finish it, would have shown that the Hollywood tycoons are really our last tycoons and that their control of this all-important medium for the communication of ideas is already on the wane. Fugitives and runaways, the early producers and their latter-day successors are no longer beyond the reach of democratic processes. Even Hollywood has repeated the quotation from John Donne made famous by Ernest Hemingway: "No man is an iland, intire of it selfe; every man is a peece of the Continent, a part of the maine."

> *"This is the end, O Pioneer—*
> *These final sands*
> *I watch you sift with meditative hands,*
> *Measure the cup of conquest."*
> —James Rorty

CHAPTER XVII

A SLIGHT CASE OF CULTURAL CONFUSION

WHEN thousands of settlers began to trek into Southern California, they came to a land strange and paradoxical concerning which they knew literally nothing and about which no available lore existed. There were no reliable guidebooks, no agricultural manuals, no soil analyses, no weather charts. Furthermore they came bearing a load of previously acquired notions, customs, practices, and concepts which they stubbornly insisted could be applied in Southern California. There was nothing tentative or experimental about their approach to this new and novel environment. What had worked in Kansas would work in Southern California. Newcomers have had to discover the novelties and paradoxes of the region by a painful trial-and-error process. While time and experience have gradually corrected some of their more egregious misconceptions, the process of cultural adaptation has been continuous. Each new wave of migrants has been compelled to discover the region afresh. Heavy and continuous migration has made it impossible for the residents of the region to undertake a thorough exploration of the land and its resources, its limitations as well as its potentialities.

"The story of America," wrote T. K. Whipple, "is the story of the process of interaction between the American country and the foreign heritage of the American people." European cultural practices imported to the Atlantic states could be adjusted to the new environment with comparative ease. A Dutch farmhouse was not only practical in Pennsylvania; it was fairly well adapted to the environment. It seemed to fit the land and the landscape. The same farmhouse probably would not have been altogether out of place in Kansas, assuming that the materials for its construction had been available. But such a farmhouse is unthinkable in Southern California. As the American settlers moved westward, many cultural incongruities did appear, but the discrepancy between the imported cultural practice and the new environment was generally one of degree. A slight variation or modification would bring the particular cultural practice into a workable relation with the new habitat. But once the jump was made to Southern California, across the mountains and the desert, the old practice had to be radically modified or altogether abandoned, for this environment differed in kind and was, furthermore, highly paradoxical. Things nowhere else available, this smiling land offered in abundance. But the newcomers knew literally nothing of the land and they had brought with them, as Stewart Edward White has pointed out, "the mode of existence they learned elsewhere, and have not the imagination to transcend." Most of the other regions of the country were settled by a process of accretion. Settlers gradually filled up Illinois and then overflowed, so to speak, into Minnesota and Michigan. But Southern California has been settled overnight, not by people from neighboring states and similar environments, but by people who have come from all over the world and from every state in the union. Out of this basic experience has come the amusingly confused culture of the region, a culture which has by no means yet succeeded in eliminating the irrelevant, discarding the incongruous, and coming to grips with the physical factors of the environment.

1. AGRICULTURAL ADAPTATION

The first settlers who came to Southern California found a region that had many native herbs, grasses, and shrubs, but the list of trees was small indeed. They looked in vain for the maple, the hickory, the basswood, the chestnut, and other familiar trees. "Oh, for the green pastures," wrote Beatrice Harraden, "for the deep lanes, and forests of trees, for the brooks and rivers, for the grass and ferns and mosses, and for everything in Nature soothing to the eye and comforting to the spirit!" About the only trees were the sycamores and cottonwoods along the stream beds and the beautiful live-oaks that dotted the rolling hills. These lovely live-oaks, dense of limb and leaf, with dark glossy spoon-shaped leaves that never changed color with heat or drought or frost, cast a solid pool of black shade on the ground. "They once covered the valleys," wrote Van Dyke, "with solid green, through which one could ride for miles in almost perpetual shade."

One of the first things the settlers did, of course, was to hack down the live-oaks. So thoroughgoing was the process that the tree soon disappeared from many sections. When the period of settlement began, the foothills were covered with a heavy mantle of shrubs, manzanita, madrona, chokecherry, live-oak bushes, lilac, wild-mahogany, and coffee-berry. All these varieties were termed "brush" or "chaparral." The chaparral provided an excellent cover for the soil and lent great beauty to the landscape. Much of the chaparral was immediately burned; in fact, it has been burning ever since. Since there were few native fruits in the region, and most of these were not edible, the settlers promptly concluded that fruit would not grow in the region. The manzanita, coffee-berry, and chokecherry, they said, were only "fit for bears to eat." The fact is, of course, that all known varieties of fruit can be grown in the region. Great herds of sheep introduced in the 'sixties were permitted to stamp out the native bunch-grass and alfileria (burr-clover) before they could seed, thereby destroying most of the range grass.

Since a dry period of two months in other sections was regarded as a calamity, "a drought," the notion persisted for years that Southern California was a desert. Elsewhere the best soils were found along the river bottoms and so these lands were sought out by the first agricultural settlers in the region. It took them almost a quarter of a century to discover that some of the best lands, particularly for citrus crops, were the foothill uplands. When artesian wells were first tapped around 1867, the notion prevailed that these wells were inexhaustible. So many wells were drilled that, at one time, the sparkle of artesian waters could be seen throughout the plains. But within two decades many of these wells had disappeared. While the first settlers knew something about irrigation, they knew literally nothing about the art of irrigation in a semi-arid climate. They wasted water wantonly and with only meager results. In fact, it was only when they began to imitate irrigation methods long practiced in Mexico and elsewhere in the Southwest by Indians that they really learned how to irrigate. They brought with them the Anglo-Saxon doctrine of riparian rights, which worked fairly well in the northern part of the state, but, when applied south of Tehachapi spelled disaster. It was not until pressure from the southern part of the state forced the adoption of the Wright Act in 1887 that the beginning of a better system of water utilization was inaugurated.

The initial success in wheat-farming in Southern California resulted in the enactment of fencing legislation that virtually destroyed the free range and with it the cattle industry. The initial success with sheep-raising resulted in such large herds of sheep that the remaining range lands were destroyed, even for sheep. Since the seasonal variations were so slight, farmers began to bet on the season, going in for large one-crop bonanza farming. All of these early successes, as Van Dyke noted, had a baneful influence on development of the region's agriculture. "Farming" was replaced by "ranching." According to Van Dyke, the principle of ranching was "to do nothing yourself that you can hire any one else to do and raise nothing to eat that you can buy." Because nature seemed to be kindlier here, slovenly farming practices developed. The land was not really plowed; it was "cultivated." "Scarcely any one from east of the Sierras," wrote Van Dyke in 1886, "knows anything about the lands of Southern California or their management, no matter what he may know of farming or gardening elsewhere. Unless one lays aside all conceit, and learns anew from those who have learned here, one may meet not only vexation, but loss."

Gradually improved farming practices were developed and, after a time, remarkably swift progress was recorded. But the progress did not occur until the settlers had been compelled to abandon their preconceptions. The fact that they were ultimately forced to reconsider established farming practices in this new environment, resulted in discoveries which have had a profound influence on agriculture, not only in California, but throughout the country. For the novel environment of Southern California has sharply challenged anachronistic methods and stereotyped procedures. The old, deep-seated, and widespread belief that a new culture would eventually arise in California, a culture fashioned not on imitation but on functional adaptation, does have this basic experience as its justification. While the idea has been grossly inflated and pompously proclaimed, it does have a core of reality. The nature of this reality becomes more apparent as one turns from agricultural practices to other cultural items.

2. ARCHITECTURE

One of the first things the settlers did, of course, was to change the style of architecture. To be sure, there was not much in the way of an architectural style to be changed. The Spanish ranch-house, however, was a well-adapted structure. With its interior patio, its low-pitched roof, its kitchen removed, in many instances, from the house itself, and with its wide verandas extending around the house (with all rooms opening on the veranda and the patio), it was certainly a comfortable and livable home. The Spanish ranch-house, however, largely vanished in the decade after 1880 (twenty-six dilapidated structures are all that exist in Los Angeles County today). The low adobe houses in the towns, with their flat asphaltum roofs, were quickly replaced by "elegant and substantial dwellings," the Mansard-roofed monstrosities of the 'seventies. Churches, hotels, and office buildings of the boom years were all done in the most florid taste of the period. "The blossoming civic vision" of the time, as one historian put it, "inspired from the East and clothed in the fashion of the day," was notable for its "gingerbread and cupolas." In many cases, the effort to eradicate the past as completely as possible was based upon a studied attempt to make the new land look as much like the East as possible. A Santa Barbara historian, for example, writes that the boosters "apparently proceeded on the theory that the Eastern Visitors would be made happiest by finding things here, excepting the climate, as much as possible like what they had left 'back east.'" To make these newcomers feel at home, and to minimize their confusion, even the names of the streets were changed, with Calle del Estado becoming Main Street.

It was not only the architecture that was changed; the physical environment underwent a kind of face-lifting. Since almost any flower, shrub, or tree would grow in Southern California, the boosters went to the far corners of the earth and imported the most heterogeneous assortment of ornamental plants, shrubs, trees, and flowers ever assembled in an environment to which they were not native. By 1880 there was scarcely a town in the region that did not have its particular show-place, an exotic, privately owned garden, in which plants, flowers, and shrubs of all varieties had been assembled and planted side by side for the delectation of the newcomers. Since the environment is highly versatile, many of these importations seemed to fit the landscape. For example, the eucalyptus, although not native to the region, is, next to the live-oak, the loveliest tree to be found in Southern California today. But other importations, such as certain varieties of the petticoated palm tree, have always been an abomination, a blot on the landscape, hideous beyond description. Today some two hundred and seventy varieties of trees are planted along the streets of Los Angeles, of which fully fifty per cent are blackwood acacias, a tree not particularly well adapted to the environment. Used to being "wide open in all directions," the Iowa contingent chopped down trees with gay abandon and trimmed hedges as hedges had never been trimmed before.

Until a comparatively recent date, the gardening manuals available in Southern California were importations, written with an Eastern or Middle Western climate and environment in mind. Not only were they useless in Southern California, but they contributed mightily to the spoliation of the landscape. Since everything would grow, everything was planted. Failing to understand that the beautiful coloring of the land is not a reflection of things, but consists in the peculiar quality of the light itself, newcomers have indulged in riotously incongruous color schemes. The misuse of the bougainvillea and the giant red geraniums (usually placed side by side) is merely one of the more ghastly examples that might be cited. Even to this day, the landscaping of the region is incongruous, confused, and shows everywhere the absence of a developed tradition within the region. In the glare of the sunlight, certain bright colors become intolerably oppressive and garish. When the hillsides were discovered as likely building sites, no thought was given to preserving contours or to obscuring roads and highways by planting shrubs and trees. "The people got busy with steam-shovels," as Frank Lloyd Wright puts it, and began "tearing down the hills to get to the top in order to blot out the top with a house." Today the hills around Los Angeles are scarred with roadways, exposed like cuts or gashes, forming a crazy zigzag pattern, with most of the damage being well-nigh irreparable.

One of the first things newcomers do in Southern California is to make themselves feel at home. "We are beginning to feel quite at home," says a character in a novel by Sidney Burchell, "having our own things around us. This morning when I woke up, and saw the old bureau and toilet glass beyond the foot of the bed, and the window chintzes, I thought for a moment I must be back in Maine." When the Iowa brigade began to arrive in Los Angeles, each family, writes Harry Carr, had a home "with a living-room that took the place of our Iowa parlors. Each one bulged out with a bunion in the way of a bay-window. Coming out nearly as far as the bay-window was a tiny porch. The Iowans had pleasant visions of sitting on the front porch in the long tropical evenings. They found that night followed day as suddenly as the dropping of a curtain, without a romantic twilight, and that the evenings, even in summer, were so cold that they would have to muffle themselves in their buffalo overcoats. Both the bay-window and the front porch were surrounded by a fringe of what we admiringly called 'art glass,' bilious patches of yellow, blue and red set in frames around the edges of the window. The front porch opened into a hall and from the hall opened a front and back bedroom. Back of the living room was a dining-room with an amazing 'built-in' sideboard; and back of the dining-room was a pantry and kitchen. All around the eaves and the roof ridge of the cottage were 'scroll work,' doodads that looked like cake frosting."

With no architectural tradition in the region, aside from the meager fragments from the Spanish period, it is not surprising that the newcomers should have imported the style of house then prevailing in the particular region from which they came. Since many of these early settlers came from New England, they dotted Southern California with typical New England homes, with high steep roofs to shed the snow that did not fall, with dark interiors that contrasted nightmarishly with the bright out-of-doors, and with deep cellars built for needless furnaces. In one booster publication appears a picture of such a home with the explanatory note, "In Los Angeles the snow-shedding roof is merely for ornament." Throughout the region today one comes suddenly on these homes, usually in a magnificent setting of orange trees and flowering shrubs, their "gloomy stupidities" standing out in the sharpest possible contrast with the land.

Fortunately the absence of durable materials, such as marble and stone, prevented most of these structures from becoming lasting monuments to the prevailing cultural confusion. But they have survived in sufficient numbers to give the region an odd appearance of being both old and new, West and South, North and East. One can still encounter ancient derelict frame structures in the older sections of Los Angeles positively fascinating by their incongruity. For in this environment, they are probably the oldest-appearing houses in America. They look as old as time, as old as the iron hills. A New England colonial structure built in 1776 appears actually modern, in its environment, by contrast with the gingerbread homes of the 'seventies which survive in Los Angeles.

Around the turn of the century, however, experience with the environment had produced a new and livable home, the California bungalow. In part the bungalow was an outgrowth of what had earlier been called "the California house": a simple structure built of rough redwood boards. But, as finally developed, it was based upon the bungalow originally built by Englishmen for use in tropical countries. British officials had found the bungalow to be a reasonably comfortable home in a tropical environment and, being inexpensive, it appealed to them, for their residence was, in most cases, temporary in character. It was precisely these qualities that appealed to newcomers in Southern California. A low, spacious, airy house, the bungalow could be built by people of moderate means and informal tastes, who were not quite sure that they intended to remain in Southern California and therefore did not want to invest a considerable sum in a home. The great merit of the bungalow was that it minimized the distinction between the exterior and interior walls, that it tended to merge the house with the landscape to which it was definitely subordinated.

Between 1900 and 1915, a few Southern California architects, in particular the firm of Greene and Greene, began to adapt the bungalow form in an interesting way, making it into a year-round home, and giving it a more substantial character while retaining its essential simplicity and absence of decoration. Universally built of redwood, these bungalows of the period 1900–1915 are among the few homes in the region that really fit the environment. To encounter one today is still a delight. As the form became more popular, however, a certain amount of gingerbread began to be added. Imitators of Greene and Greene began to use cobblestones for the purpose of converting the bungalow into a "Swiss chalet," while others began to give the bungalow an Oriental appearance by adding upturning roofs and Japanese storm-porches. A Greene and Greene bungalow, however, remains a good home in Southern California.

Unfortunately the bungalow was literally engulfed by the "rash of stucco" that swept over Southern California after 1915. The San Diego Panama-California Exposition of that year was planned several months before San Francisco decided to have, in the same year, its Panama-Pacific Exposition. Learning that San Francisco intended to have a great fair the same year, San Diego at first considered abandoning its own plans. Direct competition with San Francisco was obviously unthinkable. Then Bertram Goodhue, the architect, suggested that San Diego might give its exposition a special character by designing all the buildings in Spanish Colonial style. There had been "Spanish," and "Mission," and "Mooresque" structures in Southern California before the San Diego Exposition, but the appearance of these structures had never assumed the proportions of an epidemic. After the San Diego Exposition, all Southern California "went Spanish."

The so-called Spanish Colonial home that came out of the exposition, with its walls of white stucco and roof of red tile, was a model easily imitated by commercial contractors. It had the merit of looking a little more like the environment than the models they had been using for so many years. Furthermore, it was called Spanish and could be related, therefore, to the Mission background, and it was simply constructed. It did have one or two definite merits: a considerable amount of plain surface and low lines. By 1920 this neo-Spanish stuccoed home was the building model almost universally used by the large contractors. Southern California was Hispanized in appearance as quickly as, at an earlier date, it had been Anglicized. The style was used for residences, apartments, flats, store buildings, post offices, public structures, filling stations, roadside huts, and mortuaries. Most of Santa Barbara was rebuilt in this style after the earthquake of 1925, and, still later, an ambitious promoter built an entire village, San Clemente, in the same style. Even with some surrounding shrubbery, the glare from this village is still blinding for a distance of three miles. "As there was nothing of the Spanish there to begin with," writes Max Miller, "there is nothing there now—unless one considers the regimentation of white stucco of all the houses and all the buildings as being Spanish."

It seemed to Frank Lloyd Wright in 1934 that "the eclectic procession to and fro in the rag-tag and cast-off of the ages was never going to stop" in Southern California. "It was Mexico-Spanish now. Another fair, in San Diego this time, had set up the Mexico-Spanish as another model—for another run of thirty years." Despite the elaborate effort that went into the scheming to make these houses "original" or "different," they all looked exactly alike. "The same thought, or lack of thought," wrote Mr. Wright, "was to be seen everywhere. 'Taste'—the usual matter of ignorance—had moved toward simplicity a little, but thought or feeling for integrity had not entered into this architecture. All was flatulent or fraudulent with a cheap opulent taste for tawdry Spanish Medievalism." The neo-Spanish style just happened, by pure accident, to be a little more in keeping with the environment than the variety of styles which had been used, and it was awkwardly and clumsily adapted. "The loose rude Spanish-tiled roofs," Wright pointed out, "give back the sunshine stained pink." As far as the occupants were concerned, they felt as out of place in these homes as "the fra himself or a silken Spaniard would have looked in their little Middle-Western parlors." Although the Middle Westerner had been induced to purchase a Spanish home, he had changed but little. He still clung, as Mr. Wright observed, to his straw hat, English coat, trousers and boots long after he had moved to Southern California.

The restoration of the Missions had much to do with creating a popular acceptance of "the stucco rash." All the railway stations of the Southern Pacific Company in California were done in what the company termed the Mission style. The Franciscans who designed the Missions were not architects; they had only a faint memory of Spanish churches when they sketched out the designs for the crude structures the Indians built in California. While the Missions had some merits as structures, and could have been used as a model in the absence of any other, they became a deplorable influence. "More architectural crimes have been committed in the name of the Missions than in any other unless it be the Grecian Temple," wrote Irving Gill. At its best, the Mission style was ecclesiastical, not domestic, and the attempts to adapt it for domestic purposes were wholly grievous in effect. The same phoniness appeared in the so-called Mission furniture which was originally designed by Gustav Stickley, editor of The Craftsman. At a fair in 1900, Stickley had exhibited two clumsy chairs, with straight backs and legs made of three-inch posts, which he had labeled Mission. Since the California Missions were exciting much attention at the time, the name immediately became popular and Mission furniture was born. In a sense, the Spanish style of the Mission was as foreign to the region as any of the other styles later used. It was merely by a kind of accident, as Mr. Wright emphasized, that it seemed to be a little more apposite than, say, a New England stone house or a plantation mansion.

Once the Mission and Spanish notions had caught on, builders discovered what Herbert Croly had pointed out, namely, that "Southern California is a country in which almost any kind of house is practical and almost any kind of plant will grow." There then began the wild debauch of eclecticism which has continued unabated to the present time and which has excited the wonder and curiosity of all visitors. Even earlier, however, eclecticism had been rampant in the region. Harry Ridgway, the Pasadena architect, who specialized in "high-art styles," contended that he never made two buildings alike. He never wanted any man to be able to point to a structure and say, "That's one of Ridgway's structures—it shows the earmarks of his style." True to this prescription, he loved to combine diverse and dissimilar styles in the same structure, using Venetian, Norman, Eastlake, Old Spanish, Old Plantation, Italian, French Mansard, English and Colonial Dormers, Old English Queen Anne, and Old English Elizabethan in such combinations as his fancy dictated. He has had, of course, many imitators in Southern California.

The beginnings of a real architecture in the region date from the work of Irving Gill, a sadly neglected figure in Southern California. Trained in the office of Louis Sullivan in Chicago, Gill worked on the Columbian Exposition of 1893 and, after its completion, came to San Diego. For years he had wandered in his taste, seeking in Grecian, Roman, Italian, and early English models the style that he wanted to find. Finally, as he said, he abandoned all models and returned to the basic forms of the straight line, arch, cube, and circle, in an effort to evolve a new style. Rebelling against all gimcrack ornament, cheap construction, and false effect, he built, in the face of much opposition, the first modern homes in Southern California. Later he took over the idea of the "bungalow court," a Southern California innovation, and by designing the houses so that each had separate entrances, exits, halls and gardens, created some structures, such as the Bella Vista Terrace in Sierra Madre, that have remained wholly charming through the years. Gill used interior walls to capture the exterior light. In all his work, he sought to give real permanence, so as to avoid, as he put it, the appearance of structures erected like sets in a motion-picture studio.

Some of his comments about the architectural problem he sought to solve in Southern California have an interest that quite transcends the issues he discussed. In 1916 he wrote: "The west has an opportunity unparalleled in the history of the world, for it is the newest white page turned for registration. The west unfortunately has been and is building too hastily, carelessly and thoughtlessly. Houses here spring up faster than mushrooms, for mushrooms silently prepare for a year and more before they finally raise their house above the ground. People pour out here as on the crest of a flood and remain where chance deposits them when the rush of waters subsides, building temporary shacks wherein they live for a brief period while looking about for more permanent anchorage. The surface of the ground is barely scraped away, in some cases but a few inches deep, just enough to allow builders to find a level, and a house is tossed together with little thought of permanence, haste being the chief characteristic. The family of health- or fortune-seekers which comes out here generally expects to camp in these poor shacks for a short time and plans to sell the shiftless affair to some other impatient newcomer." A survey of apartment houses, made in Los Angeles in 1938, confirmed this impression by finding that the average tenant occupancy period was six weeks.

It is this lack of a sense of permanency that, in part, accounts for the unreal appearance of the region and the restless character of its population. "Neither was there any permanence here, any roots," observes a character in Myron Brinig's novel, The Flutter of an Eyelid. "Houses were literally builded on sand, and if not sand, their foundations were insecurely laid in clay. Men and women were in constant movement, drifting and whirling through the air like toy balloons." It is not merely that many houses are built so flimsily, however, that creates this impression. The same impression is enhanced by the circmstance that the houses have no earthly relation to the environment. They are unreal, as unreal as motion-picture sets. Turning a corner in the Hollywood hills, one comes upon, say, an elaborate Norman-French chateau or a monstrous square home, in

no style whatever, built on a curving hillside lot. As much as anything else, it is the lack of a functional relationship between these
homes and the land on which they rest that creates the illusion of
unreality. And I do believe that the character of the architecture,
while reflecting the restless character of the occupants and their
recent arrival in the region, also contributes to their rootlessness and
their feeling of unreality about the land in which they live. How can
they feel at home in such a house in such a land? It may be built
of stone and steel, but it is as unreal as though it were made of
papier-maché. Underlying these considerations, however, there is
still another paradox. Referring to the foothills of the coast range,
John Evans writes in his novel, *Shadows Flying*, "There is unrealness,
too—a theatrical beauty which is almost unbelievable. Visually very
beautiful, but somehow unalive. In summer the swelling masses, full
of voluptuous curves and undulations, are burned to a golden brown
in the strong sun; there is little or no rainfall in these months. Here
and there, sometimes singly and sometimes in small groups, the
magnificent oaks, wide-spreading and symmetrical, almost too perfectly formed, press their somber shadows against the blond land.
There is too much composition; perhaps there is too much beauty."

   Nowadays the seeds of integrity sown by Gill and Frank Lloyd
Wright, fertilized by influences from Japan and Europe, have begun
to bear fruit in some real homes in Southern California. The first of
the modern European architects to reach Los Angeles was R. M.
Schindler, who arrived from Vienna around 1922, after a short period
spent in the office of Frank Lloyd Wright. He was followed a few
years later by Richard Neutra, another Viennese, who, also, had been
first attracted to Chicago by the work of Wright and Sullivan. Both
Neutra and Schindler have been greatly influenced by Wright and
they in turn have had an important influence on some of the younger
men of the region, such as Gregory Ain and Harwell Harris, both of
whom have worked with Neutra and Schindler. It is not surprising,
therefore, that out of a listing of 136 modern homes published a few
years ago in *Twice-A-Year* 30 should be located in Southern California or that the architectural magazines should have had so many
articles, of recent years, about the extremely interesting domestic
architecture that is developing in the region (see, in particular, an
article by Talbot F. Hamlin, in *Pencil Points* for December, 1939).

3. "Scenic Arts"

The problem of cultural adaptation, strikingly apparent in architecture, the most graphic and literal of the arts, has also found reflection in the other arts in Southern California. Both in writing and in painting, Southern California has lagged behind the northern part of the state, which, for all practical purposes, is forty years older in point of settlement. The first reaction of the strangers who poured into the region south of Tehachapi was one of intense preoccupation with its scenic wonders and oddities. Both the early painting and writing of the region were largely devoted to the "scenic," the picturesque, the grandiloquent, aspects of the environment. Artists were so preoccupied with the novelty of the environment that they devoted little attention to a close study of what this environment was really like. They tended to see everything through glasses colored by preconceptions and their vision of the land itself was weirdly distorted and often amusingly inaccurate.

Most of the writers who came to Southern California after the American conquest were, as Hildegarde Flanner has pointed out, "aliens in a land toward which it is impossible to remain indifferent." The poets in particular, she thinks, might well have remained silent throughout the period of "tourist fancy," for it is only after the new and the strange have become an integral part of the poet's experience that he can express his feeling toward the land. "Quite fittingly," writes Genevieve Taggard, "there has never been a poem written about a eucalyptus tree. There could not be, until this special tree has gone into the experience of many people so long and so deeply that when a poet comes to write of it he has no sense of its novelty, but only the feeling of its everlasting uniqueness. Just now the eucalyptus tree is news; anything said of it, try as we may, has chiefly a reportorial and journalistic quality." Southern California was not at all like the faint reflection of the region that began to find expression in story, verse, and novel after 1884. For beneath the surface it is, as Miss Flanner has said, "a hard land, if a bright one, and if man cannot find water, he can die, and with less hope of resurrection than the flowers." But Southern California would not permit these newly arrived poets to wait until the land had come into some proper focus; it forced them to burst into print with consequences that have been truly appalling. With Gene Stratton Porter the desire to write poetry had remained a "suppression" as long as she lived in Rome, Indiana. But as soon as she arrived in Southern California, in 1919, "Something in the wonderful air, the gorgeous colour on all hands, and the pronouncedly insistent rhythms, all combined to force utterance."

Poetic utterance has certainly remained "forced" all through the years. The California poets, as Miss Taggard once pointed out, have tried too hard. In a strenuous effort to force some poetry out of the region the 3,000 poets of Southern California have banded together into a network of organizations that structurally resembles the National Association of Manufacturers. There are more poets per square mile in Southern California than in any other section of the United States. They have poetry societies, poetry magazines, poetry breakfasts, and poetry weekends. They meet together to chat and to sip tea, to plot and to confer. In Los Angeles, there are poetry lanes, poetry shrines, and poetry gardens. Thumbing through innumerable anthologies of Southern California verse, one can find many poems that deal with familiar scenes and themes of the region. Yet the stuff of the region is wholly lacking in these pallid verses. The few individuals who have done rather well with the land itself have been those who, like Miss Flanner, have had the wit to recognize the existence of a cultural problem: the necessity of creating, little by little, the exterior world in the image of old truths and convictions brought to the land. The imagination of the artist has not yet penetrated this exterior world; it has not become familiar; the period of awkward self-consciousness has not ended. Only within recent years, in fact, have a few poets dropped their sight, so to speak, from the ocean, the mountains, and the desert, and begun to concentrate on what the land is really like. For it is not all "sunshine and poppies."

No region in the United States has been more extensively and intensively reported, of recent years, than Southern California. Within the last decade, a dozen or more novels have been written about Hollywood alone. And yet, offhand, I can think of only four novels that suggest what Southern California is really like: *The Day of the Locust* by Nathanael West, *Ask the Dust* by John Fante, *A Place in the Sun* by Frank Fenton, and *The Boosters* by Mark Lee Luther. In a study of forty-six writers who have written novels about Southern California, Margaret Climie found that none had been born in the region and that most of them had only resided there a short time. It is worth noting that the writers who have most vividly captured the feel of the California landscape have been native sons, like John Steinbeck, or long residents like Robinson Jeffers.

"Transport a man to a remote wilderness," wrote T. K. Whipple, "and what happens? He builds himself a log cabin or a sod hut; he works and endures hardship and deprivation; he clears land and plows it; perhaps he prospers. But what happens to the mind of a man thus uprooted, and to his children's minds? The sense impressions of centuries must be obliterated before sounds and sights and smells gather full power and meaning. It will be long before these people have the feeling as a symbol for the goldenrod, say, that they once had for the rose or for heather, for maize as well as for wheat. The still where they make corn whiskey will not at once get the emotional hold upon them that the winepress had. The mockingbird and the hermit thrush will mean less to them than the nightingale had meant. When will the unfamiliar objects begin to get a grip on them and take on a symbolic content. . . . No matter how a transplanted man may thrive in his possessions, his life is to some extent impoverished, even though he may be quite unconscious of the deprivation, though he may have disliked the old and may like the new: he once had a close and vital tie with the world about him, and now he has little or none."

Of recent years there have been some indications that man is beginning to feel at home in the West, that the sense of the "scenic" is being replaced by a feeling of familiarity for the land. Reviewing a new novel by Walter Van Tilburg Clark in The New Yorker, Edmund Wilson said: "This book is a Far Western book, and, like the fiction of the Pacific slope, like John Steinbeck and William Saroyan, it does not quite meet the requirements of an Easterner. It seems too easy-going and good-natured, too lacking in organization, always dissolving into an even sunshine, always circumventing by ample detours what one expects to be sharp or direct. There is an element in all this fiction that seems to us 'goofy' or 'corny.' Yet it cannot be said that the East has had lately so much to show that is better; and it is one of the signs of the vitality of writing in the United States that the Pacific coast should be producing a literature of its own, appropriate to its temper and climate, and almost as independent of New England, New York, and the South as it is of current fashions in Europe. . . . The United States faces today toward the West as well as the East, and the West Coast is working out its own culture. The pull of the Pacific is felt in writing as in everything else."

The early landscape painters who began to work in Southern California after 1880, painters such as Elmer Wachtel, William Wendt, and Guy Rose (the only native son of the lot), experienced the same difficulty in seeing the land as did the writers. To the extent that they were successful, as Arthur Millier has pointed out, they had to narrow their sights, "choosing small, rather than grand, subjects and seeking for truth of appearance." In their early work, one can detect "the shock of recognition," as, for the first time, they actually saw or began to see, the dry arroyos, the shifting shadows, the foothill chaparral. And it must be admitted that most of them saw the land dimly and imperfectly. One can examine hundreds of these early Southern California landscapes of sunlight flickering through eucalyptus groves, of the flush that swiftly passes over the mountains before the sun falls into the sea, and recognize nothing except the strenuous, largely futile, forced effort that went into the attempt to picture a scene not yet familiar.

Many of these early artists were brought west by the railroads, among others, Fernand Lungren. An Eastern-trained artist, Lungren once wrote, "I had to unlearn most of what I had understood as light and color and especially atmosphere, or lack of it." After he had succeeded in freeing his mind, to some extent, of preconceptions, and had begun to paint the land, he was surprised to discover that local critics dismissed his later work as spurious and preferred the earlier "scenes." Another early artist of the region, J. Bond Francisco, complained of "the mocking brilliancy of the sky" and pointed out how he had only discovered, late in life, that "the light was the thing in Southern California; that the light actually changes the texture and shape of the hills." This light completely baffled the first generation of landscape painters. It has only been with the appearance of a second generation that the "quick, fluid fact" of the light has begun to show in the work of such painters as Milford Zornes, Barse Miller, Phil Dyke, Tom Craig, George Post, Dong Kingman, and Millard Sheets. "The quality of California light," writes Alfred Frankenstein, the art critic, "is not a Chamber of Commerce invention but a characteristic subtropical fact." It accounts, he believes, for the extraordinary reception given Van Gogh exhibits in California. "Take a swirl of hills, its grass burned to a golden crisp in the heat and dryness, put in a flame or two of coniferous green and a snarl of clouds in the sky and you have (1) a landscape by Van Gogh, or (2) the view from practically any window in California not hemmed in by city buildings." The early landscapists failed to bring "the California light to paper, in all its brilliance and saturation"; the spirit of the place is simply not in them.

When artists visited Southern California at a later date, after the face of the region had been lifted, they were usually troubled by a feeling that the land was unreal and impermanent. Some of them devised theories, to account for this feeling, that were close to the truth. "Like all irrigated civilizations," wrote Maxwell Armfield in 1925, "the land has a certain air of unreality and impermanence about it . . . all green things grow here with speed, continuity, and abandon, so that a sense of permanency is attained, but it is only a permanency that is skin-deep. One does not question the display of exotic flowers and trees, the palms and gigantic geranium hedges; the humming birds and gorgeous swallow-tail butterflies; but all the time there is a sense of having strayed into one of Mr. Wells' Utopias." After studying the land for some months he noted that much of the exoticism was superficial. He began to observe "the sparseness of leafage in proportion to the ground," a circumstance responsible "for those exquisite effects of blue and pale purples, with discreet orange and all manner of dim golden hues," which would be quite "vulgar in the midst of greenery." He began to detect that the land was gray and brown and that the illusion of color came with the "golden air tempered for half the year by sea-mist." And, lastly, he shrewdly discerned that the painter lives in Southern California "amidst a riot of colour that is not indigenous and yet which might well have belonged to the landscape" (italics mine).

No notion is more deeply seated, no idea has echoed more persistently through the years, than the theory that a new and vital culture would some day be born in California. "Here if anywhere else in America," said William Butler Yeats on a visit to California, "I seem to hear the coming footsteps of the muses." The historian Froude, in his book *Oceana*, predicted that a new school of art would some day arise in this rich and beautiful corner of the world, this island on the land. In most cases, the theory has been proclaimed ex *cathedra,* pompously, bombastically, rhetorically. But there has always been a basis for the belief. "The American poet," wrote Hildegarde Flanner, "living there [in California], so haplessly exploited, so rarely left to its own charm is aware not of the exciting pleasure of living in a nation's playground; not of the advantages of climate or place or ease of life. Rather, he is aware that he is part of a great movement, an ancient movement of humanity spreading and reaching out toward what it hopes is a better and happier life. *This movement has gone as far west as it can*—there is the ocean. In sight of that barrier the force of expansion is concentrated, localized, multiplied, and, in the south, we have a great metropolitan area, shut in on one side by the Pacific, on the other by mountains and the desert. *Here is a centering of human energy and desire* . . . here human energy and purpose having reached the limits of physical advance, are bound to flow back upon themselves and in doing so must either stagnate or create."

Physically attached to the West rather than belonging to the West, culturally isolated from the rest of America during decades when it grew "like a gourd in the night," California has always struggled, however uncomprehendingly, for independent expression. Visitors have sensed this struggle much more keenly than settled residents. "What America is to Europe," wrote Lord Bryce, "what Western America is to Eastern, that California is to the other Western States. It has more than any other the character of a great country, capable of standing alone in the world." Long isolated from what he called "the steadying influence of eastern states," California had been peopled by "a mixed multitude, bringing with it a variety of manners, customs, and ideas." Here on the Western shore, a society had been formed that was "more mobile and unstable, less governed by fixed beliefs and principles," than he had found elsewhere in America. "California," he wrote, "is the last place to the west before you come to Japan," a place in which he detected "a sort of consciousness of separate existence."

In the movement of American culture westward, the persistence of those cultural traits imported from Europe has gradually weakened, and, in California, they have tended to disappear under the shock of impact with an environment qualitatively unlike that to be found elsewhere in the nation. It is the last frontier of Western civilization, a land where the West faces the East. California, in fact, looks toward the East and toward the West. "You can't live for twenty summers on the hem of the Sierra Madre's magnificent purple garment," wrote the artist Anthony Anderson, "and still keep your Parisian ideals of seeing and doing. You are bound to start, sooner or later, new fashions of your own that are absolutely in keeping with your environment."

"The idea is held by everybody in Southern California," to quote from a magazine article by James M. Cain, "that some sort of destiny awaits the place." Underlying this persistent *mystique* about a renascence of art and culture in California are the cultural realities mentioned in this chapter. I refrain from adding still another prediction to the incredibly protracted list of those who have said that the arts would some day be "entempled" in California, but I do point to the fact that here, in California, when the garment does not fit, it is soon discarded. The family from Des Moines may bring their overstuffed furniture with them to Los Angeles, but, if they stay here long enough, they will discard the trash and buy something usable and comfortable. And what they buy to replace the old will, in most cases, be something that has been designed and manufactured in California.

A nearly perfect physical environment, Southern California is a great laboratory of experimentation. Here, under ideal testing conditions, one can discover what will work, in houses, clothes, furniture, etc. It is a great tribal burial ground for antique customs and incongruous styles. The fancy eclectic importations soon cancel out here and something new is then substituted. The reason the fresh growths are not more conspicuous than they are at present is that the importation-and-discarding process has been continuous. As Max Miller has so shrewdly observed, "Each decade the previous residents once again are outnumbered by a new cyclonic invasion bringing its own idea of how California should be remodeled." Each new wave of migration invariably results in the construction of still more subdivisions made up of Eastern and Middle Western homes, but, as the native life begins to grow, some of the force of this tendency is arrested and a degree of stability begins to develop. The heterogeneous architectural styles to be encountered in Los Angeles (and the same could be said of clothing and furniture) merely reflect the heterogeneous character of the population, recruited from every state in the union and from every class.

In fact, it is the heterogeneity of its population that serves to make

Southern California the ideal testing ground for ideas, styles, manners, and customs. "Let anything happen in the rest of the country," writes Idwal Jones, "in Arkansas or Maine, and there is instant repercussion inside the borders of Southern California. It has absorbed the frontier; it has become the national hot-bed and testing ground." No one has described this aspect of the region better than Farnsworth Crowder: "Here American institutions sharpen into focus so startling as to give the effect, sometimes, of caricature. Here the socio-economic class conflict is vividly posed in burning silhouettes against the walls of the factory and the hinterland. Here American scholarship and research are at their best; American cults and quasi-religions are at their shabby and shallow worst; here are America's indignant soap-boxers and pamphleteers, bigots surrendered to some over-simplified ideal, its scared reactionaries and its grim stand-patters; its baronial aristocracy, its patient poor, its sober, good natured, self-centered middle class; its promoters, racketeers, opportunists, and politicians; its fagged-out oldsters and its brash, raw youth. . . . What America is, California is, with accents, in italics. National currents of thought, passion, aspirations and protest, elsewhere kept rather decently in subterranean channels, have a way of boiling up in the Pacific sun to mix in a chemistry of queer odors and unexpected crystallizations: but it is all richly, pungently American and not to be disowned, out of embarrassment and annoyance, by the rest of the nation which is in fact its parental flesh and blood, its roots and its mentor." Here is the land where the Gothic in idea and manner, in style and expression, stands out in sharp relief and, perhaps for the first time, is recognized for what it is. For this land is not merely a testing ground, it is also a forcing ground, a place where ideas, practices, and customs must prove their worth or be discarded.

EPILOGUE

WORLD WAR II has completely revolutionized the economy of California. Since the war employment in manufacturing industries has increased from 400,000 to over 1,000,000, while the value of production, in all fields, has risen from $5,000,000,000.00 to over $12,000,000,000.00. The three west-coast states were credited with only 6.46% of the "value added by manufacture" to goods produced in the United States in 1939; but today these states have 13.23% of the national total. In California alone, cumulative war contracts through June, 1943, represented 9.54% of the national total by comparison with 4.6% in 1939. In part, this increase represents, not a net gain in national production, but an important shift in industry to the West and South. For both the Middle Atlantic and New England states have suffered a decline, as regional manufacturing centers, by comparison with pre-war levels. A large part of California's wartime increase in industrialization has been concentrated, of course, in Southern California. Between 1940 and 1944, more than $800,000,000 was invested in over 5,000 new industrial plants in the region. Overnight Los Angeles has become an important industrial area preoccupied, not with tourists and climate alone, but with such problems as "smog" and "smoke" and "strikes."

Will Southern California be able to retain these important wartime gains? Unfortunately it is impossible at this time to do more than venture a guess. In whatever direction inquiry is pursued, one comes face to face with imponderables. What will be our national policy on patent-pools and monopolies? Will discriminatory freight rates be eliminated? Can the West retain the steel mill at Geneva, Utah, and the Kaiser mill at Fontana? What, in general, will be the trend in national and international policies? No one knows. But it should be noted that the wartime industrial boom in Los Angeles has merely accelerated a trend toward industrialization apparent since the turn of the century. What the war has done in Southern California has been to telescope a quarter century's development into the brief space of a few years. "Los Angeles," writes Dr. Philip Neff, "has reached an economic development in the last 50 years that took New York City 175 years to accomplish." Many of the new industries, in particular the aircraft industry, are likely to remain in the region and even to expand production. With aircraft production, as Mr. Arthur W. Baum has pointed out, "the climate is useful, and since the factory product flies itself to market, that backbone of mountains which has always interfered with eastern marketing of western products is of little consequence." One likely prediction, therefore, is this: that industrial employment in Southern California will, by 1950, have reached a level approximating the peak of wartime production.

Paralleling the shift in industry to the West has been a sharp shift in population from the Northeast Atlantic states toward the west coast. While New York was losing 1,001,238 in population, California gained 1,013,629. During the first 150 years in the life of the republic, the center of population moved westward 160 miles, from Baltimore to Indiana; but it is now moving westward at an accelerated pace. Note the upward movement of California among the other states: from 21st place in 1900 to 12th place in 1910; from 8th place in 1920 to 6th place in 1930; from 5th place in 1940 to 3rd place in 1944 (outranked only by New York and Pennsylvania). As might be expected, most of California's wartime gain in population has been recorded in Southern California, where, since the war, the population of Los Angeles County alone has increased 662,225, with important gains being recorded in San Diego and other Southern California communities.

The whole history of migration to the region confirms the belief that Southern California will retain the bulk of its new wartime population. For the most part, westward migration is a one-way process in America. Furthermore, since the war California has been a great and lovely corridor through which thousands of American soldiers and sailors, along with a never-ending stream of equipment and material, have moved westward into the Pacific. Between seven and eight million soldiers, sailors, and marines received their training or traveled through or embarked from California. Secretary of War Patterson has estimated that perhaps 25% of these men will eventually settle on the West coast and this prediction has been confirmed by spot surveys conducted among the armed forces. In the last analysis, it has been the emergence of the Pacific in American consciousness that accounts for the shift of population and industry to the west coast.

Nevertheless it is apparent that the period of runaway growth—the "boom years"—have ceased in Southern California. Remarkable as the increase in population has been since the war, the relative increase, by comparison with earlier periods, has not been spectacular. In fact, the rate of growth has declined. The war has also brought about a regrouping of age-levels in the population, giving the west coast, for the first time, a solid population pyramid. All this is merely another way of saying, of course, that Southern California now faces, for the first time since 1880, a period of relative stability during which it has at least a chance to consolidate its gains and to integrate its population. It follows, therefore, that much of the giddy surface phenomena of the past will not reappear in the future. While not yet restored to full competency, Southern California may now safely be left to manage its own affairs.

In retrospect it will be clear that the year 1940 marks an important transition in the social and cultural life of the region. When the Spaniards landed in Southern California, they thought they had discovered an island "at the right hand of the Indies," very close to the Terrestrial Paradise, an Amazon island abounding in gold and "infested with many griffins." While time corrected this notion, California remained for many years an island remote from the centers of population in America, an economic, social, and political appendage to the rest of the continent. The war has brought to final conclusion this insular phase of the development of California as a state and Southern California as a region. Industrial expansion has now tied the economy of the west coast to the national economy in the most inextricable fashion. And by bringing the region west of the continental divide into the orbit of the west coast cities the war has unified Western America. At the same time and by the same process California has now begun to achieve a measure of internal integration. With the rate of population growth declining even as the total population continues to increase, California will now begin to outgrow some of its eccentric social mannerisms, contradictory attitudes, and narcissistic tendencies. The future will note a decline in political truculence, adolescent social noisiness, and strident cultural nativism in California. For the state, at long last, has begun to know itself and to sense its destiny.

For the first time in its history, California now feels that it is definitely a part of that fantastic world around the rim of the Pacific, the outlines of which have been so unmistakably sharpened since the war. Today California knows that in this world of the Pacific—the great world of the future—reside nearly 1,000,000,000 potential customers for west-coast products and that in this world is to be found a sizable share of the world's resources. The impact of this realization has been, of course, much greater in Southern California than in the northern part of the state. Southern California was discovered from the east, by westward-moving migrants. Looked at from its eastern approaches, the region could not be seen in proper perspective; its significance remained obscure and speculative. But when one approaches the region from across the Pacific, it begins to assume an altogether different aspect. The sense of detachment from the rest of the continent gives way to a feeling of its integral relation to the rest of the Pacific world.

Visiting California in wartime, Samuel Grafton noted the presence of "a hungry and questing crowd, and, strangely, it is like California itself, which is a questing sort of state, ever on tip-toe to peep into the future. This great coast sees itself in the future as the trade corridor between east and west. It likes that grand vision. But at the same time a good many Californians have an unreasonable private wish for peace and quiet, for fewer invasions by either the farm hungry people of Asia or job hungry people of Oklahoma, Arkansas and Texas. The state wants to be the great roaring corridor, all right, but it is not really sure that it cares for all that traffic. . . . The group as a whole moves on to its destiny, while the atoms in it dance or sit and brood. . . . Yet in spite of this resolute effort by everybody concerned to find peace at the center of the whirlpool, the state does produce greatly. The planes come off the lines and fly away. They will fly over places far from here, where men will look up to them and say they came from California, and they will be stirred by that strange hungry questing which makes this area the home of aspiration."

Perhaps this strange hungry questing is but the final expression of the impulse which has drawn, and is still drawing, thousands of Americans across the continent to where they are now assembled, crowded close to the western shore, waiting to pass "the Mediterranean torch" westward "across the fountains of the morning." Today more than ever before one feels in California the force of the lines from "Continent's End" by Robinson Jeffers:

I gazing at the boundaries of granite and spray, the
  established sea-marks, felt behind me
Mountain and plain, the immense breadth of the continent,
  before me the mass and doubled stretch of water.

I said: you yoke the Aleutian sea-rocks with the lava and
  coral sowings that flower the south,
Over your flood the life that sought the sunrise faces ours
  that has followed the evening star.

The long migrations meet across you. . . .

As one of the newcomers who came to Southern California in the great influx of the 'twenties, I have become as devoted to the region as a native son. When I first arrived in Los Angeles, I hated, as so many other people have hated, the big, sprawling, deformed character of the place. I loathed the crowds of dull and stupid people that milled around the downtown sections dawdling and staring, poking and pointing, like villagers visiting a city for the first time. I found nothing about Los Angeles to like and a great many things to detest. Without benefit of chart or guide or compass, I had to discover the charm of the city and the region for myself (one reason, doubtless, why I like it so much today). In those days, I did not know California, and, not knowing California, it was impossible for me to sense the strategic importance of Southern California, its difference, its uniqueness. More important, perhaps, was the fact that I had then seen little of America and hence could not appreciate this curious western amalgam of all America, of all the states, of all the peoples and cultures of America. . . .

My feeling about this weirdly inflated village in which I had come to make my home (haunted by memories of a boyhood spent in the beautiful mountain parks, the timber-line country, of northwestern Colorado), suddenly changed after I had lived in Los Angeles for seven long years of exile. I have never been able to discover any apparent reason for this swift and startling conversion, but I do associate it with a particular occasion. I had spent an extremely active evening in Hollywood and had been deposited toward morning, by some kind soul, in a room at the Biltmore Hotel. Emerging next day from the hotel into the painfully bright sunlight, I started the rocky pilgrimage through Pershing Square to my office in a state of miserable decrepitude. In front of the hotel newsboys were shouting the headlines of the hour: an awful trunk-murder had just been committed; the district attorney had been indicted for bribery; Aimee Semple McPherson had once again stood the town on its ear by some spectacular caper; a University of Southern California football star had been caught robbing a bank; a love-mart had been discovered in the Los Feliz Hills; a motion-picture producer had just wired the Egyptian government a fancy offer for permission to illuminate the pyramids to advertise a forthcoming production; and, in the intervals between these revelations, there was news about another prophet, fresh from the desert, who had predicted the doom of the city, a prediction for which I was morbidly grateful. In the center of the park I stopped to watch, a little self-conscious of my evening clothes, a typical Pershing Square divertissement: an aged and frowsy blonde, skirts held high above her knees, cheered by a crowd of grimacing and leering old goats, was singing a gospel hymn as she danced gaily around the fountain. Then it suddenly occurred to me that, in all the world, there neither was nor would there ever be another place like this City of the Angels. Here the American people were erupting, like lava from a volcano; here, indeed, was the place for me—a ringside seat at the circus.

Nowadays when I return from a trip to the East, I can hardly wait for the train to make that final swift descent through Cajon Pass to the floor of the plain at San Bernardino where it begins to pick up speed for the race through the orange groves to Los Angeles. Long before the descent has been made, I begin to dream of Point Sal—a favorite spot for me—where one looks down from a height of a thousand feet to the curving shoreline that stretches toward Point Conception and westward out across the forever cool blue waters of the Pacific. I dream, too, of beautiful Santa Ynez Valley and of the hills back of Santa Barbara; of Smiley Heights in Redlands and San Timeteo Canyon; of the spread of lights from Mt. Wilson on a clear cold December night or the harbor lights of San Pedro seen from the

Palos Verdes Hills; of the many times I have made the drive from San Jacinto over the hills to Palm Springs. I think of a thousand and one afternoons and evenings spent in exploring Southern California from "the foothills to the sea"; from Bunker Hill and Central Avenue in Los Angeles through the foothill homes and gardens from Montecito to San Diego. I close my eyes and I see Olive Hill, crowned with the perennially charming house that Frank Lloyd Wright did for Aline Barnsdale, with its colonnade of eucalyptus trees, and the pugnacious signs, around the rim of the hill, in which Miss Barnsdale warns the British to free India as she once warned California to free Tom Mooney. . . .

But most often I think of the first crisp days of fall after the "hot spell" which invariably ends the long summer. I think of the view from a favorite arroyo in the late afternoon, the east slope still bathed in sunlight, the far slope already full of dark shade and lengthening shadows. A cool breeze, as always at this time of day, gently ascends the arroyo. At the head of the arroyo, one can look back across the plains, out over miles of homes and trees, and hear the faraway hum of traffic on the highways and see the golden light filtering through the mist-laden air. And then I think of the sudden descent of night, when the sun catapults into the ocean—of the "sad red splendid sunsets," of the starless night skies, mysteriously vivid and luminous, full of a quick and radiant animation; and I think of the soft-silent muffled slap of the waters along the coast, far above Malibu, on nights of thick wet fog and spray and the smell of the sea. . . .

It is then that I realize that this land deserves something better, in the way of inhabitants, than the swamis, the realtors, the motion-picture tycoons, the fakirs, the fat widows, the nondescript clerks, the bewildered ex-farmers, the corrupt pension-plan schemers, the tight-fisted "empire builders," and all the other curious migratory creatures who have flocked here from the far corners of the earth. For this strip of coast, this tiny region, seems to be looking westward across the Pacific, waiting for the future that one can somehow sense, and feel, and see. Here America will build its great city of the Pacific, the most fantastic city in the world. For the American West coast, as Mr. Grafton has said, "is destined to be the world's metropolis." Nowadays one can see that the Spaniards were right after all and that we, in our technological conceit, were wrong. For with its planes whirling out over the Pacific toward China and India, California is, indeed, "at the right hand of the Indies," and, in Southern California, it does have a Terrestrial Paradise, an Amazon Island, abounding in gold and certainly "infested with many griffins."

INDEX